Thrill of the Chaste

YOUNG CENTER BOOKS IN ANABAPTIST & PIETIST STUDIES

Donald B. Kraybill, *Series Editor*

Thrill of the Chaste

The Allure of
Amish Romance Novels

Valerie Weaver-Zercher

THE JOHNS HOPKINS UNIVERSITY PRESS
Baltimore

© 2013 The Johns Hopkins University Press
All rights reserved. Published 2013
Printed in the United States of America on acid-free paper
2 4 6 8 9 7 5 3

The Johns Hopkins University Press
2715 North Charles Street
Baltimore, Maryland 21218-4363
www.press.jhu.edu

Library of Congress Cataloging-in-Publication Data

Weaver-Zercher, Valerie, 1973–
Thrill of the chaste : the allure of Amish romance novels /
Valerie Weaver-Zercher.
p. cm. — (Young Center books in Anabaptist and Pietist studies)
Includes bibliographical references (p.) and index.
ISBN 978-1-4214-0890-3 (hdbk. : alk. paper) — ISBN 978-1-4214-0891-0 (pbk. :
alk. paper) — ISBN 978-1-4214-0892-7 (electronic) — ISBN 1-4214-0890-2
(hdbk. : alk. paper) — ISBN 1-4214-0891-0 (pbk. : alk. paper) —
ISBN 1-4214-0892-9 (electronic)
1. Christian fiction, American—History and criticism. 2. Love stories,
American—History and criticism. 3. Amish in literature. I. Title.
PS374.C48W43 2013
813.009′382—dc23   2012027049

A catalog record for this book is available from the British Library.

*Special discounts are available for bulk purchases of this book. For more information,
please contact Special Sales at 410-516-6936 or specialsales@press.jhu.edu.*

The Johns Hopkins University Press uses environmentally friendly book
materials, including recycled text paper that is composed of at least 30 percent
post-consumer waste, whenever possible.

To Dave, Samuel, Isaiah, and Henry,

my four inimitable men

Contents

Preface ix
Acknowledgments xix

Chapter One

Slap a Bonnet on the Cover 3

Chapter Two

The DNA of Amish Romance Novels 27

Chapter Three

An Evangelical and an Amishman Walk into a Barn 57

Chapter Four

Taking the Amish to Market 79

Chapter Five

Is Amishness Next to Godliness? 105

Chapter Six

An Amish Country Getaway 129

Chapter Seven

Virgin Mothers 155

Chapter Eight

Amish Reading Amish 179

Chapter Nine

Something Borrowed, Something True 199

Chapter Ten

Happily Ever After 231

Notes 251
Bibliography 295
Index 305

Preface

I could have been an Amish romance novelist. Now don't get me wrong: I am not claiming that I could have become another Beverly Lewis, the grandmotherly Goliath of the Amish-fiction industry, whose Amish books have sold more than 17 million copies and have been translated into eleven languages. Nor am I under any illusion that I could have become a second- or third-tier writer of Amish fiction, with the slingshot of a killer plotline and an Amish cookbook coming out next month. I'm not even saying I could have found anyone who would have *published* my Amish novels—the ones I could have written about Fanny Byler, who longs to lip-kiss with the English man who buys her whoopie pies, or Kaitlyn Flanders, the adopted teen who travels to Lancaster County and there unearths her Amish roots and finds faith, family, and love.[1]

I'm just saying I could have written them.

Two of my favorite series as a child were Little House on the Prairie and Anne of Green Gables, whose headstrong but history-bound heroines prefigure the Rachel Lapps and Katie Yoders of bonnet fiction. I cut my adolescent reading teeth on inspirational Christian fiction, the genre to which most Amish romance novels adhere. My friends and I all checked out from our church libraries *Love Comes Softly*, by Janette Oke, the prairie romance that activated the contemporary Christian fiction market in 1979. In high school I moved from the wagon trains and full skirts of Oke's stories to the bulbous eyes and twisting appendages of Frank Peretti's demons in *This*

Present Darkness, the breakout Christian thriller that predated by ten years the *Left Behind* phenomenon. Although I soon discovered that I had no stomach for Christian horror and eventually gave up on prairie romance as well, it was not before I had become familiar with and at least somewhat fond of the conventions of Christian fiction.

Besides these early literary sensibilities, I have a few other checkmarks in the Amish-romance novelist column. I'm female, as are most current Amish romance novelists.[2] I have slept in an Amish home and eaten those proverbially smooth, mashed-by-hand potatoes in Indiana, Pennsylvania, and Ontario. My three sons have all driven an Amish buggy, a fact they brag about whenever possible—failing to mention that the elderly horse needed steering as much as they need prodding to eat their ice cream.

But the big guns on my Amish-novelist résumé are my genealogy and geography. My grandfather was raised Amish, and I've got a few dozen Amish second cousins in Ohio. I grew up Mennonite in Lancaster County, and I am a member of a Mennonite church. I used to wear a prayer covering, and some of my aunts and cousins still do.[3] My mother's grandmother spoke only Pennsylvania Dutch (also known as Pennsylvania German), the first language of most Amish people, and trace amounts of the dialect slipped into my childhood. One time in graduate school I complained to some friends about how *rutschy* I had felt during an exam we'd just taken— *rutschy* being the Pennsylvania Dutch word for "restless." For a moment I honestly couldn't figure out why they all looked so confused.

While *rutschy* confounded my grad school friends—just as *schuslich* and *dopplich* surely would have—such a childhood lexicon could have purchased me an audience with agents trolling for new entrants in the Amish-fiction field.[4] Any would-be Amish-fiction writer who has done her research will tell you that you have to convince an agent or a publisher that you have more than a thimbleful of knowledge to back up your fancy plot. "Authors don't have to be direct descendants, or practicing Amish or Mennonite, but those factors give an author a real edge," advises one literary agent who represents several Amish-fiction writers.[5] So if you're lucky, you are a dyed-in-the-wool "son of a runaway Amishman," as an ad for Dale Cramer's most recent book declares about him, or at least the descendant of someone plain, as Beverly Lewis and Suzanne Woods Fisher are. If ancestry fails you, perhaps you had the good fortune of at least being "born in the heart of Amish country," as Beverly Lewis's website proclaims, or marrying someone from Lancaster County, as Wanda Brunstetter did. A German bloodline might help—"Due to my German heritage, I feel a loose connection to the Amish and their culture," Amy Clipston writes on her website. Having had a childhood friend who was plain would "enrich your novels with authenticity," as Cindy Woodsmall's website claims, as would living within driving distance of an Amish settlement ("I already loved visiting Adams County and the stores and the shops there," Shelley Shepard Gray said in a recent interview; "So it [writing an Amish romance novel] just seemed a natural progression"). Even if you're among the less fortunate with shaky ties to the Amish, there may still be hope: "My grandfather was born in Albion, Pennsylvania," Vannetta Chapman writes on her website, "and I am currently researching whether I might have Amish roots."[6]

Although I am amused by Amish-fiction writers' claims of or longing for a plain pedigree, I also identify with it. The ancestral cord connecting me to plainness offers a measure of comfort, somehow, or even rescue. I like to imagine that if I tug on it every so often, I can reel myself and my family a little closer toward the simple goods of my heritage and a little further away from the anomie and gadgetry of contemporary life.

I now live sixty miles away from "Amish Country"—a term that always makes me want to ask after the flag and currency—but I get back there often. These days, when I drive on Lancaster County roads with names like *Schtee Bruch* ("Stone Bridge") Road and *Katzeboocle Weg* ("Cats' Back Way"), past laundry lines strung with dresses bright as irises and horse-drawn plows turning black soil, I too wonder what it would be like to belong there. Like Amish-fiction writers and readers, I sometimes long for this place that seems so far from my world of minivans, deadlines, and a daily niagara of e-mails. One can't drive far on such roads, however, before coming upon neighborhoods with names like "Fairview Farm Estates" and "Doe Run Hills"—developments with nary a farm or a doe in sight. Lancaster County, known since the eighteenth century as the "Garden Spot" of America, loses thousands of acres of farmland every year to residential development and highways.[7] As the Garden Spot is lopped into islands of farmland amid a sea of outlets and subdivisions, it's enough to make anyone scramble for an

Amish bloodline, or anything else that might rescue one from the placeless geographies of modernity.

Nostalgia is a profound force, whether born of an actual past or an imagined one. Cultural historian Leo Marx makes a distinction between sentimental and complex modes of pastoral longing, and such reflections fit squarely in his category of the sentimental. Marx would probably say that I am looking through "the soft veil of nostalgia that hangs over our urbanized landscape."[8] He'd be right, and we will investigate what nostalgia and the pastoral have to do with Amish romance novels later in the book.

For now, let me just say that when one of Beverly Lewis's male protagonists, a New York City journalist, wonders what he misses about Lancaster County when he is away from it—"Was it the tranquil, slower pace of things he longed for? The farm-fresh aroma of cows and soil?"—I first wince at the bromidic "yes" that hangs after the last question mark.[9] And then I start longing for home.

The Lay of the Book

Several scholars have studied evangelical romance fiction, the category to which most Amish novels belong. Lynn Neal's *Romancing God*, Anita Gandolfo's *Faith and Fiction*, and Jan Blodgett's *Protestant Evangelical Literary Culture and Contemporary Society* offer thorough and generous analyses of inspirational fiction and its readers. Other scholars have examined Amish life and culture, including sociologist Donald B. Kraybill in books such as *The Riddle of Amish Culture*, and popular representations of the Amish, including historian David L. Weaver-Zercher in *The Amish in the American Imagination*. But no one has yet analyzed in book-length form the marriage of inspirational fiction and the Amish—two parties that, depending on your perspective, either make the strangest of bedfellows or the perfect couple.[10] Either way, the consummation of that relationship—between evangelical literature and Amish subjects—is producing a growing brood of Amish fiction, with more than 275 titles published since the beginning of 2006. This book tells the story of that marriage.

Readers stand at the center of this study, as we will see in chapter 1 when we explore transactional reading theories and cultural criticism. Although

I read some forty Amish novels as research, I rely less on traditional literary analysis and more on the comments of the loyal readers of the genre themselves, which I gathered through written correspondence, interviews, informal conversations, and a visit to a book group in Illinois that reads Christian fiction. I visited bookstores, both Amish- and English-owned, and interviewed numerous authors, literary agents, editors, marketers, distributors, and booksellers of Amish fiction. I also spoke with several Amish women and men about their opinions of the books set in their communities.[11] I attended Amish-fiction book signings, listened to interviews with Amish-fiction authors on the online radio program *Amish Wisdom*, and kept abreast of discussions on Amish-fiction websites and blogs and Facebook pages, on which readers share thoughts and opinions about the books they love.

Another word about my approach: throughout the book I blend academic analysis with my own experiences of researching, reading, and talking with others about Amish fiction. The book alternates between a narrative nonfiction voice and a more formal academic one. Rather than disguising my social location—as a reader, a researcher who has friendships with several of her subjects, a Mennonite, and the spouse of an Amish-studies scholar— I attempt to make it visible. Rather than covering all traces of the journey I took toward understanding this genre, I decided to leave my tracks. *Thrill of the Chaste* might thus be considered "narrative scholarship," a term coined by critic Scott Slovic to describe this amalgam of story and academic writing. "Encounter the world and literature together," Slovic suggests to literary scholars; "then report about the conjunctions, the intersecting patterns."[12] While such an approach risks distracting readers from the arguments or analyses of the study, it can also illumine nooks and crannies of a phenomenon that a more distanced gaze might miss. Narrative scholarship lends itself to a study like this one, with its attention to readers, books, faith, romance, and the cultures in which they are lodged.

In chapter 1 I take stock of the size and strength of the Amish-fiction phenomenon, with particular attention to the ways two forces—hypermodernity and hypersexuality—are fueling the appeal of the genre for evangelical Christian readers. I also outline cultural criticism and transactional reading theory, the theories that undergird this study. Chapter 2 excavates the history of the Amish romance novel, which many people assume began in 1997, with the publication of Beverly Lewis's *The Shunning*. Amish fiction's lineage in fact reaches much further back—not as far back as the Amish themselves, who emerged as a distinctive group in 1693, but still more than a century into the past. We look in particular at three elements—rurality, romance, and evangelical piety—that came together in the Amish novels of the past century and that remain identifying strands of contemporary Amish fiction. In chapter 3 we look at the two discourse communities—evangelical and Anabaptist—at play in the subgenre and debunk two common myths about Amish fiction: that it is simply a milder version of general-market romance fiction, and that if you've read one Amish romance novel, you've read them all.

In chapters 4–7, then, I refract Amish novels through the lenses of four metaphors: as commodities, religious icons, methods of transport, and curators of godly womanhood. Each discloses a central trait of Amish fiction. Chapter 4 examines the production matrix within which Amish fiction is created, with particular attention to the commodification of books within a hypermodern economic era. Instead of locating the subgenre's wildfire popularity on the *consumption* end of the equation, this chapter attends to the strategies by which *producers* of Amish fiction—authors, literary agents, editors, marketers, and booksellers—are stoking the flames. Chapter 5 looks at the didactic and devotional role Amish novels play in the lives of their readers, by comparing their function to that of religious icons; we visit a book group in a small town in Illinois to learn how readers are using the books to connect with God and with one another. Chapter 6 investigates the sense of imaginative transport to a different time and place that Amish romance novels offer to readers, as well as the strategies by which they do so. Chapter 7 considers the ways the novels construct chastity, marriage, and motherhood; I argue that Amish fiction's popularity derives in part from the novels' ability to pivot between conservative and progressive notions of romance, gender, family, and female agency.

In chapters 8 and 9 we assess the phenomenon in relation to the people group that stands at the center of bonnet books: the Amish themselves. In chapter 8 we visit the bookmobile in Holmes County, Ohio, which has a

95 percent Amish user rate, and hear from appreciative, critical, and ambivalent Amish readers of Amish fiction. We also meet the only Old Order Amish author currently writing Amish fiction that is available to a broad readership. Chapter 9 surveys issues of accuracy, cultural appropriation, exoticism, domestication, and race in Amish fiction. In it I suggest that assessing the novels' level of accuracy or authenticity may be less important than considering how the Amish are being employed for particular ends. Chapter 10 looks at the future of the subgenre, directions in which it may be migrating, and the potential effects of Amish fiction on Amish and non-Amish readers.

Bonnet Books: Negotiating the Terms

Terms applied to a new genre or subgenre are notoriously slippery. Are *bonnet books*, *Amish fiction*, *Amish romance novels*, and *Amish-themed inspirationals* interchangeable descriptors, or is one more accurate than the others?[13]

Most terms that one could choose are problematic in some way. *Amish novels* and *Amish fiction* may suggest novels read or written by Amish people rather than *about* them.[14] Those two are also general enough to include mysteries set in Amish Country that lack romance narratives, such as those of P. L. Gaus, Linda Castillo, and Tamar Myers (whose books carry such incomparable titles as *Batter Off Dead* and *As the World Churns*).[15] *Amish fiction* could also refer to the bizarre worlds of Amish-themed science fiction, which includes Paul Levinson's *The Silk Code*, in which the Lancaster Amish breed fireflies for light, and Allen Kim Lang's short story "Blind Man's Lantern," in which Aaron and Martha Stoltzfoos travel to a planet eighty light-years from earth in search of farmland. And it could be applied to Amish supernatural fiction, such as Tristan Egolf's 2005 *Kornwolf*, in which a mild-mannered Amish teen morphs into a marauding werewolf with a striking resemblance to Richard Nixon. These Amish-themed genres deserve their own study, but they lie beyond the scope of this book.[16]

Bonnet fiction or *bonnet books* suggests any novel whose cover features a woman in a bonnet, which these days would include books about Mennonites, Moravians, Quakers, Shakers, Puritans, Mormons, and the Amana

Colonies. Some have protested that the term *bonnet fiction* is inaccurate and derogatory—"Please don't call it 'Bonnet Fiction,'" an Amish novelist pleaded on one blog; "The Amish wear Prayer Kapps, not bonnets."[17] And one editor confided that she thinks *bonnet books* reveals the media's dismissive attitude toward the category. "Even calling them 'bonnet books'—it bothers me," she said. "I think the reporters feel it's totally simplistic literature for a middle-America reader they overlook most of the time anyway."[18]

Inspirational Amish romance novels is probably the best descriptor, because it pays homage to both the devotional and the romance elements that characterize most Amish novels on the market, but it is more than a tad unwieldy. *Romance novel* itself is a collapsible term, and some writers and readers of Amish fiction dispute the "romance" label. "I've never thought of my books as being romance novels," Beverly Lewis told me. "There is always a love story or two along the way, but my stories are much broader-themed."[19] Several readers we hear from throughout the book agree with Lewis. Yet according to Pamela Regis's definition of a romance novel ("a work of prose fiction that tells the story of the courtship and betrothal of one or more heroines"), as well as Janice Radway's ("to qualify as a romance, the story must chronicle not merely the events of a courtship but *what it feels like* to be the *object* of one"), Lewis's novels, and most of the others on the market, do meet the criteria for romance fiction.[20]

Although I use a variety of descriptors throughout the book, including the ones that I've just debunked, I most frequently rely on the term *Amish romance novels*. It is not perfect, in that it occludes the central aspect of faith and is not necessarily used by the readers and writers themselves, but it functions well enough to mark the field that we are examining. It also clearly acknowledges that we'll pay scant attention to Mennonite or Shaker or other plain romances, Amish mystery fiction, or novels about Amish werewolves. Amish shapeshifters resembling former presidents deserve their own analysis anyway.

My other life as an Amish romance novelist beckoned as I finished revisions to this manuscript. A literary agent who knows about my research sent me an e-mail with the subject line "Any thoughts of writing an Amish novel?" Having recently met a publisher who was looking for Amish manuscripts, the agent wondered whether I might consider trying my hand at one. Yet despite her query and that of another friend, who unhelpfully observed that writing an Amish romance novel would make a lot more financial sense than writing *about* them, I decided to stick with a book about the books. Many people think that Amish romance novels must be a cinch to write, but, as we will see, the thrill of the chaste is a lot more complex than it may seem at first blush.

Acknowledgments

Thanks to the women in my writing group, who encouraged me on this project and responded to chapters with their signature blend of warm affirmation and incisive criticism: Crystal Downing, Jenell Williams Paris, Cynthia Wells, Valerie Smith, Meg Ramey, Lynne Cosby, and Sharon Baker. Special thanks to Crystal, who was a voice of encouragement the entire way and who spent hours talking Amish fiction over Pad Thai, and to Jenell, who fed me resources on religion and anthropology. Thanks to all those others who read and responded to an entire draft in very short order: Jenell, Crystal, Linda Huber Mininger, Barbara Nelson Gingerich, Nancy Adams, and David Weaver-Zercher. Their sage editorial counsel saved me from myself numerous times, even as they are not responsible for any of the mistakes that remain.

Thanks to the readers, writers, marketers, editors, and agents of Amish fiction who shared their perspectives and helped me understand the phenomenon from different angles. Although I write critically of some parts of the industry, I remain grateful for the hours of interviews and pages of reflection that their producers generously offered. Thanks to the Amish men and women, named and unnamed, who gave me their own unique perspectives on why people want to fictionalize their lives. Thanks also to Cindy Crosby, Karen Johnson-Weiner, Suzanne Woods Fisher, Richard Stevick, and Ruth Ann Swartzendruber for their help with research. Thanks to the women of Gals and Books in Plano, Illinois, for letting me listen in on their conversation and allowing me to tell their stories here, and especially to Ceil Carey, who with her husband, Jack, so graciously housed and fed me during my stay and who helped me arrange interviews.

My immense gratitude goes to Donald B. Kraybill, who believed that I could write this book and who coached me countless times along the way. I'm also grateful to Jeffrey Bach, Lucille Snowden, and the Young Center for Anabaptist and Pietist Studies at Elizabethtown College for supporting my research and writing with the Snowden Fellowship in the fall of 2011. Thanks to Cynthia Nolt, an insightful and collegial office-mate who shared citation expertise and chocolate-covered pretzels. A posthumous thanks to Stephen Scott, research associate at the Young Center, who kindly fed me numerous leads, pointed me to sources, read drafts of chapters, and generally proved a delightful person to chat with about Amish fiction and basically anything else. Steve died from a heart attack a few weeks after I finished a draft of this manuscript, long before I had asked him all my questions and long before any of us were ready to say goodbye.

Thanks to Greg Nicholl, whose warm encouragement, literary vision, and steady editorial hand moved this project smoothly from inception to publication, and to Lois Crum, whose careful copyediting improved the manuscript. Thanks to the various members of the editorial, design, marketing, and sales staff at the Johns Hopkins University Press, who believed in the project enough to take some risks. And to the outside reader whose clear-eyed suggestions helped me ease a rough draft into a final one: thank you.

I'm grateful to my parents, Richard and Ruth Weaver, who traveled several hundred miles and two days out of their way en route to a family reunion to help me make a research trip; to my mother-in-law, Alice Grace Zercher, who accompanied me on several Amish-fiction-related outings; and to all three of them for providing child care at various key junctures along the way. Many thanks to my husband, Dave, who cared for our three sons while I worked on this book and also listened to me talk about it ad nauseum. Having a spouse suddenly working in intellectual territory that one has researched for years can't always be pleasant, but Dave handled it with aplomb, even letting me raid his dissertation files in the basement. Thanks also to my three sons, Samuel, Isaiah, and Henry, for putting up with dinnertime conversation about cultural theory and Amish agency and commodification. We can talk about other things now.

Thrill of the Chaste

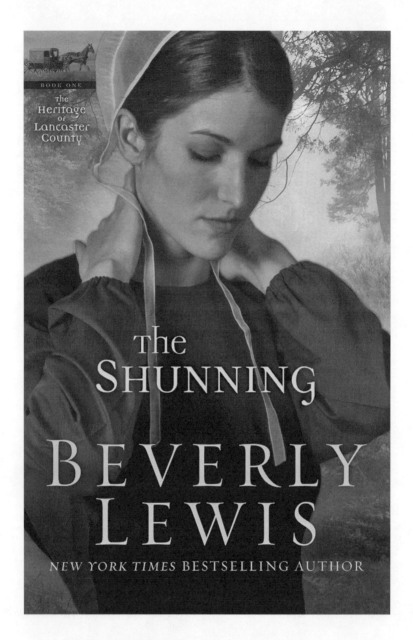

BOOK ONE

The
Heritage
of
Lancaster
County

The
SHUNNING

BEVERLY
LEWIS

NEW YORK TIMES BESTSELLING AUTHOR

Beverly Lewis's The Shunning, *published in 1997 and with a cover redesign in 2008, has sold more than 1 million copies.*
Used by permission of Baker Publishing Group.

❦ Chapter One ❦

Slap a Bonnet on the Cover

B rowse the inspirational-fiction section of most bookstores, and you will find cover after cover of comely young women wearing dresses with capes and often pensive expressions. Like Demeter, the Greek goddess of the harvest, the woman on the front of the typical Amish romance both issues from and presides over the landscape. Instead of a wreath of barley, she wears a prayer covering shaped like a heart, with gossamer strings attached. She hovers just above sun-drenched fields, in dreamy guardianship of the buggies and silos and covered bridges below her, or else she stands front stage, with the rural scene unfurling behind her. Occasionally a male figure lingers in the background, his face obscured by a hat, but more often the Amish maiden is alone in her pastoral reverie, gaze averted and thoughts inscrutable.

Demure as they may appear, Amish protagonists are annexing ever more real estate on the virtual and actual shelves of booksellers. Many Christian bookstores now sell more than forty different Amish romance titles; my local store had sixty-six at last count, and one I visited in Ohio boasted eighty-three. The Barnes & Noble near my home in central Pennsylvania had ninety-two.[1] These numbers don't include "Amishesque" novels—inspirational romances about Mennonites, Moravians, Shakers, Quakers, Puritans, the Amana Colonies, and others—that have been spawned by the Amish subgenre.

No matter the exact ecclesial affiliation of the model on the front cover, women with head coverings are the matriarchs of Christian fiction, their fortunes rising as fast as their buggies are slow. Their dominance on the inspirational-fiction shelf is just one indicator of what a marketing vice president for a Christian publishing house told *Newsweek* in a now oft-quoted chestnut: "You slap a bonnet on the cover and double the sales."[2]

The Rise and Reach of Amish Fiction

If you track the growth of Amish romance novels during the first decade of the third millennium on a line graph, you get a meandering, mostly flat line for the first six years. A smattering of new Amish titles was appearing, two or three or four a year, courtesy mostly of Beverly Lewis and a few outliers. Middecade, then, the line suddenly juts upward from gentle foothills to semi-alpine heights: from five new Amish novels in 2006 to fourteen in 2007. From then on, breathless descriptors like "exponential growth" would not be out of order. After a brief dip in 2008, the publication of Amish romance novels rises in a steep gradient. Twenty-six new titles in 2009. Forty-five in 2010. Sixty-three in 2011. Eighty-five in 2012. During both 2011 and 2012, more than one Amish romance novel appeared on the market each week. In 2012, the rate was one about every four days.

The Amish-fiction publication pie is impressive no matter how you slice it. Fourteen times more Amish romance novels were published between 2007 and 2012 than in the previous six years. Between 2009 and 2012, more than two hundred bonnet books were published.

Also significant are the types of books that these figures do *not* include: novels about other plain religious groups; titles that were self-published or released from vanity presses; young-reader novels; Amish-themed novels without a heterosexual love story, such as the mysteries of writer P. L. Gaus and the growing list of gay and lesbian Amish titles; re-releases or anthologies of previously published titles, and novels published by Anabaptist publishers for a primarily Anabaptist audience. Were all these types of books counted, the numbers would be higher and the incline more impressive. During the decade that housed a global financial crisis, the fertility rate of Amish romance novels, according to this very narrow definition, increased by a factor of eighty.

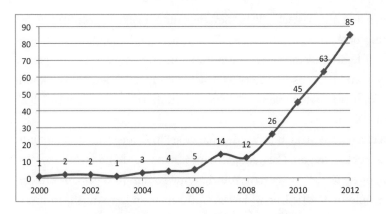

Numbers of Amish romance novels published, 2000–2012

Sales numbers and bestseller lists confirm the vigor of the Amish-fiction category. The triumvirate of top Amish romance novelists—Beverly Lewis, Wanda Brunstetter, and Cindy Woodsmall—have sold a combined total of 24 million books.[3] At least seven of Lewis's Amish novels have sold more than 500,000 copies each, and one of those, *The Shunning,* has sold more than 1 million copies. Brunstetter's fifty books, almost all of them Amish titles, have sold nearly 6 million copies. One of Lewis's recent novels sold 280,000 copies in four months.[4] Three of the top ten paperbacks listed by the Evangelical Christian Publishers Association in September 2011 were by Lewis, Brunstetter, and Woodsmall, and their books have repeatedly hit *New York Times* bestseller lists for trade fiction.[5]

Amish fiction's fertility extends far beyond the Bev-Wanda-Cindy troika. Several up-and-comers consistently see six-figure sales, and the field runs deep and wide, with at least sixty different authors having published Amish romance novels. Thirty percent of the titles on a recent Association for Christian Retail bestseller list were Amish.[6]

And although it used to be a tiny matryoshka doll nested within the genre of contemporary inspirational romance, Amish fiction has plumped up a level or two. In September 2011, publishers could begin using "Fiction / Amish & Mennonite" as an official category to help bookstores, online retailers, wholesalers, and Nielsen Bookscan classify novels for shelving, searches, and bestseller lists.[7] Several editors I talked to confirmed this widening of Amish fiction's girth. "Ten years ago, I thought in terms of historical fiction, historical romance, contemporary fiction, contemporary romance, and suspense/mystery—those were my five übergenres," Revell editor Andrea Doering told me. "By now, I think we've all added Amish as its own category."[8]

You can read an Amish-themed romance set in Pennsylvania, Ohio, Indiana, Kentucky, Oregon, Colorado, Missouri, Kansas, Montana, Maine, Wisconsin, or Mexico. You can have your heroine young, youngish, or middle-aged, single or married or widowed. You can have her Amish, formerly Amish, soon-to-be Amish, soon-to-be-not-Amish, born Amish but adopted by the English, born English but adopted by the Amish, neighbor to the Amish, or snowbound with the Amish. Within inspirational Amish romance fiction, you can now find Amish historicals, Amish suspense, Amish Wild West adventures, Amish cozy mysteries, Amish quilting novels, and multigenerational Amish sagas. One author is writing, at the request of her editor, "Sassy Amish," or what she calls "Urban Amish" (these are "totally not your mom's Amish books. Except for the Amish. They're still there").[9] Another hopeful author is writing "lighthearted romance with an Amish flavor." There is now Amish paranormal fiction, thanks to Ruth Reid's 2011 novel that folds an angel into the Amish cast and to Plain Fear, Leanna Ellis's Amish vampire series. And while you shouldn't expect to find these down at your local Christian bookstore, you can now read Amish romance novels of a quite different orientation. Yolanda Wallace's 2010 *Rum Spring*, which narrates the love between Amish teen Rebecca Lapp and English woman Dylan Mahoney, joins three series featuring gay Amish men to create a growing corpus of LGBT Amish romance.[10]

You can take your pick of series, which major in daughters, sisters, and brides: Abram's Daughters, Hannah's Daughters, Daughters of Caleb Bender, Daughters of Lancaster County, Daughters of the Promise, Emma Raber's Daughter; Sisters of the Quilt, Sisters of the Heart, Sisters of Holmes County, 3 Sisters Inn; Brides of Amish Country, Brides of Webster County, Brides of Lancaster County, Amish Brides of Celery Fields. There is also a raft of single titles, especially Christmas-themed ones. More than twenty Amish Christmas novels and novellas have been published so far, appearing right around Halloween each year.

The field of Amish fiction has attracted the astonished attention of major media outlets including the *Wall Street Journal, Newsweek, Time, USA Today, Bloomberg Businessweek*, NPR's *All Things Considered*, and ABC's *Nightline*. Editors often can't resist the high titillation quotient of headlines like "Getting Dirty in Dutch Country" and "Carrie Bradshaw—In a Bonnet?" And reporters, unaccustomed to covering what many view as the picayune genre of inspirational Christian fiction, seem baffled by the novels' sales figures and ardent fans. "Jesus Christ, do you have any idea how much money there is to be made in the Amish porn business?" one reporter marveled.[11]

So far the category seems almost as fertile as the Amish themselves, whose numbers have doubled over the past twenty years.[12] Twenty-three new Amish-themed series launched in 2012, and many authors within the subgenre have contracts for novels three or four years into the future. No editor or marketer or author or bookseller I interviewed suggested that Amish fiction was anywhere close to over. When asked about her plans for writing in the future, Beth Wiseman, who has written eight Amish novels and five Amish novellas, answered simply, "Amish, Amish, Amish."[13]

Simple Life or Soft Porn?

So wherein lies the cache of the fictive Amish *Mädchen* on the shelves and in the imaginations of contemporary readers? By what means have the Old Order Amish, who comprise less than one-tenth of 1 percent of the U.S. population, catapulted to literary stardom, so that novels about them represent 15 percent of the top religious fiction titles sold by Barnes & Noble and 30 percent of a Christian bestseller list?[14] What, exactly, is fueling the thrill of the chaste—this wildfire popularity of Amish romance literature and the virtues it contains? And what does it reveal about fiction, the Amish, and the rest of us?

Nearly everyone I talked to about this project had a theory about why Amish fiction is hot, and nearly everyone was eager to share it. Those in the Christian fiction business had theories at the ready, my brother launched into his at a family Christmas gathering, and I began to wonder whether my first-grader might also have an opinion. One writer of Amish fiction I interviewed pointed out that I had forgotten to ask her, and I didn't have the heart to tell her that I hadn't forgotten but was simply bored by all the theorizing. Indeed, the interesting thing about the rise of Amish fiction is not that no one knows why it is popular; it is that *everyone* knows.

The theories I heard carry the weight of common sense. "People are reading Amish books because society is so fast-paced and people need to slow down," one writer told me. "These books take people out of the world of cell phones and being on 24-7," a marketing manager suggested on the phone. "The family gathers around the table for meals and they pray together and they go visiting and it's all family, family, family. For a lot of people, especially moms, they're saying 'Gee, that's the life I wish I had.'" I heard countless versions of this theory, almost all of them including the sibilants *simple* and *slow.*

Another theory surfaced as well, expressed less frequently but with equal conviction, that relates not to the simplicity or slow pace of the Amish but to the sublimated sexuality of readers. An acquaintance e-mailed his opinion that by writing Amish novels, "prim and proper evangelical women use the Amish as a foil for their own stories of conflicted romance and sex." One of my friends was convinced that the subgenre's popularity lay in the submerged erotic desires of its readers and that I really ought to interview a psychologist about the psychosexual development of evangelical women. Another friend's husband passed along similar wisdom: "Amish fiction is for horny evangelical women," he told her to tell me; "Judging from the popularity of Amish fiction, evangelical women are apparently quite horny."

At times, the readiness with which people supplied their theories gave me pause. If the allure of Amish fiction was so obvious that it could be wrapped into one of two seamless sentences—(1) Amish fiction is popular because contemporary readers want to escape a fast-paced, alienated, and technologically saturated society; or (2) Amish fiction is a form of soft female porn that offers a discreet outlet for the longings of a sexually repressed readership—then what was left to investigate? And why did anyone need to write an entire book about it?

But as writers are wont to do, I became suspicious of swift or orthodox answers of both varieties. Sometimes common sense is a cloak that can hide—as well as define—the shape of the wearer. So although these theories held in their pockets elements of truth about Amish fiction's allure, I began to wonder whether they also might obscure the body of a deeper—and perhaps more interesting—rationale for the way Amish fiction was going gangbusters.

Deciphering the Thrill of the Chaste

Like most publishing phenomena, Amish fiction's popularity cannot be traced to a single, immutable seed. Various inputs are yielding the bountiful crop of Amish novels on the market: the maturation of the inspirational Christian fiction market; the widening symbolic capital of the Amish brand through the twentieth century; the 2006 Nickel Mines school shooting and the Amish community's extension of grace to the killer and his family; popular interest in simplicity that gathered force after the 2008 recession; the growing concern of evangelicals regarding the pace of social and technological change. These events, along with several others that we investigate in this book, have seeded the fertile field of Amish romance fiction.

Discrete events such as the school shooting or the recession, however, may be less deserving of credit for Amish fiction's successful season than the general contours of history and culture. To grasp the appeal of Amish fiction to its loyal readers, we must understand two attributes of contemporary life: what scholars and writers have called *hypermodernity* and *hypersexualization*. That the writing and reading of Amish fiction accelerated during the same decade in which academics and journalists began using these terms is not coincidental, and understanding Amish fiction's success apart from these forces is impossible.

Hypermodernity

Many terms have been proposed for the current historical moment: postmodernity, second modernity, late modernity, supermodernity, liquid modernity, and hypermodernity, to name a few. While each is helpful in its own right, most illuminating for our purposes is the concept of hypermodernity, which French philosopher Gilles Lipovetsky characterized in 2005 as "the frenzied escalation of 'more, always more' [that] has now infiltrated every sphere of collective life." Hyperconnection, hypertext, hyperreality, hyper-capitalism, hyperindividualism, hyperconsumption, hyperintelligence, hyperterrorism: "Is there anything now that does not reveal a modernity raised to the nth power?" Lipovetsky asks.[15] It is this hypermodern context—characterized by a high velocity of technological change, information transfer, consumption, social change, individualism, global capitalism, and even identity formation—that produced the contemporary Amish novel. The speed, anomie, and digital slavery of contemporary life have sent many readers, weary of hypermodernity, to books containing stories of a people group whom readers perceive as hypermodernity's antithesis: the Amish.

This explanation may at first appear synonymous with the "slow and simple" theory that I heard so frequently, but hypermodernity interacts with Amish fiction in a more complex fashion. Even as Amish fiction dissents from hypermodernity, the publishing apparatus behind Amish romances, with its breakneck speed of production, is situated smack-dab in the middle of it. Lipovetsky calls a hypermodern economy "capitalism in overdrive," which would appear to describe the Amish-novel-about-every-four-days phenomenon.[16] The commodifying impulse of hypermodernity is written into the genetic code of the genre itself, as we will examine. Hypermodernity is also roomy enough to contain its own contradictions, helping to shape what Lipovetsky calls "the tourism of memory," with an emphasis on folklore and "traditional" cultures, which we look at in chapter 6.[17] Amish fiction gathers momentum from hypermodernity, then, not just by dissenting from it but by benefiting from its production mechanisms and internal tensions.

Hypersexualization

Also critical to understanding Amish fiction's popularity is the extent to which it has grown up within a culture that sociologist Kenneth Kammeyer describes as hypersexual. Drawing on a word that theorist Jean Baudrillard used to illustrate his foundational concept of hyperreality, Kammeyer employs the term *hypersexual* to describe a situation in which "sexual discourse, erotica, and pornography are present in almost all aspects of society."[18] Other observers have used terms like *pornified, raunch,* and *striptease* to characterize twenty-first-century culture, evidenced by thongs and push-up bras marketed to elementary-school-aged girls and magazines targeted to tweens with articles like "Your Total Turn-Him-On Guide."[19] From fashion aesthetics and glossy magazine articles to talk-show confessionals, reality TV, music lyrics, and commercials, what media sociologist Brian McNair calls "porno-chic" was, by the turn of the millennium, inserting itself into mainstream venues. Former adult film star Traci Lords noted this transformation in 2003: "When I was in porn, it was like a back-alley thing," Lords told a reporter; "Now it's everywhere." In 2006 journalist Pamela Paul observed that the pornification of American culture was "not only reshaping entertainment, advertising, fashion, and popular culture, but . . . fundamentally changing the lives of more Americans, in more ways, than ever before."[20] Between 2000 and 2011, at least twelve academics and journalists published books that suggested, in essence, that American popular culture increasingly takes cues from Hugh Hefner and his Playmates. And the red-hot success of E. L. James's 2011 Fifty Shades of Grey trilogy—with 10 million copies sold as of May 2012—proved that bondage-themed erotica had mainstream appeal.[21]

Feeling embattled by a mass culture intent on baring all, evangelical Christians have found rare and mostly unacknowledged common cause with progressive cultural observers like McNair and Paul. Religion scholar Donna Freitas suggests that evangelicals have responded by constructing what she calls a "purity culture," in which abstinence, monogamy, modesty, and sexual fidelity are defended and promoted. Items such as chastity rings (sometimes called purity rings or promise rings), which teens wear as emblems of their commitment to abstinence, and practices such as purity balls, formal dances for teen girls that one website claims "hold high the banner of purity," have become markers of purity culture.[22] Such products and practices, stitched with notions of purity and chastity, serve as semaphores, of sorts, of evangelical purity culture: signals of a moral code that sets itself apart from hypersexual society. Amish fiction can be understood as one of these semaphores.

Thus, when readers articulate their appreciation that Amish-themed novels are "clean reads"—books largely free of sexual scenes and passion-driven plotlines that would offend their conservative sexual ethic—their words express not just a personal literary preference but a dissident value system. Sexual chastity is imprinted in the genre, as we will see in chapter 7. The heroines of Amish novels are, almost without exception, chaste—either virginal or in monogamous marriages—and chastity is widely celebrated in the category. Like the wearing of a chastity ring, the reading of Amish fiction reinforces the morality of an evangelical subculture, becoming for some Christian readers another way to bind themselves to a set of values and to be reminded of their faith commitments.

The exponential growth of Amish fiction during the first decade of the twenty-first century cannot be understood apart from these "hyper" cultural developments. And since hypersexualization can be seen as one prong of hypermodernity—Lipovetsky suggests that hypermodernity entails that "in *every* domain there is a certain excessiveness, one that oversteps all limits, like an excrescence"—at times I will use hypermodernity to encompass both concepts.[23]

Chastity in Triplicate

The thrill of the chaste that animates Amish fiction is rooted not just in sexual purity, however, but in the broader sense of moral innocence. *Chastity* descends from the Latin term *castus*, meaning a state of being "morally pure" or "holy," and this concept fuels the genre in several ways, as we will see. The Amish are often viewed as chaste residents of an otherwise defiled larger culture. Like the mythic virgins of literature and lore, whose rejection of sex earned them respect and even beatification, the Amish are frequently imbued with power commensurate with their ability to abstain from what many view as essential intercourses of a technological age: driving cars, flipping light switches, using a laptop, owning a cell phone. In *Selling the Amish,* an investigation of Amish-themed tourism, Susan L. Trollinger argues that the Amish are frequently perceived as having avoided "entanglements in unseemly worldly concerns" and thus are seen as "innocent technologically, socially, and politically."[24] This rejection of mass culture has earned the Amish a reputation of being set apart, inviolate, and even virginal: *in* a hypermodern world but not *of* it.

The Amish aren't viewed as literally virginal, of course; their large families stand as a ready correction to any thought that the Amish might be kin to the celibate Shakers (who, incidentally, are now also subjects of inspirational romance novels).[25] Rather, the Amish are seen as premodern virgins, of sorts, in hypermodern times: people who have not given themselves over to the desires and distractions of contemporary affairs. Many readers articulate the vast distance between their own harried, tech-filled lives and what they perceive as the slow, offline lives of the Amish. Readers often expressed to me disappointment with their own families' and churches' inability to say no to the digital and material seductions of the era.

While actual Amish negotiation with technology and contemporary life is much more complex than such a view would suggest, it is true that the Amish have managed to remain untouched by much of hypermodern discourse, activity, and gadgetry. As such, they have become a kind of vestal, vestigial community from the past. Historian Eric Miller, writing about Amish fiction in *Christianity Today,* suggests that there is a wistfulness to Amish-fiction readers' literary tastes, a longing for a "world that's refused to simply go along with it all, the mad dash to freedom be damned."[26] One reader told me that the heroines of Amish novels are generally "wholesome, ethical, religious, honorable, and righteous," and another described them as "simplistic" and as "looking through the eyes of a child." Thus, through their ability to withstand the probing of hypermodernity, the Amish are viewed, in some sense, as the last virgins standing.

Reading Amish fiction, then, results in an even stronger experience of chastity than reading other Christian fiction, since the virtues of the protagonist and her community extend beyond sexual innocence to cultural purity. Not only are Amish novels "clean reads" about modest young women; they are novels set within a subculture conceived of as unsullied by modernity. The genre thus becomes for its readers a tripartite literature of chastity: chaste texts about chaste protagonists living within a chaste subculture.

The particular way in which the novels construct and appropriate Amishness also begs for brief examination from the start. What is the essence of

Amishness—this distinctly "Amish" way of being in the world? And who gets to define it? Linguist Karen Johnson-Weiner suggests that "Amishness" is an English construct, a non-Amish notion that "acts implicitly to certify the authenticity of goods and behaviors, investing them with value by linking them to a particular people who . . . remain tied to the historic past, its behavioral norms, and its pace of life."[27] While it is not always clear what constitutes Amishness in the popular imagination—chastity? simplicity? faith? community? authoritarianism? a slower pace?—it is clear what Amishness is *not:* promiscuity, materialism, agnosticism, alienation, chaos, speed. In that sense, Amishness takes shape in readers' minds in proportion to their rejection of its binary opposite: non-Amishness, or "Englishness." Throughout this study, we will observe how Amish romance fiction serves as a conduit conveying Amishness to readers, many of whom articulate a deep dissatisfaction with the norms and values of hypermodern, hypersexualized culture. How closely this constructed Amishness resembles *actual* Amish subjectivity and practice is another question, and one we will examine. But since we look primarily at readers' *uses* of Amish fiction instead of at Amish life itself, we entertain that question relatively briefly.

By using the tools of cultural criticism and transactional reading theory, *Thrill of the Chaste* investigates the ways Amish romance novels function in the lives of their loyal readers, who are largely—although not entirely—evangelical Christian women. Yet even as we study the rather fancy cultural and religious tasks that Amish novels perform, we will keep in mind another critical element of fiction reading: as just plain fun. Ludic reading, or reading for pleasure's sake, can occur even within a category like inspirational fiction, known also for its instructional and devotional qualities. Like the Amish themselves, who frequently fold work into play and chore into pleasure, Amish fiction aptly combines the two, and readers find both education and enjoyment in its pages.

The Ghosts of New Criticism Past

Speaking of pleasure: although I level several criticisms at Amish fiction throughout this study, at times I liked Amish novels enough to forget that reading them was supposed to be research. I would suddenly realize how absorbed I had become in a certain plot, or how curious I was about how a heroine was going to finagle a happy ending out of this or that dire plight. Eager to keep reading my latest Amish romance but unwilling to admit it, I would sometimes tuck the book under my sweatshirt when going to the gym or under a notebook when entering a doctor's waiting room.

The deeper I got into this project, the more fascinated I became by the surreptitious nature of my Amish romance reading. While I remained interested in the question at the heart of the book—that is, what exactly is fueling the thrill of the chaste?—I became just as intrigued by the responses of people who, when they hear about the popularity of Amish romance novels, shake their heads in befuddlement. I became startled by the ferocity of criticism of the genre, such as that of one blogger who suggested that Amish novels celebrate "dullness, misguidedness, and insularity" and are written by "artless, hammy, sappy, cliché-ridden romance novel hacks."[28] I began to wonder why the recent baby boom of Amish titles produced such distaste in some circles and why, when I told friends that I was working on a project about Amish romance novels, they sometimes wrinkled their noses and asked, "Does that mean you have to actually *read* them?"

So what is causing the lament that attends the popularity of the genre, the critical hand-wringing that in certain circles accompanies any conversation about the ascendancy of bonnet books? Is it because Amish romance books *are* actually poor fictions—because when you pull back the layers of text and wield the scalpel of the close reading, you find nothing except nostalgia for pre-industrial America and sermons on born-again evangelical faith and ideal Christian womanhood? Is it because bonnet fiction is one more sign of our dismal publishing times, in which easily consumable books of negative-integer literary merit make authors a boatload of money, while "serious" writers can't get agents? Or is it merely because of worry that those poor Amish are once again being bought and sold for outsiders' financial gain: commercialized, romanticized, exoticized, fetishized, demonized, trinketized, evangelicalized, or patronized beyond recognition?

Perhaps. But I began to wonder whether the pooh-poohing of Amish titles is evidence of something else: a narrow view of literacy that privileges certain types of literate material and behavior over others and that attempts to apply the standards of one aesthetic community to another. Maybe critics of Amish fiction were guilty of the self-same unimaginative and pedantic thinking with which authors and readers of Amish fiction have been charged. All those questions led me to the invisible world of theory.

I first met the ghosts of New Criticism in the halls of my college English department. As an English major in the early 1990s, I had no idea that New Criticism had, for all intents and purposes, been declared dead decades earlier or that my professors, like many others schooled in New Critical thought in the 1950s, were simply unable to accept its demise. In my classes I learned that texts could be judged by objective aesthetic criteria and that the text was autonomous: as separate from its author's purposes as it was from its reader's response. New Critics attacked both the "intentional fallacy" (that an author's intention controls the meaning of a text) and the "affective fallacy" (that a reader's emotional response does). Authority lay not in the author, nor in the reader, but in the text itself.[29] The task of the reader, then, was to extract, critique, compare, contrast, and classify; if you weren't able to do that, you had failed. Interestingly, New Critics, or formalists, viewed the text much as we "English" (non-Amish) folks often view the Amish: as a separate, sacred, immutable entity from which one can extract meaning.[30]

New Criticism's "battery of critical instruments was a way of competing with the hard sciences on their own terms," literary theorist Terry Eagleton has written.[31] The novels and poems occupying me and other English majors were a far cry from the cadavers our premed friends were examining, but we were learning to take a similar position in relation to our objects of study. We learned that literature could be quantified, dissected, and calibrated, and our razor-sharp pencils probed beneath the skin of the text for the organs of theme, metaphor, and irony.

So it was that I donned the habitus of an educated reader, learning to distinguish between literary hard-hitters—Dostoyevsky, Faulkner, Cather, and Morrison—and the hoi polloi—L'Amour, Clancy, Steel, and Grisham. I learned to thumb my nose at any book with a whiff of the formulaic and to expect from writers a certain level of intellectual and poetic rigor. Victor Nell would say that I fell for the "elitist fallacy," which claims that there are two classes of readers: one with a taste for high literary quality and one with an appetite for baser literature.[32] When I did occasionally concede defeat to a novel so demanding or amorphous that I figured I simply wasn't smart enough to follow—or, on the other hand, when I binged on three Tony Hillerman mysteries in a row—I kept it quiet and hoped to God that I wasn't backsliding from highbrow to middlebrow, from literati to lit lite.

This hierarchy is visible to many Amish-fiction readers and writers with whom I spoke, and many are aware of the low register to which their beloved texts are assigned. A friend from church admitted her Amish-fiction habit after a Wednesday night Bible study. "I guess you could say it's my fluff reading," she said to a group of us as we chatted, as if to make sure that we knew that she could distinguish between literary weight and genre-fiction weightlessness. When I asked one Amish-fiction author how others view her work, she laughed. "My family makes all kinds of fun of me," she told me. "They're like, 'Oh, a little Amish writer!'"

Listening to my friend's deprecation of the books she loves, and to that author's words, I began to wonder whether the ghosts of New Criticism were haunting not only my analysis of Amish fiction but also that of its readers and writers. Although those ghosts make some good points, I began to wonder whether they might also be standing in the way of a more illuminating perspective on Amish fiction. So I began casting about for theory that might open up the intense allure of the fiction for its readers and the meaning they make from it. Hurling analysis from a safe distance would be one approach to studying these novels; listening carefully to their loyal readership is quite another.

A caveat: I don't want to unmake my literary affections, forged in the halls of New Critical thought, and I'm holding on to my dissection tools. I'm grateful for literary fiction, and I affirm literature that refuses to play the game of limbo that consumer capitalism increasingly requires publishers to play: lower the literary bar, bend toward the aesthetic whims of the masses, publish authors willing to contort their bodies of work toward the sensational and pleasant and exotic, and you just might win. That is, of course, how we have ended up with Amish vampires.

Yet I have learned how fascinating the world below the limbo bar can be. Readers' interactions with texts—including texts of genre fiction—are much more nuanced, rich, and fascinating than critics used to think. Deciphering the nature of the thrill of the chaste in Amish fiction was going to require paying attention to loyal readers and the meaning they were making from the novels they loved, and I needed theory that would help me discern those interactions.

Transactional Theory's Attention to Readers

Literary theory has taken several turns since my college days, including a brief stopover in transactional theories of reading, which assume that the reader and her context contribute as much to the reading act as the author's intention or the text's immutability. Louise Rosenblatt's 1978 *The Reader, the Text, the Poem,* one of the signal texts of the transactional movement, argues that reading events are not neutral or self-contained, that readers are not tabulae rasae awaiting the imprint of the text, and that the texts themselves are only one variable in the reading equation.[33] Rather than assuming that readers simply imbibe meaning from text as if quaffing beer from a mug—with external substance (the meaning), poured from an external source (the text) into internal space (the reader)—transactional theories like Rosenblatt's, also called reader-response theory, let the reader make her own drink, mixed from ingredients including the text; her social location, emotional life, and past experiences; and elixirs from a host of other containers. In a transactional reading framework, you and I can read the same novel and manufacture completely different meanings from it.

Thus, in terms of Amish fiction, Beverly Lewis and her peers aren't the only actors on the stage of bonnet fiction—and maybe not even the most important ones. From this perspective, those who read Amish novels and pass them around become the main performers, the ones most worthy of investigation. "Works of art have a kind of 'unconscious,' which is not under the control of their producers," writes literary theorist Terry Eagleton. "We have come to understand that one of those producers is the reader, viewer or listener—that the recipient of a work of art is a co-creator with it, without whom it would not exist."[34] It is these voices—the voices of the readers—that will command much of our attention.

Cultural Criticism Redefines the Literary

Eagleton represents a more recent and perhaps more significant turn in literary theory toward cultural criticism, also known as cultural theory. Born of the populism of the 1960s and 1970s, cultural criticism both argues with and borrows from several other theories (chief among them Marxism and postmodernism) and disciplines (including anthropology, linguistics, philosophy, and art). Cultural theory not only debunked New Criticism's marginalization of the reader, as transactional reading theory had. It also appended the claim that works of literature and art disclose a great deal about the historical and cultural moment in which they are created. Rather than asking critical questions about a small canonical body of art, cultural theory asks what Eagleton calls metaquestions: questions less about the quality of one particular text than about the nature and conditions under which the text is created and consumed. "Instead of asking whether the clarinet concerto is slightly too cloying to be entirely persuasive," Eagleton writes, "it [cultural theory] inquires about the material conditions which you need to produce concertos in the first place, and how these help to shape the work itself."[35]

Thus, when looking at Amish romance novels through the lens of cultural criticism, I ask fewer questions about whether a particular Amish novel is any "good," or even whether it portrays Amish life in an accurate way. Instead, in *Thrill of the Chaste,* I will ask metaquestions: What cultural and religious work do bonnet books perform in the lives of their readers? How does the sensation of living within a hypermodern and hypersexualized context affect the meanings that readers create from the books? Under what conditions are the books produced? What ideologies constitute them? And how do they function as maps of the evangelical discourse community largely responsible for creating and consuming them?

Cultural theory also widens the field of what scholarly inquiry can pursue, thus making it possible for this book, which examines popular fiction, to be published by a university press. "Culture is ordinary," Raymond Williams, the progenitor of cultural studies, famously wrote. This might not sound radical to twenty-first-century ears, but it was mind-boggling to many scholars in 1958, when "culture" often referred only to the artistic production and consumption of the elite. Although Williams learned from anxious professors in graduate school that "the masses were coming, and that they would trample and destroy the fine fields of culture," he came to believe that so-called high and low forms of culture are less connected to inherent aesthetic quality and more to power and ideology.[36] Those who wield power get to determine what constitutes true "culture," and they tend to look askance at the aesthetic products everyone else is consuming.

Cultural critic Herbert Gans suggests that there are at least five *taste publics*—people who make similar cultural choices according to "shared or common aesthetic values and standards of tastes." Critics and reviewers who belong to the high and upper-middle taste publics tend to view popular culture "as an aberration born of commercial greed and public ignorance," Gans writes.[37] This derogation results from judging the products of popular culture according to the standards of high culture, which, Gans maintains, is unfair to a taste public that operates according to its own internal standards of quality, artistry, and sense of the good life. Critics must evaluate cultural products according to the standards of the particular taste culture from which they emerge, rather than applying standards external to them. While high-culture aesthetic standards are "explicit and to some extent even codified"—by my alma mater's English department, for example, or by the "great books tradition" articulated by Allan Bloom—the standards of other taste cultures "are rarely discussed and taught, and are thus implicit, uncodified, and for all practical purposes invisible."[38] And although evangelical aesthetics are increasingly being codified, thanks to the appearance of prizes like the Christy Awards, established in 1991 to recognize and honor excellence in novels written from "a Christian worldview," such rubrics remain largely invisible to those outside evangelical circles.

Eagleton comes to conclusions similar to Gans's, but from the field of literary theory. "One can think of literature less as some inherent quality or set of qualities displayed by certain kinds of writing all the way from *Beowulf* to Virginia Woolf, than as a number of ways in which people *relate themselves* to writing," Eagleton declares. The consequences of such a line of thinking are radical, he admits. "The suggestion that 'literature' is a highly valued kind of writing is an illuminating one. But it has one fairly devastating consequence. It means that we can drop once and for all the illusion that the category 'literature' is 'objective,' in the sense of being eternally given and immutable. Anything can be literature, and anything which is regarded as unalterably and unquestionably literature—Shakespeare, for example—can cease to be literature."[39]

The notion that novels like *Her Amish Man* or *Ella Finds Love Again* could, at times, constitute "literature"—whereas *To the Lighthouse* might, at times, not—can be disquieting. During the months when I was knocking back one Amish novel after another, I sometimes longed for Allan Bloom's literary clarity. Yet it's not a new idea. Despite the ragings of literary border guards, an objectively definable literary canon was declared an illusion years ago—or if not an illusion, a product of what critic Richard Ohmann has called a "troubled historical process" in which one powerful class's aesthetic wins out over all others'. Cultural theory is no longer novel, and many literary scholars now affirm, at least in part, the idea that, as Nell claims, "the reader's expectations create the quality of literariness in a text, not the text itself."[40]

Women's Suspect Reading Habits

Disdain for Amish fiction may also descend from a historically male academy's denigration of women's reading habits. In the history of reading in the West, novels, especially romances, have had a gendered reputation, with an assumed female readership. During the nineteenth century, female readers and their tastes were often viewed as suspicious, pathetic, or even dangerous. "Novels were held suitable for women, because they were seen as creatures of the imagination, of limited intellectual capacity, both frivolous and emotional," write historians Guglielmo Cavallo and Roger Chartier. Yet, while seen as suitable for the weaker sex, novels also appeared dangerous when critics realized the possibility that novel-reading "could excite the passions, and stimulate the female imagination."[41] By encouraging women's longing for a place at the center of their own life's narratives—not to mention helping them waste time they should have been devoting to their families—novels threatened the bourgeois patriarchs of the nineteenth century.

Claiming that the critical disdain for romance fiction in general and Amish fiction in particular is based on gender would be an oversimplification. Academic theory-making and literary criticism are as much the purview of women as of men in the twenty-first century, and Pamela Regis points out that some of the harshest critics of romance novels are women. Already a century and a half ago, George Eliot critiqued her gender's taste in literature in an essay titled "Silly Novels by Lady Novelists," which she called a genus with species including "the frothy, the prosy, the pious, [and] the pedantic."[42] Working similar critical ground 150 years later, Melanie Springer Mock, professor of English at George Fox University, suggests that reading Amish fiction is akin to "eating an Amish shoo-fly pie: the first bite is always really good, but pretty soon the taste becomes too treacly, and the rest is exceedingly difficult to swallow."[43]

Just as not all the critics of Amish romances are male, not all of the readers of Amish fiction are female. The marketing manager at a major publisher of Amish fiction told me that their Amish authors have a "significant male readership." "We get lots of confessions from the guys sitting in the easy chairs in the bookstore while the book signing is going on that they're reading the books," he relates. "A lot of guys read them. Their wives buy them and then they read them." He attributes the appeal of the books for male readers to the "whole horse and buggy life" and the rural settings. Many Amish novels have at least one point-of-view male character, such that the perspective toggles between female voices and male ones. One of my uncles, a retired farmer, is an avid reader of Amish fiction; and I overheard one man at church say that he had picked up the Amish novel on his wife's bedside stand one night and couldn't put it down. A family friend trades Amish novels back and forth with a man who works in the dining hall of her retirement home, and at one performance of *The Confession,* the musical based on Beverly Lewis's first Amish series for adults, I glanced down the row during the final nuptial scene and saw two men wiping away tears. The boom in e-readers, which we examine in chapter 10, now makes it possible for men—or any other readers who might be ashamed, for whatever reason, of their love of Amish fiction—to enjoy Amish novels on a bus or in a waiting room without others' knowledge.

Still, since Amish romance novels are largely written and read by women, we must consider the nexus of gender and reading. Three out of four readers of Christian fiction are women, and Amish fiction, as a subgenre of

Christian fiction, is likely no different.[44] Pamela Regis points out that although the *New York Times* reviews genre fiction such as mystery, science
fiction, and horror, it does not review romance novels, the most popular
form of the novel in twentieth-century North America and one almost exclusively read by women. And while Amish fiction adheres more solidly
to the forms of inspirational Christian fiction than to those of general romance, it shares attributes with the romance genre, which Regis suggests
is frequently attacked by critics who discount "the most personal hopes of
millions of women around the world."[45] If, in addition to guarding literary
borders, academic discourse's police work includes giving medals to some
readers (often men) for having sophisticated literary tastes and sentencing
others (often women) for pedestrian sensibilities, I'm not willing to serve
in that line of duty.

Readers at the Fore

Theory would determine the endpoints of my analysis, so choosing my theoretical lens carefully was critical. Because meaning resides not in a text
but in the interaction between the text and the reader and the culture in
which both were created, hazarding a formalist literary analysis of these
novels would run the risk, as Janice Radway points out in her landmark
ethnographic study of romance readers, of analyzing "something that does
not even remotely resemble the text as they [the readers] encounter it."[46]
And since the assumptions I had made about what constitutes literature
were rooted in my own particular taste culture, refusing to acknowledge the
existence of other aesthetic rubrics meant that I risked misreading Amish
fiction—and misunderstanding its appreciative readers—altogether.

   I also discovered that for many of those readers, Amish romances represent only a small fraction of their reading. Thus, claiming to understand
readers' longings and anxieties by examining one subgenre of many that
they like to read becomes a futile exercise. One evening during a conversation with Ceil, who has read sixty-seven Amish romance novels, I watched
as she opened up a Word document containing the titles of all the books
she has read since 1983. It is 118 pages long, with about thirty titles on each
page. That's 3,540 books (not counting all the children and young-reader

books she reads for her work at the library), which translates to about eleven books a month. Three a week. One every 2.3 days.[47] Clearly, Amish stories are not the only narratives to which Ceil turns when she wants a good read. Overplaying the role of Amish fiction in the lives of its readers would do a disservice to their often wide-ranging literary tastes and other interests.

As I talked to and corresponded with more and more readers and writers of Amish fiction, and as they hosted me in their homes, fed me, and gave me hours of their time with nothing in return except the chance to talk about books, I recognized how profoundly I wanted to represent them with the generosity and graciousness with which they had treated me, even when I asked them questions that certainly revealed my own latent judgments. I began discovering that women I already knew and loved—my widowed aunt, the fabulously kind women at my church, the chair of the chemistry department at a local college—were also fans of Amish fiction. Slowly I began recognizing the thick overlap between taste publics and the fact that my loved ones don't all belong to mine.

These readers entrusted me with their honest assessments of the fiction they love; their distaste for a society with seemingly few technological and sexual limits; and their desire for community, coherence, and "the simple life," however they define it. Transactional reading and cultural theory had already suggested that paying attention to readers' words and worlds was critical; growing regard for the people I was interviewing confirmed it. Although these readers' favorite books might not get high marks according to the assessments of my taste public, and although I question whether novelists can write about another culture without in some way domesticating or exoticizing it, I came to respect the impulse and conscience underlying their readings.

After all, longing for community and coherence and even a happy ending doesn't mean you're unsophisticated or uncultured or the victim of false consciousness. It just means you're human.

Everything Old Is New Again

Having said all that I have about my fascination with the critical responses to Amish fiction, the question of why bonnet fiction has suddenly become so blisteringly popular still holds me rapt. The question of why chaste texts about chaste protagonists in a chaste culture are so alluring to readers remains the focal point of this book.

The first step toward understanding the popularity of the novels and the cultural and religious work they perform begins with an excavation of Amish romance novel history. Many observers espouse a young-earth theory when it comes to the genre, assuming Beverly Lewis created it out of a formless void in the mid-1990s, when she wrote *The Shunning*. But to discover the ur–bonnet book, you must dig way past the alluvium of the millennial Amish novel boom, past the topsoil of Lewis's early career success, way down to the primordial sands of the early twentieth century.[48]

For that is when this story begins, in a stately brick house in Harrisburg, Pennsylvania, just twenty miles from the Lancaster County line.[49] There, at 1168 Mulberry Street, novelist Helen Reimensnyder Martin and her musician husband lived with their two children. Harrisburg seemed backward to the Swarthmore- and Radcliffe-educated Martin, and she and her husband traveled frequently; in Martin's opinion, Harrisburg was "a provincial town."[50] Yet provinciality was the very engine of most of Martin's short stories and novels, which are set in what she saw as the uncouth domain of the Pennsylvania Germans. Martin's *Sabina: A Story of the Amish,* published in 1905, lays legitimate claim to being the first Amish romance novel ever written. Thanks to the heroine's strange psychic powers, *Sabina of the Amish* could also be considered the first paranormal Amish romance novel—thus proving songwriter Peter Allen's jazzy assertion that, in literature and life, everything old is new again.

Helen Reimensnyder Martin's novel Sabina: A Story of the Amish *(1905)*
was the first Amish romance novel ever published.

Chapter Two

The DNA of Amish Romance Novels

The Amish heroine lives with her parents, siblings, and widowed aunt on a verdant farm in Lancaster County. She is all but betrothed to her suitor, an Amish man whom she does not love. Enter a handsome English stranger, an artist who boards with the protagonist's family to paint the picturesque folk and their surrounding locale. Our heroine falls hopelessly in love with him, and he with her. Underneath various subplots, including a brother's romance, the mysterious death of a secondary character, and the protagonist's clairvoyant intuitions, throbs the essential question: which guy will get the girl?

So goes a story line as intelligible to contemporary readers of Amish fiction as the now-familiar concepts of *Rumspringa* and shunning. Yet this narrative comes from a book over a century old: Helen Reimensnyder Martin's 1905 novel *Sabina: A Story of the Amish*.[1] In its reliance on rural particularism and its use of romance as an engine of plot, *Sabina* carries two of the three genetic strands that characterize contemporary Amish romances. The third strand—evangelical piety—would be encoded into Amish fiction several decades later, through the midcentury novels of Clara Bernice Miller. Although this blend of rurality, romance, and religiosity did not prove its appeal to a wide swath of readers until the 1997 publication of Beverly Lewis's *The Shunning*, these three characteristics had formed the backbone of the genre for decades. Tracing the accrual of the three elements also sheds light on the character of contemporary Amish fiction.

The history of Amish romance reveals a dialectic at work in popular representations of the Amish, in which the Amish are alternately idealized as American saints and denigrated as a fallen people. It is a dialectic that we will observe throughout the twentieth century, one that draws force from the contradictory poles of mystification and denigration. This dialectic may be emerging again within the subgenre, as we will see in ensuing chapters.

Chronicling the history of the bonnet book takes us past well-known and lesser-known landmarks in the twentieth century: the advent of leisure reading for the privileged classes and white Americans' anxiety about immigration in the early 1900s; the appeal of the pastoral to industrializing and modernizing populations; the two-mindedness of midcentury Mennonites regarding how to represent their ecclesial cousins; the post–World War II boom in Christian publishing that has continued, with a few hiccups, to the present; the swelling eroticism of the modern romance novel and the dissenting chastity of the evangelical romance novel; and the expanding domains of evangelicalism and the marketplace of Christian retail. These forces, combined with the marketability of the Amish within an increasingly hypermodern and hypersexualized cultural situation, led toward the breakaway success of *The Shunning*, the first contemporary, commercially successful Amish novel.

Prior to all this twentieth-century literary, social, and religious cacophony, however, stands Sabina, Martin's protagonist and the maternal ancestor of the countless Amish women who now populate bonnet fiction. Sabina's story, what Martin calls the "primitive rural drama that was being enacted under his [her English suitor's] eyes," was the first of many such primitive rural dramas to be enacted under the eyes of fiction readers to come.[2] So it is that any investigation into the contemporary Amish romance novel must begin here, with the fustily named love triangle of "Biney" Wilt, Augustus Acker, and Ulmer Popple.

Sabina: The Ur–Bonnet Book

Were you to leaf through the antique, sepia-edged pages of *Sabina* in search of the "respect" and "love" and "admiration" for the Amish that characterize current bonnet novelists' descriptions of their work, you would be looking for a long time. Martin's portrayal of Sabina and her family is unabashed in its derision. The non-Amish male protagonist, Augustus Acker, who is lodging with Sabina's family, uses adjectives like "queer" and "ignorant" and "commonplace" to describe them, and Martin offers no authorial irony to suggest that his impressions are wrong. Martin has Sabina looking out at the world from under her "ugly purple bonnet" with a gaze as blinkered as that of her family's horses, a stance from which women who can't make lard don't make good wives and that views grammar as a field "where learns you how to speak correct."[3]

Throughout the book, we mostly view Sabina and her Amish family through the eyes of Augustus. In a conversation with Levi Wilt, Sabina's father, Augustus tells Levi that the Amish people he has seen at the Lancaster market are "'certainly robust, healthy-looking specimens of humanity. But there is a remarkable sameness of type among them.'" Levi responds:

"You think?" Levi's tone was uninterested. Such speculation was too subtle for him. "The reason we marry our cousins so much is that we like to stick close to each other and form Amish settlements, still. We try to make farmers of all our sons and give 'em farms near us when they get married, so they don't move away. To keep 'em satisfied to be farmers, we darsent leave 'em get too much educated, so we just send 'em to the district school a while, and that has to do 'em."

"And of course you must keep your daughters uneducated, too, or they would not be willing to marry the farmers—is that your principle?"

"Yes, them's our ways."[4]

Martin's portrayal of her Amish characters and their speechways seals *Sabina*'s identity as a work of regional fiction, sometimes called "local color" writing, which constituted a good portion of American literature in the latter half of the nineteenth and early part of the twentieth centuries. Regional fiction attempted to capture the particularities of mostly rural landscapes, peoples, and languages. According to Richard H. Brodhead, a scholar of nineteenth-century literature, regionalist writing "requires a setting outside the world of modern development, a zone of backwardness where locally variant folkways still prevail." Readers of local-color writing had only recently acquired leisure time sufficient for activities such as pleasure reading, and regional fiction like Martin's *Sabina* offered such upper-crust readers a "rustic vacation," of sorts, which "dealt with the threat of the foreign from within an apparently detached entertainment realm."[5]

Reading books like *Sabina: A Story of the Amish* would have enabled readers, Brodhead argues, to bring themselves "within hearing distance of the 'stranger in the land'" but at a safe remove from the actual realities of an increasingly diverse America. Not inconsequentially, Brodhead adds, regional fiction also substituted "safe" native communities like the Creole or Tennessee mountain folk or, in the case of Martin's writing, the Pennsylvania Dutch, for the new immigrants who were crowding into American cities: Chinese, southern Italians, Russian Jews, and Slavs. In an era when the immigrant had become a "phobic embodiment of all imagined threats to elite superiority, from cultural mongrelization and racial dilution to political anarchism and class war," Brodhead says, regional writing like Martin's became a way for readers who considered themselves socially superior to manage their anxiety about the darker-skinned masses who were appearing on their doorstep.[6]

Although Brodhead's analysis may seem an outsized burden for *Sabina* to carry, it helps to explain how Martin's readers—privileged Americans who considered themselves "nonethnic"—would have actually found solace in the ostensibly tragic ending of the novel. In violation of one of the primary conventions of the contemporary Amish romance, the heroine and her beloved do not get together. Sabina's psychic intuitions, which have centered around the frightening appearance of "the Face" in her mind's eye, ultimately land her in a feverish stupor after she sees a man on a streetcar whose features are exactly the same as those in the vision that has haunted her. Her near-death illness erases all memory of her love for the non-Amish artist, all the events of their truncated courtship, and all the education she had begun pursuing at a local teachers college. Augustus goes to Paris to study art, returning to Lancaster two years later to see the lovely face that has been haunting *him*—not in a terrifying manner but in an appealing one. Throughout the book, Augustus has longed to paint Sabina; one could even suggest that Augustus's desire to reproduce an Amish woman is stronger than his desire to reproduce *with* one. In the end, he comes to see Sabina one more time before attempting to paint her portrait. He finds her married to Ulmer Popple, her boorish Amish suitor, and the mother of two children. The final scene has Augustus walking away from Sabina, who "picked [her baby] up and crooned over it, too absorbed in it, and its need of her, to notice him further."[7]

By keeping Sabina safely Amish and Augustus safely English in the end, Martin gave her early-twentieth-century readers the happy ending that they desired: a temporary tryst, rather than a permanent alliance, with the Other. If Brodhead is correct, the fictional Sabina and her family, their affection for inbreeding, and their bastardized tongue were performing a pleasurable scene in their native habitat for an audience with a taste for a judicious amount of the primitive. The novel thus offered turn-of-the-century readers a dalliance with difference, a chance to court the Other without consummating the relationship.

Sabina also proffered a feminist reminder of modernity's beneficence to women, and it includes more overtly feminist commentary than most Amish novels do today. While many current Amish novels address the self-actualization and wish fulfillment of its female characters, as we will see in chapter 7, almost all end in contented marriage and the promise of motherhood. The protagonist may work in a bakery or a harness shop or a restaurant, but any paid labor is generally tangential to her caretaking offices. Any feminism within the pages of current Amish novels is of a gentle variety, cloaked in language of self-actualization and finding oneself. But Helen Reimensnyder Martin was a suffragist and a socialist, and her ideological commitments are clear.[8] In a scene in which Aunt Susanna carries heavy chairs out to the porch, Martin suggests that Amish men's views of women were as primitive as a progressively minded reader at the turn of the century could imagine: "Levi made no movement to help her, for an Amishman's idea of the relation of the sexes is not unlike that of a North American Indian—it is the part of the female to wait on the male and make him comfortable. This, indeed, is the chief end of woman." From Martin's perspective, Amish women lived not only without fulfillment or joy but without subjectivity at all. Three pages from the end of the book, Augustus asks Sabina's aunt whether Sabina, now married and a mother, is happy. "Whether she's happy?" Aunt Susanna responds, bewildered; "it was a question too searching for the average Amish intellect. 'I never ast her if she is or no. I guess mebbe she is. She ain't never said nothin'.'"[9]

Sabina's pathetic destiny—marriage to a man she does not love, self-abnegating motherhood, and amnesia regarding the brief era when she stood on the brink of passion and education—simply underscores Martin's feminist point by counterpoint. There is no way, in Martin's view, for Sabina to be both Amish and self-actualized. Unlike contemporary readers of Amish fiction, who often admire Amish resistance to hypermodernity, readers of the ur–bonnet book likely had their modernizing impulses confirmed. If resisting modernity required marrying one's cousin and pegging a wife's worth to her knack for making lard, Martin seemed to suggest, then it was better to get with the progressive program of the twentieth century.

Cora Gottschalk Welty's Whiter-Than-White Amish

Three years after Martin's *Sabina* appeared, *The Masquerading of Margaret*, by Cora Gottschalk Welty, offered an inverse portrayal of Amish life, albeit one still containing the two constitutive elements, rurality and romance, that defined *Sabina*'s narrative.[10] In Welty's work, the Amish remain exotic and strange and rural, but now they live in an Eden of rustic, agrarian simplicity, unsullied by modernity. Unlike the doltish yokels of Martin's prose, Welty's Amish hold, in the words of one character in *The Masquerading of Margaret*, "a happiness and contentment that rivaled and outwitted luxuries" and are "utterly removed and apart from the surrounding contentions and strife."[11]

In the same manner in which Virgil's Arcadia, a rural region in Greece, became an idealized location of bucolic purity, the Amish have frequently embodied the pastoral ideal for people who feel caught in the machinations of urban and technological advancement.[12] Welty's characters reside in this

Amish Arcadia, a location that anticipates the pastoral conventions of contemporary bonnet fiction.[13]

When wealthy New York socialite Margaret Habecker visits her Amish relatives, she is captivated by the simple surroundings. The bedroom "was a joy in its quaintness!" and "everywhere there was an air of order, cleanliness and serenity, and she [Margaret] loved it."[14] Margaret decides to dress in Amish garb during her stay—"I'm going to be in harmony with my surroundings. . . . No one is to know otherwise than 'Margaret Habecker, Amish,'" she says—and she finds herself longing for a life apart from the "flitting through society" that she has done thus far.[15] "Oh, how I wish our lives were different," Margaret says, musing about her life back in New York. "How I wish that we were as simple and sincere as these good people are!" Margaret soon falls in love with Robert Jackson, an English boarder at her Amish relatives' home, who agrees with her assessment of Amish life: "I honor and revere these noble Amish folk. . . . Their simple life is so refreshing," he tells Margaret, adding that it would be wonderful if "this great surging world would pause to listen and to learn at the feet of the Amish." Pastoral convention frequently inserts bewildered city-dwellers into the rural landscape and has them finding themselves drawn to the pristine simplicity they find there. As cultural theorist Crystal Downing points out about the pastoral conventions of several Amish-themed films, the outsider then returns to the city, as Margaret and Robert do, having been transformed by their pastoral immersion.[16]

The distance between Martin's and Welty's narrative approaches to fictionalizing the Amish would be reproduced over and over again in the coming century of Amish-themed stories. The dialectic between denigration and sacralization of the Amish is repeatedly rehearsed in contemporary culture.[17] It's a dialectic we will observe again in chapter 10, when we hear from several would-be Amish novelists frustrated with what one calls the "sugar-coating" tendencies within contemporary Amish fiction.

Despite its binary opposition to the representation of the Amish in *Sabina,* however, *The Masquerading of Margaret* still functions as regional fiction: literature that helped a socially privileged readership manage anxiety about the ethnically and economically different Other. With her wedding to

Robert, "the supreme moment of her life," Margaret's story culminates in blissful radiance rather than in amnesiac and loveless trance, as Sabina's does. But the finales of both *Sabina* and *The Masquerading of Margaret* keep the Amish maritally and genetically cordoned off from the English. Reading *The Masquerading of Margaret*, like reading *Sabina*, would have allowed an early-twentieth-century readership to don the costume of the Other, as Margaret herself does, for a masquerade of identity. But in the end, both Margaret and her reader can strip off their Amish garb while keeping notions of ethnic purity intact.

The brutish, unenlightened Other that appears in Amish guise in Martin's novel also resides in Welty's book. But in Welty's tale, this Other appears as horse-thieving Gypsies with "dirty women and children" and as the "antagonistic natives with their superstitious beliefs" whom one character plans to save when he goes as a missionary to the Philippines.[18] Here, the Amish are definitely white—ultrawhite, even, when contrasted with Roma and Filipinos. Welty's novel, when set against Martin's, demonstrates the dichotomy that poet Julia Kasdorf discovered in racial representations of the Amish in contemporary poetry. In some poems, "they [the Amish] are raced as white. . . . In fact, they might even embody the myth of racial purity," Kasdorf asserts; in others, they are depicted as nonwhite, demonstrating the country's deep investment "in positioning Amish people outside the mainstream, as Other." In Martin's books, the Amish are essentially "nonwhite"; in Welty's, they are whiter than white. Either way, such portrayals of the Amish tend to normalize the "'we' that is whiteness."[19]

Whether portrayed as nonwhite primitives or whiter-than-white Arcadians, the Amish characters that people these early romances are distinctly Other from the novels' assumed readership. It is doubtful that either Martin or Welty ever intoned, as at least one contemporary author of Amish romance has, that the Amish are "just like the rest of us." Although the computerless and largely carless readers of these early twentieth-century novels lived more like the Amish than contemporary bonnet-fiction readers do, the incipient Amish literature available to them underscored difference rather than concurrence. The eager embrace of the Amish by evangelicals, demonstrated by a 2011 headline about Amish fiction that proclaimed that the Amish are "Just Like Us," was still almost a century away.[20]

Dobson's Fallen Saints and Yoder's Saving Remnant

The dialectical swing of denigration and mystification of the Amish continued in ensuing decades. Ruth Lininger Dobson's *Straw in the Wind*, published in 1937, saw the Martinesque derogation of the Amish and raised it one. In her setting of choice, a northern Indiana Amish community, Dobson paints an unforgettable character: the domineering and egoistic Amish bishop Moses Bontrager. He forbids one daughter to marry the man she loves and forces another daughter to marry an elderly widower she does not love, and his wife dies from overwork. The book won the prestigious Hopwood Prize from the University of Michigan and went into four printings in its first year.

Straw in the Wind elicited indignant responses from Amish and Mennonites. One Amish bishop wrote in a local newspaper that, having known nearly every Amish leader in the United States for several decades, he had never met one "that would in any way fit the description of this avaricious potentate." A Mennonite reviewer methodically slammed the book for its many inaccuracies, some of which appear to be rather trivial points of contention, and one Amish man held a lengthy and testy correspondence with Dobson, questioning what qualified her to write about his people.[21]

A similar outrage about Dobson's work inspired Mennonite writer Joseph W. Yoder, who grew up Amish, to attempt to set the record straight. "Being Amish born, raised Amish and still belong [sic] to the Amish Church, I wish to protest against the many misrepresentations of that novel," Yoder wrote in 1938. Thus he began writing the story of his mother's life, which became *Rosanna of the Amish*. The novel, self-published in 1940 and then published by the Mennonite Publishing House, has sold more than four hundred thousand copies and was reissued in 2008. It tells the story of Yoder's mother, Rosanna, born to an Irish-American family and adopted by an Amish woman as a baby when her mother died. It also narrates her courtship and marriage to Little Crist. Unlike most Amish romance novels today, the book covers a wide chronological swath, from Rosanna's birth through her marriage and childrearing years and all the way up to her death; it includes gentle anecdotes about family life and extensive exposition of Amish folkways.[22] Though not written as a romance novel and perhaps more accurately described as autoethnography, as Kasdorf asserts, *Rosanna* functions as a romance novel according to the definitions of Regis and Radway.

The pastoral is writ large all over Yoder's book, what with its chestnut parties, blacksmith shops, powwowing, and visits from Rosanna's urban siblings, who are impressed with the fact that the Amish "all bore the stamp of health and strength and vigor." When Rosanna's sister Margaret, an urbanite, comes to visit Rosanna, Margaret is delighted by the "pure clean air, the unobstructed sunshine, the abundant foliage of the trees, the delightful freshness of the fruits and vegetables on the table and the aroma of the country cured ham." Another English woman, a local villager who comes to buy cream from Rosanna, says at one point, "Rosanna, I envy you; you're a happy woman. I wish I had your philosophy of life."[23]

Yoder's prose is as elevated as his portrayal of the loved ones he wished to memorialize, as demonstrated in his final paragraph: "Thus closed the last chapter of the love-life of Rosanna of the Amish, and Little Crist, her devoted husband, but the memory of their devotion to each other and to the church and their untiring kindness to all who were in need will linger in the beautiful Kishacoquillas Valley while the memory of man endureth." As Mennonite professor John Umble observed, the idyllic and mystifying tone by which Yoder mediates Amish life was likely determined by the defensive posture in which he wrote the book.[24]

But a trustee-like approach to the Amish is certainly not the only stance available to a novelist raised in that tradition. Two decades after *Rosanna* was first published, Clara Bernice Miller, who, like Yoder, grew up Amish, would write four romance-inflected novels, all of them as unflattering to the Amish as Yoder's was generous.[25]

Escalator Amish: Clara Bernice Miller's Midcentury Evangelism

Ethno-rural particularism and heterosexual romance had carried Amish novels into the middle of the century, and Clara Bernice Miller threw those items into the pot. But more than any previous Amish romance novelist, Miller added religious piety to her work. Some critics grumbled that Clara Bernice Miller had sold her Amish birthright for a pot of evangelical message, but it is also true that she had come across a central ingredient in the Amish fictional stew. Evangelicalism, with its attendant emphases on a personal relationship with Christ, born-again salvation, and evangelism, was the flavor enhancer that would continue to both satisfy and stimulate readerly appetites years after her death.

It takes only a few pages of *Katie,* Clara Bernice Miller's second book, published in 1966, for a reader to determine which dialectical pole Miller inhabits. Her heroine, a spunky Amish girl who strained against her family's suspicion of reading books, thought "God must be a great, angry being who frowned on everything that was nice and desirable, if He demanded all her church said He did." Over time, however, through reading Christian romance novels, Katie learns the evangelical message of personal salvation. When Katie eventually kneels beside her bed and asks God to save her soul, Miller observes that "few of her people would have thought it anything special." She longs for her family to become born again, and her mother accuses her of heresy for her convictions: "I told Pop that you were getting heretical ideas way last spring," her mother tells her. "What's the matter with you anyway? Since when does a young girl like you know more about the Scriptures than the preachers do?" Katie considers leaving the church for a more liberal Mennonite group but decides to stay Amish, at least as long as "our people accept any spiritual light."[26] In the end she marries an Amish man, Mark Hochstettler, who, like her, wants to be an undercover missionary to the Amish. In one conversation, Katie asks him,

"Aren't you going out to some mission field?"

"Not in the sense of it being a place in some other country."

"Where are you planning to go then?"

"Katie, have you ever thought what a big field our own people are?"

She gave a sad, short laugh. "Have I? That's all I have been thinking the last few days."[27]

Miller's books, which included *The Crying Heart* (1962) and *The Tender Herb* (1968), don't stop at portraying the majority of Amish people as legalistic followers of rules rather than Jesus. On Miller's fictional landscape, Amish theology leads to immorality of all kinds, especially among the youth, whom Miller portrays as largely interested in fornicating and drinking. Katie and some of her friends become known as the "covering bunch" because, when dating boys in the evening, they decide to leave their coverings on and their lamps burning. They are ridiculed as prudish and self-righteous by the youth and many of the adults in their community, who say that old, looser courting ways worked well enough for them. Katie and her peers in the covering bunch are clear predecessors of the virginal heroines who populate contemporary Amish fiction.

Like Beverly Lewis, who published her first Amish novel thirty years after Clara Bernice Miller published her last, Miller hoped her books would be read by Amish people, who then might become born-again Christians. There is a long history of evangelicalism's ministrations among the Amish, beginning around the time that Clara Bernice Miller was writing her novels and coalescing in the Amish "mission movement," when some Amish individuals began arguing that faith must include witnessing to others.[28] A 1966 division among the Lancaster County Amish occurred when one group began agitating for greater expressions of personal salvation, more wholesome youth activities, and less stringent authority for church rules. Today there are forty distinct Amish affiliations, each with different levels of acceptance and use of individualized expressions of spirituality. "Higher" and more progressive affiliations such as the New Order Amish often encourage individuals to articulate personal faith narratives, and "lower" ones, such as the Swartzentruber Amish, usually discourage it. While a few Amish people move from higher to lower affiliations because of marriage or changing understandings of faith, the more frequent trajectory is from lower affiliations to higher.

The "Anabaptist escalator," first identified as such by sociologist Donald B. Kraybill, helps to explain this movement from low-church, world-rejecting plainness to higher floors of progressive, world-accommodating Anabaptist churches and beyond.[29] Clara Bernice Miller herself rode the Anabaptist escalator: having been raised Amish, she joined the church at sixteen but had become a member of the Beachy Amish, a car-driving Anabaptist group, by the time she wrote her first novel. She had become Mennonite by the time she wrote her second. Powered by individualism and modernization, the Anabaptist escalator frequently has implications for

*Clara Bernice Miller, who was raised Amish, published three Amish-themed
romance novels in the 1960s, including* Katie *(1966).*
Used by permission of Herald Press.

spirituality. Evangelical vocabulary places the individual, rather than the
church community, in a privileged position with regard to understanding
God's will and purpose. It can be perceived as threatening by Amish people,
such as one Old Order Amish man in Holmes County, Ohio, with whom
I spoke.

David Kline has actually gone *down* the up escalator, having been New

Order Amish for a time before becoming Old Order because he became weary of New Order understandings of salvation. An organic farmer, Kline is not normally suspicious of literature and is himself a writer of more than a little acclaim.[30] Somehow managing to be both curmudgeonly and effervescent, Kline has opinions about everything from late capitalism to what he calls evangelicalism's "Western industrial plan of salvation." Yet just as quickly he can move on to rapturous descriptions of a red-shouldered hawk or of the strange half-inch of ice that coated his farm overnight.

"We had Harry Potter, we had Mark Twain," Kline says, describing the books on his shelves when his children, now adults, were at home. It is a frigid February day, and Kline is speaking with me from his phone shanty, the small enclosure outside of some Amish homes where a phone is allowed. "But we did *not* let Clara Bernice Miller books into our home," Kline tells me firmly, his syllables distinct as hand claps. "They're anti-Amish." Considering Miller's twin portrayals of the Amish as both mission field and seedbed of immorality, one can see why Kline would keep Miller's books out of his home, why he would view this restriction as a lesser evil than the whirring motor of evangelicalism, which can carry away one's children and drop them off far from home.[31]

Hence, more than three decades before Beverly Lewis penned *The Shunning*, Miller and her Mennonite publisher, Herald Press, had unwittingly discovered the third element of the quintessential Amish romance novel: evangelical devotion. The recipe worked well enough that Miller's first two books, *The Crying Heart* and *Katie,* sold a combined two hundred thousand copies. Many of the copies were paperbacks printed by Moody Press, which was the first evangelical publisher to enter the Amish-fiction fold.[32]

Although Miller's work succeeded, with its tripartite blend of rural particularism, chaste romance, and evangelical piety, it would take another forty years for other evangelical publishers to figure out what an appealing and lucrative alliance that could be. Miller's heroine herself offers a canny comment on the genre that houses her when she describes for her sister the inspirational novels she has been reading. "'Well—' Katie tried to find the right words. 'They are romances—but they also tell you how to be saved.'"[33]

The Birth of Prairie Romance

Carol Johnson read several of Clara Bernice Miller's books when she was in her early twenties. Like most people who try to recall novels they read more than forty years ago, Johnson can't remember much about the plots or the characters except that they were Amish. The daughter of Christian missionaries in Borneo, Johnson was attending a small missionary recruiting and training center called Bethany Missionary Fellowship in Minneapolis at the time. By 1978 Johnson had become the editorial director at the newly expanded publishing arm of the Bible college.

One day she sat down at her desk to read four chapters of a manuscript sent over the transom by an unknown writer, a forty-two-year-old mother of four teenagers. Johnson was not the first editor to read the manuscript; the writer had already sent it to a large New York publishing house that had summarily rejected it. Set on the Western frontier, the novel revolved around a determined young protagonist whose husband dies just after they reach the land they plan to claim. Pregnant with her first baby, she quickly marries a widower whom she does not love, since it's the only way she and her child will survive the harsh conditions of pioneer life. Her new husband is a Christian, and his slow imparting of the gospel to her mirrors the gradual but certain ripening of their love.

"Something about her simple story and her simple writing style connected with me on an emotional level that I can't really explain," Johnson recalls.[34] She took the manuscript to her colleagues and advocated on its behalf. The editorial board finally agreed to its publication, somewhat reluctantly. Most of their publishing program to date had centered on theological and devotional nonfiction, written largely by male authors. When the novel was published in 1979, booksellers were similarly cautious about stocking it. Bethany House decided to market the book through a company that held home parties, like those that sell Tupperware.[35]

Janette Oke's *Love Comes Softly* is now widely credited as the novel that launched the contemporary Christian fiction movement. What Oke had thought would be a stand-alone novel morphed into a multigenerational, eight-book saga. More than thirty years after her first book was published, her novels have sold nearly 30 million copies.[36] The small publisher to which she sent her manuscript is now powerhouse publisher Bethany House, a division of Baker Publishing Group, and the editor who discovered her is now known as the midwife of the modern evangelical romance novel.

Before Johnson acquired Oke's manuscript, the fiction shelf in most Christian bookstores was just that: a shelf, Johnson recalls. "It was twenty-four inches long, and everything was there," she says. The shelf had stray titles by Grace Livingston Hill, whose fiction equation consisted of "boy plus girl plus conservative Protestant Christianity equals a happy marriage," according to religion scholar Lynn Neal, and a few by Catherine Marshall, whose 1967 novel about a schoolteacher in North Carolina, *Christy*, honed the formula.[37] But evangelicals were still largely suspicious of fiction, especially romances, and the marriage of the terms "Christian" and "novel" was still mostly a shotgun affair.

But during the two decades following the publication of *Love Comes Softly*, Christian fiction grew more quickly than any other segment of Christian retail, becoming what one writer called "the 500-pound gorilla of the Christian publishing industry."[38] And although *Love Comes Softly* does not even have Amish characters, its blend of rurality, romance, and religion and its birthplace at Bethany House render it a close ancestor of contemporary Amish fiction. Had Oke's prairie romance not proved readers' craving for chaste, faith-filled, romance-infused rurality, Bethany House editors may have been less willing to take a risk on the Amish story that one of their children's authors would propose almost twenty years later.

Fabio, Harlequin, and Musical Beds

In the general market, contemporary romance novels had taken off through the 1972 publication of Kathleen Woodiwiss's *The Flame and the Flower*. Before Woodiwiss's success, writes Janice Radway, gothic romances like Daphne du Maurier's *Rebecca* had centered on "love relationships between wealthy, handsome men and 'spunky' but vulnerable women," often in some type of physical peril.[39] Publishers did very little advertising of gothics; instead, they placed them in grocery stores and drugstores, locations populated in the 1960s largely by women, the target readership.

But by the early 1970s, romance sales had begun to decline, either be-

The blockbuster prairie romance novel Love Comes Softly (1979), by Janette
Oke, is an ancestor of Amish fiction in its combination of rural setting,
heterosexual romance, and evangelical piety.
Used by permission of Baker Publishing Group.

cause the market for them had become saturated or because the feminist movement and the sexual revolution had led readers to long for more exploration of female agency and sexual desire. Woodiwiss's novel, which included sexual scenes and a near rape, became the quintessential "bodice-ripper" and sold more than 2.3 million copies. Published as a paperback original, it signaled the advent of a new era of romance publishing. By 1977, the year before Carol Johnson sat down to read Janette Oke's manuscript, premier romance publisher Harlequin boasted sales of $75 million.[40] The Harlequin at the end of the cereal aisle had become a staple of many American women's reading diets, even as denigration of the genre as empty-headed and regressive was becoming the standard response of critics. By 1999 more than half of the mass-market and trade paperbacks sold in North America were romance novels.[41]

Some of those mass-market romances were actually Amish romance novels. At least six mass-market Amish romance novels were published by trade and romance publishing houses between 1986 and 2005, with covers that revealed nothing of their Amish location or characters. On the front covers of these novels, the people are stripped of any signs of Amishness—and, in one case, of any clothing at all.[42] The cover of Sharon and Tom Curtis's 1986 romance *Sunshine and Shadow,* which narrates the liaison between Amish widow Susan Peachey and a jaded Hollywood film director, shows a woman and a man lying in bed, their naked torsos only partially hidden by a gold-flecked comforter. The cover of Annette Blair's 1999 *Thee, I Love*—which tells of a love affair between Amish schoolteacher Rachel Sauder and her brother-in-law Jacob—shows Rachel in a décolletage-baring dress hiked to her thigh and lifting her lips to Jacob's (see the figure on page 71).

The steamier that general-market romances became, however, the less appeal they held for evangelical readers and other women offended by a bare-chested Fabio Lanzoni, the Italian model whose sex appeal dripped off countless romance novel covers in the 1980s and 1990s, and by story lines that increasingly featured casual and explicit sexual encounters. In her study of evangelical romance novel readers, Lynn Neal notes the frequent indictment of romance novels by the Christian women she interviewed. "The problem for these women revolves around not only the 'musical beds' message of secular romance, but also its explicit portrayal," she writes. Neal cites a reader's letter to one author: "Have you ever read any of those secular books they have in stores? I bought one once and boy was it bad. I hadn't even gotten past the first chapter when I had to throw it away."[43]

It was this reader—the evangelical Christian woman who wanted her romantic fiction more closely aligned with her faith than with Fabio—whom Carol Johnson knew and understood. It was this reader who had been waiting for writers and publishers to comprehend the delicate blend of rurality, chaste romance, and Christian devotion that she was seeking. Like Clara Bernice Miller's Katie and her friends in the covering bunch, this reader definitely wanted her heroines to keep their lamps lit and their coverings on.

Beverly Lewis's "Little Amish Story"

Almost thirty years after Johnson read Oke's manuscript, Beverly Lewis, a children's author with modest sales, approached Bethany House with an idea. One of Lewis's series for young readers, Summerhill Secrets, had featured a non-Amish teenager with Amish friends and neighbors in Lancaster County, and Lewis was ready to try her hand at writing fiction for adults. She proposed a story loosely based on the life of her maternal grandmother, Ada Ranck Buchwalter. Buchwalter was actually Mennonite, but Lewis chose to migrate her grandmother's story from the lesser-known and less-restrictive Mennonites to the Amish. There is no way to know whether, had Lewis made Katie Lapp Mennonite rather than Amish, we would be discussing a different phenomenon—or no phenomenon at all.[44]

When Lewis's editor approached Johnson with the idea, Johnson remembered the Amish novels by Clara Bernice Miller that she had read as a young adult. "I had a connection with the Amish people and the story from there," Johnson says; "I was captivated immediately by what Bev had come up with. So we published it, probably slightly cautiously—not sure how it would be received."[45]

For despite Oke's success with prairie romance and the stunning triumph of a title from a different Christian fiction subgenre—the 1986 suspense thriller *This Present Darkness*, which spent ninety-six months on the Christian Bookseller Association bestseller list—there were no indications

that an Amish romance novel would have broad appeal.[46] Herald Press,
the publisher of *Rosanna* and Clara Bernice Miller's books, was continuing
to publish Amish-themed novels, but their audience remained relatively
small and was composed mostly of Mennonite readers. Johnson and her
colleagues at Bethany House knew that the 1985 romantic suspense film
Witness had done well, grossing almost $40 million in the first six weeks.
Starring Kelly McGillis as an alluring Amish widow and Harrison Ford as
a police officer seeking safety among the Amish as he flees corrupt cops,
the film received eight Academy Award nominations.[47] And Amish-themed
tourism, along with the market for faceless dolls, handcrafted quilts, and
shot glasses emblazoned with horses and buggies, was on the rise as well,
drawing millions of onlookers to Lancaster County and other Amish settlements around the country.

But *Witness* was a star-studded Hollywood movie with a little sex and a
whole lot of violence, and a good tourist doesn't necessarily a fiction-buying
reader make. There was no promise that a gentle, chaste Amish story, told
within the conventions of the Christian market, would sell at all. "We didn't
perceive then what the interest would be," says Steve Oates, vice president
of marketing at Bethany House. "Bev just wanted to write these books and
we said, 'Oh, okay.' It seems like this little Amish story . . . maybe we could
sell about 25,000 of that." Oates guffaws with the confidence and self-
deprecation of someone delighted to have been proved wrong. "That's the
biggest sales projection number I've ever missed in my life," he says with
glee. *The Shunning* sold 150,000 copies in its first year and over 1 million in
subsequent years.[48]

The Shunning was followed by two more titles in the series The Heritage
of Lancaster County, and the trilogy was repackaged with updated covers
in 2008. The books were adapted into a Hallmark Channel movie directed
by Michael Landon Jr., which aired to an audience of 2.9 million viewers.
Lewis went on to write seven more Amish series, several stand-alone Amish
novels, an Amish cookbook, and a book of Amish prayers. A musical, *The
Confession*, based on her first trilogy, played to record audiences in Indiana,
Pennsylvania, and Ohio ("We are weekly setting new ticket sales records,"
said the director of marketing for The Blue Gate, a restaurant and theater in
Shipshewana, Indiana).[49] By 2012 Lewis's thirty Amish novels for adults had

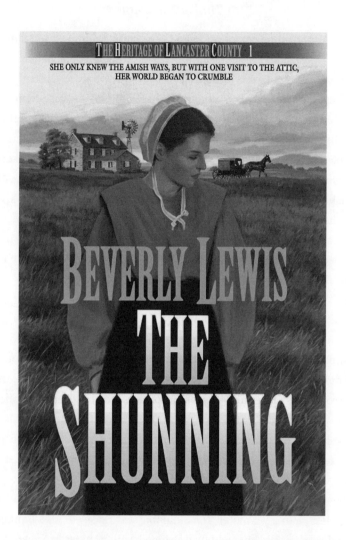

THE HERITAGE OF LANCASTER COUNTY · 1

SHE ONLY KNEW THE AMISH WAYS, BUT WITH ONE VISIT TO THE ATTIC,
HER WORLD BEGAN TO CRUMBLE

BEVERLY LEWIS

THE
SHUNNING

The Shunning *(1997) was the first commercially successful*
contemporary Amish romance novel.
Used by permission of Baker Publishing Group.

sold some 17 million copies and had been translated into eleven languages, and her work had become the apotheosis of Amish fiction against which all others would come to be measured.[50]

Johnson is circumspect in reporting her company's Amish-fiction grand slam. "Fairly soon, probably within two years, we knew it was a franchise," she tells me on the phone. "Beverly Lewis's Amish stories were something that people were fascinated with and wanted to read. We have kept that going and sold a lot of copies." Oates is considerably less retiring. "Other publishers probably wouldn't have touched Amish stories five or six years ago. They would have stuck their noses in the air, sniffed, and said, 'If you guys want to do that, that's fine, but we're not doing that,'" he tells me with barely submerged glee. "But all of a sudden, they're like, 'Oh, Amish fiction! We could sell a few of those.'"[51]

The Amish Trek from Liability to Asset

Attempts by other publishing houses to replicate Lewis's sensational success did not unfurl immediately. Whether other publishers were initially too arrogant, as Oates suggests, or simply unsure how deep and wide readers' desires for Amish stories were, is unclear. Now that Lewis and Bethany House had become so proficient at Amish fiction, Christian publishers may also have wondered whether it was even possible to romance readers away from them.

One evangelical publisher, Multnomah, did produce an Amish-themed trilogy less than a year after *The Shunning* was released. Like Bantam, the general-market publisher who had stripped Amish character Susan Peachey of a lot more than her covering for the front cover, Multnomah chose not to call attention to the Amish setting and characters. Although the characters on Multnomah's covers were duly clothed, only one cover features anything Amish at all: on the cover of *The Key*, written by Gayle Roper and published in 1998, a buggy passes behind a man and a woman sporting jeans, dress shirts, and feathered bangs. The other two covers on Roper's *The Amish Trilogy*, released in 1998 and 1999, feature nothing that would suggest Amishness. But a little more than ten years later, in a move revealing the rising prominence of the Amish, evangelical publisher Harvest

House bought rights to Roper's three books and re-released them as The Amish Farm Trilogy. This time around, in 2010 and 2011, the reincarnated covers of the books are clearly marked with the requisite buggies, barns, and bonnets.[52]

For at least five or six years after the publication of *The Shunning*, many Christian publishing insiders doubted the capacity of the market to hold more than one Amish-fiction author. Wanda Brunstetter had begun writing Amish-themed novels for Barbour, but she was also writing other inspirational Christian fiction. Andrea Doering, now an editor with Revell, says she wised up to the fact that the Amish-fiction market was largely untapped when she was editor-in-chief at Crossings, a Christian book club, from 1994 to 2007. With three-quarters of a million members at the time, Crossings represented a fairly large and reliable sampling of evangelical-fiction readers. As she perused sales figures, Doering began noticing that Lewis's Amish novels, which consistently sat in the bestselling fiction slot, were outpacing the sales of second-place novels at a staggering rate. Based on Crossings' sales data, she began telling the Christian publishers she worked with that they should try to acquire Amish-themed manuscripts. Doering was not at liberty to share sales figures with them, but she gave them the contours of what she was observing. "I can't tell you how popular this is," Doering recalls saying to several publishers, with the oblique but emphatic tone of an informant unable to reveal her sources. "The difference between what she [Lewis] was selling and that number-two spot was so significant," Doering says. "You couldn't help but think that these people might want to read something while they waited for Beverly Lewis to write her next book."[53]

When Cindy Woodsmall began pitching her Amish-themed fiction at a Christian writers' conference in 2003, editors and publishers were still largely convinced that readers were content to do just that: wait for Lewis's next Amish book. Woodsmall received affirmation for her work but no contracts, she says, although she did receive "a potential offer from one publisher to put me under contract if I'd write anything except Amish fiction." Woodsmall decided to stick with Amish settings and characters and continued making the rounds of Christian writers' conferences. Finally, Woodsmall recalls, "After a lot of disappointing feedback, I met with one editor who felt that my writing and story were strong enough to sell regardless of its Amish setting." WaterBrook, an imprint of Random House, published Woodsmall's *When the Heart Cries* in September 2006, and it quickly became a bestselling title in the Christian publishing world. "Her success seemed to unlock something for publishers," Doering says. They saw "that this was a risk worth taking, that there was more room in the market, and that they could confidently publish in that space and not just be left on the shelf."[54]

The distance between a manuscript selling *in spite of* its Amish setting, as Woodsmall's did, to manuscripts selling *because* of it, as was arguably the case by 2009, was traversed in less than five years. "Five years ago, I wasn't interested [in Amish-themed manuscripts]," Sue Brower, editorial director for fiction at Zondervan, told me in 2011. "Four years ago, I was desperately looking." One day in 2007, Brower received three Amish-themed manuscripts. She acquired one of them, and the other two were quickly bought by other publishers. By 2010 author Mindy Starns Clark was leading "Amish 101" workshops at Christian writers' conferences, helping attendees figure out how to write in the very genre that, a few short years earlier, editors and agents had summarily rejected. By 2012 one literary agent was boasting on a blog, "I have never circulated an Amish romance . . . I haven't sold to a major Christian publisher."[55]

The peregrination of a people from publishing liability to publishing asset in such a short time is stunning, and our task is to figure out how it happened, and happened so quickly. One could argue that it was a result of the visibility of the Amish in the wake of the Nickel Mines shooting in October 2006, when a gunman killed five Amish girls and wounded five more before killing himself. The Amish community's expressions of forgiveness of the shooter and gestures of grace to his family became international news, and several readers of Amish fiction suggested to me that their admiration of the Amish and desire to learn more about them grew in the wake of that event. The surge in publication of Amish romance novels two years later suggests that writers and agents and publishers were indeed at work on manuscripts in the aftermath of those shootings. The recession of 2008–9 was also fueling America's interest in traditionalist fiction in general. "During tough economic times, there is always a return to historic American values," literary agent Chip MacGregor told me; "Economic crashes are always followed by an upswing in nostalgic writing."[56] Eight of the fifteen member publishing houses of the Evangelical Christian Publishers Association reported a growth rate of 14.5 percent from 2009 to 2010.[57] In an era of belt-tightening, it makes sense that readers would gravitate to the Amish, who seemed largely unfazed by economic terrors, not to mention capable of canning and freezing their way through anything.

The advances of hypermodernity and hypersexualization in popular culture were likely even more influential in the growth of the genre during the first decade of the twenty-first century. When Woodsmall was shopping her first Amish manuscript in 2003, the sense of contemporary life as excessively harried and excessively indecent was beginning to overspread the cultural landscape. The hyperactive nature of contemporary culture had not yet been widely identified by writers and academics, and the metamorphosis of fictionalized Amish folk from literary burden to literary boon was still at an incipient stage.

And nowhere was the Amish makeover of Christian fiction more obvious than at the yearly trade convention of evangelical Christian publishing houses.

Christian Retail and an Amish Masquerade

Levi Miller (no relation to Clara Bernice) chuckles when he recalls conventions of the Christian Booksellers Association in the years around 2005–7. Miller was raised Amish in Ohio until he was nine years old, when his parents left their Amish community and joined a Mennonite church. As a former editorial director of the Mennonite publisher Herald Press, Miller can't help but laugh when he recounts watching Christian fiction begin donning Amish garb—literally. "My last several years at CBA conventions were spent dodging pretty Amish-clad maidens in the aisles directing traffic to the booths of Beverly Lewis and Wanda Brunstetter," he recalls. Wearing capes and coverings, the young saleswomen mimicked the dress-up game of the protagonist of Cora Gottschalk Welty's *The Masquerading of Margaret*—although in this case it was not to be in "harmony" with their environment, as Margaret's masquerade was, but to be at odds with it.[58]

From the 1960s through the late 1990s, when *The Shunning* appeared, Amish-themed novels had largely remained the property of Mennonites. Levi Miller himself had written an Amish-themed novel, *Ben's Wayne,* which was published in 1989. A Kansas Mennonite couple, Carol Duerksen and Maynard Knepp (he grew up Amish) began in 1995 self-publishing Amish-themed fiction, often with a romance element, and their nine Amish novels sold fifty thousand copies.[59] And Herald Press, Miller's employer, produced several more rounds of Amish romance novels in the decades following Clara Bernice Miller's last novel. Most notable among these were Mary Christner Borntrager's series Ellie's People and several series by an Old Order Mennonite woman, the daughter of a prominent bishop, writing under the pseudonym Carrie Bender. The ten books in the Ellie's People series sold almost seven hundred thousand copies, and Carrie Bender's twenty-six books sold handily as well.[60]

But in the same years when Johnson and Oates and others at Bethany House were stumbling onto the commercial cache of the Beverly Lewis franchise, and only a few years before Cindy Woodsmall's Amish novels proved the market's viability, Herald Press was leaving the Amish-fiction fold. Miller chuckles again when he talks about shutting down Herald Press's Amish-fiction publishing apparatus at the same time that larger evangelical publishers like Bethany House and Barbour began revving up theirs. "I guess you could say that I'm the villain," he admits ruefully, noting that his predecessor at Herald Press had enthusiastically supported the publication of Amish books. While Bender's and Borntrager's gentle Amish romances were selling well, especially among older female readers, a retail price of under ten dollars and a royalty structure that heavily favored authors meant that even relatively robust sales numbers didn't create substantial revenue for the press. In addition, the books that Miller calls "Amish folk fiction" didn't jibe, in his opinion, with the mission of Herald Press as a denominational publisher. Herald Press had a mandate to "equip the church to experience and share the gospel of Jesus Christ from an Anabaptist perspective," regardless of whether that perspective sold many books.[61]

Miller confesses that he sometimes second-guessed this decision when he attended CBA trade shows and observed the success that novelists of the Amish and their publishers were enjoying. As he watched the Amish-fiction train gain steam year after year, having just hopped off, he was also watching Herald Press teeter on the brink of financial insolvency. With $5.1 million in operating losses and debts, Mennonite Publishing House, which owned Herald Press, was facing what one church leader called a "financial challenge of immense proportions," a challenge that placed the two Mennonite denominations that owned the publishing house in significant financial peril themselves.[62] "I'd go home from those conventions thinking that maybe we should reconsider our decision, that maybe this [Amish fiction] would be our financial savior," recalls Miller. Ultimately, however, the marketing dollars Herald Press would have had to invest to reenter a market now dominated by Bethany House, and the nagging sense that its mandate from the Mennonite Church didn't include made-up stories about runaway buggy rides and Amish wedding feasts, kept Herald Press from pursuing any more Amish-fiction projects.[63]

Dressed like so many Amish Vanna Whites, the saleswomen Miller observed in the aisles of CBA conventions might be viewed as a creative marketing strategy: canny advertising in an era when publishers must scrap for every inch of shelf space and every minute of a populace's vanishing fiction-reading time. Their masquerade could also be seen as commodified pastiche, a kind of cultural hodgepodge in which elements of a religious tradition are, according to theologian Vincent Miller, "fragmented into discrete, free-floating signifiers abstracted from their interconnections with other doctrines, symbols, and practices."[64]

The "Amish" saleswomen's masquerade might also be considered a performance, what theorist Richard Schechner calls "ritualized behavior conditioned/permeated by play."[65] In the cavernous exhibit hall of an urban convention center, saleswomen performed Amishness for the retailers, suppliers, distributors, and others in attendance at the trade show, such that attenders could freely interact with women who were, if not Amish, at least Amishesque. It is possible that some trade-show attenders imagined they were shaking hands with real Amish people. Most, however, probably quickly figured out that they were being greeted by mascots: costumed characters in a play of identities, in which any cleft between evangelicals and Amish people was concealed by a covering and a cape.

The Evangelical-Amish Marriage

This masquerade would be reproduced on cover after cover of Amish fiction in years to come, when young models with plucked eyebrows would sport Amish garb and gaze into the near distance. By taking up sectarian "habits" for a day, the salespeople-cum-Amish-women whom Miller watched also mimicked the narrative act of Amish-romance novelists throughout the preceding century—from Helen Reimensnyder Martin to Cora Gottschalk Welty to Ruth Lininger Dobson to Clara Bernice Miller to Beverly Lewis—who had to inhabit their protagonists if they were to write convincingly. It is essentially what Amish-fiction readers do as well, when they psychically exit hypermodernity and slip on the heroine's habitus for a few hours of vicarious canning, egg-gathering, and hand-holding in the buggy.

Whether the bonneted representatives of evangelical publishing houses were agents of creative advertising, purveyors of crass commodification, or actors in a postmodern performance remains open for debate. In any case, they were striking embodiments of the evangelical-Amish marriage that would be consummated in the coming decade. In chapter 3 we scrutinize evangelical and Amish discourses to discover the attraction of one to the other.

The saleswomen also served up an amusing if slightly sour reminder to Levi Miller of the lucrative bonnet book business that his company had so recently exited. It's doubtful that the little Miller boy, growing up Amish in Ohio in the 1950s, could have imagined that one day he would watch as women dressed like his mother pressed the flesh in the vast, echoing exhibit hall of Christian retail.

Mennonite Romance, *by Jon Stich, accompanied the article "Getting Dirty in Dutch Country" that appeared in a 2010 issue of* Bloomberg Businessweek. Used by permission of the artist.

❦ Chapter Three ❦

An Evangelical and an Amishman
Walk into a Barn

My friend Jenell is a white feminist academic who votes Democrat,
reads books on spirituality by a Buddhist-informed Quaker, and
knows how to choose the pitch-perfect swear word. She is also an evangelical Christian. Bishop T. D. Jakes is an evangelical Christian, too. Jakes, who
is African American, is pastor of a thirty-thousand-member church based
in Dallas, Texas. With an evident taste for designer suits, Jakes reigns over a
media empire that includes a record label, feature films, plays, books, and a
sitcom. Thousands of miles away from Jakes's congregation, in northwest-
ern Ohio, my cousin Lois is homeschooling her children. She wears skirts,
covers her head when she goes to church, and picks berries and apples to
preserve for winter. Evangelical? Definitely.

To understand the Amish masquerade that Levi Miller observed on the
floor of the trade convention of Christian publishers, it is less important to
know anything about the Amish than to know something about evangelicals. With few exceptions, contemporary Amish romance novels are texts
produced by and for evangelical Christians. Only one writer of generally
marketed Amish fiction is currently Amish, and a few do not reveal their
faith commitments. But because the majority of the writers, literary agents,
editors, publishers, and marketers—the main architects and framers of the

Amish-fiction barn—are evangelical Protestants, it is imperative to know a bit about them.

Evangelicals can be considered a discourse community: a group that shares conventions for interpreting language and text and that forms its adherents' understandings of the world. Media theorists Quentin Schultze and Robert Woods Jr., themselves evangelicals, suggest that evangelicals are a "mediating tribe" or a "tribal community of discourse."[1] Discourse communities often overlap, and one person may belong to several. But the idea helps to explain the distinct ways individuals communicate based on the norms of their particular discourse community, as well as the occasional unintelligibility of their speech and ideas to those who stand outside of it.

After examining the basic vocabulary of evangelicalism, we will look at the other discourse community that is a stakeholder in this publishing phenomenon: Anabaptism, which includes the Amish. Although they are not the main producers or consumers of the subgenre, the Amish stand at the eye of the bonnet book storm and deserve a brief explication.[2] Understanding these two discourse communities will prepare us to take on two common myths about Amish fiction: that Amish novels are slightly cleaned-up versions of the proverbial "bodice rippers" and that once you've read one Amish novel, you've read them all. Only after we have dispelled these myths can we view the field with any clarity.

The Evangelical Discourse Community

As my cursory descriptions of my friend Jenell, Pastor T. D. Jakes, and my cousin Lois make eminently clear, defining the prototypical evangelical person is almost as difficult as defining the typical Amish one. Practices, theologies, politics, and lifestyles differ between and within communities, both Amish and evangelical, and holding forth about "*the* evangelical mind" or "*the* Amish perspective" is likely to lead to simplistic formulation and stereotype. Evangelical Christians may not even use the term to refer to themselves; many prefer the term "born-again Christian" or simply "Christian." And evangelicals belong to many different Christian denominations—or none at all—so identifying evangelicals by denominational affiliation is difficult.

Modern evangelicalism, what sociologist Christian Smith calls "engaged orthodoxy," grows out of conservative Protestant ferment in the 1940s.[3] The early-twentieth-century debates between modernists and fundamentalists had rent Protestantism in two, resulting in the retreat by fundamentalists from the realms of both wider society and ecumenical Christianity, on the one hand, and the loss of religious distinctives by progressive Christians absorbed by the academy and culture, on the other. But a disenchanted group of young moderate fundamentalist reformers, evangelist Billy Graham and *Christianity Today* founder Carl Henry among them, began agitating against what they saw as the judgmental properties of fundamentalism, which, in the words of Smith, had "guarded doctrinal purity at the enormous cost of sacrificing the spread of the Gospel."[4] Observers often overlook this distinction between fundamentalism, which remains a subset of evangelicalism, and the more culture-engaging form of evangelicalism. Fundamentalist Christianity remains stricter in its doctrinal and practical positions, including positions on biblical inerrancy, eschatology, and separation from the world. This story—evangelicalism's journey out of midcentury fundamentalism—comes to bear on the Amish-fiction story, as we will see in chapter 5.

Evangelicalism remained largely inconspicuous in American life until the late 1970s, when evangelical Jimmy Carter was elected president of the United States and Jerry Falwell's Moral Majority began proposing ways for Christians to wield political power. Since then, evangelicals have become known for the rise of the Religious Right and even for the desire to wrangle the United States back into the theocratic "Christian nation" that some claim it was founded to be. But current evangelical engagement with politics is not reducible to rightist politics, and evangelicals are not a homogeneous political or religious bloc.[5] Nor does the label "evangelical" always equate with patriarchy, homophobia, religious triumphalism, environmental apathy, and affection for kitsch. As Joseph Loconte and Michael Cromartie suggest, critics of evangelicalism often make a "gross caricature of the 100 million or more people who could be called evangelicals" and ignore "evangelicalism's deepening social conscience."[6] Loconte and Cromartie and others cite evangelical engagement in social issues such as AIDS, racism, global poverty, modern-day slavery, refugee concerns, and climate change as examples of what some have called "the new face of evangelicalism."

New or old, fundamentalist or not, evangelicals do share certain beliefs, practices, and history. Scholars have demarcated the boundaries of contemporary evangelical Christianity in various ways, with one of the most frequently used heuristics coming from historian David Bebbington. His four-pronged definition of evangelicalism, known as the "Bebbington quadrilateral," includes (1) biblicism, the priority given to Scripture; (2) crucicentrism, the belief in the atoning work of Jesus on the cross; (3) conversionism, a conviction that persons need to be converted; and (4) activism, a focus on efforts of the faith such as evangelism and, increasingly, social activism.[7]

While evangelicalism separates itself less rigidly from mainstream culture than fundamentalist Christianity has, it remains uncomfortable with many manifestations of "worldly" values and ethics. Historical stances against abortion, gay marriage, and divorce, although increasingly contested within evangelical circles, still set conservative evangelicals apart from their more liberal evangelical and mainline peers, and an increasingly sexualized public sphere has led to evangelical calls for chastity, modesty, and holy living. Some evangelicals mourn what they see as the passing of Christian influence in schools, families, and communities; this view has led to the Christian homeschooling movement and support for organizations trumpeting "family values," such as James Dobson's Focus on the Family and Nancy Leigh DeMoss's Revive Our Hearts. The centrality of family and holiness to evangelical discourse, as well as a persistent if not always lived-out desire to remain separate from the world, also help to make sense of evangelical identification with Amish narratives, as we'll see in chapter 7.[8]

Many evangelicals are convinced that people outside evangelicalism disdain them. "The feeling of being disliked and alienated has worked its way deep into the evangelical consciousness," writes sociologist Bradley Wright, in the evangelical flagship publication *Christianity Today;* "We feel it in our bones." Wright cites a 2009 study from the Pew Forum on Religion and Public Life, which found that 43 percent of evangelicals think that there is "a lot of discrimination" against evangelicals. This sense of being despised by the wider culture persists, Wright says, despite evidence that only about 20 percent of Americans say they have negative impressions of evangelicals. A conviction that most of their neighbors do not like them, whether or not it is rooted in fact, may also contribute to evangelical readers' identification with the Amish, who are, in the words of one Amish-fiction writer, "an often misunderstood sect of people."[9]

This sense of separateness drives the increasingly rapid-fire production of evangelical media.[10] While the Bible remains the central text of evangelicalism and has experienced its own product proliferation (the Bride's Bible, the Police Officer's Bible, the Green Bible, the Precious Moments Bible), it must compete for attention now divided among Christian magazines and newspapers, radio, online media, nonfiction, and fiction. Especially fiction. According to a 2009 report from the Evangelical Christian Publishers Association (ECPA), Bibles make up a lower percentage of purchases than Christian fiction by "active Christians," the category of consumers who made 61 percent of Christian book purchases in 2009. Christian fiction accounted for 20 percent of Christian book purchases by this group in 2009, and Bibles made up only 18 percent.[11] "That's right, among the core consumers of Christian books, Christian fiction has already eclipsed Bible purchases in units," Michael Covington, former information and education director for the ECPA, marveled in a blog post. "If you had made this assertion 20 years ago, no one would have believed it." But now, among the primary consumers of Christian books, Christian fiction is selling better than the Bible. "You know what they say: 'Truth is stranger than fiction,'" wrote Covington. "We may also add that it doesn't sell as well either."[12]

Not all evangelicals are reading Amish fiction, of course; like all other discourse communities, the larger evangelical tribe contains clannish preferences based on race, age, geography, gender, education, and aesthetics. While it's possible that T. D. Jakes is a big fan of Beverly Lewis, the almost unilateral absence of characters of color in Amish-themed novels makes Amish fiction a largely white phenomenon on both the publishing and the reading end. Several marketers and editors told me that the readers of their authors' novels are mostly white, mostly female, mostly forty-five to sixty-five years old.[13] "It's sort of a rural, *Saturday Evening Post* crowd," one marketer told me. "We can go to a town of three thousand and have a huge book signing. We can go to Phoenix and have five people come out."

Also essential to understanding the nuances of evangelical life is that evangelical scholars have issued some of the most incisive criticism of inspirational fiction to date. Narrow-mindedness is a common charge against evangelicals, from critics both within and without. Although they weren't writing about Amish fiction specifically, Susan V. Gallagher and Roger Lundin, both professors at evangelical colleges, contend that the writing that characterizes inspirational romances "purports to be morally righteous, and readers may be thankful for its lack of profanity and chaste bedroom scenes, but its mechanical structure reflects its moral shallowness. It follows rote formulas and holds the reader's interest with titillating fantasy, rather than with realism." Schultze and Woods agree: "Evangelical media generally lack originality," they write, summarizing one of the arguments contained in their anthology of essays about evangelical communication. "Without being cultural elitists, we can probably conclude that evangelical productions tend to suffer from a lack of artistic quality."[14]

Evangelical discourse, then, housed in a plethora of nonfictional and fictional texts, may befuddle observers, even evangelical ones. But understanding its contours clarifies some of the reasons that many evangelical readers are identifying with a religious group that, on the surface, could hardly appear more different.

The Anabaptist Discourse Community

The Amish are the best-known branch of the Anabaptist family tree, which includes Hutterites, Brethren in Christ, Mennonites, the Church of the Brethren, and several other groups and subgroups. Anabaptist discourse is as contested as evangelical discourse, insofar as no one owns its definition. There are evangelical Amish people and evangelical Mennonites who draw deeply from both traditions, and some scholars locate Anabaptism as a subcategory of evangelicalism.[15] Because evangelical and Anabaptist discourses merge at times, demarcating where one ends and the other begins becomes difficult. Still, cursory knowledge about Anabaptist history and life will aid our later examination of how Amish fiction portrays its subjects. Here we look at two Anabaptist discourses: Amish and Mennonite.

Amish Discourse

Amish discourse is inscribed with a centuries-old communal memory of persecution and separatism. Growing out of the Radical Reformation in the sixteenth century, the Anabaptist movement held that believing adults should be baptized rather than infants and maintained that Protestant reformers such as Ulrich Zwingli and Martin Luther had not gone far enough in their critiques of the ruling Catholic church. In rebaptizing adults, the Anabaptists placed themselves at odds with civil authorities, who used baptismal records to tax, manage, and count citizens. Anabaptists were persecuted for their refusal to baptize infants; they faced torture, imprisonment, and execution. Some two thousand Anabaptists died for their faith during the 1500s, gaining attention for their pacifism, or lack of violent resistance, rooted in obedience to the words of Jesus in the Sermon on the Mount contained in Matthew. In addition to pacifism, also known as nonresistance, separation from the world became a key value in Anabaptist thought, and today the Amish and many other Anabaptists still hold themselves at some remove from what they perceive as "the world."

A split among the Swiss Anabaptists in 1693 left one group holding fast to the use of church discipline. This faction continued to hew to a more world-rejecting way of life than many other Anabaptists, and separation from the world became a key component of their discourse. As followers of the seventeenth-century leader Jacob Ammann, this group became known as the Amish.

The Amish came to the United States from Europe in two waves during the eighteenth and nineteenth centuries and now live in 463 settlements in thirty states and one Canadian province. The total population of Amish is approaching three hundred thousand, spread among at least forty different affiliations, each with practices and traditions and beliefs that can diverge greatly from one another.[16] The number of Amish in the United States and Canada doubles about every twenty years because of robust rates of both birth and retention. The average Amish family (including parents and children) has 8.5 members, and despite the infamy of *Rumspringa,* the time before baptism during which Amish youth sometimes taste the pleasures of English life and which many outsiders assume becomes a cultural exit door, Amish retention rates hover around 90 percent.[17]

Gelassenheit, which means "yieldedness," can be seen as a central container of Amish identity that frequently appears in conversation, written texts, and church life. An attitude of yieldedness should manifest itself, the Amish believe, in internal qualities such as humility and patience and in external commitments such as plain dress, horse-drawn transportation, retention of Pennsylvania German as a first language, and other issues of lifestyle that the church codifies in the *Ordnung,* or set of expectations for right living.[18]

Since the mid-twentieth century, the Amish have found themselves to be magnets for tourists, especially in Lancaster County, Pennsylvania; Holmes and Wayne counties in Ohio; and Elkhart and LaGrange counties in Indiana, where vendors of all things Amish serve more than 19 million tourists each year.[19] And representations of the Amish have appeared in many venues, including Peter Weir's 1985 movie *Witness,* the 2002 documentary *Devil's Playground,* and the 2012 reality series *Breaking Amish.* For most Americans, Amish discourse itself is less accessible than discourse *about* the Amish, and although the Amish often represent their culture to tourists in the form of commerce, they have not generally produced written texts that are widely available to outsiders. There are signs that this is changing; the novels of Amish writer Linda Byler, for example, are finding a broad readership. But in general, the Amish discourse contained in Amish fiction is whisper-down-the-lane Amishness: fictionalized, edited, published, marketed, and sold by non-Amish actors.[20]

Mennonite Discourse

Scattered throughout eighty-three countries of the world, Mennonites are much more racially and ethnically diverse than the Amish. In fact, most of the 1.7 million Mennonites live outside of North America and Europe. Although, like the Amish, Mennonites descended from the early Anabaptists, they generally separate themselves less rigorously from the rest of the world than the Amish do; many Mennonites move inconspicuously through the larger culture. Some conservative Mennonites resemble the Amish more closely than they resemble their more liberal Mennonite cousins, but Mennonites in general have accommodated themselves to technology, higher education, missions, urban life, and the professions to a greater extent than the Amish. Additionally, many Mennonites have been heavily influenced by evangelicalism, such that visitors to some Mennonite congregations on a Sunday morning would pick up a much stronger evangelical vibe than an Anabaptist one.[21] Others have retained Anabaptist distinctives such as a nonresistant theology and ethics of service and simplicity.

Mennonite discourse comes to bear on Amish fiction in terms of both the readers and the content of the books. While some Mennonites partake freely of the offerings of literary and commercial fiction and popular culture in general, many others seek the kind of clean, Christian read that Amish novels offer. "We talk about selling a lot of books around Amish communities," Steve Oates of Bethany House told me. "That's not because we're selling to the Amish; it's because we're selling to the Mennonites and those who live around them. There's a little dot of Amish, and then there's a huge circle of Mennonites around them." Oates's claim is evidenced in a recent issue of the *Mennonite,* the news and theology magazine of the Mennonite Church USA, in which the only two full-page ads were for Amish novels.[22] An employee at an Amish-owned store in Franklin County, Pennsylvania, told me that Mennonites are frequent buyers of the Amish novels they stock.

Mennonite discourse also intersects with Amish fiction in that the heroines in the novels sometimes end up becoming Mennonite or joining the Beachy Amish, whose members can drive cars, use public electricity, and worship in church buildings.[23] The Mennonite and Beachy Amish faiths, in Amish romance novels, are depicted as less authoritarian and more warmhearted in spiritual expression. Amish characters at odds with their strict, *Ordnung*-heavy communities frequently take refuge with Mennonite neighbors or cousins, who are depicted as having more personal relationships with God and more reasonable relationships to technology.

In Shelley Shepard Gray's *Autumn's Promise,* for instance, English protagonist Lilly and her Amish fiancé Robert decide to join a conservative Mennonite church to synthesize their cultures of origin. "As a Mennonite, you could retain some of your technologies," Robert tells her. "They would let you have a car. A phone. They would not look upon our marrying as wrong."[24] In Cindy Woodsmall's Sisters of the Quilt trilogy, Amish-born Hannah marries her Mennonite boyfriend, Paul, and becomes Mennonite, and she thus is able to pursue a master's degree in nursing while still remaining plain. Katie Lapp, the prodigal daughter in Beverly Lewis's first Amish series, ends up conservative Mennonite, too. Mennonites within Amish novels are often portrayed as an ideal fusion of evangelical and Amish: appropriately converted to Christ, sufficiently plain.[25] Mennonitism becomes a contact zone of sorts between evangelical discourse and Amish discourse, a shared precinct where heroines can combine the best of evangelical orthodoxy with the best of plain orthopraxy.[26]

Understanding these discourse communities—especially evangelicalism—is one step toward debunking two myths about Amish fiction that people unfamiliar with the genre often hold. These myths—that Amish fiction is a stepchild of the general romance novel and that Amish novels are essentially indistinguishable from one another—are potent reminders that in some circles, an evangelical taste public, especially an evangelical female one, is frequently ignored, derided, or at the very least misunderstood.

Myth: Amish Novels are Bonnet Rippers

The bare-chested hunk with the mane of black hair looks like he just stepped out of the 21st Century Skins Native American Men's Calendar. His skin is bronzed, his cheekbones high, and his nose broad and aquiline. His pecs and biceps suggest the assistance of a personal trainer. One beefy leg covers the skirt of the woman he clutches in his arms, who is vaguely Amish-looking. She is wearing a light-blue dress and a white head scarf that does little to contain her own mane of black hair. Pressed so hard against the man's chest that her left breast pushes up at an impossible angle, the woman looks about as comfortable as if she were having a mammogram. Yet she is raising her lips to his and pressing her left hand against his burnished chest. Behind them, a barn on the horizon owes a debt to Andrew Wyeth, as does the field of indeterminate crop that spreads out behind the couple. At the right, a sober Holstein looks on.

This is *Mennonite Romance,* an acrylic-and-pencil illustration in mostly blue and ochre by Jon Stich, featured in a summer 2010 issue of *Bloomberg Businessweek*. The artwork accompanies an article titled "Getting Dirty in Dutch Country," which investigates unusual microtrends in romance publishing including the Amish, knitting, quilting, and the paranormal. In order to "satisfy as many lust-filled imaginations as possible, the romance fiction industry has ripped the bodice from seemingly every niche group," concludes writer Spencer Morgan. He places Amish fiction solidly within the romance-novel industry, citing romance sales of $1.4 billion for 2009, a 7.7 percent increase from the year before, and offers gleeful quotes from Harlequin public relations folks ("We're going gangbusters!") and the requisite bonnet humor (Amish romances covering bestseller lists "like a giant headscarf").[27]

None of this is exactly untrue—although the article's assertion that the Amana Colonies featured in several recent romances represent an "ultraconservative strain of the Amish" is. (Too bad that *Businessweek* fact-checkers didn't check Wikipedia.)[28] Amish-themed romances do indeed represent one piece of a romance industry increasingly splintered into niche markets, and they do share certain sensibilities with the romance genre. Most current Amish novels follow some romance conventions: a young female protagonist with an incomplete identity; the appearance of the love interest in the first chapter; a trajectory of romantic encounter, conflict, and resolution; and a comfortable textual environment that eases readers' access to the narrative. In addition, the big names among Amish romance writers regularly receive awards from the Romance Writers of America— Beverly Lewis received a Career Achievement Award from the trade publication *Romantic Times* in 2009—and some of the newcomers to the Amish-fiction party started their careers writing romance for general audiences.[29]

But as we saw in chapter 2, contemporary Amish fiction was born not of Harlequin flesh but of Bethany House spirit. The preponderance of Amish fiction is written by and for evangelical Christians, and with the exception of a few forays by the general romance houses, Amish romance novels are the province of purity culture rather than "pornified" culture. Few contain the conventional Byronic hero of general-market romance novels, the "swaggering, rough-hewn, mythic man" who populates Harlequins, according to one romance novelist. Rather, Amish heroes have thoughts that are "not sexual but concerned," as Rebecca Barrett-Fox suggests about heroes in Christian romances; "He talks with her—a lot. He listens, and he shares. If any physical contact occurs, it is never 'punishing' or 'cruel' but earnest."[30] And Amish romance novels operate according to their own internal narrative arc, linguistic code, and devotional sensibility, which differ greatly from conventions of general-market romance.

More relevant, then, than the $1.4 billion romance-novel sales figure that Morgan offers as context for the Amish-fiction phenomenon is a surprisingly analogous number that emerges from Christian publishing. Mark Kuyper, chief executive of the Evangelical Christian Publishers Association, estimates the Christian book industry's annual revenue for 2011 as also $1.4 billion, up slightly from 2010. Another relevant metric would have been the $4.6 billion "Christian products industry," which includes books, collectibles, music, gifts, and other items.[31]

That Morgan fails to even mention the term *Christian* or *evangelical* in his piece exemplifies the failure of many observers of the Amish-fiction phenomenon to grasp the Christian genealogy and character of the genre.[32] Reporting on the trend of Amish romance novels in 2010 without mentioning North American evangelicalism is akin to tracing your family genealogy and forgetting to find out your mother's last name. "A lot of people covering this [publishing trend] don't understand how Christian the customer is," Steve Oates, vice president of marketing at Bethany House, told me. "There are very, very few secular readers."[33]

Harlequin and other general romance publishers, although they are now getting with the Amish program through their inspirational romance lines, are relatively late adopters. The same year that Beverly Lewis's *The Shunning* appeared, Harlequin was just birthing its line of inspirational fiction, Love Inspired, which didn't bring out an Amish title until thirteen years later. By 2010, when Love Inspired finally published *Katie's Redemption*, an Amish-themed novel by Patricia Davids, it entered an already crowded field of Amish books that evangelical houses had published in intervening years.[34] Compared to evangelical publishers, the big romance houses are Johnny-come-latelies to the fact that bonneted women sell books as well as heaving bosoms do.

To be fair, the *Businessweek* article was looking at several microtrends in romance publishing and thus could give only a cursory description of each. The illustration is mostly satirical, and its conjuring of the traditional bod-ice-ripper cover is both amusing and clever. Magazine editors and illustra-tors owe nothing to the Amish or to those who fictionalize them. But here's the thing many observers miss: sexed-up contemporary romance novels and steamy encounters between hunks with long black hair and lusty hero-ines like the one depicted in *Mennonite Romance* are exactly what Amish ro-mance novels are *not*. Amish-themed romances are defined by the absence of overt sexuality, and loyal readers of the subgenre are as articulate about what they *don't* want in their books as what they do. The extent to which observers overlook the centrality of chastity speaks to the unintelligibility of evangelical tribal discourse to the ears of many outside critics. Too many observers simply miss this point: Amish novels turn not on the titillation of the carnal but on the thrill of the chaste.

Businessweek's coverage of the Amish-fiction phenomenon is the most egregious of the mainstream media reports in terms of its situating of Amish fiction. But *Businessweek* isn't the only venue in which the nature of Amish romance novels is misunderstood. Lisa Miller of *Newsweek* says that much of the press coverage of the trend has been "snarky," and my own friends and acquaintances sometimes echoed this perspective. When they heard about my research, many would smirk and crack Amish-themed bed-room jokes ("Wouldst thou untie thy covering strings?") or offer title sug-gestions for the Amish novel they think someone should write (*Amish Girls Gone Wild*). Beneath jokes about covering stripteases and X-rated Amish girls rests the same inaccurate assumption evident in *Businessweek*'s cov-erage: that Amish romance novels are, as one acquaintance of mine sug-gested, "the religious equivalent of bodice-ripper romance novels," major-ing in lust and arousal and minoring in anything of consequence. We'll look at the specific ways Amish novels construct romance in chapter 7, but it's important to note here that loyal readers often don't even use the term *romance* to describe the category. "I like the classification of 'Amish fiction' versus 'Amish romance fiction' because I don't necessarily read them for the romance," said one responder. When I mentioned "Amish romance novels," another woman I spoke with furrowed her brow and said, "Really? These are romances? I don't think of them as romance."[35]

This myth also positions the Christian world as borrower and the "secu-lar" world as owner. That arrangement accurately describes many cultural forms (think Christian rap), and some theorists have made it their business to prove that evangelicals essentially xerox popular culture products, result-ing in a bowdlerized subculture.[36] While there is some truth to this argu-ment, and while Christian writers like Janette Oke and Beverly Lewis rely on some hand-me-down conventions of general romances, the linear Chris-tian-appropriation-of-secular-forms argument doesn't work here. Amish protagonists are not simply Danielle Steel heroines cinched into capes and coverings. As indicated by Harlequin's and Avon's relatively late release of titles, and as demonstrated by the recent entrance of Penguin and Simon & Schuster imprints to Amish fiction, Christian writers and publishers have added so much value to the Amish subgenre that general romance and trade publishers are now wanting to get in on the action. Like a daughter embarrassed by her mother's risqué fashion choices, Amish novels pub-lished by Harlequin's Love Inspired line display the name of their parent company in one inconspicuous spot: a lower corner of the back cover.

Now that romance houses are boasting lines of squeaky-clean inspira-tionals, it is unclear who is borrowing from whom. Evidence that inspira-tional Amish fiction has placed pressure on the general trade market can be seen nowhere more clearly than in the fact that Sinful Moments Press, an imprint of Canadian publisher Lachesis Publishing, repackaged, retitled, and rereleased *Thee, I Love* as *Jacob's Return* in 2011. Rachel Sauder, the bodice-bursting vixen on the cover of the 1999 *Thee, I Love*, is redressed as a fully clothed Amish woman, standing in a field and fingering a covering string, on the cover of the 2011 *Jacob's Return*.

Rachel Sauder's journey from cleavage to cape suggests that by 2011 Amishness had gained powerful currency. In 1999 the Amish sign was still worth less to publishers than some choice views of skin. Only twelve years later, the bonnet had become so celebrated and successful an insignia within Christian fiction that even a publishing imprint with a name like Sinful Moments Press—which also publishes erotic fiction—would trust the force of the Amish brand.[37] Clearly, the borrowing of form and aesthetic between Christian and popular cultures goes both ways.

Thee, I Love, *a novel by Annette Blair featuring Amish characters and setting, was published in 1999.*
Used by permission of Kensington Books.

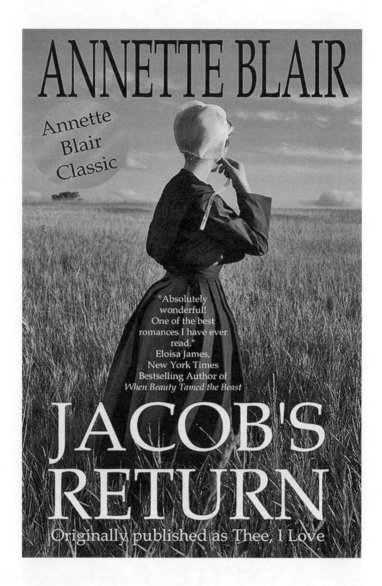

ANNETTE BLAIR

Annette
Blair
Classic

"Absolutely
wonderful!
One of the best
romances I have ever
read."
Eloisa James,
New York Times
Bestselling Author of
When Beauty Tamed the Beast

JACOB'S
RETURN

Originally published as Thee, I Love

Thee, I Love *was repackaged and reissued as* Jacob's Return *by*
Sinful Moments Press in 2011.
Cover art by Laura Givens. Used by permission of Lachesis Publishing Inc.

To reach the same loyal Amish-fiction reader who has funded the Amish novel craze, however, romance houses and trade publishers will have to keep the zippers up and the carnality quotient down. "They [general romance houses] have to bend over backwards to abide by the guidelines of our [Christian] market, or they'd get slaughtered," one marketer with an evangelical house told me. "They tend to be looked at askance by the Christian bookstores because of their DNA." *Jacob's Return,* despite its front-cover renovation of Rachel Sauder from strumpet to saint, can't be purchased from Christian Book Distributors, Crossings Book Club, or any other major Christian bookseller.

So mainstream publishing is beginning to embrace the Amish-fiction reader as eagerly as the bulked-up man in *Mennonite Romance* is clutching his Amish maiden, and it has even cleaned up its act for the sake of getting the girl. It remains to be seen whether Amish-fiction readers will return the affection, or whether general publishers will have to go elsewhere to find themselves some love.

Myth: Read One Amish Novel and You've Read Them All

A second myth circulating about Amish novels suggests that the books are pure potboilers—hack-work featuring stock characters, predictable dialogue, refurbished backdrops, and recycled plots. "They're kind of like Nancy Drew books," one Amish woman told me. "If you've read one, you've read them all."[38] An Amish man I spoke with referred to them as "Amish drivel novels," and a February 2011 article about Amish fiction in *Publishers Weekly* began with this "Recipe for an Amish Novel":

Take
One young woman (Sarah, Katie, or Rebecca).
One young man (Jacob, Daniel, Samuel).

Add one, or more, problems:
Someone is 21 and unmarried.
Someone has a family secret.

Someone is tempted by life outside the Amish community.
Someone's heart has been broken.

Mix together with one Daed, one Mamm, assorted siblings.
(Optional: add grossdawdi and/or grossmammi).

Bake together for 352 pages till resolved.
Garnish with Pennsylvania Dutch glossary or recipes or quilt pattern.[39]

This "Amish fiction as formula" myth contains more than a kernel of truth. Amish novels often *do* cook up best according to a particular recipe. They are genre fiction, which means they rely on certain conventions of plot, character, dialogue, and setting. Even a convinced apologist for the concept of taste cultures like Herbert Gans concedes that stereotypes and templates are more common in mass-marketed works of art than in "higher" forms. "Popular culture is more standardized, making more use of formulas and stereotypical characters and plots," he writes.[40] Amish fiction as a whole contains countless stern bishops, buggy accidents, midwives, shunnings, barn raisings, quilting bees, tables groaning under the weight of home-cooked food, forbidden romances with Englischers, and widows surprised by love. Almost without exception, there is a dusting of Pennsylvania Dutch in the dialogue, a heterosexual love story, a redemptive ending, and a character's trust in God.

Not only are Amish novels genre fiction; they are *evangelical* fiction. Lynn Neal, in her study of women readers of inspirational fiction, writes, "In this [evangelical Christian] religio-aesthetic world, mediocrity, predictability, utility, and sentimentality reign. What many would call creative flaws are labeled by evangelicals as artistic achievement and theological truth." These four qualities—mediocrity, predictability, utility, and sentimentality—combine to create a distinctly evangelical imagination, claims Neal, who is also careful to define *mediocrity* not in the pejorative sense of inferior quality but as "the mean between two extremes."[41] Such use of patterns serves a purpose, in that it prompts readers to "recapture the feeling of faith, reestablish a sense of community, and revisit a variety of practices and beliefs, including prayer, forgiveness, and patience," Neal writes. "It [repetition of forms] affirms their sense that they are maintaining the historical evangelical faith amidst the innovations of contemporary secular culture."[42]

Since Amish novels are generally considered genre fiction, marked by the qualities Gans describes, and since they are situated within an evangelical imagination, as Neal outlines, *and* since they are set within a community that itself values uniformity and utility and predictability, it is possible that they offer a triple shot of potboiler aesthetic. One reader, in response to the question, "When you read an Amish novel, do you usually know how it is going to end?" answered with a nonchalant "Yep."

Yet this myth, while it contains a measure of truth, may obscure as much as it illumines. It exaggerates both the uniformity of Amish fiction and the innovations of literary fiction. Gans suggests that each taste culture, operating according to its own internal aesthetic standards and expectations, "is sensitive only to its own diversity and judges the others to be more uniform."[43] Because no objective barometer of the predictability of genre fiction and literary fiction exists, readers of each taste culture are left to generalize about the others.

The readers of Amish fiction I spoke with had no trouble generalizing about the "secular" fiction that most of them avoid. But between Amish novels they drew fine distinctions that might go unnoticed by people unfamiliar with the genre. Whenever I asked Amish-fiction readers to respond to the criticism that Amish books are all the same, they begged to differ. "I don't think they're the same story just being told different ways," Jodie told me. "I think there are similar themes, but I don't think they're all the same," Louise said.[44] "You do have to remember that they are all romance, so there is going to be some romance in every one, but there are different characteristics to each one," another reader told me. One reader pointed out the variety of barriers to love that the protagonists must overcome, noting a tremendous diversity in terms of what that barrier is. Readers named authors they liked and authors they didn't, plotlines they loved and ones they disliked, protagonists they liked and protagonists they found annoying.

In my own Amish-fiction reading forays, I also encountered a great deal of diversity in quality, even according to my own taste culture. I found some books rather appalling in their clunky prose and didactic sensibilities, but I and other critics have found others to be well written and narratively appealing. Dale Cramer's *Levi's Will* earned a starred review in *Booklist*, which called it an "accomplished work" and a "beautiful and original story"; *Publishers Weekly* skewered an Amish novel by Amy Clipston for a narrative that "drags repetitively around the lovers—how many times can Timothy raise his eyebrows in surprise and eat Miriam's crumbly peach pie?—and misses chances for conveying greater emotion in central family relationships."[45]

Although in some books the ending was clearly in sight from the first chapter, in others the resolutions were not visible at all until I neared the end. The supersonic pacing, skip tracers, cutting-edge gene therapy, and gun-toting intruders of Mindy Starns Clark's Amish suspense stories are a far cry from the meandering plots of family dinners, fishing trips, and hope chests of Wanda Brunstetter's novels. Cramer's impressively plotted historical novel *Paradise Valley*, about an Amish family that moves to Mexico in the 1920s and there learns about poverty, racism, and the Mexican Revolution, could hardly be more different from the anodyne dialogue and unlikely proposals of Emma Miller's *Miriam's Heart* ("She was crying, tears flowing, her lower lip quivering. 'Will you marry me, Charley?'"). And the sexually charged scenes in Kelly Long's *A Marriage of the Heart*, replete with husky voices, double entendre, and suggestively thrown towels, are of a different character entirely from the chaste handholding and blushes of Beverly Lewis's characters in the Courtship of Nellie Fisher series, in which the most erotic phrase is "How's the prettiest baker in Honey Brook?"[46] In addition, the spectrum of representations of Amish faith in the novels—as a works-based, not fully Christian form, on the one hand, to true Christianity in suspenders and coverings, on the other—is wide.

Thus, to claim that "all Amish novels are the same" would be to overlook polysemy in much the same way that someone who says "all Amish are Luddites" does. Critic Raymond Williams admonishes that, when considering works within a particular genre, one must look not only at their "essential community" but also at their "irreducible individuality."[47]

Metaphors for Amish Fiction

These latent but powerful myths obscure two essential characteristics of Amish fiction: the centrality of chastity within the novels and the heterogeneous nature of the subgenre. Expelling these myths makes it possible to listen more carefully to the writers and readers of the novels, as well as to the meaning that they make from the books they love.

Chapters 4–7 offer four metaphors through which we can refract the Amish-fiction phenomenon. The first metaphor—Amish novels as commodities—focuses on the production end of the thrill of the chaste, which is situated within what Lipovetsky calls "hypercapitalism."[48] The remaining three metaphors—Amish novels as devotional icons, as vehicles of transport, and as curators of chaste womanhood—center on the consumption of Amish fiction: the thrill of the chaste as articulated by readers. Each illuminates the success of the subgenre in a particular way, bending our attention toward certain qualities of the texts themselves and their cultural and religious functions in the lives of readers.

The light that these four metaphors shed on the subgenre's production gears, its religious qualities, its capacity to imaginatively transport readers, and its constructions of godly womanhood could illumine the popularity of the larger category of inspirational Christian fiction. These metaphors are particularly apt for our purposes, however, in that they highlight the even more significant sense of departure from hypermodernity that *Amish* fiction offers, relative to inspirational fiction in general. While Christian fiction peopled with non-Amish characters and set in non-Amish contexts may provide readers with a measure of relief from the stresses of hypermodernity, only Amish fiction offers such substantial psychic distance from it.

Ironically, however, even as the subgenre effectively positions itself as an alternative to hypermodernity, the stunning success of Amish novels can be credited, in part, to hypermodern production and sales mechanisms. In chapter 4 we view Amish romance novels as commodities. Like all metaphors, this one risks being reductive. Yet when used appropriately, the commodity metaphor sheds light on a central aspect of Amish fiction: the production matrix within which it is conceived, represented, published, marketed, and sold.

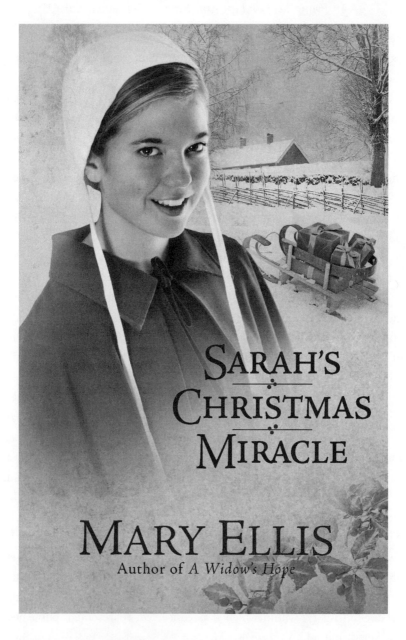

Sarah's Christmas Miracle *(2010)*, *by Mary Ellis, is one of more than twenty*
Christmas-themed Amish romances.

Used by permission of Harvest House Publishers.

Chapter Four

Taking the Amish to Market

I meet novelist Suzanne Woods Fisher at a Starbucks on a cloudy Saturday morning in May, an hour before she is due at a book signing. Dressed in khaki pants and a sky-blue cardigan, Fisher greets me warmly before we head to the counter to order. She is to fly back to San Francisco this afternoon, after a whirlwind three-and-a-half-day trip to Pennsylvania that includes two book signings, a meeting with her coauthor about an upcoming series, and visits with Amish friends in Lancaster and Somerset counties.

Fisher is not only a novelist of Amish fiction but also the host of an online radio program, *Amish Wisdom*, which began three months after her first Amish novel appeared. Smooth as amber and inflected with optimism, Fisher's voice seems made for radio. *Amish Wisdom*, broadcast every Thursday afternoon, promises to help you "slow down, de-clutter, find peace, and live a simpler life." Guests on the program have included all the big-name Amish-fiction authors and many of the recent entrants to the field.[1] In her role as host of *Amish Wisdom*, Fisher has likely talked to more authors of Amish romance novels than anyone else on the planet. "It's time to capture the simple peace of the Amish in your own life, right now," intones a male voiceover at the beginning of each show. "So pour a cup of coffee, settle into your favorite chair, and tune into 'Amish Wisdom,'" the website invites. The slow chords of a George Winston piano solo at each fade-in and fade-out create a dreamy, almost somniferous soundscape.

The ratings for Fisher's radio show and the sales of her novels, however, are anything but sleepy. *Amish Wisdom* is one of the highest-rated shows on Toginet Radio. Her book *The Search* has been nominated for a Christy Award, a prize for fiction written from a Christian worldview, and Fisher's books make regular cameos on the bestseller lists of the Association for Christian Retail and the Evangelical Christian Publishers Association. They also claim spots on the Christian Book Distributors' Top 20 list.

While it may sound as if Fisher has been at this a long time, she hasn't. Her first Amish novel came out in January 2010, and her first Amish non-fiction title appeared only a few months before that. She is contracted with Revell through 2016; as of 2012 she had ten Amish books on the market and eleven more in process, including a three-book series of Quaker historical fiction. That's twenty-one books in about seven years. In one particularly busy stretch, Fisher had five books appearing within seven months.[2]

Fast Texts about a Slow Culture

In 1993, new works of fiction were appearing in the United States at the rate of about one a day. In 2002 there was one every twenty minutes, and today a new fiction work is published about every twelve minutes.[3] "Consumers are impatient, and attention spans are short," one branding expert has written to her colleagues in the Christian products world. "A traditional publisher's ability to rapidly slice, dice and deliver is now a core competency for survival."[4] In this climate, it is incumbent upon publishers to bring out books as quickly as possible.

Many individual Amish-fiction novelists are doing just that. Several of the authors have three books appearing each year, necessitating what some would consider a supersonic writing pace. "Many of my readers have been asking me to 'write faster,'" says Cindy Woodsmall in an automatic reply to explain her lack of a personal response to each e-mail. "My publisher and I agree that it's time to heed the call. I'm settling in to write two novels per year for the next three years, plus two novellas and one nonfiction book." When I ask Fisher whether writing a novel is a six-month-long process for her as well, she replies with some longing, "Oh, I wish it were. . . . I'm on more like a three- to four-month cycle." Amish-fiction author Shelley Shepard Gray published nine books during 2011.[5]

This is what publishing looks like in "fast capitalism," sociologist Ben Agger's term for an economic system in which commerce, information, and social trends have rapidly accelerated. Fast capitalism, or what Gilles Lipovetsky calls "hypercapitalism," could be seen as the economic prong of hypermodernity, in which ever-increasing speed and efficiency are applied to all domains of life. "There is no longer any choice or alternative other than that of constantly developing, accelerating," writes Lipovetsky; "everywhere the emphasis has been placed on the need to keep moving, on hyperchange." Agger calls the books published in this epoch "fast texts." "Writers write more quickly . . . as the pace of the culture industry accelerates," he explains in his book *Speeding Up Fast Capitalism.*[6]

The expedited pace of publishing in fast capitalism means that writers like Fisher face time pressures not unlike those of line workers in the Fordist era, in which mass production dictated efficiency and speed of assembly. Journalist Julie Bosman calls the rising productivity of novelists the "literary equivalent to the double shift," a phenomenon she attributes to e-books, which have raised readers' expectations that books by their favorite authors will be instantly downloadable. Add a few publishing successes along the way, such as Fisher has garnered, and the velocity increases further. "As soon as an author has a tipping point and becomes a big brand, then other forces come into play," literary-agent-turned-editor Peter Straus told the *Guardian.* "Sales and marketing and publicity departments want that author's next book as soon as possible." Lisa Scottoline, a bestselling author of thrillers who has increased her yearly output of novels, recently told the *New York Times,* "Today the culture is a great big hungry maw, and you have to feed it."[7]

Fisher is not unaware of the incongruities of writing fast texts about a people group whose example, according to her radio show, helps us "slow down." And her working life is beholden not only to the imperatives of a caffeinated publishing climate but also to those of her caregiving roles as mother, grandmother, and daughter. "Sometimes I wish I had two days for every one day in life in general," she muses during a phone conversation. "A writer's life—you need a lot of quiet, and a lot of time undisturbed, and I have four kids and a little grandbaby who just arrived, a dad with Alzheimers, and a mom who needs a lot of help."[8] Both times that I spoke with her,

Fisher's husband, a finance executive with a consumer products company, was in South America on business.

It is this sense of contemporary life as frenetic, excessively mobile, and technologically complex to which Fisher attributes the appeal of Amish fiction. The category is popular, she says, in part because it is "a response to the feeling that people have of being out of control with technology and change that's coming so fast. The feeling that you have a cell phone and you are never off the hook, you are responsible to be available all the time—it's just overwhelming. I think there's a longing for a life in which you're unhooked and detached, and we can't do it; it's too hard. I mean, it's really hard to put the brakes on." A few seconds later, as if on cue, the iPhone sitting beside her latte jangles. "There," she says, flashing an ironic half-smile and rubbing a thumb quickly over her phone's face. "See what I mean?"[9]

Commodities: Amish Novels as Hypermodern Goods

That novels like Fisher's are fast texts about an ostensibly slow culture points to the first metaphor through which we will examine the bonnet book phenomenon. Before a text reaches the hands of readers, where it can be used for culture- and meaning-making, its journey parallels that of any other commodity, from manufacture and distribution to marketing and sales.

The idea of literary texts as commercial commodities, subject in production and distribution and form to the vagaries of capitalism, is not a new one. Historian Laurence Moore traces the new avenues for profit-making that the Reformation offered to printers and booksellers, who began producing devotional materials, tracts, and eventually religious novels. The rise of popular literacy and the responsive strategies of people in the book trade thus resulted not only in more reading but in more buying. "People learned to read through a book quickly," Moore writes, "less to savor its story or to pore over its wisdom again and again than to get done with it and buy something else." This migration of reading from a mostly public, oral practice to a private, consumptive ritual moved books solidly into the marketplace of culture, where they remain today. Since Protestants were pioneers in the movement of printed texts into commodity form, religion itself, Moore says, "took on the shape of a commodity."[10]

Janice Radway, in her landmark study of romance-novel readers in the early 1980s, suggests that the "institutional matrix" of publishing is an essential if often overlooked chapter in the story of books. Failure to take into account the publishing matrix and the profit motive can lead to faulty theory-making about the popularity of any given genre. Radway maintains that disdain for romance novels issued in part from critics' disregard for the fact that books are market-bound goods. By assuming that the books were solely literary events, critics ended up drawing erroneous conclusions about the nature of readers' desires or the effect of cultural changes.[11]

For example, some critics attributed the explosion of the romance genre in the early 1970s to women's dissatisfaction with feminism. Average women were sick and tired of second-wave feminists' messages of sisterhood and equal rights, this line of thinking suggested, and their sudden propensity for romance reading constituted a lipstick-covered backlash against the movement. According to this theory, Gloria Steinem might have needed a man like a fish needs a bicycle, but your regular American woman just wanted to be ravished by a beefcake like Fabio. But Harlequin's propitious sales figures of the time had less to do with backlash than with business, Radway argues, and with the company's increasingly savvy production and marketing strategies. "The astonishing success of the romance may constitute evidence for the effectiveness of commodity packaging and advertising and not for actual changes in readers' beliefs or in the surrounding culture," writes Radway.[12]

When I asked after their theories on why Amish novels have become so popular, most people, from readers to writers to publishers to outside observers, pointed to a variety of psychological, cultural, and religious factors: postrecession nostalgia, a longing for the pastoral or simple life, anxiety about technological dominance, and desire for marital and familial coherence. These answers point out important aspects of the phenomenon, and we will examine them in the next few chapters. Yet if culture must be understood in light of the mode of production that undergirds it, as cultural criticism suggests, these answers tell only half the story.[13] In considering

culture, writes critic Raymond Williams, one must look at "all forms of sig-
nification, including quite centrally writing, within the actual means and
conditions of their production."[14]

So it is that we can trace the Amish-fiction boom not only to emotive or
social factors on the reading side of the equation but also to strategies on
the production end. Writers, literary agents, publishers, distributors, and
booksellers have become increasingly adept at keeping Amish novels in
the publishing pipeline and thus in the hands of readers, and any explanation for the ascendancy of Amish romance novels must include attention
to these processes. Simply put, readers would read fewer Amish novels if
fewer of them existed. Ignoring the production matrix might lead us to a
faulty conclusion: that Amish fiction, in its emphasis on the serene lifestyle
of a counterculture, only *critiques* hypermodernity instead of also *benefiting*
from it. Investigating the ways in which Amish fiction is conceived within
a hypermodern economic context, what Lipovetsky calls "capitalism in overdrive," allows us to view the more complex relationship between the genre
and the era.[15]

While looking at the production of Amish romance novels, however, we
must be careful not to suggest that a few Christian-publishing elites steer
culture as a buggy driver controls a horse. Conversely, although some publishers may claim that the runaway horse of reader desire for all things
Amish is determining the speed of the buggy, we shouldn't attribute the
phenomenon solely to readers either. Each argument—that a sudden bur-
geoning of reader desire singlehandedly created the Amish-fiction phenomenon, *or* that publishers' directives did so—is only half right. Only
when we look at both the driver and the horse can we understand how the
Amish-novel carriage system works.[16]

The producer least visible to Amish-fiction readers is the literary agent.
Within the institutional matrix of publishing, literary agents play a critical
position, poised between writers' fervid desire to get published and editors'
longing to acquire strong front-list books. Agents, who get paid a percentage of authors' royalties in exchange for representing manuscripts to publishers, negotiating contracts, and offering literary advice, receive the talent
from one side of the cultural field and parlay it to the other. So positioned,
within range of what's being written and what's being asked for, agents

have unique predictive abilities regarding the future of the subgenre. During the prosperous years of the Amish-fiction game, literary agents have made essential plays—not only by delivering Amish-romance manuscripts to the market, but by instigating their production in the first place.

The Literary Agent with No Agency

It wasn't quite a setup, but it wasn't entirely innocent. When I called a literary agent who represents several Amish-fiction authors, I wasn't really planning to trap him in an untruth, but I didn't try to rescue him, either.

Early in our conversation, before I stumble onto what I've come to call the Great Amish Agent Cover-Up, I begin to suspect that this agent, whose identity I'll conceal and whom I'll call Warren, may not be entirely forthcoming. As we chat about the astonishing growth of Amish fiction, Warren tells me that just five years ago, none of his clients were writing Amish fiction. Now quite a few of his clients are. Warren marks his entrance into the Amish-fiction business with a call he received from an editor who wanted to publish an Amish-fiction manuscript. By that time several of his clients had begun writing Amish stories, so Warren says, "We pursued it more aggressively" after that editor called.

"What do you mean you 'pursued it more aggressively?'" I ask Warren, in what I think is a kindly tone. His answer suggests a sudden defensiveness, perhaps some regret for his word choice. "I sent [the editor] a bunch of them," he answers. "I sent her . . . yes, I sent [the editor] several Amish books when she told me. Yes. That's what I mean." Clearly, this agent does not want to be perceived as aggressive.

Whether it's payback for his oblique reply or simply the next question that comes to mind, I'm not sure, but in a split second, I decide to lead my interviewee where he definitely does not want to go. "Have you encouraged some of your authors to think in the direction of writing Amish fiction who weren't doing it before?" I ask. There's an almost imperceptible pause at the other end of the line. "No, not really," Warren tells me. "They have to . . . it has to be in your heart."

Here's where my guilty conscience comes in. Before I called Warren, I had come across an interview in which one of his clients said that she began writing Amish books after her agent suggested she try her hand at Amish fiction. So a little later in my interview with Warren, I bring up this author's quotation to give him a chance to revisit his claim that he does not solicit Amish-themed writing from clients. Again, there is a brief pause on the other end of the line before he responds. "[My client] wrote a number of different things, and honestly, that's so long ago that I can't remember."

Since I'm not an entirely malicious person, I decide to give his amnesia defense the benefit of the doubt and change the subject. After I get off the phone, however, I do a little research and discover that at least four more of Warren's clients have chronicled their agent's suggestion that they try writing Amish fiction. Several were writing in other genres without much success when their agent mentioned that they might try Amish fiction.

That a literary agent would point clients toward a particular subgenre is not the notable action here. Good agents know what kinds of manuscripts publishers are buying, and good agents shepherd clients toward a sellable style or genre or voice. For agents, as literary matchmakers, it's all in a day's work. Several Amish-fiction authors, represented by other agents, tell similar stories of having been guided by their agents toward writing about the Amish. A marketer describes an agent he knows who "specializes in beating the bushes to find every imaginable little bit of Amish he can find." And agents aren't the only ones soliciting Amish-themed writing; an editor told me of an editorial meeting in which another editor said to her colleagues, "I have this author, and she's kind of been floundering and not sure what to work on. If I told her to do Amish and she would be interested, what would you think?" One novelist of Amish fiction tells me that editors and agents at Christian writers' conferences have been known to ask their audiences, "Can anyone here write Amish?"[17]

So Warren is far from alone in steering writers toward Amish Country narratives. What *is* notable is that an agent would deny playing such a role. By implying that Amish-fiction manuscripts were flooding his inbox simply because writing about the Amish was suddenly "in the heart" of so many of his clients, this agent appealed to what Mary Louise Pratt, in her study of colonial travel writing, has called "strategies of innocence": representations of oneself as caught in a matrix of others' making. European explorers wrote what Pratt calls "anti-conquest narratives," in which they positioned themselves as sentimental, noninterventionist observers, rather than as active agents of colonial hegemony and commerce.[18] Buffering oneself from capitalism, imperialism, or anything that might be construed as aggressive actually legitimates one's continued position in an expansionist project.

When I ask Warren whether writers or agents or publishers of Amish fiction might be cashing in on the Amish, he denies that, too:

> No, I think if you try to write an Amish romance novel with the thought of cashing in, I'm going to see right through that when I read it. If you don't have a genuine interest in the Amish and a love and caring attitude toward the Amish, it's going to show. . . . I mean, [Warren names several of his clients]: they reflect a true love for the Amish. . . . They go to church with the Amish. They've been to their houses for dinner. I mean, they know Amish. And they love them. And most of all, they respect them. And a publisher would know before they ever accepted a book where the author was just cashing in on the Amish; they would never publish it. So I have to safely say that I don't think there are really any published books out there that have taken that tack.

Since this agent's schema erases the very possibility that anyone who manages to get an Amish novel published, or anyone connected to that act, might be opportunistic in any way, he may be surprised that several of his colleagues readily own up to such a motive. When I ask another literary agent of Christian fiction, whose agency represents several Amish-fiction authors, the same question—whether people like him are capitalizing on the Amish—he snorts good-humoredly and answers posthaste. "Of course!" he says. "Has it [Amish fiction] been commercialized? Well, of *course* it's been commercialized. We're selling dozens, if not hundreds, of titles on this. This is a business; we're out to make a profit." This agent is quick to clarify that the authors represented by his agency are sticklers for accuracy and that they are respectful of Amish culture. But he doesn't shrink from the fact that lots of folks are benefiting from the boom in bonnet books, nor from the fact that he is one of them.

After the Great Amish Agent Cover-Up, I find such honesty refreshing. Ironically, the second agent's candid appraisal of his and his writers' roles as vendors in the Amish-fiction market seems less jaded than Warren's claims: that "it has to be in your heart" or that one must have a "true love for the Amish." And while many mediators' motives—including my own—are a mélange of the professional, the personal, the literary, the spiritual, and the financial, when it comes to articulating why their work centers on the Amish, many are loath to admit to anything even vaguely resembling a profit motive.

What the Great Amish Agent Cover-Up reveals is not that this particular agent is constitutionally untruthful. I have no reason to believe that massaging the truth is Warren's modus operandi. His elision may, in fact, be rooted in a deep-seated moral impulse, an unease regarding his location in the Amish-fiction matrix. His unwillingness to admit that he *does what agents do*—both in the sense of literary representation and in the sense of one who acts of his own accord—may indeed reveal a soulful disquiet about consumer capitalism itself, an economic system that, as theologian Vincent J. Miller has written, "creates a world where everything is transformed into a commodity that can be brought to market, exchanged, and consumed: selves, others, culture, religion."[19]

Warren's equivocation demonstrates that, regardless of the measures to which they go to affirm or deny it, literary agents are active on the incipient leg of the journey of Amish fiction from concept to commodity. It reveals that the buying and selling of books about the Amish, a people often assumed to be unsullied by mammon, can bring one's own merchandising actions into stark and uncomfortable relief.

Publishers Gone Corporate and Amish

The most visible vector of the Amish-publishing matrix, after the author, is the publishers themselves, composed of the editorial and marketing staff from acquisitions to sales and points in between. The extent to which books have become commodities is clear within publishing houses, in the notoriously fragile balance of power between editorial and marketing departments. Many publishing insiders say that during the past several decades, the scales have tipped in favor of marketing. The advent of mass-marketed paperbacks midcentury, usually reprints of the previous year's bestsellers, is responsible for shifting the balance for many publishers, according to publisher Jason Epstein: "Marketing was now the essential function and the editors at paperback houses were its servants, an inversion of the traditional relationship." Many observers suggest that the inversion continues today. One tribute given when legendary editor Bob Loomis retired from Random House in 2011 speaks to this waning authority of old-school editors. "The publishing business has been turned on its head," a literary agent commented. "The authority that people like Bob Loomis had has been captured by the marketing side of publishing."[20] Consolidation in the publishing industry, which morphed from a landscape of many small, privately owned publishers to a scene dominated by a few multimedia conglomerates, has also been blamed for shrinking the job security and professional purview of editors.

Christian publishing is not immune to this agglomeration trend. Cindy Woodsmall's publisher, WaterBrook, is a division of Random House, which is owned by Bertelsmann AG, one of the largest media conglomerates in the world. Zondervan, which publishes the work of four Amish novelists, has been owned by HarperCollins since 1988. In October 2011, Harper-Collins also announced its acquisition of powerhouse Christian publisher Thomas Nelson, the publisher of seven Amish novelists' work, and the deal was finalized in July 2012. This means that long-time rivals Zondervan and Thomas Nelson, the two largest religious book publishers in the nation, are now part of the same blended family.[21]

And what a family it is. HarperCollins itself is a unit of News Corporation, which also owns Fox Broadcasting Company, the *Wall Street Journal*, and Hulu. Although figures are hard to come by, one estimate suggests that owning both Zondervan and Thomas Nelson gives HarperCollins a 70 percent share of the religious book market.[22] Most readers are likely unaware that books such as *Naomi's Gift* and *An Amish Kitchen* issue from the empire of media mogul Rupert Murdoch. But if critic Raymond Williams is correct—that cultural items are shaped by the mode and condition of their production—this fact is not entirely irrelevant.

The metamorphosis of Christian publishing houses from small independents to divisions of multinational media corporations underscores the focal argument of this chapter: that Amish novels are commodities marked

by the hypermodern, globalized economy in which they have been conceived. Although it behooves publishers to disguise the hypermodern strategies that fuel the genre, such strategies can actually influence the content
of the novels, as we will see at the end of this chapter.

Hypermodernity can also leave a mark—literally—on the covers of the
books themselves. To achieve such a breakneck publishing pace and to keep
costs down, some publishers are turning to image subscription services to
get a jump on their cover design. One Amish-clad model, lifted from such
a service, appears on at least ten Amish romance novel covers, including
that of *Jacob's Return,* where she represents a scrubbed-up Rachel Sauder.
Wearing a cape dress and pensively fingering a covering string, the model
stands with her back to the camera. On several covers she has been placed
in a field, on one she stands in front of a window, and on the first Amish
vampire novel she is shown beneath a brooding sky, her dress bleeding into
a gravestone. In her various incarnations, this cover model is becoming an
insignia of Amishness, symbolic of the way that, through commodification,
Amishness can be extracted and dropped into a variety of contexts. She becomes what theologian Vincent Miller calls a "free-floating cultural object
. . . ready to be put to whatever use we desire."[23]

Such commodification is part and parcel of a hypermodern economy,
as we will see at the end of this chapter—a shorthand for communicating
meaning to consumers being pummeled with ever more images and information. It is on this competitive and ever-shifting media slope, where readers have countless choices regarding which texts to read and how to read
them, that editors and marketers of Amish fiction seek to gain purchase.

Editors

Disempowered as they may be relative to the historic power of their office,
the editors of Amish fiction with whom I spoke were an articulate and per-
ceptive crew, cognizant of the three-way tug-of-war between religious, literary, and economic forces on their industry. They are dedicated to strengthening the role of print in the devotional lives of their readers; helping their
authors write better; and competing for readers' time, attention, and money
in an era when a proliferation of entertainment options and a recession

have reduced the amounts of all three. Acquiring books has increasingly entailed learning to identify a product that will sell. Whether halcyon days in which editors could simply hunt for good writers and spruce up their prose ever actually existed is debatable, but it is clear that even if they did exist, those days are over. One editor of Amish-themed fiction made a Freudian slip on the phone when he was telling me about future acquisitions of Amish fiction. "If we find the right products—*projects*, rather—we're open to doing more," he said.

Identifying the right project/product in a crowded subgenre like Amish fiction means that editors must both help authors stake out their own unique, sellable territory within the broader category *and* help them stay within a genre's parameters so that expectant readers won't be disappointed. One editor told me that she and her Amish-fiction author went back and forth several times on her first proposal for an Amish-themed novel. "There was nothing wrong with her style—her lovely way of putting things together was all there," the editor said. "But what I wanted her to see was what someone comes to Amish fiction for. What are they looking for? So we had a conversation: here's what they [the readers] want, here's what they're looking for, here's what we need to deliver. Once she knew that, she went back, completely rewrote the proposal and the first chapters, and said, 'Is this what you're talking about?' and I said 'Yes!'"

Not all editors are as proactive in terms of helping Amish-fiction authors sculpt their narratives according to what readers are seeking. But as category literature, with a well-defined readership expecting certain conventions of format and content, Amish fiction works best within parameters with which readers are familiar. "They [readers] want a clean read," this editor told me. "They want a sweet story."

Nor are all editors as sanguine about delivering what readers want. The director of acquisitions at one publishing house confessed to me that he has never read an Amish romance novel—including those written by his own authors—in its entirety. "I wouldn't consider myself a fan of the genre," he told me in one e-mail, his diplomacy leveled by a smiley-face emoticon. At the same time, this editor is very aware of his and his colleagues' indebtedness to the readers of a category for which he expresses a measure of distaste. Although he belongs to a different taste public than his readers, he knows better than to bite the hand that feeds him. "We editors can be kind of a smug lot," he tells me on the phone. "There's the tendency for us to look askance at Amish fiction and wish that more serious fiction was selling. At the same time, we're very grateful for the fact that we still have jobs partly because of the people clamoring to buy Amish novels."

Marketing

Point your browser to Amishliving.com or Amishreader.com, and you can find voluminous virtual helpings of all things Amish.[24] There, beneath banners emblazoned with the silhouette of a horse and buggy or a field of pumpkins and a barn washed in amber hues of sunset, you can get Amish recipes for scrapple and haystack dinners. Clicking on a "Lifestyle" tab, you can link to sites that will find you a "cozy place to stay in Amish country" or quilts you can use to "wrap yourself in the warmth of the Amish." You can respond to polls such as "Would you be interested in reading an Amish novel that included a mini-Amish cookbook in the back?" or you can request an Amish pen pal.[25]

What might not be immediately apparent, either to the casual site visitor or the regular user, is who owns these sites. If you click on the "About" tab on Amish Reader, you will find the sponsor of the site, Harvest House Publishers, in small font. But on Amish Living, the much more sizable and active of the two sites, the name of the sponsor is as nonexistent as a plasma TV in an Amish living room. "Amish Living created this Ning Network" is the only phrase suggestive of a source, but in a frustratingly recursive whorl, the clickable text takes you to the main page for, well, Amish Living.

If you are in the mood for some sleuthing, you might discover that, although many different Amish-fiction authors are discussed and are even members of the Amish Living site, the only novels that the site links to for purchase come from one publisher. The only book giveaways come from the same house. And although you're welcome to bring up any Amish novel on the site's book club, the only moderated discussions revolve around books from said publisher. One member of Amish Living told me that she figured out who sponsored the site only after she had become a book-discussion host and began to notice that all the books flowed from the same source. It takes a little detective work for even a savvy visitor to discover that Amish Living is a marketing tool for Thomas Nelson, the Nashville-based evangelical publisher estimated to generate about $200 million in annual revenue.[26]

That Amish Reader and Amish Living are portals to publishers of Amish fiction demonstrates a fairly recent turn in marketing, a seemingly nonsensical one to many people unfamiliar with the field. If marketing is all about introducing people to your business and then creating customer loyalty, don't they need to know your name? Why conceal your brand so completely that someone could spend more than an hour trying to figure out who owns the site—as my own mother did with Amish Living—only to finally give up?

But marketing-that-is-not-marketing is an indispensable method for companies in an era of social media, and it's one that many publishers of Amish fiction are taking seriously. Conversational marketing is based on the idea that, as Rick Levine and his coauthors point out, "markets are conversations" and that "companies that do not belong to a community of discourse will die."[27] In conversational marketing, also dubbed "word of mouse" for its location in online media, consumers are conversation partners, not receptacles. Demographics and psychographics are out; sharing and reader-generated content are in. Instead of broadcasting or persuading or using the traditional "spray-and-pray" method, in which you strafe a massive crowd of potential customers with advertising messages and hope that a few take notice, companies must listen and engage. Rather than starting from one point (the company) and going to many points (the audience), effective marketing in a hypermodern age is initiated from many points and moves out to many points.

These originating points are often *prosumers,* a term coined by futurist Alvin Toffler in 1980 to describe "producing consumers." Toffler forecast that in an increasingly saturated marketplace, the line between consumption and production would blur and that companies would need to customize products by relying on the opinions and expertise of purchasers. Thirty years later, prosumers do appear omnipresent on the Web, creating buzz for companies by reporting on their experiences with particular products or by giving feedback to the company, which becomes vital to future product development. When they buy a ticket on Fandango or a new book on Amazon, marketing expert Joseph Jaffe writes, prosumers, whom he also calls "proactive consumers," are "definitely going to tell you about it—whether you asked to be told or not." After highlighting several examples in which bloggers and other web-users radically influenced companies' fates—for good or for ill—simply by posting about their products, Jaffe asks, in a question reminiscent of my mother's futile search for the source of Amish Living: "Where does advertising figure in this story? Nowhere. It is less than visible. It is invisible. . . . It doesn't even exist in a world where conversation prevails and marketing fails."[28]

Such a recondite marketing approach is a nice fit for publishers of Amish fiction for several reasons. As the Great Amish Agent Cover-Up demonstrates, it behooves producers of Amish fiction to camouflage economic interests behind more edifying ones, such as "community," which appears as a conveniently clickable tab on Amish Living and sounds positively Amish. And because reviews and conversations have long been drivers of book sales, and women's relationships around books are notoriously effective if accidental tools of the trade, conversational marketing also makes sense. Furthermore, because Christian marketers often think of their work as a hybridized vocation of mission and business, creating conversations between consumers can feel a lot like setting up a women's Bible study. "There is a communal feel among Amish-fiction readers," Terry Glaspey of Harvest House told me. "The idea with Amish Reader is to try to get people who are interested in Amish fiction to feel like they're part of something. It's also a way to help them build more of a relationship with the authors themselves."[29]

In addition to social media sites specifically devoted to Amish fiction, Facebook and Twitter have become central gathering places for Amish-fiction readers and venues in which they can interact with their favorite authors. Zondervan hosts the "Amish Life" Facebook page, which bills itself as an "online community for people who love all things Amish" and beckons Facebook users: "The Amish are known for their hospitality—so come on in." Most authors of Amish fiction have at least an author's page on Facebook where readers can become fans, and publicists sometimes organize Facebook release parties for new Amish novels. Several Amish-fiction authors regularly post updates about everything from a husband's upcoming surgery to how they spent Mother's Day to page proofs for an upcoming novel. In a classic "prosumptory" move, some even use Facebook to help them determine content for future books. "It's time for another poll!" author Amy Clipston posted on her author's page. "Which characters would you like to see featured in future Kauffman Amish Bakery books? Check out my poll tab and VOTE!"

Another effective publishing strategy in an era of presumption is giving free books to readers who agree to review them. Bloggers can get free Christian books from sites like Litfuse or BookSneeze, which is also a program of Thomas Nelson and which demonstrates that company's supreme flair for this business. In exchange, all readers have to do is write a review of the book on their blog, on Amazon, or on some other consumer website. Launched in October 2008, BookSneeze now has a database of twenty thousand bloggers, whom the company calls "influencers."[30]

One of the influencers, Karla, who writes reviews of inspirational fiction on her blog, is an ardent reader of Amish fiction, especially Beth Wiseman's novels, and has developed both virtual and in-person friendships with Wiseman and several other authors. A retired teacher who says she has probably read "hundreds" of Amish novels, Karla flew from Ontario to Texas for several days in spring 2011 to go to one of Wiseman's book signings. Karla also met Kathleen Fuller, another Amish-fiction author, when she and her husband went to Ohio, and made a prayer quilt for her. Influencers such as Karla play a vital role for publishers these days. More traditional marketing approaches, such as the book tours, magazine ads, and bookstore displays, are by no means extinct. It's just that they've been joined by other strategies that, instead of broadcasting or persuading or blitzing, gently insinuate themselves into conversations and relationships that are already taking place.

None of the readers and writers with whom I spoke seemed disturbed at the blurring of lines between marketing and friendship, advertising and conversation. For them, Amish novels are less products to be exchanged than textual links between people who share a common faith, as we will see in chapter 5. Suzanne Woods Fisher speaks genuinely and with gratitude about her relationships with readers, many of which have developed through Facebook. "I see it as sincere connection," she says, adding that she takes readers' prayer requests very seriously. Her website contains a section where visitors can submit prayer requests, and every Friday morning she prays for them. "I'm not looking at people just as an opportunity for me," Fisher says, and despite my tendency toward cynicism, I find that I believe her. "I'm doing the best I can to put good work out there, work that gets people thinking about faith."[31]

Sales: Amish Fiction's Point of Purchase

Investigating the popularity of Amish romance novels also requires considering the locations and manner in which they are sold. The term *bookseller* in the twenty-first century is less likely to refer to a bricks-and-mortar bookstore than to a virtual point of purchase, where readers buy books with the tap of a key, or to a mass merchandiser such as Costco, where shoppers can toss a book in the cart on top of a pair of flip-flops and a new garden hose. From chain bookstores to big-box retailers to the online behemoth Amazon, bookselling has clearly grown into a big if not always lucrative business.

In the last four decades of the twentieth century, bookselling became increasingly rationalized—designed with an eye toward efficiency of production, marketing, and sales—writes Laura Miller in a study of the contemporary book trade. In her chapter on price-cutting and publishing, Miller examines how the practice of discounting books has driven the rise of chain bookstores and the entrance of nonbook retailers into the book trade, even as it has hurt independent sellers and publishers. This is now an oft-told story, especially among those who mourn the slow strangulation of the independents at the hands of corporations large enough to offer deep discounts, and the subsequent narrowing of the field of books one can find for sale. Yet even beyond contributing to the demise of the independent bookseller, price-cutting practices have "taught consumers to view books as potential bargains rather than as unique embodiments of culture," Miller writes. The systematic discounting of books and other consumer goods has led to "a more single-minded focus by consumers on price and a concomitant cultural understanding of the consumer as a rational actor out to obtain desired goods at the lowest possible cost." Throughout the 1990s, she continues, mass merchandisers such as Walmart, Costco, and Target began selling books in earnest, and the Walmartization of literature in general and Amish fiction in particular began.[32]

More than half of Beverly Lewis's Amish-novel sales are now occurring through mass-market chains, such as Walmart and Kmart, as opposed to bookstores.[33] Fisher is pleased that her books have broken into Target, a notoriously difficult big-box retailer for publishers to crack, and while Harlequin's Love Inspired imprint used to try hard to get their books into CBA bookstores, now, thanks to the success of big-box bookselling, it's no longer worth their while. "As time went by, about 2006 or 2007, we thought, 'Why are we banging our head against the wall?'" recalls Melissa Endlich, senior editor at Love Inspired. "We do very well in Targets and Walmarts. These wonderful Christian women go in to buy laundry detergent and they pick up our book."[34] Some Amish romance novels, published in the mass-market paperback format like the ones at the end of the cereal aisle, are now available for less than four dollars, and Amish e-books can be had for less than three.

In the same way that books have penetrated traditionally nonbook retailers known for selling products, products have insinuated themselves into spaces formerly reserved for books. In the Christian market, for example, the surround sound of jewelry, music, movies, collectibles, gifts, and glow-in-the-dark crosses now muffles the book trade. Books now represent only 35 percent of the items sold in Christian bookstores. The trade association CBA dropped its full name, Christian Booksellers Association, in 1996, because for many of its member retailers, books had dwindled to only a fraction of what they were selling. It has retained its acronym, CBA, but is now also known as the Association for Christian Retail.[35] Two large Christian bookselling chains have scrubbed "book" from their titles: Family Christian Bookstores became Family Christian Stores, and Baptist Bookstore became LifeWay Christian Stores. In 1986 the magazine for Christian booksellers changed its name from *Christian Bookseller* to *Christian Retailing*. The increasing spread of Christian products into the territory that Christian writers used to command counts as one more indicator of the more-than-metaphoric way in which books have become commodities.[36] Many Christian bookstores have not survived, going the way of independent booksellers everywhere: out of business. But by folding Christian products into their retail offerings and operating as chains themselves, some have been able to weather the bookselling storms of recent decades.

The bookselling vector of the institutional matrix producing Amish-fiction titles also includes other actors: book distributors such as Biblica and Choice Books, subscription services of publishers such as Harlequin's Love Inspired, and book clubs such as Crossings and Doubleday. Book club sales, for example, help publishers save on production and inventory costs, since they don't have to print or warehouse book club titles; the lower costs at which book clubs sell books are counterbalanced by the immense volume of sales that book clubs help to ensure. Readers agree to buy a certain number of titles per year and receive deep discounts on them (along with sign-up deals like four books for ninety-nine cents). Book club sales usually represent a modest percentage of a publisher's complete output, but book clubs remain an essential strategy for publishers of Amish fiction to get their books to their audience. A recent list from Crossings Book Club contained eleven Amish novels in its top one hundred bestselling books. Only twenty-one novels in all made it onto that list.

Electronic publishing is also remaking the field of Amish fiction, as we will see in chapter 10. No one knows how many Amish novels are being bought as traditional books versus e-books, but several readers with whom I spoke read their Amish novels exclusively on e-readers.

When combined, these sales and distribution channels ensure delivery of inexpensive Amish novels to their loyal readers. Despite creative strategizing over the past decades, the book trade remains a rocky one, and few people get wealthy from participating in it. But as the last stop on the journey of Amish fiction into readers' hands, booksellers contribute to the success of the subgenre through their own particular blend of discounted prices, efficient sales channels, and, for businesses like Walmart and Costco, by not being "booksellers" at all.

Commodification: Liquidating Tradition

Amish people aren't literally bought or sold in any of the exchanges between Amish-fiction authors and agents and editors and marketers and booksellers and readers. It is not Amish bodies or souls that are traded, but rather items associated with the Amish.[37] Yet *commodification,* the transformation of goods or people or ideas into commercial goods, remains an instructive concept with regard to the process by which the Amish or any other religious group are rendered into cultural products. Although books are literary events in a way that quilts, faceless dolls, and furniture are not, novels about the Amish function much as these more easily recognizable Amish-themed commodities do: they are products that convey to the consumer some essential quality of Amishness.[38] So it is that those in the publishing matrix and those who are buying books exchange not only books but, in some sense, the Amish themselves.[39]

This is John Bomberger's concern when he talks about his organization's "ambivalence" regarding Amish fiction. Bomberger is CEO of Choice Books, a book distributor with Mennonite roots that stocks book displays in airports, supermarkets, gift shops, and travel centers across the United States and sells 5.2 million Christian books annually. "There is a concern among many in Choice Books about exploiting the Amish," Bomberger told me on the phone, pausing occasionally as if carefully choosing his words. Some of Choice Books' staff grew up Amish, and many are Mennonites. "It's always a question of what is being communicated in a particular book," Bomberger said. "What will the reader find in this book about Jesus, and about the Anabaptist-Christian tradition? Or is it written by somebody who is trying to profiteer? Now anything about the Amish will sell."[40] One young Amish woman in Indiana told me something similar: "It seems like word has gotten out that if you write about the Amish, you can sell books. I think it's getting out of hand."

Commodification of religion is not new, and it is not always distinguishable from other forces. Nikki Bado-Fralick and Rebecca Sachs Norris point out in their study of religious games and dolls that Christianity and commerce have linked arms in American religious life for hundreds of years. Religion is lived out in the marketplace as well as in the home and the sanctuary, and it's inevitable that expressions of religious belief sometimes take commercial form. Also, many novelists reject the idea of commodification completely, essentially arguing that one person's charge of commodification is another's artistic prerogative or religious call. Most authors of Amish fiction see their writing not merely as a career but as an exercise of their gifts for the glory of God. "I really look at this work as God's work," Fisher tells me. "With each book I just pray that one life will be positively affected," Beth Wiseman told an interviewer. "Then I will know I have done my job for Him."[41]

Yet while commodification does not always display clear lines between profiteer and object, and while there's no consensus on what constitutes commodification as opposed to artistic license or religious call, the concept remains essential to understanding the social world in which bonnet books are exchanged. Vincent Miller, in his incisive study of how consumer culture forms American religion, writes that commodification of culture is the single most important factor in the development of consumer capitalism in the twentieth century; his analysis situates commodification as a central and inevitable outcropping of our economic system. The commodification of culture, he explains, is a process "in which the habits and dispositions learned in the consumption of literal commodities spread into our relationships with culture."[42]

So on a visit to a bookstore, I might casually leaf through Fisher's latest Amish novel or an Oprah biography or a treatment of Muslim prayer practices or a sports encyclopedia or a devotional book about Christian hospitality. I browse through all these books, containing radically different content, in the same posture: as a shopper. My approach to cultural objects like books is, as Miller writes, "highly informed by the channels" through which I receive them. I may be a person of a particular faith tradition or none; either way, commodified religion allows me to graze on whatever practices or convictions I find most appealing. The bookstore example manifests one way in which consumer culture results in the "liquidation" of traditions, as Miller calls it, "whereby the elements they comprise (beliefs, symbols, practices, and so on) are abstracted from their traditional contexts and engaged as free-floating signifiers, put to decorative uses far removed from their original references and connections with other beliefs and practices." Miller cites several examples: Buddhist meditation techniques used as stress management in a corporate world devoted to extreme profit, the crucifix as a marketing tool for Catholic education, religious chant listened to via ear buds at the gym. Such shattering of traditions into shards, pieces from which consumers construct their own spiritual mosaics, is commonplace in a hypermodern context, which, as Lipovetsky writes, spreads "the model of the market and its operational criteria" to domains like history and religion.[43]

Given their highly visual distinctives, such as dress and transportation, the Amish are particularly ripe for commodification. The emblems of Amish life—coverings, capes, beards, hats, quilts, buggies—render them especially useful in a consumer culture and help to explain why Amish novels, as opposed to Presbyterian or Lutheran ones, are selling so well. Miller suggests that "religions that lend themselves to visual intensity and symbolism have greater appeal in consumer culture."[44]

That the Amish, rooted for centuries in traditions of self-denial, communal life, churchly authority, and pacifism, have come to function decoratively in the bricolage of commodified religion is fairly clear. Although authors of Amish fiction may argue that their books reconnect the picturesque aspects of Amish life with the spirituality and history and internal religious logic that undergird them, thus reassembling Amish signs by connecting practices with beliefs, critics maintain that the books further sever Amish signifiers from their signifieds. Fictional accounts of Amish life slice it into serving sizes such that readers can consume the tasty parts—Amish Christmases and midwives and brides and quilts—without needing to digest the ecclesial authority, pacifist orientation, or communal practices that stick in a modern craw. "Traditions are valued as sources of 'poetic and imaginative imagery,'" Miller writes, "while their logics, systems of doctrine, and rules of practice are dismissed for their rigidity and exclusivity."[45]

Hypermodernity marks Amish novels in decided and sometimes ironic ways. There is the sweepstakes entry that visitors to the website Amish Living can obtain by filling out a survey about why they love Amish fiction ("Complete our survey for a chance to win $10,000").[46] There is the Facebook release party for an Amish novel with giveaways that include an iPad and gift certificates to Starbucks, Amazon, and iTunes. There's the website photo of a tanned Amish novelist leaning against a boat railing with the caption, "with hubby . . . on a much-needed cruise!"—right under photos of Amish boys, buggies, and silos. There are the Amish Christmas novels and novellas (more than twenty in all) that enter the consumptive bacchanal each fall—even as actual Amish Christmas observances are relatively muted, centering mostly on family gatherings, special meals, and small gifts.

And when the commodifying impulse of hypermodernity is superimposed on Amish life, the novels themselves, and the portrait of the Amish that the novels contain, can be affected. One anthology of Amish novellas is interesting in this regard. "Three Amish women yearn for the perfect wedding," reads the marketing copy for *An Amish Wedding,* and the titles of the novellas—"A Perfect Plan," "A Perfect Match," and "A Perfect Secret"—further underscore the idea of nuptial perfection. While Amish women may indeed want to have a lovely wedding, or one that goes off without a hitch, the notion of a "perfect wedding," with all its attendant preoccupations, is largely a construct of popular culture, courtesy of the $161 billion American wedding industry.[47] At least twenty-five Amish novels contain the word "bride" or "wedding" in the book or series title. When commodification becomes the lacquer through which the Amish are viewed, it is indeed possible to end up with Amish bridezillas.

Whether any particular Amish novelist or agent or publisher is "guilty" of commodification is beside the point. Commodification is less the atomized acts of an individual or publisher than an irrevocable element of what Lipovetsky calls "hypercapitalism."[48] Commodification, whatever its gains or losses, happens. It is the central air system of the Starbucksized, Walmartified, iPadded home in which we live. As anyone who has seen a buggy parked outside the local Kmart can affirm, the Amish live here as well, albeit in a room of their own.

Commodities or Sacred Products?

To suggest that the work of authors, agents, publishers, and booksellers belongs only in the realm of hypermodern commerce would be unfair.[49] None of the metaphors through which we refract Amish romances should be used reductively, especially this one. While books are commodities, they are also venues through which people experience the sacred. And although they are caught in the gears of fast, commodifying capitalism, the people who produce Amish romance novels are also people who love books—writing them, editing them, handling them, talking about them, reading them, and persuading others to read them. "I really admire beautiful writing and I aspire to be better and better at that: where you just have an economy of words and you capture something with a little bit of poetry," Suzanne Woods Fisher tells me. She reads widely, from literary fiction to biography, and puts great priority on the craft itself. "I always tell authors at writers conferences that I'm looking for 'books that change me,'" agent Chip Mac-Gregor writes on his blog. "Words can do that. . . . Jesus was described as being the 'word'—the very word of God come to life. To me, that not only says something about Christ, but about the importance of words."[50]

From viewing Amish novels as commodities, we move to a surprisingly proximal metaphor: Amish novels as religious icons. Consumer desire and spiritual longing are both "about the joy of desiring itself, rather than possessing," Vincent Miller writes. It is the similarity between consumption and redemption that has allowed consumer culture to so deeply domesticate religious symbol and belief. Consumer desire, according to Miller, "resembles more profound longings for transcendence, justice, and self-transformation enough to be able to absorb the concepts, values, and practices of religious traditions into its own forms without apparent conflict."[51]

Listening to the meaning that readers make may help us avoid deterministic equations that would reduce writing about the Amish to commodification and reading about the Amish to consumption. To learn how readers construct religious meaning from Amish novels, we go to a small town in northern Illinois. There, in Plano, population 10,500, a group of Christian women meets monthly to talk about fiction, faith, and, on the night that I visit them, the Amish.

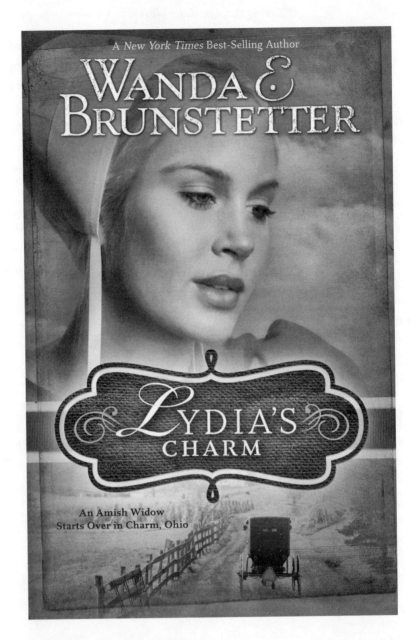

Like many other Amish novels, Lydia's Charm (2010), by Wanda Brunstetter,
narrates both a human and a divine love story.
Used by special permission of Barbour Publishing Inc.

꽃 Chapter Five 꽃

Is Amishness Next
to Godliness?

From O'Hare International Airport it takes about an hour to drive to
Plano, Illinois, thanks to the omniscient eye of the I-Pass, which extracts its invisible toll and requires no slowing. Only a few years ago, before the electronic payment collection system made travel on the toll road
"faster, safer, and more convenient," as the website advertises, it took a lot
longer. Traveling west on the Illinois Tollway toward Plano at night, on my
way to visit a book group that has invited me to its discussion of an Amish
novel, I'm relieved that I decided to spring for a transponder from the rental
car company. Merely imagining my other option—switching lanes, slowing down at the many toll plazas, fishing for exact change, merging back
onto a highway coursing with semis and SUVs—makes my hands sweat.
What Gilles Lipovetsky calls "the society of hypersurveillance" may be on
the march, I think, but as I trundle past the spreading office parks and
hotels of the western suburbs with no need to brake, I am grateful for the
telepathic square of plastic mounted on my windshield.[1] Who knew Big
Brother's gaze could feel so indispensable?

   The first sign of Plano as I approach from the north is its white water
tower, rising like a gargantuan garlic bulb into the sky. The low end of the
radio dial offers me a choice of at least eight Christian radio stations, and a

sign in the cornfield on the right announces the future home of the Plano Christian Church. Low-slung bungalows line the streets leading into downtown Plano, where the storefronts along Main Street have the weathered faces of those who have stared down the Great Depression, two world wars, a globalized economy, and a recession and have survived, if barely. Torresmania Mexican Restaurant, a block from the square, advertises ten tacos for $10.99. Torresmania, Chapala Family Restaurant, and a *mercado* along Route 34 announce a growing population of Latinos, drawn by jobs in the nearby Caterpillar plant and other industries in neighboring towns.

I am in Plano to visit not only members of an Illinois community but members of an interpretive one. Interpretive communities, as literary theorist Stanley Fish famously proposed, are bound not by geography but by a predisposition to interpreting texts in a particular way. Meaning is created neither by the text nor by the reader, Fish claims, but by interpretive communities, which share strategies for constructing meaning—strategies that "exist prior to the act of reading and therefore determine the shape of what is read rather than, as is usually assumed, the other way around."[2] The women of the book group I am here to visit are part of a larger interpretive community that appreciates the conventions of Christian fiction. Driving into Plano near dusk, I am eager to learn what meaning they find in Amish novels and the strategies by which they construct it.

Gals and Books: Literature's Ligatures to Faith

In a yellow-sided ranch house on East Church Street, on the north side of the railroad track that runs through town, a dozen women gather on a chilly Monday evening in early April for "Gals and Books," or GAB. They've been meeting monthly since 2000 to read and discuss Christian fiction, eat refreshments, and, well, gab. All but three attend the Plano Bible Church, an independent fundamentalist church in town that one of the women calls Plano's own "Bible Belt." GAB has a rotating attendance of about twenty women, many of whom have been acquainted for years; Linda and Karen knew each other in high school, and Mardel and Nancy lived on the same street. Carol is the church secretary, Loni is a retired nurse, Jackie has taught piano lessons for fifty-five years, Nancy worked as a receptionist, Pam is an at-home mom, and Julia, who arrives late, is an artist.

Throughout the years, the women of GAB have read books by the big names in inspirational fiction—Karen Kingsbury, Jan Karon, Francine Rivers—as well as literary fiction with religious themes such as Marilynn Robinson's *Gilead*. A few years ago they read Beverly Lewis's *The Secret*, the first in the Seasons of Grace series, although several of the women didn't like it because they thought it left too many loose narrative threads. Many of them read Amish fiction on their own.

GAB is holding a potluck tonight, and I take a chair at the dining room table beside Pam, an at-home mother of four. Pam has read numerous Amish-fiction titles, the first of them Cindy Woodsmall's book *When the Heart Cries*, after her seventeen-year-old daughter recommended it to her. Woodsmall's books remain Pam's favorites; "I never want to put them down," she tells me.

The women gather in the living room after dinner to discuss *Lydia's Charm*, their book for the evening. The novel, written by Wanda Brunstetter, features a young Amish widow who, along with her young son, moves back to her mother's house in Charm, Ohio. There she is courted by two Amish men: Menno, a middle-aged widower with four unruly sons, and Levi, a younger man who comes from a family of little people but is himself of regular stature. As with most Amish romance novels, Christian devotion and a sense of God's leading are braided throughout the entire text. Characters frequently reflect on God's presence and God's will for their lives. Lydia wonders at one point in the narrative, "Could marrying Menno be God's will?" and the book's epilogue confirms that a divine hand has guided the plot toward its culmination. "So much had happened since she'd lost her job in Illinois and moved to Charm," Brunstetter writes; "some good, some not so good, but all leading her closer to God."[3]

GAB's conversation swerves between the content and characters of the book itself and the stuff of their own lives, especially faith. Always they return to faith. The women pause halfway through the session to pray for a member who has shared tearfully about her frustration with a relative, and one woman tells us of a miraculous sign she received years ago. Another woman speaks of her inner peace despite the facts that her husband died only six weeks ago and that, since his death, she has become the primary caregiver for a granddaughter with brain injuries. "God takes care of all of us," she says simply and without affectation.

The first half hour or more of the book discussion includes scant reference to the novel. Even when the women do talk about *Lydia's Charm*, it seems to serve more as an aperture than a focal point. When discussing Lydia's transition to Charm, Pam says how thrilled she was to meet someone she knew at the bank soon after she moved to Plano. When the group speaks of one character's losing of herself in care for an aging father, Ceil describes a recent episode with her own elderly mother. As they discuss Lydia's mother's prejudice against little people, a woman confesses her own prejudice against someone less educated than herself. When they discuss Lydia's son's death, Nancy shares about her young son's death years ago and the comfort that friends offered.

The conversation seems to list away from the text on its own, but discussion questions at the back of the book, which the leader of tonight's session uses, tack that way as well. Ten of the twelve questions ask readers to link the plot and the characters to their own experiences and opinions, and the two remaining questions ask them to reflect on what the Bible says about prejudice and what they learned about the Amish through reading this novel. Many of the discussion guides at the end of Amish romance novels similarly lead readers to make personal associations between the text and their experiences; readers are invited to make explicit connections between literature and life much more frequently than to critique or analyze.

As the women chat about everything from Plano's welcome wagon to who was in the young marrieds Sunday school class the same years that they were, I sip my lemonade and try not to worry about how salient this visit is going to be for my research. Somehow I had expected to discover a cipher in tonight's conversation, some key to unlocking how a particular interpretive community reads and views Amish fiction and its conventions. I had hoped to find out how these women position themselves as readers within the narrative, whether they resist aspects of the text, and what larger cultural forces they might identify as making the novel more appealing. If the women barely got around to talking about the Amish novel itself, where did that leave me?

After the discussion is over and we begin moving toward the door, Cindy tells me that she is glad I joined them for their discussion. Cindy opened up to the group earlier in the evening about a personal struggle she's been having, and now she turns to me before she leaves. "This is a great group," she says, surveying the living room, where some women are still chatting and gathering up books and purses and empty cups. "If there's any group of people I'll share things with, this is it."

Later, as I reflect on GAB's discussion and on Cindy's parting words, I remember Neal's study of evangelical romance novels, in which she found that women use inspirational fiction as a means to connect with each other and to fuel their faith. By passing the books back and forth with daughters and mothers and friends and women at church, and by discussing them informally online or offline or in more structured settings such as GAB, women readers of inspirational romance transform reading, an essentially solitary action, into a communal practice. The author's voice and narrative elements matter, but only inasmuch as they illuminate readers' own lives and connect them with the experiences of others. Rebecca Barrett-Fox reports a similar pattern of response in the readers of Christian romance novels whom she interviewed. Their comments to her "did not focus on the book (for example, praise about diction or criticism of plot devices) but instead focused on their personal responses to the books."[4]

Neal theorizes that evangelical romance fiction, the category to which most Amish novels adhere, represents a ministry "by, for, and about women"—a ministry that underscores women's agency and experience in a religious arena still largely led by men. It is a ministry that I observed in GAB's discussion and in the connections between text, life, and faith that the women made over and over again. The novels become avenues for what Neal calls "fictional devotion," a manner by which readers are "both devoted *to* and *through* the genre in ways that reflect and configure the contours of their conservative Christian piety."[5]

Recalling Neal's schema, I begin to see that GAB's wide-ranging conversation wasn't simply getting off topic or going on nontextual tangents.

Rather, if Amish romance novels serve as apertures through which readers view God and life and relationships, then the quotidian stuff of these
women's conversation becomes essential to answering the question of what
cultural and religious work the novels perform. Through discussions that
move seamlessly from the faith struggles and love life of the Amish protagonist in *Lydia's Charm* to whether Shirley and Trish were charter members
of their book group, the women of GAB utilize Amish fiction to reinforce
their Christian commitments and nurture relationships. Their operative
interpretive strategy, which I initially failed to recognize, is viewing texts
as channels through which one can connect to others and to God. In that
sense, a book group like GAB functions as an antidote to the "detached hyperindividualism," as Lipovetsky calls it, which characterizes hypermodernity.[6] Amish novels, for these women, are not commodities but conduits:
openings in daily life through which both sisterly support and divine grace
can flow.

Icons: Amish Stories as Channels to God

The realm of Christian art contains an older, better-known type of doorway
to the divine, one that illuminates the work that Amish novels perform. An-
glican artist Linette Martin writes that religious icons, which in Eastern Orthodox tradition are egg-tempura paintings on wood panels depicting saints
and church events, are "sacred doorways" through which "what we call 'our
world' and what we call 'the spiritual world' are opened to each other."[7] The
term *icon* as used in popular discourse refers broadly to any symbol, but in
Orthodox Christianity, an icon is much more than a symbol; it both stands
in for the divine and participates in it.[8]

   When judged by the standards of nonreligious art, critic Titus Burckhardt says, religious icons may seem to fall short because of their apparently flat dimensions or unrealistic proportions. But as art intended to lead
a viewer into prayer and awareness of the divine, icons have a "conscious
and established doctrinal character" that determines their highly symbolic
content. In Russian iconography, for example, a protruding forehead is a
code for wisdom and blue is a sign of heaven. Icons are "rule-bound in both
form and content," writes iconographer Solrunn Nes. Thus, predictability

and a level of standardization of form and content are written into the very character of iconography.[9] Similarly, Amish romance novels operate within highly determined aesthetic conventions and with particular codes that, while apparently limited in scope or conventional in arrangement, allow readers immediate and comfortable access to devotional and didactic meaning.[10] So it is that within Amish novels, bishops are frequently a code for religious authoritarianism, barn-raisings for communalism, and quilts for female artistic expression and agency. Such codes contribute what Konrad Onasch and Annemarie Schnieper call "communicative efficacy": the ease with which icons, or novels, communicate the messages encoded in them.[11]

The metaphor of Amish fiction-as-icon also illuminates the interpretive community that surrounds the genre, which shares certain strategies for constructing meaning, and the ways Amish fiction often connects readers with other believers. Icons are communitarian in that they require an agreed-upon set of symbols and a shared sense of what those symbols mean. Orthodox artists, including iconographers, seek "not so much self-expression as expression of the community," writes critic Anthony Ugolnik.[12] Similarly, Amish novels are created, viewed, and validated within a particular interpretive community and are expressions of a communal ethos.

The Amish novel-as-icon trope is problematic in some ways. The word *icon* comes from the Greek *eikon*, meaning "image," "figure," or "likeness," such that icons are, by definition, *not* written texts (although iconographers speak of "writing" icons rather than drawing or painting them, to emphasize them as a form of prayer rather than of art). Although the production and use of icons has spread from Orthodox Christianity into mainline Protestantism, they remain a foreign sign for most evangelicals, one far outside their religious domain. Given Protestantism's historic suspicion that icons approximate idols, some readers of Amish fiction may take offense at the metaphor. Orthodox believers may reject the metaphor as well, because icons for them carry a liturgical, sacred weight that genre fiction cannot, and because their metaphoric use in this context may be the appropriation of religious signs for purposes other than that for which they were intended. So instead of comparing any actual properties of icons and Amish-themed novels, we will look at the ways Amish novels *function*. When we view the functions of Amish fiction as parallel to the functions of icons, it gains a certain internal cohesion as a subgenre, a unity of purpose and voice, and the appeal of the category to readers becomes more apparent.

In this chapter we look at the *devotional* and *didactic* functions of Amish novels. By relying on certain conventions, Amish novels, like icons, both inspire reader-viewers to greater devotion to God and instruct them in the faith. GAB's discussion leader, Ceil, articulated the dual function of Amish fiction in this way: "[The readers] could read other clean fiction . . . but I do think they want some instruction, and for this time to be well-spent and to be drawn closer to the Lord."[13]

The Devotional Role of Amish Fiction

When I asked readers of Amish fiction why they like the novels, many responded that their relationships with God were strengthened by reading them. "I often feel God's presence in one way or the other when I am reading Amish Fiction novels," one fan posted on the Amish Living website. "After reading these novels, I came to fully realize that I am craving even a deeper and closer relationship with the Lord my Savior, just plain and simple."[14] At least two responders added that the spiritual inspiration they find in Amish-themed novels is greater than that they find in other Christian fiction.

Many Amish-fiction authors confirm that their fondest hope is that their writing would serve in this devotional way, bringing readers closer to Christ. "I write to impart the things that Christ has taught me in my walk with the Lord," Beverly Lewis told me. "A lot has do with forgiveness and redemption and extending mercy and going outside our comfort zones to assist or help or pray for others. . . . Maybe it [my work] can make a heart more tender and realize that they're hungry for the Lord, just as some of my characters are."[15] And the connection that loyal readers feel to their favorite Amish-fiction authors goes beyond a fan's adoration of a celebrity to a sense of Christian sisterhood. Readers at book signings have sometimes recounted to authors the ways their books encouraged them through major life crises and have ended up crying and praying with the authors. In these ways and others, Amish novels become devotional texts for many readers, icons communicating the presence of an invisible God.

The Amish: Saints

Devotional texts of evangelical Christianity often include stories of people who function as heroes of faith. Many readers told me that the Amish characters in their favorite books were role models, of sorts—exemplars of spiritual virtues such as forgiveness, simplicity, acceptance of the will of God, morality, neighborliness, commitment to family and marriage, and compassion. While clarifying that they know the Amish aren't perfect, many still communicated a deep admiration for the faith and practice of both real and fictionalized Amish persons. "I have been so impressed with how they walk the walk besides just talking the talk," Amish-fiction author Mary Ellis told Suzanne Woods Fisher on her radio show. "Their relationship with God is just right there. It's so easy to compartmentalize my spirituality, but in the Amish, God is the focus in every one of their thoughts, in the words that come out of their mouths, and in their actions. . . . They keep God central, and I respect that so much."[16]

In this way, the Amish characters in novels serve as saints, as do those depicted in icons: sanctified individuals whose virtues and character both outstrip our own and nudge us toward greater piety. While they are given much more flexibility and agency and humanity than the transfigured saints depicted in religious icons, they still serve to point the reader toward the divine. As we will see in chapter 7, the virginal character of the protagonists serves to heighten their saintly status, raising them to a position that is simultaneously in the world but not of it. So it is that, in the devotional function of bonnet fiction, the Amish serve as the "saving remnant" in the dialectic outlined in Weaver-Zercher's *The Amish in the American Imagination.* The other half of the dialectic—the Amish as fallen people—will become apparent later in this chapter, when we look at the didactic function of Amish novels. Devotionally, however, Amish characters serve as models of people pursuing relationship with the divine.

The notion of an intimate, personal relationship with Jesus, which stands at the center of evangelicalism, is the cynosure of most Amish romance novels. In fact, while human romance is one engine of plot in the novels, just as essential is the devotional one, in which the protagonist is drawn closer to God. Many readers told me that they liked to read about women who, in facing adversity, learn to trust in God. Several mentioned that the Amish women in the books have the "same problems" they themselves have and said that as readers, they are personally challenged as they observe protagonists rising to meet challenges such as unrequited love, infertility, loss of a loved one, marital disagreement, and economic uncertainty. Some heroines are depicted as having strong Christian faith at the beginning of the novels, and the ensuing events simply confirm or purify their piety and devotion; other protagonists embark on more radical devotional journeys in which they move, as many evangelicals construct it, from "religion" (a set of rules) to "relationship" (friendship with the living Christ). As saints in the icons of Amish fiction, protagonists become role models, agents through which readers view God.

God, the Great Romancer

The devotional momentum of many Amish novels is so great that any romantic plotline becomes a facsimile, of sorts, of the devotional arc of the story. Neal claims that most evangelical romance novels portray God as "the great romancer," who offers the protagonist—and by extension, the reader—unconditional love.[17] Many readers of evangelical romance novels say that reading such fiction helps them rekindle passion for their faith that humans stand always on the verge of losing. Beverly Lewis confirms Neal's claim: "The love stories that people seem to crave, or the romance novels they seem to devour, are just an indication of our hearts, in that we are longing for the Great Love, that of Christ for his church. . . . The bride of Christ [the church] longs for our husband, Jesus, because that's the Great Love."[18]

Such narratives of God as initiator of sacred romance with humanity are not unique to contemporary evangelicalism; they have permeated all manner of religious discourse for centuries. The sexuality-infused Song of Solomon in the Hebrew Scriptures is often read as a metaphor for God's love and longing for people, and Christian writers including the twelfth-century mystic Mechthild of Magdeburg and the sixteenth-century Spanish mystic Saint John of the Cross frequently relied on imagery of God as a lover. More recently, evangelical writers like John Eldredge and Brent Curtis have pictured God as a romancer, and the image of Christ as a lover appears in much of the contemporary worship music sung by and performed in evangelical churches.[19]

Amish romance novels participate in this tradition of viewing God as longing for and pursuing humanity. In many of the novels, a romancing God becomes a full-fledged character whose actions, though invisible, influence outcomes and draw the protagonist's affections. In Cindy Woodsmall's *When the Heart Cries*, Hannah Lapp is ready to turn her back on God after she becomes pregnant from a rape and after a series of scandals follow in its wake. When her Mennonite beau, unaware that she has been raped, rejects her, Hannah plunges into deeper sadness and renunciation of her faith. But after hearing the baby's heartbeat, Hannah remembers the unmarried mother of her Savior and finds comfort and sustenance in the idea that her child shares the same parentage as the Christ child. "As the thoughts gave her courage, she knew what had to be done. This infant didn't belong to its father; it belonged to the Father. That's who Hannah would pray the child would take after: its heavenly Father. . . . Love—real, God kind of love— gave the infant worthiness." The book ends with Hannah leaving both her Amish community and her Mennonite boyfriend; "Hannah's relationship with Paul was over. Nevertheless, God's strength would pull her through. If everything ended with God, then those who were in Him had a good ending—eventually. A deep warmth comforted her."[20] Hannah reunites with Paul in the third novel of the Sisters of the Quilt series, but her relationship with God precedes and informs her romantic decisions.

Images of God as a lover factor prominently in many other novels as well. In Beverly Lewis's The Courtship of Nellie Fisher series, God functions as the vertex of a love triangle, a divine suitor who sometimes complicates, in the short term, the protagonist's earthly romance. In the third book, set in the 1960s as the Old Order and New Order Amish split, a friend asks Nellie why she and her boyfriend, Caleb, stopped courting. Nellie has become part of the New Order group, which emphasizes assurance of salvation and a personal relationship with Christ, and Caleb remains among the Old Order. "Jah, and strange to say it, but the Lord came between Caleb and me," Nellie replies. "That's all I'd best say."[21]

Mennonite, New Order Amish, Beachy Amish, and evangelical Christian characters frequently serve as models of intimacy with God for the

Amish characters. In the early part of Beverly Lewis's *The Shunning*, Katie Lapp wonders at the prayers of her mother's Mennonite cousins, who "seemed comfortable talking to the Lord." Hillary Manton Lodge, in her urban Amish novel, writes in the voice of Sara Burkholder, who fled her Amish community to become a fashion designer. At one point, reflecting on the faith of her new friends and her brother, who has also left the Amish, Sara thinks, "Jayne, Levi, and Gemma described a God very unlike the one I'd been told about for eighteen years. I knew I needed to reintroduce myself now that we were meeting under different circumstances. Maybe a part of me was waiting for Him." By the end of the novel, as she stands as a bridesmaid at her brother's wedding and reflects on her own romance, Sara has gained clarity: "I knew that no matter what, I was loved by God, and I was loved by Will."[22]

As Neal writes and as these scenes make clear, in evangelical romantic fiction "Christianity itself becomes a love story as the novels narrate the power of God's love, not the force of his judgment." Readers of Amish novels, then, become not just observers of the human love story told in the pages of the book; they become protagonists in a sacred love narrative that supersedes the textual one, a story in which they are both loved and lover. In the Greek parlance well known to many evangelical Christians, the divine love narrative is the *agape* love that places the *eros* in its proper context. Indeed, the chaste quality of this divine love can be seen as another way Amish novels dissent from an oversexed culture, which many readers think exaggerates *eros*. Amish novels serve as doorways through which readers reenter divine love; as iconographer Paul Boyce has written of Orthodox icons, Amish novels remind readers that they "are deeply loved by God."[23] Amish-fiction author Shelley Shepard Gray says, "I feel lucky to be spending much of my days writing about people loving the Lord and falling in love at the same time."[24]

The Didactic Role of Amish Fiction

Like religious icons, which communicate to viewers the stories, history, and substance of faith and impart information about correct belief and practice, Amish novels serve a didactic function. Philosopher Constantine Cavarnos suggests that in an earlier, preliterate era, Orthodox icons schooled viewers in faith by efficiently delivering information in visual form; he quotes a patriarch who said that icons offer "a representation of knowledge consonant with piety."[25] Amish novels serve a similar function for an evangelical audience: reminding readers of what faith is (relationship with Jesus), what it is not (rules for living), and how to discern the difference.

God as a lover or God as a judge is a central dialectic upon which many Amish romance novels turn. Narrating the devotional power of God's love, as Neal writes, often requires narrating a protagonist's erstwhile view of God as a judge. This is apparent in several of the examples above, in which the Amish heroine journeys from the ostensibly empty "religion" of her forebears to a vibrant "relationship" with Christ. It is at this point where, in many novels, the Amish become less figures of devotional inspiration than avatars for instruction in an evangelical faith.

In Gayle Roper's *A Stranger's Wish,* English protagonist Kristie details for her Amish friend Jake the difference between his faith and hers. First she scolds him—"You keep using your family's Amish-ness as an excuse for not becoming a Christian"—and then boils down the essence of his faith and hers: "Being a Christian has nothing to do with traditions of any kind, no matter how much you love or hate them," she tells him. "It has to do with a personal faith in Jesus as the Christ. Either you choose to believe in him or you don't." This thread of distinction runs through Hillary Manton Lodge's *Simply Sara* as well. "The stern, unbending God I grew up with who demanded obedience from His children seemed so different from the God present at Jayne and Livy's church," Sara reflected, as she contrasted her Amish childhood with the church of her new friends, which, while it remained unnamed, appeared to be nondenominational, informal, and wholly evangelical. "Their God was stern yet loving, unyielding in faithfulness, slow to anger, and quick to love."[26]

The journey of many Amish heroines like Sara, from viewing God as judge to viewing him as lover, becomes a lesson for evangelical readers in the character of God, the definition of salvation, and the contours of the faith. Historian Eric Miller, writing about Amish romance novels for *Christianity Today,* suggests that the books confirm for readers the rightness of their own faith narrative. Referring to Woodsmall's first book, *When the*

Heart Cries, Miller writes, "As the story unfolds, it's clear that for Woods-mall, what Hannah needs is what her whole community needs: to embrace a freer faith, one more personal, spiritual, biblical. In short, they need to become evangelicals."[27]

Miller points to a fascinating conundrum of the Amish-fiction phenomenon: that evangelicals are reading about the Amish to learn how to be better evangelicals. As we saw in chapter 3, many evangelicals have emerged from what Miller calls the "strict, idiosyncratic code" of fundamentalism, which they now view as constraining and legalistic.[28] In many Amish novels, then, as readers watch protagonists strip off repressive Amishness and outfit themselves with liberating evangelicalism, they see a replica of themselves and their own ecclesial journey.

Whether it's the *Ordnung* of a midcentury fundamentalist Protestantism or the *Ordnung* of the Amish, readers are reminded that rules don't save you: a relationship does. "You don't have to wear a prayer bonnet or ride around in a horse-drawn buggy to follow God," says one English character in Beverly Lewis's *The Mercy,* and while he is speaking to his Amish wife, he is also clearly speaking to readers.[29] While readers are encouraged to view "the loyalty, the fidelity, the willed innocence of the Amish" as noble and virtuous, in the writings of some Amish-fiction authors, Eric Miller claims, "for freedom to ensue, they [the Amish] need a complement. For Woods-mall and Lewis, this complement comes compliments of American evangelicalism—dual, dueling identities, deeply enmeshed."[30] Thus, in their teaching role, some contemporary Amish novels echo the timbre of the mid-twentieth-century novels of Clara Bernice Miller, which taught readers what faith *is* by placing it next to what faith is *not.*

During the same years when novelist Clara Bernice Miller was riding the Anabaptist escalator out from the Amish and toward the Mennonites in Iowa, Beverly Lewis's father, an Assemblies of God minister in Lancaster County, was serving as a stopover for Amish people on a similar journey. Lewis remembers that during her childhood, her father met frequently with Amish neighbors and friends who would come to him for counsel on matters of faith. On the phone, Lewis recounted her father's role in the lives of their Amish friends: "So many Amish people said [to my father], 'You know, it's just all rules here, we don't truly know the Bible, we don't know the

Lord, we want what you have.' So they'd invite us to their houses, and we'd have dinner with them, and Dad would open the Bible and read the New Testament to them. I didn't know until I was probably in high school that less than actually 20 percent of Amish in Lancaster County know Christ as their Savior. It was really remarkable to me. I don't know if some people might think it's a mission field. It's . . . definitely something I pray about a lot." More than most Amish novelists, Lewis expresses hope that her books can serve an instructive function for Amish as well as English readers. In that sense, she desires that her real-life Amish readers follow her Amish characters on this road to salvation. "I never set out to write books for the Amish to read, necessarily, but they do," she says. "And then many of them [Amish readers] will say, 'We've been told we shouldn't read your stories because we'll end up outside of the Amish community if, you know, we end up becoming Christians.'"[31]

Lewis's comments bring into stark relief an enigma at the center of some Amish novels' didactic function: that the very characters portrayed as saints might not necessarily even be "saved," according to readers' definition of salvation. This figure of the not-necessarily-saved Amish saint appears, at first, inscrutable. How can books that, on the one hand, sanctify the Amish also question whether the Amish are even Christian? How can a sectarian religious group be viewed as both model and mission field? Nonpareil but not necessarily going to heaven? Worthy of emulation but requiring of prayers for their salvation?

Evangelical Salvation: Born Again

Answers to this paradox are threefold. The first clue lies in the nuances of evangelical soteriology, or doctrine of salvation, which sees salvation as independent from one's church affiliation and based entirely upon one's confession of sin, acceptance of Christ's atoning work on the cross, and personal relationship with Jesus. Thus, while some Amish novels, especially Lewis's early ones, portray many of the characters as rule-bound rather than Jesus-filled, many evangelicals would say that their own churches have a mix of "cultural" Christians and genuine ones. One woman in Plano tells me that she grew up Catholic but only later "became a Christian," although in another conversation she speaks of a Catholic friend who *is* "a believer." Evangelicals may posit that their churches, compared with Amish ones, contain a higher percentage of people who, in Lewis's words, "know Christ as their Savior"—her 20 percent figure for Lancaster County Amish sets a pretty low bar—but most would be loath to judge any particular church group as monolithically filled with believers or otherwise. "You have to remember, Kristie, that there are two types of Amishmen, religious and cultural," an Amish friend of the protagonist says in Gayle Roper's *A Stranger's Wish*. "My parents are religious Amish. They love God and believe the church's teachings." He contrasts his parents to Isaiah and Ruth, who are "Amish because that's the life they've been raised to live." Kristie, the protagonist, immediately understands. "There are people like your parents and people like Ruth and Isaiah in my church too," she tells him. "Even the Bible talks about people who have the form of faith but not the substance."[32] The evangelical distinction between believers and unbelievers, then, falls less along lines of ecclesial membership or virtuous action or even right belief than personal relationship with Christ.

In novels that emphasize the difference between Amish unbelievers and Amish believers, the protagonist, by the end of the narrative, has always become a believer. Readers may still be convinced that the heroine is a minority among her people—when I ask a member of GAB who loves Woodsmall's novels whether she thinks the Amish are Christians, she replies, "Not the Old Order; they're not allowed to read the Bible. The Old Order ones are lost according to our Christian standard; they're basically living by works." But if you are an evangelical reader concerned about the eternal (if fictional) fate of a protagonist's soul, you will ultimately be assured that she, too, knows Jesus.

In many novels, especially more recent ones, the protagonist's journey is not from unsaved to saved but from immature to mature faith. But even within those novels that do draw most Amish people as either unsaved or hovering dangerously close to it, the protagonist always ends up as, well, an evangelical. Ceil, the leader of the Plano book discussion group, who has read more Amish novels than almost anyone else I talked to, said that she has seen a change in the subgenre over the past ten years regarding whether the Amish are portrayed as what evangelicals would define as "Christians"

or not. "When I first started reading the novels, it seemed like the big conflict was, 'Here's Christianity, accepting Christ as your Savior, living like
the Bible says,' and then there was always a group of people or the father
in the family who said, 'No, you don't have to speak personally to God and
you don't have to do this.' So then there was this conflict of the characters
coming to know what it *really* meant to be a Christian. Now I don't see that
anymore. Now in the books it seems that they're all Christians, and that
they all have a personal relationship with Christ." Ceil's sense of a shift in
the portrayal of Amish spirituality in the books may have something to do
with the fact that the early work of Lewis and Woodsmall, two of the most
successful Amish-themed novelists, emphasized the distinctions between
Amish believers and unbelievers more than the writings of recent entrants
to the field or even the more current novels of Lewis and Woodsmall. Lewis's
early writing, especially, delineates between Amish believers, whose warmhearted faith results in spontaneous prayer and devotional practices, and
unbelievers, who are beholden to the *Ordnung* and other "man-made" rules
devoid of grace. "The Ordnung can't save us, Katie," says the protagonist's
suitor, Daniel, in *The Shunning*. Daniel has begun hanging around with
Mennonites, who are known for "seeking out the truths of God's Word."
"Our forefathers weren't educated in the Scriptures. . . . They didn't study
the Bible so they could teach it to the People. They made rules for the Old
Order to follow. Man-made rules." By the end of the trilogy, Katie has experienced a personal conversion and tells her Amish mother, "But, Mamma,
following the Ordnung isn't what matters. Don't you see, being a follower
of *Jesus* is what counts?"[33]

Amish Salvation: The New Birth

The second idea that helps to answer this riddle of the fictional Amish being saintly but not necessarily saved is the fact that the Old Order Amish,
in general, use a very different soteriological vocabulary than evangelicals.
Rather than using the term *born again,* the Amish are more apt to speak of
the *new birth,* which refers less to eternal salvation of the individual than
to joining a community dedicated to holiness and discipleship. And rather
than assurance of salvation, the Amish speak of a living hope of salvation,

claiming that to be certain that one is saved would be presumptuous and vain.[34] So if the Amish themselves aren't sure whether they are "saved," is it any wonder that writers like Lewis aren't?

When outsiders focus on the Amish reluctance to speak of being born again or having the assurance of salvation, they may be missing some theological subtexts. First is the Amish indictment of what one Amish bishop has called the "two-track system of salvation" that characterizes evangelical theology. By "two-track" system, write the authors of *The Amish Way*, the bishop is referring to "a theology that separates belief and obedience, placing personal faith on one track and matters of lifestyle on another." "I just don't like the two-track view of salvation," Bishop Eli told the authors, because "it separates grace from ethics."[35] This grace-versus-works argument has dogged Christianity for millennia, and in Lewis's early books and several others, the Amish religious system lands squarely in the works column. Readers of those Amish-themed novels are schooled in salvation-by-grace via the negative example of Amish characters who appear to be trying to shoo-fly and shun their way into heaven.

Outsiders to Amish life may also miss the overtones contained in what the Amish call the "living hope" of salvation. When I mention this topic of evangelical assessments of Amish salvation to an Old Order Amish woman I'll call Esther, it quickly becomes clear that I have brought up a sensitive topic. "There's this great big rift between English people and Amish people," she tells me, leaning forward and speaking in measured tones. Esther's speech gradually gains the speed and ire of someone forgetting her intention to be polite. "Because we [Old Order Amish] dwell on the humility so much, we say, 'We *hope* we are saved.' Other Amish and Mennonite and English people say they *know* they are saved. The difference is absolutely not tangible; you can't even talk about it. It makes me so mad. It's our *humility* that has us saying it that way." She pinches her index finger against her thumb as if to measure the proximity of assurance and hope. "The difference is about this much," she says. "If Beverly Lewis wants to say we're not saved, she can. Excuse me. I don't care; she can." Esther pulls a tissue out of her purse and blows her nose. "I get a little passionate on that subject, as you can see. It upsets me."[36]

Not all Amish novelists would raise this Amish woman's hackles in that regard. It is possible that the Amish demonstration of forgiveness after the Nickel Mines shooting in 2006 silenced many people's doubts regarding the spiritual integrity of Amish individuals. One reader of Amish fiction told me that, in his opinion, the Amish novels published post–Nickel Mines have a kinder, gentler view of Amish spirituality than the ones published before the tragedy. When I ask author Mary Ellis whether she thinks the Amish are Christians, she looks at me, baffled. "*Absolutely!*" she answers, as if I just asked whether water is wet. Suzanne Woods Fisher is quick to say that Amish Christians simply emphasize different parts of the gospel than evangelical Christians do. "The Amish aren't evangelical," author Adina Senft wrote on one blog. "These folks are Christian, but not mainstream evangelical Christian. They look at the world, at salvation, at God's laws differently."[37] And even Beverly Lewis's more recent novels play less along the born-again versus not-born-again line, emphasizing the spiritual growth of the characters rather than any initial conversion.

Critical, too, is that not all Old Order Amish people reject the evangelical vocabulary, as Esther does. One Old Order Amish woman in Lancaster County sounds a lot like the protagonist in an Amish novel when I ask her about Lewis's claim that only 20 percent of her people "know Christ as their Savior." While I expect her to take offense at the notion of calculating the ratio of saved Amish souls to unsaved, she doesn't. "Personally, I can say that I have a relationship with Jesus. I love him with all my heart," she tells me, pausing from her task of hanging up laundry near the woodstove. Her eyes look a little moist. "And I know—I *know*—there are many, many Amish people who do also. I just have wonderful, amazing fellowship at church and in my group of friends and with my neighbors. I just believe that they're on their way to heaven. I have *no* doubt. So I would feel that figure is much, much more than 20 percent." She concedes that there probably are Amish people who go through baptismal instruction class "because it's part of the culture, but don't really get a grip on the fact that if I were the only person on earth, Jesus would have died for *me*." Thus, while this Amish woman may dispute Lewis's numbers, she wouldn't dispute her terms.[38]

The Bishopric

The third clue to this enigma of the sainted-but-not-saved Amish lies in the novels' ability to displace the traits of Amish life that evangelicals find abhorrent—the mere hope of salvation, an emphasis on works, communal control of behavior—onto one character. This allows estimable Amish qualities—neighborliness, fidelity, good humor, commitment to family, a relaxed approach to time—to be spread among the remaining characters. There is no better carrier of all things unpalatably Amish than the bishop.

In many of the novels, the Amish bishopric functions as part law enforcement and part papal authority, and almost always as mediator of God's judgment. In Amy Clipston's first novel, *A Gift of Grace,* Rebecca Kauffman and her husband come under the bishop's scrutiny because of the rock music and bikini tops belonging to one of Rebecca's English nieces, who are living with them since their mother died. Rebecca's husband, Daniel, is convinced of the danger of the bishop's disapproval long before Rebecca is: "Gaining negative attention from the bishop would bring problems that he didn't need for the family. The bishop would pressure Daniel to get the family in line."[39] Daniel's fears are confirmed on the afternoon when the bishop pulls his buggy into Daniel's driveway. "When the bishop arrived unannounced it could never be good," Daniel thought to himself, and he clearly understood the bishop's cryptic message: "The community is *very* concerned about things that are going on in your house." Daniel could "read between the lines, and he knew what could happen," Clipston writes. "If the community turned against him, he'd be an outcast, possibly shunned. He couldn't risk that."[40] In Woodsmall's *When the Heart Cries,* Hannah's jealous sister Sarah operates as an informant, of sorts, for the bishop, feeding him all kinds of information, both true and false, about her sister's behavior. "So, someone had been watching her that day, and they'd told the bishop," Hannah realized at one point.[41] Many novels contain characters' similar fears that either the bishop himself is watching or that his gumshoes are.

One Old Order Amish woman with whom I spoke, who is married to a bishop and who has read a few Amish novels, told me that she has also been struck by this panoptic quality of the bishop figure in the books. "Always the bishop was looking," she said, with more than a hint of exasperation, as she recounted one of the novels she read. "The minute she [the protagonist] made a misstep, the bishop was there. Apparently he didn't have a life."

When characters in the novels do manage to escape out from under the bishop's thumb, some express relief. For Hillary Manton Lodge's ex-Amish heroine Sara, who was on her way to becoming a fashion designer, even the freedom to love a particular color was a reminder of her emancipation from the bishop's omnipresent eye. "Here I was free to love yellow. I loved the sunshine of it. Loved the brightness, the way it attracted attention without me worrying about what the neighbors or the bishop thought. How nice it was never to worry anymore about what the bishop thought!" reflected Sara, and she began to cry.[42]

Occasionally the bishop figure in Amish novels becomes more than an annoying mediator of communal sanction or enforcer of dull colors and becomes a malevolent force. In a move reminiscent of the tyrannical Moses Bontrager in Ruth Lininger Dobson's 1937 *Straw in the Wind*, the bishop in Laura Hilton's *Patchwork Dreams* sets about "forcing Becky to marry Amos Kropf," an old, unattractive widower. In Woodsmall's first novel, when the bishop and the preachers show up at Hannah's house to investigate rumors about her, Hannah wonders whether they came so quickly "because they were willing servants of the people, or if they were simply vultures swooping down on a fresh carcass"; in the ensuing encounter, all signs point to the latter.[43]

And in Lewis's novel *The Crossroad*, Bishop Seth is possessed by a demon and has "kept the People in the grip of the enemy" during his tenure as bishop. Years ago he put a hex on the protagonist's great-uncle, and now, in *The Crossroad*, Bishop Seth is on his deathbed and still truculently evil. Lavina Troyer, a relative of Rachel's who is under the *Bann* because she joined the car-driving Beachy Amish, is convicted that the dying bishop needs to be given the chance to accept Christ as his Savior. "The spreading of the Light was what she also desired for the old, now ailing bishop, a former powwow doctor in the community. Jah, Seth Fisher needed to hear that the Light has come." Lavina goes to visit the bishop on his deathbed and prays that he will become born again and released from the powers of darkness. What follows is an exorcism in which, as Lavina later recounts to Rachel, "the bishop began to shake and twist on his bed, winding the ends

of his sheet into what looked like a coiled rope, holding on to it as if convuls-
ing. His face broke out in heavy perspiration, and his eyes kept rollin' back
in his head. Then he began to cough and sneeze repeatedly." The demon is
successfully exorcised, and both Bishop Seth and his wife Rosemary accept
Christ in that scene, much to Lavina's delight.[44]

Some novelists resist using the Amish bishop as an antagonist. Suzanne
Woods Fisher sounds weary when she talks about the "stern bishop" trope
in many Amish novels, and she states that the real-life Amish bishops she
has met are among the nicest and most compassionate people she knows.
One Old Order Amish man told me that he doesn't fear his bishop but
pities him, because of the unremunerated workload of leadership and the
conflicts that are part and parcel of the job. In most Amish communities,
the bishop brings items to the table for the congregation to discuss, but any
changes to the *Ordnung* or issues of excommunication must be voted on by
the congregation.

But while some novels portray bishops more sympathetically, and while
few bishops are as ominously portrayed as the possessed Bishop Seth, many
fictional Amish bishops still occupy the important role of scapegoat, the carrier of Amish dysfunction. Ruth Reid's character Deborah summarizes the
role of the bishop in much of Amish fiction when she warns her friend
Judith to stop talking as if God is speaking to her directly, asking nervously:
"What would the bishop say?"[45]

That some novels depict the Amish as both models for life and objects
of mission remains something of a conundrum. But distinctions between
evangelical and Amish doctrines of salvation and the subgenre's displacement of unappealing Amish attributes onto the shoulders of fictional
Amish bishops help to make sense of the matter.

Temporary Exile

In their devotional function, Amish romance novels successfully nurture
in their loyal readers a greater sense of God's love. In their didactic one,
they instruct readers in evangelical doctrines of what faith and salvation
are—and aren't. Reading and writing Amish novels help readers and writers to "demonstrate and maintain their religious identities," as Neal claims.

Whether it is by nurturing a person's belief in an all-loving, all-powerful God or instructing a person in the grace, assurance, and freedom of personal salvation, Amish novels function in a way similar to that of icons: they are portals through which readers can connect to each other and can gaze toward the world beyond. A religious icon "is merely a signpost, a window only 'through a glass darkly,'" one iconographer has written.[46] While people outside of the interpretive community to which the women of GAB belong might view Amish fiction as flat or lacking in imagination, the subgenre's conventions serve to open this window a little farther, clearing away textual clutter that might obscure a view of the divine. Like religious icons, Amish novels function as signposts, orienting readers toward the sacred and pointing them toward the God they cherish but cannot see.

Just as I was ambivalent about the transponder on the Illinois Tollway on my way to Plano, because the device heightens convenience but also surveillance, many Amish-fiction readers find themselves both grateful for the accoutrements of hypermodern life and worried about their side effects. Is the gaze of the scanner suspended from a gantry above the highway, as well as that of all its electronic cousins, that of a benevolent, brotherly bishop or of a tyrannical Big Brother? Are efficiency, freedom, and speed worth the panoptic structures that proffer them, or do they rack up losses we have not yet begun to tally?

It is this mix of gratitude for hypermodernity and disenchantment with its disciplines that creates the urge to "leave it all behind" for a few hours of Amishness. So while readers of Amish fiction are consumers, as we saw in chapter 3, and icon-gazers, as we saw in this chapter, they are also travelers who temporarily exile themselves from the world as they know it. In that sense, Amish novels become methods of transport: narratives that carry readers away from their lives and deposit them on foreign soil and among a foreign people. We turn now to the methods by which Amish novels transport readers to an alien clime—alien, that is, except that it feels more like home to many readers than the developments, office parks, and highways that their bodies inhabit.

TRICIA GOYER

A BIG SKY NOVEL

BESIDE
STILL
WATERS

"When I opened *Beside Still Waters*
I was transported into the world of
the Amish. This book is a keeper!"
—ROBIN JONES GUNN

An endorser of Beside Still Waters *(2011), by Tricia Goyer, said the novel
"transported" her "into the world of the Amish."*
Photography by Steve Gardner / Pixelwork Studios. Used by permission of
B&H Publishing Group.

❦ Chapter Six ❦

An Amish Country Getaway

Deanna's office is almost within spitting distance of William Penn. The building where she works at a global real estate firm in center-city Philadelphia places her about as close as one can get to the bronze statue of the Pennsylvania founder that stands atop City Hall. The massive statue faces northeast, toward the site where Penn supposedly signed a treaty with Tamanend, the Leni Lenape chief whose people inhabited the land that came to be known as Penn's Woods.

The Amish settlement an hour's drive west of Philadelphia, which Deanna visits several times a year and which she reads about in one of her favorite types of fiction, exists in part as a result of Penn's utopian vision. Penn's religious toleration drew to his colony settlers of many traditions, including Mennonites, Quakers, and the Amish, the latter arriving in the 1730s. While some historians have suggested that Penn's vision of a European–American Indian relationship was simply a gentler shade of imperialism than that of the colonists around him, his mythic power as a broker of the peace with the indigenous people of the northeast woodlands remains untrammeled. Many of nineteenth-century artist Edward Hicks's one-hundred-odd versions of *The Peaceable Kingdom* add the legendary signing of the treaty by Penn and the Leni Lenape chief to the image of a cow being nuzzled by a bear and a cherubic child lolling about with lions.

Deanna travels the highways that now crisscross Penn's Woods several times a year on her way to Lancaster County. There she and her family browse in the outlets along Route 30 east of Lancaster, visit tourist sites like the Amish Village, shop for the Amish-made furniture that fills her home, and relax. Along with 11 million other visitors who make their way to Lancaster County each year, Deanna and her family consider it a great place to vacation.[1] They have been traveling to Lancaster at least three times a year for more than fifteen years. "We have fallen in love with Lancaster County," Deanna tells me on the phone one Monday morning from her office in the center of the city. "I'm a city girl as a worker but a country bumpkin at heart."[2]

Deanna, who is vice president of a company that has more than 40,300 employees in sixty countries, first discovered Amish fiction while browsing at Walmart. In the past four years she has read more than thirty Amish novels, many of them on her Kindle. "I know some of those back roads better than I do the ones around here," Deanna tells me with a laugh, as she recounts her trips to Lancaster County. "The Amish are just so genuine. When you're talking to them, you know how they feel. There's nobody putting on airs. There's no keeping up with the Joneses. It's a nice, laid-back, relaxed feel, even as they are extremely dedicated and hardworking."

I think of the Edward Hicks paintings, with their brokered peace and their toddlers frolicking with wild animals. I wonder whether the painter felt a little like Deanna does, whether his many depictions of a peaceable kingdom are evidence that he felt more at home in the idylls of his paintings than in his rapidly modernizing nineteenth-century life. "It's just a day away," Deanna tells me matter-of-factly about Lancaster County and the Amish delights it contains. Several stories below her corner office, the traffic that clotted the downtown an hour ago has thinned out, signaling the end of another Monday-morning rush hour in the City of Brotherly Love.

Transport: Amish Fiction as Intensified Tourism

"The exotic is uncannily close," anthropologist James Clifford has written.[3] Thanks to globalizing forces such as mobility, tourism, urban sprawl, and immigration, formerly "exotic" people groups no longer exist at a remove from those who imagine themselves vacant of anything racially, ethnically, or culturally idiosyncratic. While *coca-colonization*—the disappearance of local cultures in the face of exported American goods and values—may be an oversimplification of the complex relationships of globalization, perceptions of an increasingly global monoculture are strong. The idea of the American landscape as more and more "placeless" has spread beyond the academy, and the losses of a colonized world gather in many readers' minds.

Now, thanks to Amish fiction, America's own exotic but homespun religionists are as close as the book on the bedside stand. Whether in a car or through a novel, Deanna's frequent travels to Amish Country transport her to a place both foreign and familiar, far away from her known world yet somehow closer to her "country bumpkin" self than her office downtown. Historian Eric Miller suggests that readers use the Amish "as an adequately alien, adequately familiar community to imaginatively work out persisting cultural and theological questions."[4] Like the "noble savages" shaking hands with the Europeans in Hicks's paintings, the Amish are for many Americans an alloy of the familiar and the foreign.[5] For many readers of Amish fiction, as for Deanna, they are "just a day away," both literally and imaginatively: far enough away to be a destination, close enough that one can get back home before dark.

Images of transport populate the words of readers describing their reading of Amish fiction. "When I opened *Beside Still Waters,* I was transported into the world of the Amish," Christian novelist Robin Jones Gunn writes in an endorsement of Tricia Goyer's Amish novel. "This is a book that has certainly taken me to another world, another time, another place," a reviewer on Amazon wrote about Cynthia Keller's *An Amish Christmas.* "'The books take me to another place,'" says Steve Oates, marketing vice president at Bethany House, summarizing what Amish-fiction readers repeatedly tell him: "I feel so peaceful and calm when I read the books. It's so nice to go to a place where everything isn't so rushed." He characterizes the books as "mini-vacations."[6]

Some readers experience the sensation of being transported even more intensely when reading an Amish novel than when visiting an Amish settlement. One reader told me that although she enjoys going to Amish tourist sites, she likes reading Amish fiction even more because it enables her to "actually get into their homes." This reader is not necessarily physically as close to the Amish as when she visits Lancaster or Shipshewana, yet

Amish fiction produces a greater psychic transport for her than tourism does. Scholar Beth E. Graybill calls this phenomenon "tourism of the imagination."[7]

Amish novels can be viewed as textual carriages that transport readers away from their actual worlds to imagined ones. Narrative theories of transport, according to psycholinguist Richard Gerrig, posit that "someone ('the traveler') is transported, by some means of transportation, as a result of performing certain actions. The traveler goes some distance from his or her world of origin, which makes some aspects of the world of origin inaccessible. The traveler returns to the world of origin, somewhat changed by the journey."[8]

I have deliberately chosen the term *transport* as opposed to *escape*. *Escape* is frequently employed, as D. W. Harding has noted, "as a term of disparagement to refer to an activity that the evaluator believes has no merit in and of itself."[9] This is apparent in the words of one editor at a publishing house with a full stable of Amish-fiction authors, who told me bluntly that Amish fiction is popular because it is escapist. Its popularity, he maintains, "shows some weakness in evangelical readership—a desire to avoid the moral quandaries of contemporary living."[10] Escapism, the use of mental diversions to avoid a mature encounter with reality, is seen by this editor and many others as a weakness, an immature response of flight away from complexity and ambiguity. But the notion that Amish romance novels are *escapist* simply does not capture the fullness of what readers say they experience when they read Amish novels. As critic Lev Grossman writes about genre fiction, "You don't read it [genre fiction] to escape your problems, you read it to find a new way to come to terms with them."[11] So even though readers themselves sometimes used the word *escape* to explain why they read Amish fiction, I will rely on the more neutral concept of *transport*.

How do Amish romance novels transport readers and—considering their popularity—do it so effectively? In this chapter we look at the four elements of Gerrig's notion of narrative transport as they relate to Amish fiction: (1) the reader's *world of origin*, which I characterize here as hypermodern and hypersexualized, based on readers' descriptions; (2) the *text* of the novel itself and the strategies by which it transports readers; (3) the nature of the *fictive world* to which the reader is transported; and (4) the *return to the world of origin* and the change that the traveler-reader experiences as a result of the narrative journey. By considering these four elements in turn, we can trace the journey of readers like Deanna, who, when she wants to be close to the Amish, can now go either by car or by Kindle.

The World of Origin

Hypermodern

Hypermodernity, as we saw in chapter 1, describes the historical moment when Amish fiction emerged as an identifiable genre. French philosopher Gilles Lipovetsky characterizes hypermodernity as a "headlong rush forwards, of unbridled modernization comprised of galloping commercialization, economic deregulation, and technical and scientific developments being unleashed with effects that are heavy with threats as well as promises." Amish fiction's appeal exists in direct proportion to the distance that the books carry readers from a world they experience as hyperactive. While readers of Amish fiction reflect a certain diversity—rural, suburban, and urban; male and female; evangelical, Catholic, and Amish; politically conservative and liberal—they share this larger context of hypermodernity. The academic analysis of hypermodernity articulated by Lipovetsky and other philosophers squares with the way many readers of Amish fiction characterize their world of origin: as a place of excess, individualism, chaos, speed, and overconsumption.[12] Lipovetsky suggests that the spirit of the hypermodern age is marked less by immediate gratification of desire or unbridled hedonism than by "anxiety about a future fraught with risk and insecurity."[13]

And although readers sometimes attribute their love of Amish fiction to a distaste for the moral licentiousness and agnostic soupiness of the "secular" world, their dissatisfactions with their world of origin seem to have at least as much to do with the threats of hypermodernity, a sense of too-muchness, as with any threats of secularity. "All of the conveniences that we as non-Amish have—the cell phones and the microwaves and the constant contact we have through e-mail and Twitter, . . . all of these advances that we have made—it has *not* simplified our lives," an author told me; "It has actually made them more complicated." "My theory is the pacing of our lives," said a literary agent when I asked about the popularity of the subgenre. "A lot of young moms read Amish fiction. They might be single. They're catching a bus in the city to get to work. Their lives are *crazy*. They get home from work, they have to get their son to soccer, their daughter to ballet, cook dinner, do the laundry. But they can sit down on a Sunday and read an Amish fiction book—go back in time, and slow their lives right down."

Whether the Amish actually lead slow lives is debatable, of course. One Amish man with a wife and six sons, a full-time job, and a market stand giggled when I told him about this perception of Amish life as slow. The question of how the Amish themselves experience the passage of time, however, is less salient here than that readers *perceive* that the Amish lead slow lives. The idea that Amish life moves in creeper gear has gained renown in popular culture at the same time as hypermodernity is metastasizing. Observers such as Lipovetsky and Albert Borgmann place the inception of hypermodernity during the 1990s, which means that it came into its own during the same decade in which the contemporary Amish novel first fledged from the Bethany House nest.[14]

Hypermodernity is also vast enough to hold internal tensions. Hypermodernity has resulted in increased attention to the preservation of memory, to heritage, and to simulations of the past. Lipovetsky explores the proliferation of what he calls the "tourism of memory," with its emphasis on folklore, history and archaeology, vintage artifacts, and—especially pertinent to our study—cultures perceived as conjoined to traditional practices.[15] The Amish are not merely residents of the past, but as the literary agent's comment about going "back in time" demonstrates, the past is where the rest of us often deposit them.[16] Amish-fiction readers sometimes slip into past tense when talking about Amish practices or mention that the Amish remind them of "how things used to be." "Amish fiction is like we used to live and we've kind of marched on and left all that behind," one of the women in the GAB book group said. In that sense, the Amish become, as cultural historians Malcolm Chase and Christopher Shaw write, "talismans that link us concretely to the past."[17]

Along with its cursory interest in history, hypermodernity also nurtures an openness to spirituality, especially as it connects to personal identity and tradition. "The hypermodern age does not put an end to the need to appeal to traditions of sacred meaning," Lipovetsky writes. "It merely re-vamps them to give them greater individuality, a wider spread, and a more intensely emotional set of beliefs and practices." Lipovetsky's understand-ing of hypermodern spirituality helps to explain the potency of the Amish-fiction mashup, mobilizing as it does both a sacred tradition and a pro-tagonist with an increasingly individuated self. Amish fiction features a history-bound community, but one that houses a heroine who seeks and finds private happiness and self-actualization. Like Lilly, Shelley Shepard Gray's protagonist in *Autumn's Promise*, many of the heroines articulate the goal of being "true" to themselves. "Now is the time you should be discover-ing who *you* are," an older sister advises the protagonist in Dale Cramer's *Paradise Valley*. "I've been cut loose to discover who I truly am," reflects Beverly Lewis's Katie Lapp at the end of *The Shunning*, and although she returns partway to the Amish by becoming Mennonite at the end of the trilogy, her actualized self remains intact.[18] Whether religion and the self are portrayed as at odds or in sync matters less than that the self's jour-ney remain central. In hypermodernity, religious traditions are employed in the project of individual identity construction. Hypermodern readers are gripped by plotlines involving an Amish adolescent during *Rumspringa*, in the throes of an identity crisis, or those of a young woman choosing be-tween two suitors. Thus, as we observed earlier, Amish fiction emerges from within the body of hypermodernity even as it critiques it.

The Amish themselves aren't immune to hypermodernity, as I learned when I received e-mails from an Amish teenager with a "sent from my iPhone" tag within seconds of sending messages to her. Yet they manage to hover somewhere in premodernity. They stand as comforting, calm, and controlled figures, silhouettes in an imagined country far from readers' own.

Hypersexualized

Readers and writers of Amish fiction frequently describe a sense of em-battlement by a sexually saturated society, in which a ten-year-old in stiletto heels and a sultry gaze poses on the cover of the French edition of *Vogue* and dolls marketed to four- to eight-year-olds wear miniskirts and fishnet stockings. One study of television shows popular among twelve- to seventeen-year-olds found that 93 percent of sexual incidents involving underage female characters could be classified as "unhealthy" by the American Psychological Association and that the female characters only rarely displayed any negative response to being sexualized. "We have laced the sleazy energy and aesthetic of a topless club or a *Penthouse* shoot throughout our entire culture," *New Yorker* staff writer Ariel Levy claims.[19]

It is within this context that Amish fiction stands out in stark, discreet relief. Lisa Miller of *Newsweek* suggests that the oversexualization of popular culture, in which little girls vamp it up for Halloween, is indeed pushing readers to stories of sexual chastity and modesty and characters who wear two layers of fabric over their cleavage instead of none. One Amish-fiction author writes of her dismay upon discovering that she had accidentally bought "skinny jeans" for her very young daughter. "They fit over the diaper but the legs were way too tight," records Tricia Goyer, author of an Amish-fiction series set in Montana, on her blog. "Skinny jeans for a 10-month-old baby . . . SERIOUSLY!" It's likely that Goyer speaks for many of her readers when she muses, "Why do we sexualize young girls? Don't get me wrong. I don't think my daughters need to wear Amish dress and bonnets, but I do like for them to be girls. I hate the fact that retailers fill their shelves with clothing that's more sexy than sweet."[20]

Many readers of Amish fiction concur. "I'm definitely concerned about way things are going, as younger and younger ages are focused on looking sexy," one young Amish-fiction reader, Betsy, tells me over coffee. She falls silent for a moment, then adds, "It's as if very long ago, women were treated just as pieces of property, and then women worked so hard to get their rights, and now it feels like we're putting ourselves back in that position, making women look, like, not as people, just 'use me.' It's almost as if we're going backwards." Patrice Oppliger, author of *Girls Gone Skank*, sounds an echo to Betsy's concern. "Instead of advancing women's power, popular culture trends in the United States appear to be backsliding into sexual exploitation of women," Oppliger writes.[21]

Living within a hypermodern era, which has birthed a hypersexual culture, many evangelical Christian readers find themselves longing for transport to some other realm. For many of them, Amish fiction proves to be the conveyance they've been seeking.

The Vehicle of Transport: Amish-Fiction Texts

When reading for pleasure, many readers prefer that the text be less an item that draws attention to itself and more an unassuming or even invisible vehicle to take them where they want to go. Immediate and ostensibly unmediated access to the fictive destination is the priority for these readers, rather than prose that calls attention to itself with metaphor, metonymy, or other fancy detailing. They appreciate modes of narrative transport that are efficient, comfortable, and affirming, such that the act of reading is subsumed in the experience of the story itself. At least four mechanisms of transport are at work in many Amish novels: a welcoming textual environment, parasocial relationships between characters and readers, strategies of suspense, and satisfying endings.

A Welcoming Textual Environment

When I asked loyal readers of the genre about the difference between a good Amish novel and a mediocre or bad one, few mentioned stylistic features, deftness of prose, or anything having to do with the writing at all. Instead, they spoke of the relative depth or shallowness of the characters, unpredictability versus predictability of outcome, devotional elements that felt authentic versus a false or tacked-on piety. Like Dot, Janice Radway's primary informant in her study of romance readers, the readers of Amish fiction seem to "judge writing solely on the basis of the efficiency with which it gets its job done, that is, tells the story."[22]

Readers' desire for efficient delivery of the story dictates that Amish novels operate within a relatively straightforward semantic and syntactic register, with few obscure vocabulary words or disorienting metaphors to distract from the procurement of meaning. This characteristic prose style produces not only efficiency of story delivery but reassurance for the reader that she is on the correct track to comprehension. In many Amish novels, gestures are rarely allowed to stand without explication and images are rarely left unannotated. After the death of her fiancé, Ella, in Jerry Eicher's *A Wedding Quilt for Ella,* feels lonely and asks how God could allow such a thing to happen. A final sentence reassures readers that they have correctly interpreted Ella's internal state. "Her eyes searched the heavens, studied the stars—those very stars she and Aden had shared. *Do they know the answer?* She waited but was greeted only with silence, with mockery, as if they laughed at her distress and promised her nothing with their stony silence. She was truly alone and forsaken in life."[23]

Another strategy to make readers feel at home in the text is the posing of rhetorical questions. "The evening sun broke through the rain clouds at that moment, creating a streaming shaft of light over the house and property," writes Beverly Lewis, from the point of view of a character whose wife has just returned from an unexplained absence. "Was it an omen of good things to come?" No guesswork is required in Shelley Shepard Gray's *Autumn's Promise,* either, when Amish widower Robert asks Lilly, his English girlfriend, to marry him and she agrees. Again, a question serves to orient readers, assuring them that their inferences about the imagery are correct: "Around them, the air smelled sweeter and the stars seemed brighter. Everything felt better and exaggerated and like new. Perhaps because he was so ready to begin a new life, too?"[24]

While it may be tempting to indict these writers for telling instead of showing, these passages also demonstrate that authors of Amish fiction are skilled at creating welcoming textual spaces, such that readers can expend their energy less on decoding or interpreting and more on identifying with characters, conjuring images in their minds, and wondering what will happen next. Anita Gandolfo, in her analysis of Christian fiction, notes, "Since the simplicity of language and directness of presentation require minimal interpretation, the reader's energy can focus on more emotional involvement in the story, thus lending the illusion of reality."[25] Unlike literary fiction, in which any comprehension difficulties are chalked up to the brilliance of the author and the dimness of the reader, writers of Amish fiction are mindful of readers who may doubt their interpretive abilities or who may be looking for a ludic experience as opposed to an intellectual one.[26] Ceil, the leader of GAB, told me that some of the women in the group have disliked the literary novels they have read. "Not everyone wants to go through all that trouble for a story," she said. "I was looking for light reading when I picked up this [Amish fiction] trilogy, and that's exactly what I got," a reader wrote to me from China, where she is teaching English. "So I am thankful to have run across this work when I did."[27]

The gentle interpretive space of most Amish novels also affirms readers' literate abilities. By throwing up few if any textual roadblocks, the prose confirms a reader's hope that she is capable of the task of meaning-making. "For [romance readers], redundancy and overzealous assertion perform important and particular functions," writes Radway. "Together, these functions combat ambiguity, imply that all events are definitively comprehensible, and reassure the reader that whatever minimal inferences she might construct, they will be adequate and accurate."[28]

Parasocial Relationships

When I began speaking with readers of Amish fiction, I expected that they would identify with the protagonist at the center of an Amish novel, perhaps even imagine themselves *as* her. Instead, they describe a sense of *relationship* with the protagonist—a feeling of being present in the story as a friend, not as the protagonist herself. "I don't feel like I'm her, but like she's somebody that I'm getting to know," Jodie told me.[29]

This points to another trait that enables Amish-fiction texts to transport readers: parasocial relationships that readers develop with the characters. While this is not a strategy of the text itself, it is a characteristic of readers' interaction with the text. Communication theorists Donald Horton and R. Richard Wohl first used the term *parasocial relationship* to describe the sense of intimacy that television viewers sometimes experience with a media persona, and the idea has been used to explain the connection that viewers feel to soap opera characters and romance-novel readers feel to fictional characters.[30] Gandolfo writes that one reader of Janette Oke's *Love Comes Softly* reported that the characters in the book had become so real to her that she had found herself praying for them. Even after Oke finished the series, Gandolfo writes, "readers continued to ask for more information about the family, begging her to at least tell them what happens even if she wasn't going to write any more novels about them." One author of Amish fiction recounted to me her surprise at the intensity of reader interest in two of her minor characters. "I cannot tell you how much reader e-mail I get: 'What happens to Bess and Billy? We have to know. Are you going to have them marry?'"[31]

Parasocial relationships help to explain these readers' absorption in Amish narratives. One Amish-fiction author at a book signing in Lancaster County asked a reader whether she had any Amish friends. "No, but I have all your books," the woman responded. "So you do have Amish friends," the author replied with a smile, placing her palm on the book she was signing; "In here."

Suspense

Contrary to the perception that romance novels are predictable, many Amish novels have endings impossible to see from the outset. In Suzanne Woods Fisher's *The Choice,* for example, the heroine doesn't meet the hero until chapter 7. The first and second books of many Amish series keep the reader in a great deal of suspense. Cindy Woodsmall's *When the Heart Cries* ends with the heroine on a train, leaving the man she loves. Some Amish novels do contain clear indications of what is to come—the appearance of the love interest in chapter 1, for example, is a convention of the romance genre that Amish romance novels often use. But even these more formulaic novels can retain a suspenseful quality, thanks to two strategies, one on the part of the writer and one on the part of the reader.

Many Amish-fiction authors rely on what Pamela Regis, in her study of romance novels, calls the "point of ritual death," in which the union of the protagonist with her beloved appears impossible. Also called a "false end-ing," the point of ritual death occurs when a barrier, often one that has ap-peared earlier in the book, reemerges as the novel or the series approaches the denouement, thus placing the hope of a happy ending in jeopardy.[32] In some books the false ending comes in the person of a false hero or heroine, one who almost or apparently succeeds in capturing the affections of one of the main characters. In others a misunderstanding between the main characters nearly leads to the death of their relationship. In Beverly

Lewis's *The Mercy*, the false hero is Isaac, a New Order Amish man whom the heroine nearly marries, although she loves another. In Gayle Roper's *A Stranger's Wish*, the heroine sees another woman kiss the man she loves—a woman we find out later is his sister. In the Amish vampire novel *Forsaken*, the point of ritual death approximates actual death, when the protagonist Hannah surrenders to the vampire Akiva (her former beloved Jacob Fisher) so that the hero, Jacob's brother Levi, might be saved. However the point of ritual death is utilized, it serves in many Amish novels to heighten the suspense that keeps readers immersed in the fictional world.

Another strategy of suspense, this one initiated by the reader, is the willing suspension of knowledge about how the story is going to turn out. *Anomalous suspense*, according to Gerrig, occurs when readers essentially pretend not to know what the outcome will be. "Readers must participate in a narrative world in such fashion that the knowledge critical to sustaining suspense is not immediately accessible," Gerrig writes. "This added complexity is necessary because *readers often experience suspense even when they know what will happen.*"[33] So even if it is apparent from the beginning that Lilly will end up betrothed to Robert, or that Miriam will marry Charley, or that spouses Rebecca and Daniel will fall in love again, readers can essentially suspend such knowledge and read *as if* they did not know.

"Eventually everything will work out," Jodie, an avid reader of Amish fiction, tells me. "I know that whenever I get to the end . . . things will work themselves out, because that's how it has to be." She ripples her hand through the air, as if to trace a rollercoaster's path, and adds, "It's the whole ups and downs and twists and turns and getting to how things will work out that makes the story so good." First-year college student Betsy, another Amish-fiction reader, says she likes both the knowledge that the books have happy endings and the suspense inherent in getting there: "I like them partially because I know they're going to end well. When I'm reading it, and I'm at the climax, I know that it's going to end well, but I don't know *how*. I'm like, 'How could this possibly end well?' Then somehow it wraps up and I'm like, 'Oh, *that* is awesome!'" Thus there is no conflict for readers of Amish romances between their desire for unpredictability and their demand for a happy ending. Thanks to the reader-contributed anomalous suspense, both are possible.[34]

Happy Endings

Jodie's statement—that "things will work themselves out [in Amish novels], because that's how it has to be"—demonstrates her trust in one of the signature conventions of inspirational fiction: the happy ending. Beverly Lewis promised her readers in one interview that in the then soon-to-be-released final book in her Rose Trilogy, they would "see all the loose ends tied up nice and neat."[35]

A majority of the romance readers Radway surveyed considered a pleasurable ending an indispensable narrative feature of the books.[36] The twin forces of anomalous suspense and happy endings offer readers complementary sensations of excitement and peace, risk and security.[37] Amish romance novels, in their consistently happy endings, resemble the myths of oral cultures, Radway suggests, for they all "retell a single tale whose final outcome their readers always already know."[38] The repetitive quality of the myth and its known outcome do not subtract from the pleasurable experience of hearing it, as we just saw. When critics voice hostility toward inspirational romance novels or other genre fiction because of the books' consistently happy endings, they may be underestimating the mythic quality of the novels.

With the exception of the initial books in a series, which may leave many loose narrative ends, the resolutions of Amish romances almost always include heterosexual love, betrothal, or marriage—or, if the heroine is already married, a renewal of love that has been lost. Almost without fail, the concluding scene of a book or a series has the hero and heroine declaring love for each other, and often love for God as well. Many include at least the promise of childbirth, sometimes ending with the protagonist telling her husband that she is pregnant.

The finales of Amish romance novels almost invariably include a conviction on the part of the hero and the heroine that God's providence has won out, such that the culminating romance is ensconced in a sense of divine plan. "I'm thankful God brought us together," Martha tells Luke at the end of Brunstetter's *A Sister's Hope*. "Whatever they might have to face in the future, she could be at peace, knowing their love for God and for each other would see them through." At the end of Beth Wiseman's novella *Heal-*

ing Hearts, Levina Lapp considers the mysterious way God has rekindled her love for her husband, Naaman, despite a series of strange events. "'A *man's heart deviseth his way; but the Lord directeth his steps.*' Levina smiled as the Scripture came into her head. The Lord always had a plan." God's providence is even more transparent in the first Amish-and-angels novel by Ruth Reid. "It's God we must thank," Andrew tells Judith in *The Promise of an Angel*, when she wishes she could thank the angel Tobias for his role in bringing them together. "'He sent Tobias.' Andrew cupped her face and lightly stroked his thumb along her cheekbone. 'I have so much to be thankful for.'"[39] Not all Amish novels end in a stroked cheekbone; sometimes endings highlight a restoration of broken family bonds or other conflictual relationships, the solving of some mystery of personal identity, or emotional healing from grief or guilt or a secret too long kept. But in both their romantic and nonromantic conclusions, Amish romance novels invariably end propitiously, at least for the protagonist and her beloved.

While these final scenes may strike some as religious catharsis of the most jejune variety, for the genre's loyal readers, they serve to strengthen faith, renew what Neal calls "a theology of hope and perseverance," and reassure that good triumphs over evil. The happy endings of Amish novels echo one of the well-known verses in Romans in the New Testament, which many readers have likely memorized: "All things work together for good to them that love God, to them who are the called according to his purpose."[40] Reveling in a happy ending isn't the same as denying that suffering exists; as I learned when I visited the GAB discussion group, readers are reminded of tragedy whenever they close their books. But when we take the voices of these readers seriously, as Neal suggests, "the decision to read becomes not the act of a child but that of a woman trying to maintain her faith amidst the ups and downs of daily life." Another critic suggests that the romance novel is "narrative eschatology," a story about how to get to an "eschaton of love, completion, fulfillment, happiness, generational continuity, maturity, and hope."[41] The promise of a satisfying ending, then, serves both as an effective narrative strategy and as a prefigurement of heaven itself.

The Fictive World

If hypermodernity is the world from which readers depart, and if Amish novels are the vehicles into which they climb, what is the narrative destination to which they are taken? Keeping in mind readers' varying imaginative constructions of the fictive world, we can nonetheless make a few generalizations about the diegetic space, or the "world of the story," that readers enter when they open an Amish novel. The terrain of Amish fiction is heavily marked by focal things; it is a pastoral place; and it is populated by chaste characters.

Focal Things

Horses, barns, gardens, home-cooked meals, woodstoves, hymn sings, wood carvings, canned goods: Amish novels are filled with what philosopher Albert Borgmann has called *focal things* and the practices that surround them. A focal thing, writes Borgmann, is "something that has a commanding presence, engages your body and mind, and engages you with others."[42] It "provides a center of orientation" and exudes a "gathering and radiating force."[43] Focal things, such as a fireplace that provides warmth for a family or a meal that is prepared and eaten communally, order one's affections and labors. A focal thing requires tending by humans who, in guarding and nurturing and learning to care for the thing, become practiced in crafts and traditions. By learning focal practices, people devote themselves to habits that draw them toward the natural and communal world and away from the hyperreal and hyperactive.

Characters in Amish novels routinely engage in focal practices, either as aspects of their jobs or as requirements of home-tending, and practices such as these ratchet up the appeal of bonnet fiction to readers living under the reign of hypermodernity. Activities like harness-making, quilting, beekeeping, cider-making, and baking fill their days and their dialogue. Readers follow the characters through tasks like hovering over a pan of hot rolls to check for doneness, checking a ewe in labor, finishing a seam on a new dress, or driving a wagon of newly baled hay back to the barn before the rain starts. The extent to which authors elaborate on these practices varies between novels, in ways perhaps related to the amount of specific knowledge the author has about agricultural and domestic domains. Regardless of the depth to which these descriptions run, however, the narration of such focal practices fuses them together to create a portrait of what Borgmann calls "eloquent" or "focal" reality, which he says lies on the other side of hypermodernity and is characterized by "an attitude of patient vigor for a common order centered on communal celebrations." Patience, vigor, order, communality, celebration: Borgmann wasn't writing about Amish fiction, but his description of eloquent reality parallels what readers find in the pages of most Amish novels.[44]

That Amish novels themselves are focal things and that reading them constitutes a focal practice are defensible theories, although I'm not ready to advance them. Those theories may indeed be true, depending on the hold the novels exert on a particular reader and the extent to which she orders other priorities in life as a result of reading them. But it is safe to say that Amish novels draw strength from their *depiction* of focal concerns, appealing to readers in ways commensurate with readers' growing awareness of the clutches of hypermodernity.

A Pastoral Place

The opening pages of Amish novels, and those that follow, are rife with rurality. One protagonist stumbles across her missing mother's handkerchief in a cornfield. Another carries freshly gathered eggs in a basket toward a neighboring farm. Another tells stories to children gathered under a crimson maple tree. Like *Country* magazine, which offers its 1.2 million readers space "to show their pride in and passion for a simpler, better life close to the land, people and traditions they love," Amish novels celebrate the rhythms and rituals of country life.

While the term *pastoral* has been widely contested and variously employed—as a name for a classical genre of poetry, for example—I use it here to refer generally to a literary tradition that constructs rural life as Edenic and that situates urban life as diametrically opposed to agrarian innocence, purity, and charm.[45] As we saw in chapter 2, pastoral literature turns on this tension between sacred and profane, natural and artificial, premodern and hypermodern. Amish novels, in their representation of rural spaces as sacred and urban life as rife with sin and sadness and SUVs, and in their frequent depiction of outsiders who retreat to rural Amish life and then return, invigorated, to their urban English lives, clearly operate within the pastoral tradition.

Pastorals have largely been written for urban audiences, literary critic Terry Gifford points out. Authors of pastoral literature, including writers of Amish fiction, are usually not native to the Arcadias about which they write but are residents of the urban spaces they directly or indirectly indict. Many of them create characters that mimic their own narrative journey as writers—characters who retreat to an Amish place, find there succor and strength, and return to their lives somewhat changed. In Amish novels with English point-of-view characters, the Amish often become agrarian models of the good life.

We frequently follow an English protagonist as she journeys to the world of the Amish from some location outside of it, such that our own narrative transport as readers mirrors her actual one. We travel with nurse-midwife Lexie Jaeger in *The Amish Midwife*, for example, as she drives from the Philadelphia airport into Lancaster County and slams on her brakes when she sees her first Amish farm. "The matching clothes, immaculate farms, and whitewashed houses and barns had a stylized appeal," Lexie reflects. "It was all very much alive. The people. The scents wafting through my open window. The vibrant colors snapping on the lines. It was orderly and patterned and obviously it all had a purpose."[46] By the end of the novel, the purpose and order that Lexie encountered with her first view of an Amish farm has insinuated itself into her own life, and she returns from her pastoral sojourn to her former life having been transformed by her time among the Amish.

Deanna, the reader with the corner office in Philadelphia, calls herself a "country bumpkin" at heart, thus asserting that she contains within herself the pastoral duality that many readers feel: in the city but not of it. One of Beverly Lewis's point-of-view characters in *The Crossroad*, a New York journalist, personifies this fracture between a city-dwelling body and a country-dwelling soul. In one scene she has him sitting in his lonely urban apartment. He "rose after a time and pulled the cord, blocking out the enormity of the population, noise, and vibrations of the city that surrounded him, threatening to strangle him. Sitting down at his desk once again, he thought of Lancaster County, where farmers talked to their cows and went to bed with the chickens. A world set apart. And not so surprisingly, a place he missed more than he cared to admit."[47]

The pastoral mode is so dominant in Amish fiction that it obscures one of the central transformations of Amish life: that less than half of Amish people actually farm. Only one-third of Amish men under thirty or over fifty years of age now farm, and in Holmes County, Ohio, the number of Amish men who are farmers is less than 10 percent.[48] Many characters in the novels work in small businesses such as carpentry, harness-making, and construction and in tourist-related enterprises, but by far the majority of fictional Amish are depicted as living and working on farms. Also absent from most novels is any mention that in a few Amish communities, Amish children attend public schools. The pastoral ideal feeds on the "little red schoolhouse" as the iconic Amish educational experience, and most Amish novels deliver in that regard.[49] It's doubtful that an Amish novel in which the male protagonist works in a recreational vehicle factory and the Amish children face peer pressure at public schools would appeal to readers trying to imaginatively exit those very realities.

In its emphasis on the aesthetically pleasing, "simple" nature of the rural life, most of Amish fiction represents a popular, sentimental mode of pastoralism that, as Leo Marx writes in *The Machine in the Garden*, is characterized by "an urge to withdraw from civilization's growing power and complexity." Marx suggests that such sentimental pastoralism is "a simple-minded wishfulness, a romantic perversion of thought and feeling" that is rarely rooted in the realities of rural life.[50] The rural landscapes on the front covers of the novels attest to this sentimental mode, as do the many novels that fail to mention crop failure, exhausting physical labor, or the increasing manufacturing or other nonfarm employment of Amish men who can no longer afford to farm.[51] Most Amish fiction retains a sentimental pastoral flavor, avoiding entanglement with issues facing rural residents and small-scale farmers such as competition from agribusiness, the encroachment of development and the ensuing loss of farmland, and increasingly challenging markets for farm products.

Occasionally the pastoral mode of an Amish novel works its way into what Marx calls complex pastoralism, in which the writer acknowledges the presence of the machine. Marx calls this the "interrupted idyll," or a pastoral account that includes the impingement of technology. In *The Waiting* by Suzanne Woods Fisher, Cal, one of the Amish characters, disagrees with his brother, who is being swayed toward no-till methods by a sales representative of a chemical company. "If I used those herbicides on my fields, every time it rained, those chemicals would leach into the streams and creeks that run into our neighbors' properties," Cal says to his brother. "Tell him this: how can we love our neighbor and do such a thing?"[52] Occasionally a character in an Amish novel mentions the complications of living on the land or the financial hardships of small-scale farmers who compete against industrialized agriculture.

Such manifestations of complex pastoralism, however, are exceptions to the rule. The pastoral vision of most Amish novels is an uncomplicated and apolitical one, given more to bucolic scenery, gentle animal husbandry, and a pleasing sense of connection to the seasons.

Chaste Characters

Like evangelical fiction in general, Amish romance novels are immaculate textual spaces, within which no profanity or promiscuity may be enacted. The conventions of publishers within the CBA (Association for Christian Retail) market dictate this, as do the expectations of readers. The readers of Amish fiction I interviewed frequently described the novels as "clean reads": unsullied by promiscuity, profanity, or anything else that might offend their Christian sensibilities. "They [readers] want a clean read," one editor of Amish fiction told me; "They want a sweet story."

Readers frequently express relief regarding the G-rated nature of Amish-novel romance, and the assurance of chastity and fidelity is what frees them to share the books around to daughters, granddaughters, and friends at church. One woman attending an Amish-fiction author's book signing told me that she likes the books because she can let them lie around the house without worrying that her young daughter might pick them up and find sexual scenes beyond her ken. Another mother told me that she likes being able to let her young daughter read the books without having to preread them herself. Cindy Woodsmall told ABC News that most Amish novels would not be too explicit for a ten-year-old. Sarah, a first-year college student, told me that her mother and father were strict with regard to what their children read and watched on TV and that it was her mother's Beverly-Lewis habit that got her interested in reading Amish fiction. "If I go to a bookstore and find an Amish fiction book by a Christian author, I know that I'm not going to get to anything that would be inappropriate to read," Sarah, who is now eighteen, told me. As Lynn Neal found in her study, inspirational romance readers on the whole believe that "sexuality belongs in the bedroom, not in the book" and thus prefer texts about "veiled marital beds" rather than ones about "visible 'musical' beds."[53]

Even marital sexuality almost always occurs offstage of the diegetic space of the novel, described as backstory or foreshadowing or as suggestion of a scene that is not narrated. The most frequent method of obscuring marital relations is via the epilogue, popularized by Beverly Lewis and utilized by several other authors of the genre. In an epilogue, the action of which usually occurs eighteen months to several years after that of the final chapter, news of pregnancies and births is often divulged. Thus, the moment of conception is slipped into an envelope of unnarrated time between the final chapter and the epilogue. "My gift to you is a son or daughter of your own," the pregnant Barbara Hilty declares as she places her new husband Paul's hands on her stomach in the epilogue of Wanda Brunstetter's *On Her Own,* and protagonist Miriam in Beth Wiseman's *Plain Proposal* announces to her mother during that novel's epilogue, "We are in a family way." In the epilogue of Brunstetter's *Lydia's Charm,* Lydia watches her one-year-old daughter play on the floor; in the final chapter Lydia was still only imagining her future as "Mrs. Levi Stutzman."[54]

The books are such chaste spaces, in fact, that many readers and some writers of the novels say that Amish novels aren't really romance novels at all. As we saw in chapter 1, Beverly Lewis does not consider herself a writer of romance novels, and when I used the phrase "Amish romance novels," one reader, Louise, said to me, "In my mind I'm going, 'Really? These are romances?' I don't think of them as a romance. It's a fiction story. Oh yeah, there happens to be a romance story in it. . . . I like characters who are coming of age or struggling to make a decision. That's what appeals to me more than the romance part." Readers Wendy and Ellen agreed: "I like the classification of 'Amish fiction' versus 'Amish romance fiction' because I don't necessarily read them for the romance," Wendy told me; Ellen wrote, "I like authors who focus on a heroine's whole life and family with romance being a secondary interest."

Readers of evangelical romance novels disagree on exactly how much romantic content they want in their novels, and in chapter 7 we will look at the differing amounts of romance and sexual tension contained within Amish novels.[55] By figuring out how to imply sexual couplings without narrating them, authors offer readers of Amish fiction what they are looking for: a chaste textual domain, absent of fleshly intercourse and marked by essentially immaculate conceptions.

Return to the World of Origin

The last element of Gerrig's notion of narrative transport is the idea that the reader-traveler returns to his world of origin "somewhat changed by the journey." When I asked readers and writers whether or how they had been changed by Amish fiction, I received a wide assortment of answers, from "Not at all," to "I don't think a day goes by that I don't feel changed." This wide and diverse register of responses suggests that readers carry different goods home with them from their Amish-novel journeys and that some bring little home at all. "I'd love to say yes, but no," one reader, Jodie, responded, and several readers also reported not feeling changed.

Many readers, however, mentioned critical changes they'd made since reading Amish fiction. "One of my greatest joys is hearing from readers who say my stories have touched them significantly—even changed the direction of their lives," Beverly Lewis writes on her website. "On almost every book tour, there will be people who squeeze my hand and tell me, 'Please don't *ever* stop writing. I glean so much spiritual truth [from your books]," Lewis told me on the phone. "I am more trusting," one reader told me. "I read the Bible more as I look up some of the quotes from the Amish fiction," another said. "Your books always make me want to be a better person," a reader wrote on a Facebook page for a book tour of three authors.[56]

The tangible ways readers report being changed by Amish fiction range from reading the Bible more to learning to quilt. "Other than the Bible, the Amish books have changed my life more than any other books," a reader named Marilyn wrote on Thomas Nelson's Amish Living website in September 2010. "I am now more aware of keeping life simple, of putting family and community high priority, relishing the simple in what I buy, etc." "Since reading these books, I have started making most everything from scratch, gardening, quilting, all kinds of things like that," wrote another Amish Living respondent,[57] and one reader told me that as a result of reading Amish novels, she is trying "not to purchase items just for the sake of purchasing them." Other readers mention going online less frequently or trying to declutter their lives.

Some readers, on returning to their actual world and finding it lacking, appear to decide they want to dwell among the Amish rather than the English—like Natalie, a reader who posted on the Amish Living website: "I know I have learned so much and I hope one day, I can call myself Amish."[58] But readers' words are more frequently characterized by a longing for Amish life than by active pursuit of it, and I found no indication that Amish-fiction readers are en masse buying up plain apparel or purchasing horses and buggies.

Still, many readers enjoy asking themselves whether they could handle being Amish. In response to a question about whether you could give up "the life that you have now" and become Amish or Old Order Mennonite, many members of Amish Living said yes. "I truly believe I could," wrote one woman. "I know in my heart that parting ways with the world I know now would be quite easy," another added. "I disdain the fast paced, anonymous, angry society we live in and find my solace in my family, my home and my gardens."[59] Others were less certain, mentioning items like air conditioning, hair dryers, and college that they would have a hard time giving up.

For the most part, readers remain residents of a hypermodern culture even as they long to be exiled from it. But dwelling among the fictive Amish for as long as it takes to read a novel allows them to entertain the "could I be Amish?" question. Judging from the rapid rise of the subgenre, it appears that, for many readers, this is a tantalizing question.

Nostalgia: Dysfunction or Resistance?

Noting the transportive quality of Amish fiction raises the question of whether these narrative trips to Amish Country are fueled largely by nostalgia: the "longing for a home that no longer exists or has never existed," as theorist Svetlana Boym defines it. Edward Hicks's painterly retreats to Penn's peaceable kingdom, Deanna's trips to Lancaster, readers' returns to the focal, pastoral, and chaste spaces of Amish novels: are these evidences of pining for the past, a sense of loss and displacement from some imagined home? And if these journeys are essentially nostalgic, perhaps they point to deficiencies in the reader-traveler—an inability to deal with present reality, say, or entrapment in fantasy. Insofar as nostalgia is packaged in ways pleasing to consumers, it becomes a symptom of hypermodernity, representing, as Lipovetsky writes, "the transformation of memory into entertainment and spectacle."[60]

Nostalgia is frequently viewed as a particular person's childish or dysfunctional response to change. But rather than diagnosing nostalgia as a syndrome within individuals, Boym suggests that it is "the incurable modern condition" and that it has displaced early-twentieth-century optimism regarding the future. Nostalgia, in this view, may be less a private response or an individual sickness than a communal "alter ego," of sorts, to progress. Some theorists suggest that nostalgia may not be a regressive or commodified force at all, but rather a psychological location in which people can find solace, meaning, and even impetus to action.[61] While this view admits that nostalgia can at times be dysfunctional or packaged, it suggests that nostalgia can also provide people with a mechanism for critiquing current conditions of the self and society and imagining a different future. By reading about the Amish, who seem to have somehow escaped history's inexorable march, non-Amish readers get to rehearse alternatives to hypermodernity.

The impossibility that lies at the root of nostalgia—we want to go home but we can't—helps to explain the longing that many Amish-fiction readers articulate to "live like the Amish" even as they confess that they could never actually do it. Many intuit that Amish fiction must, in fact, remain *fiction:* an imagined location, a Swiss-German Brigadoon. As pastoral fiction, Amish romance novels create an Arcadian setting that exists only to the extent that readers cannot penetrate it; as theorist Crystal Downing suggests, were an Amish Arcadia accessible to all those desirous of it, it would cease to be.[62]

Nostalgia, then, is the pursuit of the unattainable: the thrill of the chase. Romance fiction is furnished with the same thrill; "the chase, in fact, is more important than the capture," romance novelist Brittany Young has written, "because the chase is where the romance is."[63] Few genres combine the thrill of the *chase* and the thrill of the *chaste* as well as Amish fiction.

Just as Amish fiction transports readers to places they could not otherwise access, it also has the capacity for transport with regard to notions of womanhood. What Lynn Neal writes about evangelical romance novels in general could be said for Amish romance novels as well: "While upholding contemporary evangelical ideas about gender, [the genre] transports these women from the periphery to the center of evangelical life."[64]

In chapter 7 we will observe the ways that Amish novels manage to both guard traditional notions of womanhood and gesture toward more progressive ones; as the reader in this chapter pointed out, within a hypersexualized culture it is sometimes unclear which is which. To find out more about Amish novels' construction of gender and romance, we go first to the campus of a Christian college and meet eighteen-year-old Betsy, a nursing student who happens to love Amish fiction.

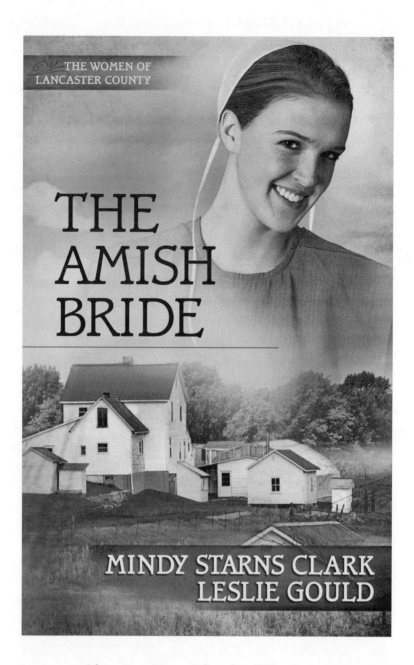

On many Amish romance covers, such as that of The Amish Bride (2012),
the heroine is depicted between heaven and earth.
Used by permission of Harvest House Publishers.

Chapter Seven

Virgin Mothers

B etsy's friends call her a hopeless romantic when it comes to her taste in fiction. In ninth grade, having picked up Beverly Lewis's *The Preacher's Daughter* at a discount store while looking for a book by Nicholas Sparks, Betsy was hooked. Now in her first semester of college as a nursing major, Betsy tries to persuade others to read Amish-themed romances, with spotty success. "They often say things like, 'They're going to be boring!'" she tells me, wrinkling her nose in imitation of friends' responses.[1]

But to Betsy, boring they are not. While she likes learning about the Amish and feels that the books strengthen her Christian faith, the romance is an integral part of why she loves the genre. Her summary of the novels is punctuated by a playful irony: "Oh, these two people love each other; oh, they can't be together; whoops, they find some way to get through it!" She likes the fusion of comfort and suspense that we looked at in chapter 6: knowing that the characters will surmount the obstacles between them, but not knowing how they will do it.

Betsy attends a Christian liberal arts college in Pennsylvania, where the "ring by spring" imperative—pressure to get engaged by one's senior year—is both joked about and, for many women, keenly felt. Many Christian colleges contain some version of this phenomenon: the MRS degree, the shoe factory ("you come in single and they box you up paired"), the senior scramble. Donna Freitas, in her 2008 study of sex and romance on college campuses, describes senior women at evangelical colleges as stressed if they weren't yet dating or married, smug if they were. "Failing college for these young women is not about grades or jobs," Freitas writes. "Failing college is about graduating without a husband, or at least a fiancé."[2] Freitas may overplay the pressure on women at Christian colleges to find a mate before they find a vocation, but her analysis points to the centrality of marriage and family in evangelical life, the way they factor prominently in the imagined futures of many young women (and men too, although they are less likely to say it).

Barely into her first month of college, Betsy does not articulate the ring-by-spring anxiety that grips many of her older peers. As far as Amish fiction goes, Betsy isn't bothered by the fact that the protagonists invariably end up engaged or married with at least the hope of childbearing in the near future. "I definitely want to get married," she tells me near the end of our conversation in her college's snack shop. "In Amish books, there's always just like that one guy who was meant for them, you know . . . yada yada." She smiles and rolls her eyes a bit and then turns quickly serious. "But like, that's what I want. Is that realistic or is that just fiction? I don't know."

Curators: Amish Novels as Keepers of Chastity

We come again to the title question of the book: what, exactly, is the thrill of the chaste? And how does it fund the popularity of Amish fiction?

Chastity can refer specifically to refraining from sexual intercourse outside the bounds of a particular code of morality or religion or culture. For most evangelical Christians, that means virginity before marriage, fidelity after, and celibacy for those who never marry. "Saving oneself" stands at the center of this definition of chastity, even as exactly what is saved is open to interpretation. "Rose was glad she'd saved her kisses for him alone," writes Beverly Lewis in The Mercy, pointing to one of the more stringent definitions of the concept.[3]

But chastity, as we saw in chapter 1, can suggest a moral posture that goes beyond sexual temperance, referring more broadly to purity of thought and action, a state of being undefiled. Chastity can mean a virginal perspective on the world—an intentional innocence and a commitment to reining in the passions of the body. The Amish as a people have gained a virginal status in the American imagination, so that even though heroines of Amish novels may marry and have children, they can remain "virgin mothers" in readers' minds. Undefiled by the stains of hypermodernity and bound together by their common rejection of the technological impurities and moral murkiness of larger culture, the Amish function as a "chastity ring," of sorts, in the evangelical imagination. Thus, while the chastity that animates Amish fiction includes the first definition of sexual purity, the thrill of the chaste has at least as much to do with this more general sense of moral purity that imbues the novels. In that sense, Amish fiction serves up a triple shot of chastity. As chaste texts about chaste women in a chaste culture, Amish novels become keepers of both the sexual purity and the moral innocence that some Christians consider to be rapidly vanishing.

Having already examined their roles as commodities, devotional icons, and vehicles of transport, we now consider Amish romance novels as curators of chaste womanhood: custodians of that assemblage of assumed female traits and prescribed roles privileged within the evangelical discourse community. Lynn Neal suggests that evangelical romance fiction has become an "important site for articulating and defending the subculture's beliefs," and this is true of Amish fiction, particularly with regard to beliefs about gender and sexuality. "I read Amish fiction for the same reason I read non-Amish Christian fiction," one reader, Lisa, posted on the Amish America website; "I want only Godly values coming into my mind and I need examples of the type of Godly woman I aspire to be."[4]

This is not to say that Amish fiction is a univocal defender of a return to the cult of domesticity, with the corsets and crinoline of the Victorian "angel in the house" simply replaced by Amish capes and coverings. The category is roomy enough to contain dissenting ideas regarding gender, and Amish novels sometimes reflect more progressive notions of gender roles than observers might expect. The same author may even write one novel that appeals to conservative notions of womanhood and another that narrates a protagonist's struggle against patriarchy.

Thus, we will focus on the ways Amish novels pivot back and forth between competing notions of womanhood, even as they keep one foot solidly planted in traditional expectations for women.[5] By viewing the three basic installments in the typical Amish protagonist's life—virginal youth and courtship, complementarian marriage, and willing motherhood—we will look at the ways the novels construct romance, marriage, and the family. These three stages of ideal womanhood form the spine of many Amish novels, even if they are sometimes only implied in foreshadowing or in backstory.[6] This typical progression, when placed next to dominant cultural narratives about sexuality, romance, and marriage, helps to explain the strength of the subgenre. The subgenre's ability to straddle conservative evangelical discourse about gender and more progressive ideas that lie mostly outside of it is one of the keys to Amish fiction's success.

Virginal Youth and Courtship

At the center of almost all Amish-fiction reading experiences stands a virginal protagonist, who is usually but not always Amish. She is the focal point of most front covers, the main actor we follow in the novel itself, and an avatar of chastity who demonstrates both sexual and moral restraint. Like the protagonists of romance novels through most of the genre's history, the vast majority of Amish protagonists are young and unmarried and have never had intercourse.[7]

Many scholars have explored the mythic power of the virgin in literature and legend. From the Virgin Mary, whose immaculate conception gave rise to Christianity; to the vestal virgins of Roman mythology, whose vow of celibacy enabled them to tend the sacred fire of the goddess Vesta; to the virgin martyrs of medieval hagiography, who rejected pagan suitors and died graphic deaths for Christ; to Elizabeth I, the virgin queen whose rejection of sexual activity constituted a strategic move for political power: these and other virgins in history and lore have become prototypes of female autonomy and agency.[8] Looming large on the landscape of imagination and myth, the virginal heroine still wields authority in modern romance novels, remaining, as romance bloggers Sarah Wendell and Candy Tan write, "one of the more peculiar constants of most romance novels, from historicals to contemporaries to paranormals to even erotica."[9]

There are several theories regarding why the virginal heroine remains so appealing, but the one most helpful in understanding the virginal Amish protagonist has been advanced by general-market romance novelist Doreen

Owens Malek. Malek writes that her novels featuring virgins always sell better than her books that feature sexually experienced protagonists.[10] "Why
are virgins so special?" Malek asks. "It is because they are *in* the world but
not completely of it, since they have not participated in that essential earth-
bound activity which transforms a girl into a woman."[11] Like the Amish
themselves, who also speak of being "in the world but not of it" as a way of
rendering their ultimate fealty to a heavenly kingdom instead of an earthly
one, the archetypal virgin in the popular imagination transcends normal
realities. She is located somewhere between the profane and the sacred, the
worldly and the otherworldly, the hungers of the flesh and the attainments
of the spirit. Her frequent position between land and sky on the front covers
of the novels exemplifies this liminality.

In addition to virginity, modesty characterizes the youthful heroines of
Amish fiction. As we saw in chapter 1, in an era in which three-year-olds
strut around on TLC's *Toddlers and Tiaras* in costumes à la Julia Roberts's
Pretty Woman prostitute, modesty gains particular appeal for evangelical
readers. Little is more modest than Amish dress: elbows are covered, hair
is shrouded, knees are hidden, and cleavage is closely wrapped in several
husks of fabric. In intimate moments in Amish novels, the female characters rarely reveal more than their hair, which sometimes inadvertently
tumbles out of their prayer coverings before getting hastily pushed back
underneath ("He knew he shouldn't be staring at her hair," writes Emma
Miller of love interest Charley, who was watching Miriam; "That was for a
husband to see in the privacy of their home").[12] The male characters' bodies are rarely described except through shirts or coats. Indeed, there is little
need to recite the references to modesty made in the pages of Amish novels,
since all of them presuppose that characters are duly clothed.

Along with Amish fiction's defense of modesty comes its de-emphasis
on physical beauty. There is a nearly total lack of dissatisfaction by female
characters regarding their bodies or appearances. With a few exceptions—
including, interestingly enough, the ever-dieting protagonist in the Lizzie
Searches for Love series, written by an Amish woman—body type and
beauty are rarely mentioned in the characters' thought lives or conversations. Male point-of-view characters occasionally comment on women's
beauty or appearance, but they often affirm the value of her character as

highly as the allure of her body. "You're so beautiful," Paul tells Hannah early in the pages of Cindy Woodsmall's *When the Heart Cries*. "Beauty is vanity," Hannah protests, backing away, "and I'll thank you not to put any stock in it." Paul quickly clarifies, "Oh, you are beautiful, but that's not why I'm interested." The novels become sanctuaries, of sorts, from the body-sculpting rituals of a culture that, to many readers, feels increasingly both immodest and dangerous to women's sense of self. While the trim, radiant, and acne-free cover models usually fill in any narrative blanks about the protagonists' appearances, the texts of Amish novels themselves are relatively lacking in the infamous Barbie-doll ideal.[13] Rebecca Barrett-Fox suggests that one of the main differences between Christian romances and general ones is that Christian romance novels "do not depict women as . . . sexual objects."[14]

The courtships narrated in Amish fiction follow directly from the virginal identities of its protagonists. Few Amish-themed novels depict any premarital or extramarital sexual activity, and the romantic interactions of characters, while sometimes hinting at their desire to consummate their passions, lie mostly in the sphere of hand-holding, kissing, and hugging. Characters occasionally long to do more, but the limits of physical expression are clear. "He kissed her on the head and was taken aback by the softness of her skin," Cindy Woodsmall writes of Paul, the male point-of-view character in her Sisters of the Quilt trilogy; "The longer he stood so close to her, the stronger the need to kiss her lips became. But he was afraid she might not appreciate that move." One of Beverly Lewis's characters, Leah, feels guilty for kissing her beau on the day of her baptism, and another, Rose, reluctantly agrees with her boyfriend when he says, "We'll wait until our wedding day to lip-kiss."[15] How Amish novels manage to fuel the passions of readers when the parameters—kissing, hugging, some stroking of faces and cascading of hair—are so tightly cinched befuddles many observers outside of purity culture. Lacking vocabulary for chaste romances or novels that feature them, many observers find *repressed* or *sublimated* the only terms available. But for those within purity circles, these scenes serve as markers of the subculture, signals of an author's commitment to premarital sexual limits.

The presence of modest, chaste gestures does not mean that passion is absent. Writing scenes of chaste romance requires attention to details, on the part of both the writer and the reader, according to author Suzanne Woods Fisher. "The more you get into it, the more sensitive you grow toward the subtleties, the sweet little gestures," Fisher says. "To keep that magic in a scene—it really takes work." Recovering the sensuality of a glance and a shy smile and a chaste touch is no easy task, but it's a worthwhile one for authors like Fisher. Fisher says that Amish romances are sometimes skewered by reviewers not accustomed to this style; "They're like, 'Where's the plot? Where's the romance?'"[16] In that sense, authors of Amish or other inspirational fiction set about resensitizing readers to the thrill of the chaste.

The titillation factor of a chaste romance should not be overplayed. The thrill of the chaste in Amish fiction is not the same as that in Hollywood or BBC film productions of novels by Jane Austen or the Brontë sisters, in which the subtle eroticism of skin peeking out between a sleeve and a glove becomes a driver of the narrative. Writing of the 1995 BBC adaptation of *Pride and Prejudice,* for example, critic Lev Grossman describes a scene in which Mr. Darcy (played by Colin Firth) emerges, wet and dripping, from a pond: "It's an iconic moment precisely for what it doesn't show," Grossman writes. "No skin is revealed, nobody touches anybody, but there's more sex in the air, in invisible, intangible form, in those 2 minutes than in 100 hours of softcore Cinemax writhings."[17] Nor does the thrill of the chaste in Amish fiction resemble that of the sexually charged scene in *Witness,* in which Rachel Lapp, Kelly McGillis's character, hands a sweaty Harrison Ford a glass of ice water and is visibly engulfed by his heat. With a few exceptions, Amish novels do not tread in the aphrodisiacal aura of which Grossman speaks or that *Witness* contains. Arousing the reader is rarely the project of Amish novels, and the thrill of the chaste remains situated in the sweetly romantic rather than the suggestively sexy.

Evidence of this fact—that Amish romance novels trade in chastity rather than titillation—lies in the general absence of reference in the genre to bed courtship. Also known as bundling, bed courtship is a dating custom still alive in some conservative Amish communities in which an unmarried couple lies together, clothed, in bed until early morning.[18] Brought to North America from Europe and a relic of days when houses were unheated and lacked private spaces for courting couples, bundling has been a much-commented-on ritual of early Pennsylvania German life in general and Amish life in particular. Although estimates suggest that it is practiced in less than 10 percent of Amish communities, it has frequently caught outsiders' attention. In fact, in the 1930s and 1940s, booklets about bed courtship were some of the most popular and readily available sources of information about Amish life. An article in *Esquire* in 1937 suggested that the custom offered a discreet outlet for the Amish libido in an otherwise repressive culture. But few contemporary Amish romance novels include any reference to the practice. Kelly Long's historical Amish novel *Arms of Love* includes a bundling scene, although the heroine has no interest in bundling with her partner and slips out of bed as soon as he is asleep, and Long's novel seems to be an exception to the genre's no-bundling rule.[19] Were Amish fiction driven by eroticism or sensuality, bed courtship would be a rich natural resource, a fount of prurient potential waiting to be tapped.

Amish novels do differ when it comes to the level of sexuality present in the prose, however, and it is in this diversity that the subgenre pivots between chaste encounter and more racy material. Wanda Brunstetter's and Beverly Lewis's characters rarely do more than kiss, and sometimes they feel guilty about having done that. But Kelly Long's characters in *A Marriage of the Heart,* perhaps because they marry during the first chapter of the novella, do a great many things that involve the "husky pull of his voice" and his mouth finding "the warmth of her shoulder through her blouse." Outside the boundaries of *inspirational* Amish fiction, anything goes. The first Amish vampire book, *Forsaken,* is rife with scenes in which the protagonist's skirt has "scooched up over her knees" and her lover glances at her "exposed leg, his tanned, work-roughened hand against the delicate whiteness of her thigh." And the book description on the Amazon page for *Jacob's Return* warns, "Please Note: This is a Sexy Historical Romance in Amish setting with sexual content."[20] Still, it is safe to say that most Amish fiction trades less in the arousal or consummation of their characters' sexual desires than in the emotive warmth they long for and eventually find.

The purity culture in which Amish fiction resides has its detractors; Freitas derides the purity ideal for its "extreme restrictions" and its creation of "terrible angst and disappointment for young adults, who are often shattered by their failure to live the fairy tale."[21] Yet purity culture makes room for those who fall short of its standards, with notions such as forgiveness, healing from past sexual sin, and even the idea of "born-again virgins"— those who have had sexual intercourse in the past but confess and commit to refraining until marriage. Within the Amish-fiction field, several plot-lines center on the failure to be pure. Beverly Lewis's Seasons of Grace series revolves around the long-ago premarital rendezvous of the mother figure, Lettie Byler, and the resulting child she gave up for adoption; and Lewis's Abram's Daughters series also hinges on the births of two children conceived out of wedlock. *The Amish Midwife,* by Leslie Gould and Mindy Starns Clark, contains a florid mix of family lines and uncertain paternity, and unwed pregnancy is not an infrequent story line in other novels. Such extramarital sex is even more delicately narrated than the chaste romance scenes—"There in a hunters' shack hidden deep in the trees, she willingly gave up her virtue" suffices to describe one such premarital tryst—and the consequences of giving in to such temptation are clearly drawn: heartache, broken relationships, community sanction.[22]

Such story lines correct the common perception by those who have not read the books that Amish fiction tells only the sanitized loved story of the virginal Amish woman. The subgenre is rife with all manner of departure from this, so that while the subgenre as a whole remains rooted in chastity, it rotates to include territory in which passions are consummated. By narrating only the chaste encounters but suggesting illicit ones, Amish fiction remains anchored in the directives of purity culture while also pivoting toward the ways that they are breached.

Complementarian Marriage

Just as Amish fiction gathers salience by being what hypersexualized culture is not, it gains momentum from its depiction of marriage within what some have called a "postmarital" society.[23] Sociologist Andrew Cherlin, in his book *The Marriage-Go-Round,* suggests that not only do people in the United States divorce frequently; they marry frequently, and they cohabit for shorter periods of time than other Westerners. The result, he claims, is a nation of "sheer movement: frequent transitions, shorter relationships." Research suggests that this is the case within evangelical Christian circles as well. A 2008 study by the Barna Group found that "born-again" Christians and non-born-again adults had statistically identical divorce rates: 32 and 33 percent.[24]

Divorce is virtually unheard of among the Amish, and I know of no Amish romance novels in which Amish characters divorce. There may be marital strife, or coldness, or even separation, but by the end of the novel it resolves into marital accord and renewed commitment.[25] While remarriage between Amish characters occurs in several of the novels, it is always the result of having been widowed. And although heroines may remain unmarried through the course of a series, fearing what one author calls the "*alt Maedel* stigma," by the end of the series they are invariably depicted as betrothed or married.

Marriage in inspirational Amish romances is assumed to be monogamous, heterosexual, lifelong, and *complementarian*, a favored concept by some evangelicals to describe gender spheres that are separate but equal. Complementarian marriage, which construes both men and women as divinely valued but tasked with different functions, is the ideology in which Amish fiction plants itself, even as it pivots away from it at certain points, as we will see. The headship theology that animates Amish family and church life is a suitable match for the gender ideology of conservative evangelicals.[26] Amish marital emphases—"biblically prescribed" gender domains, the spiritual authority of the husband, with a dash of mutual submission thrown in—make, for many evangelical readers, a comfortable theological fit. "My struggle with the Old Order prayer veiling has come to a blissful end," Katie Lapp, protagonist in Beverly Lewis's The Heritage of Lancaster County series, reflects in the epilogue. "Reverently, I now wear the formal Mennonite covering in obedience to God and to my husband. Such a blessing and delight it is to follow my dear Lord Jesus in this simple act of faith."[27]

The trajectory of Wanda Brunstetter's English-turned-Amish heroine Laura in *Plain and Fancy* elaborates on this complementarian perspective. "I'm a slave to piles of laundry, dirty dishes, and holey socks," Laura shouts at her Amish husband Eli, prior to her personal salvation. She has become Amish only to snag Eli, and she plans to lead him out of his plain life and into her modern English one. Her husband is befuddled by her rebelliousness. "Eli blinked. Was there no pleasing this woman?" Eventually, however, Laura accepts Jesus into her heart, which leads her to acceptance of and pleasure in her wifely lot. By the epilogue she is counting the blessings of her now-domestic life. "'I have two *wunderbaar* children and a *gut* husband who loves us all more'n anything, and—' She looked up. 'And I have you, Lord. Thank You for takin' a fancy, spoiled English woman and turnin' her into a plain Amish wife, who loves You so much. God, You've truly blessed me!'"[28]

The reflections of Philip, the male point-of-view character in Beverly Lewis's *The Postcard* and *The Crossroads*, also exemplify the complementarian nature of many Amish novels. Philip, who is not Amish, here reflects on a former girlfriend. He is soon to fall in love with the Beachy Amish protagonist, Annie, whose submissive manner this passage anticipates: "No, what their relationship had granted him—literally—was the realization that he was now able to describe in words the kind of woman he wanted to marry someday. First and foremost, she must be a lady, someone mannerly and appreciative. He also did not think much of married women who felt they had to invent their husbands. He had decided the day after Lauren and he broke up that if ever he was to marry, the girl would have to be demure—a nice change. A young woman who allowed him to lead, though he was no tyrant."[29]

Passages like this, as well as the inevitable ending of an Amish romance novel or series—complementarian, heterosexual marriage and at least the suggestion of motherhood—raise the question whether the subgenre feeds women readers, especially young ones, the ideology that the only future worth imagining necessitates snaring a husband and birthing babies. First-year college student Sarah admitted that the assurance of marriage at the end of the novels is problematic. "You shouldn't find your fulfillment in getting married," she told me. "Your fulfillment should be in doing what God wants you to do." And the identifying sign on the covers of Amish novels—the covering on the head of the model—may suggest that the category reinscribes patriarchy. Amish rationale for the head covering comes from 1 Corinthians 11; immediately after the apostle Paul claims that "the husband is the head of his wife," he admonishes women to cover their heads when praying as a "symbol of authority."[30] Branded with a woman wearing a head covering, every Amish or Amishesque novel has, in one sense, women's submission and male headship written into its very DNA.

While many observers find such signs of female obedience offensive, Amish and non-Amish evangelical readers of Amish fiction likely do not. "Honestly, I don't mind the old-fashioned roles," first-year college student Sarah told me. "I think that men and women are equal but different. I see nothing wrong with women just staying at home and being a mom and a housekeeper and not having a career. I hold the traditional belief that the man is the head of the household. I feel like I'm very old fashioned in that way." Sarah is an honors student with majors in math and biology and uncertain about what she wants to do vocationally. Part of Amish fiction's appeal for her, she says, lies in its depiction of "what a woman would do, being a mom and working at home." Describing herself as frequently stressed by schoolwork, Sarah said that Amish fiction provides a release from the demands of academic achievement. "The opposite life of what I'm living now would be kind of refreshing," Sarah tells me. "The only thing I know is I want to be a mom, because I love little kids. Not that I don't want to have a career, it's just . . . I don't know what it's going to be."[31]

Even if Sarah ends up employed rather than or in addition to being a wife, she may manage to retain what she calls her "old-fashioned" beliefs, thanks to a dichotomy that Sally K. Gallagher and Christian Smith describe in their study of evangelical gender understandings. Many contemporary evangelicals uphold the "symbolic traditionalism" of male headship language even as they function, practically speaking, in an egalitarian manner. Gallagher and Smith found that although many evangelicals maintain that feminism has stripped away supports for families, the imperatives of a postindustrial economy have meant that women committed to conservative gender vocabulary have entered the workforce. Headship language in many evangelical circles has changed from "breadwinner" to "spiritual leader" terminology, thus allowing evangelicals to preserve a feeling of separateness from the world even while accommodating to it. Gallagher and Smith write that the "transformation of headship from authority-breadwinner to symbolic spiritual head and protector continues to provide an ideological framework within which individual evangelicals may maintain a sense of distinctiveness from the broader culture of which they are a part." This combination of symbolic traditionalism and pragmatic egalitarianism has allowed evangelicals to "manage social and economic change while maintaining a distinctive subcultural identity."[32]

Gallagher's and Smith's analysis illumines the way Amish fiction can defend a subculture's values while pivoting away from them. Many Amish novels contain protagonists known as much for speaking their minds as for listening to their boyfriends or husbands. "I want you and Jorie to end up together because she's so right for you," one brother tells another in Suzanne Woods Fisher's *The Choice*. "She's smart enough and she speaks her mind." In *Autumn's Promise*, non-Amish heroine Lilly considers becoming Amish in order to marry her Amish fiancé. Ultimately, however, she decides that she can't. "Robert, I love you, and I love the Lord, but I can't become Amish. I can't give up everything that I am. Not even for you." Robert understands: "Part of what made her so vibrant was her zest for life," he reflects. "Her spark of independence. . . . No, she wasn't a moldable girl, ready to rely on him to help her through things. She was strong. And she wanted what she wanted."[33]

When asked to describe the female protagonists in Amish novels, readers often oscillate between terms of female agency and female submission. Kathie wrote, "They are respectful of elders and church leaders and they are strong women but not harsh and obnoxious." Anna told me that Amish heroines are "strong, slightly rebellious, true, virtuous, Christian, giving, loving, caring." This commingling of adjectives, some emphasizing dutiful Christian womanhood (respectful, virtuous, loving, caring) and some underscoring women's empowerment (strong, rebellious), reflect the paradoxes embedded within an evangelical doctrine of submission.

Complementarian marriage and literature that privileges it operate as a marker of difference for many conservative evangelicals: signals of the distance between themselves and the marriage-go-round that Cherlin describes. On the one hand, Neal writes, "Whether through language of male headship, the practice of homeschooling, or endorsement of traditional gender roles, evangelicals see beliefs about family as a way to differentiate themselves from the world and to provide a heritage of faith for their children."[34] On the other hand, as Gallagher and Smith point out, such traditionalist language is increasingly symbolic, such that it overlays a more complicated and egalitarian reality. Reading Amish novels, then, in which the spiritual authority of men is assumed even as the consciousness and fulfillment of women is privileged, may help evangelical readers straddle the traditional scripts of their faith community and the evolving gender and economic realities of American life.

Willing Motherhood

Were one feeling bold enough to connect dots to form a line that no evidence yet draws, one could suggest that Quiverfull, the movement toward large families among conservative evangelical and fundamentalist Christians, is filling not only the quivers of husbands across the country but also the coffers of publishers of Amish fiction.[35] The belief that couples should turn family planning over to God and accept as many babies as God grants them is becoming increasingly popular and is requiring women to remain at home to raise—and frequently to educate—their ever-expanding broods.[36] Michelle and Jim Bob Duggar, parents of nineteen children, homeschoolers, and now media moguls with their own TLC show and books, are the best-known faces of the Quiverfull movement. Although they are far from Amish, it is possible that the ideology fueling the rise of the Duggars is at least adjacent to, if not synonymous with, the one feeding Amish fiction.

The typical married Amish woman in Lancaster County gives birth to 7.1 children, whereas the typical non-Amish woman bears 2.8.[37] Large families are typical both among the real-life and the fictional Amish and are perceived as gifts from God. Although some Amish couples use birth control methods, either natural or artificial, birth control is mostly frowned upon. Large families have historically functioned in Amish life to increase economic productivity on farms, because children begin contributing labor at an early age.[38]

But evidence that the Amish-fiction phenomenon is a direct cognate of the Quiverfull movement does not exist. No Amish-fiction reader or writer I interviewed had an overwhelming number of progeny; while many were mothers, and some had homeschooled their children, most had no more than three children. None of them responded to the question "How has reading (or writing) Amish fiction changed you?" with anything approxi-mating plans for extreme motherhood. While the heroines in the books themselves often yearn for a lot of children—"They had a big finished attic that would someday, God willing, offer bedrooms for a large family of chil-dren," writes Emma Miller in *Miriam's Heart*—there's no proof that their readers do.[39] Thus, it is best to limit any claims regarding the portrayal of motherhood in the subgenre to something other than an Amish quiverfull.

It is safe to claim, however, that constructions of motherhood in Amish fiction are closely linked to evangelical *familism,* which privileges the moral and social prerogatives of the family over the desires of the individual. Evan-gelical familism, according to sociologist W. Bradford Wilcox, seeks to "pre-serve marriage's social status as the institutional anchor for sexual activity, childbearing, and childrearing."[40] While evangelical Christians have not been entirely successful in living up to their familistic ideals, with divorce rates closely aligned with those of nonevangelicals, Wilcox suggests that family-centered beliefs have indeed strengthened active, churchgoing evan-gelicals' commitments to their families. One marketer, whom we heard from in chapter 1, described the appeal of Amish fiction to me this way: "The family gathers around the table for meals and they pray together and they go visiting and it's all family, family, family. A lot of people, especially moms, are saying, 'Gee, that's the life I wish I had.'" Evangelical sacraliza-tion of the heterosexual nuclear family, and readers' frequent references to the appeal of Amish family life, help to explain the popularity of Amish fic-tion—although the church district, not the nuclear family, is arguably the central social unit of Amish life.

Amish novels contain a mosaic of motherhood realities—widowed motherhood, stepmotherhood, adoptive motherhood, mothering of adult children, motherhood as the result of premarital sex, motherhood while separated from one's children, child loss, inability to conceive, and future motherhood—so it is difficult to make hard and fast claims regarding how the category constructs the office. Underlying these varying representations of motherhood, however, lies an assumption that motherhood is a high, if not the highest, calling for women, and one that deserves utmost respect and support. Little ambivalence regarding the role is depicted, and few fe-male characters express a desire *not* to be a mother or any internal conflict regarding the role. The prominence of midwives in the casts of characters of Amish novels suggests the lofty role of motherhood in the pages of the books; midwifery becomes an almost priestly calling.

Most novels reference motherhood for the protagonists only in the future tense, for their young heroines are usually not yet married. Motherhood becomes a kind of veil through which young adult protagonists will someday pass, a gauzy location of coming contentment. Heroines frequently articulate a desire for children—"As the Lord wills, I wish for a lifetime of joy, and children, and peace, with the husband of my heart," Abigail tells her husband in Kathleen Fuller's novella *A Marriage of the Heart*—and almost without exception they assume that they will be mothers.[41] Motherhood is a status to which they aspire and becomes a site where they work out the divine purpose of their lives.

One dissenting note in this generally positive motherhood tenor includes several books in which a widowed Amish man wants to marry the protagonist so that his children might have a mother and he a housekeeper. The protagonist usually considers marrying him or is nearly forced to do so, but she always intuits the instrumental nature of his intentions. "I knew well and good that John Beiler had one important thing on his mind: He needed a mamma for his children," Beverly Lewis's Katie Lapp reflects.[42] Lydia in Wanda Brunstetter's *Lydia's Charm* is pursued by Menno, the widowed father of a passel of unruly sons, and widowed bishop John Frey in Brunstetter's *On Her Own*, also trolling for a wife for himself and a mother for his children, sets his sights on protagonist Barbara Zook, fifteen years his junior. Barbara resists the slightly lurid advances of the bishop, who seems to be forever licking his lips, and is convinced that even the high calling of motherhood is not sufficient reason to marry Bishop Frey. She and Lydia and Katie all end up marrying for romantic love rather than maternal commitment. In that sense, the genre remains planted in traditional notions of motherhood while gesturing toward women's emotional fulfillment as a priority of an even higher order.

While some of the Amish protagonists stop working when they marry or have children, others find satisfaction and support from their husbands for their employment, circumscribed as it may be. Cindy Woodsmall's heroine Hannah, who has become Mennonite by the end of the Sisters of the

Quilt trilogy, has a master's degree in nursing and a husband who is "always proud of her work and school accomplishments" and calls her "Lion-Heart." Abigail Graber's husband Daniel, in Mary Ellis's *Abigail's New Hope*, similarly supports her career as a midwife. "Don't be in a hurry to dismiss this, Abby," he tells her, after a work opportunity presents itself. "Don't doubt or second-guess yourself. If your heart leads you back to work, then go with confidence."[43] Thus, the subgenre roots itself in a traditional gender ideology—motherhood as the highest calling for women—while also pivoting away from it.

Regressive Fairy Tales or Texts of Female Freedom?

So the questions remain: do Amish novels fete chastity, submission, and Duggar-like procreation, all with conservative religiopolitical zest? Or do they offer narratives in which girls develop free of the reign of oversexualization and in which women negotiate work and family in a manner of their choosing? Does the genre restrain its readers' imagined futures by propagating fantasies and patriarchal ideologies, or does it free readers to see themselves as worthy protagonists in their own life's narrative and people who construct their own happiness in the midst of constraints?

Some observers maintain that romance novels in general "extinguish the heroine and bind the reader."[44] By constructing marriage as the only route to happiness for women, these critics argue, the novels enslave the protagonist's—and thus the readers'—imaginations. Critics of the romance genre argue, as Tania Modleski does, that "romances provide women with a common fantasy structure to ensure their continued psychic investment in their oppression."[45] Modleski summarizes a widely held opinion that romance novels are infantile and regressive texts that legitimate patriarchy and the oppression of women. Women tranquilize themselves in privatized worlds of dashing heroes and submissive heroines, this line of thinking goes, rather than working corporately to undermine patriarchy and to better their station in life.

Observers of Amish romance novels are marshaling similar arguments about the harm bonnet books do to women readers, especially to young adult readers like Betsy. "I find the novels nearly as damaging to women as

far less innocent-seeming shows like *The Bachelor*," writes English professor Melanie Springer Mock: "The settings seem dramatically different: for
one, a pimped out mansion; for the other, an austere Amish community.
But really, *The Bachelor*'s fantasy suite, complete with hot tub, wine, and
rose petals, is no less idealized than the simplified perfection of an Amish
farm: both suggest a transport to another, more faultless world, apart from
the flawed places we stumble through. . . . The narrative trajectory is also
similar, as is the underlying message: the love of your life is waiting! God
will find a way! Sit back, relax, and enjoy the ride—in a limo or a buggy—
because a man's agency is all that matters, not your own!" *Washington City
Paper* blogger Amanda Hess agrees, calling Amish fiction a "romanticized
account of a community where women's rights don't exist. Beyond the
genre's unsettling conservative bent, the Amish romance novel strikes me
as a more offensive version of the Regency romance. They both rely on sentimental ideas of antiquated societies, except that the Amish are still alive."[46]

In this view, Amish romance novels become antifeminist treatises
squared: regressive novels that valorize a regressive culture. Given that
Amish novels are still largely the literary productions of evangelicalism,
with its historic commitment to male headship, it is possible that the novels are indeed advancing a traditionalist gender politics. Amish heroines, in
this perspective, become miniatures of conservative Christian womanhood,
sacred wives and mothers acting out the scripts of religious patriarchy.[47]

Alternatively, one could argue that Amish romance novels are texts of
freedom for their mostly female readership. Amish fiction privileges the
stories of women, narrating their identities and subjectivities. "By fore-
grounding women's spiritual lives, as well as their concerns about marriage and family, the genre validates women's experience of evangelicalism
and their role as wives and mothers, friends and leaders," writes Lynn Neal
about inspirational romance fiction. "In a subculture where men continue
to dominate religious leadership, the genre offers fictional worlds where
women occupy center stage." Rebecca Barrett-Fox agrees, suggesting that
Christian romance novels are "gynocentric tales" in which "heroes defy stereotypes of men as brutish, emotionally distant, and attracted to jobs with
power and status" and "heroines defy the roles to which many Christian
gender manuals would assign them."[48]

Regis's argument in *A Natural History of the Romance Novel* traverses similar theoretical terrain, although her point refers to romance novels in general. By overcoming two elements of the romance novel's plot—the barrier, which is outlined early in the text, and the point of ritual death, which occurs near the end—the heroine experiences "two great liberations," such that romance novels serve not to oppress the heroine but to free her and, by extension, the reader. "Her [the protagonist's] freedom is a large part of what readers celebrate at the end of the romance," Regis writes. "Her choice to marry the hero is just one manifestation of her freedom. . . . Heroines are not extinguished, they are freed. Readers are not bound by the form; they rejoice because they are in love with freedom."[49] The barriers in Amish romance novels vary greatly: from intra-Amish or Amish-English religious difference, to the inability to trust after the death or betrayal of a previous lover, to geographic distance, to assumptions that the lover is interested in someone else, to rancor between two families, to disability or deafness or blindness or emotional trauma. Always, however, the argument asserts, there is freedom.[50]

It could also be said that the novels use Amish culture as a generative space in which female protagonists resist male-dominated structures. Dale Cramer's heroine Rachel, whose father has decided to move the family to Mexico, expresses a fairly overt feminist sensibility when describing her lot in life to her boyfriend, Jacob: "A girl has no say over her own life, that's all," she tells him. "Men in the government—men I don't even know—decided I should go to school every day, and so I go, like it or not. Because of this, my father decides we should move to Mexico, and so I'll go, like it or not. One day I'll get married, and then my husband will decide everything for me, like it or not. A girl has no more say-so than a dandelion seed. It's just not fair, that's all." And Beverly Lewis told one reporter: "For every lineup of Amish women at a gathering of any kind, you'll always see one of them that has her hand kind of on her hip. That's my character. She's the one that's pushing boundaries."[51] Of course, having chafed against gender prescriptions, by the end of the book the characters almost inevitably choose to live within them. Still, the hand-on-the-hip stance of many Amish heroines could be seen as a feminist posture.

The very act of reading an Amish romance novel may, for some women, represent release from caregiving duties that structure their lives, thus becoming a liberation from traditional women's work. "Not only is it a relaxing release from the tension produced by daily problems and responsibilities," Janice Radway writes about the reading of romance novels; "it creates a time or space within which a woman can be entirely on her own, preoccupied with her personal needs, desires, and pleasure."[52] Readers of Amish romance novels with whom I spoke echoed Radway's finding. "Sometimes you reward yourself for having done a task that you hate," Karen told me. "You just washed a floor, you think, 'Oh, I'm so glad that's done, I'm going to sit down and read.'" Another Amish-fiction reader told me that women who love to read will do it anywhere and everywhere: "At lunch, at work when you have a few minutes, at night, when you have everything else done, when you go to bed at night. When you go to the doctor's office, you take your book with you. When you go for any kind of meeting or appointment you take your book with you. In your car you listen to books on CD. . . . So in other words, for people who really love to read, it's just every opportunity that you get." In that sense, the simple act of picking up an Amish novel—or any other novel, for that matter—may itself be a strategy by which women readers exert selfhood.

Reducing Readers to Their Romances

To suggest that Amish fiction is either antifeminist polemic or liberating narrative would be brash. Claiming either would elide the differing ways in which readers receive and create meaning. Some readers of Amish fiction likely find their preexisting conservative gender ideologies confirmed, and others likely emerge from the fiction calling those ideologies into question. As we have seen, the popularity of Amish romance novels rests in part on the genre's ability to oscillate back and forth between competing notions of gender roles. Were the novels to play only one side of the line, the genre would fail to engage the affections of contemporary readers. But by pivoting back and forth across debates surrounding contemporary womanhood, even as it remains firmly planted in conservative religious understandings, Amish fiction can reflect back to readers their own two-mindedness regarding these issues. For readers like Betsy, the college student, the novels serve both as custodians of a subculture's beliefs about chaste womanhood and as explorations of the tensions within that subculture.

Although the subgenre as a whole draws deeply from conservative ideologies regarding gender, readers' interactions with Amish-fiction texts are much more complex than simple ingestion. Reader-response theories suggest that readers like Sarah often filter texts, accepting what they like and eschewing what they don't. Many readers I spoke with held their appreciation for Amish fiction in tandem with critical or even oppositional reading. "Sometimes I even argue with the books," a young conservative Mennonite woman in Pennsylvania told me. And within the discussion group in Plano, Illinois, there was both affirmation and dissent as they talked about Wanda Brunstetter's *Lydia's Charm*, which uses a famous passage from Proverbs 31 about a "virtuous woman" as an epigraph and ends with the protagonist's husband quoting that verse and thanking God "for giving me such a woman."[53] The women disagreed, albeit gently, about what a "Proverbs 31 woman" would look like today. One woman suggested that such a woman "puts her husband's and children's needs front and center before she even goes out and works," while other women brought up counterarguments, about their own desire or need to work full time while also caring for their families. "God calls us to different things," one woman asserted, in counterpoint to any hearth-and-home message of the novel itself.

In addition to sometimes arguing with the text, most readers of inspirational romance, as Neal points out in her study, read in other genres as well: "We must remember that these women cannot simply be reduced to the romance novels that they read, since this genre represents only one aspect of their religious [and, I would add, romantic] lives."[54] For some readers I interviewed, Amish novels sit on their shelves beside books like William Powers's *Hamlet's Blackberry*, a nonfiction exploration of technological change, and *The Poisonwood Bible*, Barbara Kingsolver's fictional treatment of Christian missionaries behaving badly. College student Sarah pointed out that although she reads Amish fiction, she reads a lot of other novels as well and that Amish is just one of many categories of fiction that she enjoys. "I very rarely meet a book I don't like," she told me.

Calling Betsy's or Sarah's enjoyment of Amish fiction the mere outworking of false consciousness would require ignoring the complex transactions at the heart of the reading event and the sometimes contradictory messages contained in the subgenre itself. Claiming that Betsy or Sarah or any other reader of Amish fiction is always freed by her reading of Amish fiction would be erroneous as well. Betsy and Sarah are bright young women who read widely and who think a great deal about how they want their futures to look. Like many other readers of Amish fiction, they are ambivalent about the scripts of gender and sexuality and marriage that they have been handed both by their churches and by the wider culture. Suggesting anything more than that about them—that their enjoyment of Amish fiction will lead them to small-minded domestic dreams, on the one hand, or to feminist libera-tion, on the other—would be, frankly, immodest.

The Amish behind the Fiction

Thus far we have heard mostly from people like Betsy and Sarah: non-Amish readers of Amish fiction. Chapters 8 and 9 turn our attention to the Amish themselves: what Amish readers are saying about Amish fiction, and what representational issues are operative as non-Amish writers seek to fictionalize the Amish. In chapter 10 we inquire after what effect Amish fiction might be having on its readers, including Amish individuals and communities, and consider in what directions the Amish-fiction flock may migrate in the future.

We now entertain one of the most frequent questions I received from people when they heard I was writing about this genre. Do Amish people read Amish novels, and if so, what do they think of them?

by Linda Byler

Lizzie's Teen Years *(2005), the fifth book in a self-published series by Old Order Amish novelist Linda Byler, was read widely in Amish communities.*
Used by permission of Linda Byler and Good Books.

❧ Chapter Eight ❧

Amish Reading Amish

Ceil, the discussion leader of the book group in Plano, Illinois, is an ebullient and well-spoken woman with close-cropped hair and the wide vowels of a midwesterner. During my days in Plano, I stay with her and her husband, Jack, who is recently retired and spends his weekdays in his basement workshop. Jack's whimsical wooden carvings fill their house—angels on the bookshelf in the living room, fishermen in orange rain slickers and waders on the kitchen table, a googly-eyed sheep with a cuffed sweater. The figurines bespeak the work of a master whittler and a fanciful vision carefully and lovingly wrought. Shortly after my visit, I receive an e-mail from Ceil. "I guess all of our talk about the Amish inspired Jack," she writes. "He bought a book about carving Amish and has started on an Amish woman." A few weeks later, I receive a package in the mail from Ceil. It is Jack's first Amish carving, a wide-hipped Amish woman with a white covering, a blue dress, and a basket glued to her left palm. She is a sturdy little figurine who now sits on my desk, a pleased and slightly startled expression on her face.

Ceil and I talked a lot about Amish fiction during my stay. Having read almost seventy Amish novels, Ceil was eager to hear the opinions about the genre that a few Amish folks had shared with me. "I've sometimes wondered what the Amish think about these books," Ceil mused one evening as we chatted in the kitchen. A faceless Amish doll in a purple dress and a black bonnet slumped on a tiny rocking chair behind the couch, revealing nothing.[1]

Searching for *the* Amish opinion on Amish romance novels would be a fool's errand. Though abiding by a core set of practices, beliefs, and conventions, the Amish are a diverse religious sect made up of at least forty different affiliations, each of which contains local church districts differing from one another. Thus, generalizing about what "the Amish" think about a topic is nearly as egregious as claiming to know what "the Methodists" or "the Baptists" think.[2] Within the parameters of their religion and culture, the Amish contain several of the taste publics that cultural theorist Herbert Gans describes, and it is fairly apparent that if Amish people are reading Amish fiction, some probably like it and some probably don't. Additionally, no quantitative data on Amish readers of Amish fiction have been collected, and using anecdotes to build a composite claim would be erroneous.

Nevertheless, as my research on Amish-themed fiction progressed, the question that Ceil raised dogged me as well. What do the Amish themselves think about the novels being written about them? Is it startling to walk down an aisle in Walmart and see airbrushed versions of yourself on book covers? Or is it a relief to find books featuring chaste characters from your faith community, books that you trust are safe to share with your daughters? So despite the impossibility of the task, I decided to do some sleuthing to find out what I could about Amish readers of Amish fiction.

The Bookmobile: Portal to Amish Reading Tastes

At a McDonald's in Holmes County, Ohio, one summer afternoon, I ask an Amish man sitting at a nearby table if he can point us toward the Evener Shop. Although I do not yet know what an evener is or what it does (later I find out that it's a device that distributes weight evenly on a team of horses), I want to visit the shop because the Holmes County bookmobile is to be parked there this afternoon. The man gives me directions to the shop, which turns out to be only a few miles from the restaurant. My parents and youngest son and I climb into the car and head out. With an hour to spare before we need to start toward a family reunion, we decide to try to find the bookmobile.

One of sixty-six mobile libraries that operate in the state of Ohio, the Holmes County bookmobile travels along the narrow back roads of central

Ohio, where one feels slightly criminal just for riding in a car.[3] Making monthly stops at sites like Shady Hollow School and Bowman Harness and the Evener Shop, it trundles its literary freight to residents who live far from the library branches in Millersburg and Walnut Creek and who may have only a buggy or a bike to get around. Ninety-five percent of the patrons of the Holmes County bookmobile are Amish, so its use is a barometer, of sorts, of Amish reading tastes. If I don't find Amish readers of Amish fiction here, I think, as I climb into my parents' car, it is doubtful that I will find them anywhere.

A few miles north of town, a small sign, "The Evener Shop," directs us to turn left off the state road. We wind our way past farms with large garden plots strung across bottomland and slightly disheveled shocks of wheat dotting the fields. We are only a few miles from where my mother's father grew up, an Amish boy who loved books and dogs and who eventually moved away and sent his daughters to nursing school and college. Now, driving past farms like the one where my grandfather was a child one hundred years ago, we have no sign of my grandfather's Amishness to qualify us as belonging. We are simply four of the 4 million tourists who visit Holmes County each year, some of whom happen upon the bookmobile at its more visible stops and take pictures of Amish children with their bags of books.[4]

When we finally reach the Evener Shop, several miles off the main road, we see the bookmobile parked partway down the lane. A whimsical mural of squirrels and turtles reading books is painted on its side, advertising its purpose. As we arrive, two Amish girls in their early teens are emerging from the bookmobile, each carrying a plastic bag of books and heading toward two bicycles leaning against a nearby fence. I climb the steps into the thirty-five-foot-long bus, where rows of novels and biographies and how-to manuals and magazines along the interior wall create a kind of uterine lining of the printed word.

It only takes a sentence or so from librarian Marty LaVigne for me to realize that I need to revise a nascent hypothesis that Amish people don't read Amish fiction. "Oh yes, we have lots of holds in Amish fiction—people request them a lot," she tells me. "Amish novels are very well-received, for the most part."[5] Wanda Brunstetter is popular with the bookmobile's mostly Amish users, she says, as are Beverly Lewis, Kathleen Fuller, Mary Ellis, and

Jerry Eicher, among others. In fact, the only author of Amish fiction she can think of who doesn't do well with bookmobile readers is P. L. Gaus, whose crime stories set among the Amish do not contain romance elements.

Some of the Amish patrons get Christian book catalogs in the mail at home, LaVigne tells me, and then bring the catalogs to the bookmobile, having circled the Amish-novel titles they hope the library will order. LaVigne pays special attention to the marked-up catalogs of one Amish reader in particular; "I will literally go straight to my computer and order the books she requests, because I know that they will be checked out a lot," she says. When LaVigne orders copies of new Amish titles, she generally orders three or four (although if it's a new book by Beverly Lewis, she orders five). The Herald Press Amish titles by Carrie Bender and Mary Christner Borntrager remain very popular; the bookmobile has six or seven copies of each of those.[6]

Only occasionally do the librarians hear from a patron that the Amish novel she has just read isn't accurate in its representation of Amish life. LaVigne's coworker on the bookmobile tells me about one Amish woman who told him that she has gotten tired of Amish novels because "they're all the same." For the most part, however, they just keep checking out the books. None of the bookmobile patrons choose Amish fiction exclusively, and the bookmobile contains many other varieties of inspirational Christian fiction. But in the past few years, Amish fiction has become one of the most popular fictional categories for the bookmobile, LaVigne says; five years ago it had only stray copies of Beverly Lewis's and Wanda Brunstetter's novels.

Later, as we pull out of the lane, I learn that my father decided to help me with my research. Just after I entered the bookmobile, he called out to the two young Amish teenagers who were leaving. "Do you read those Amish love stories?" he asked them as they mounted their bicycles. One of the girls had already set off down the lane, but the other one paused briefly to answer him. "*Ja*, we do," she said with a smile, and rode off with a bag full of books.

Appreciative Amish Readers

The Holmes County bookmobile offers just one of many clues that Amish fiction's wide ambit now includes Amish communities themselves. The

Swartzentruber Amish, having splintered from the Old Order Amish in 1913 because of concern that the Old Order were becoming too liberal, can serve as an indicator of how far an innovation has reached into Amish life. If a technology or practice or type of literature has shown up among the Swartzentrubers, it likely is found among the more progressive affiliations as well. Linguist Karen Johnson-Weiner, who has many friendships among the ultraconservative Swartzentruber Amish in New York, says that several of her Swartzentruber friends are reading Beverly Lewis's and Wanda Brunstetter's novels—although when they read them, they don't feel that they're reading about their "own" people. One Swartzentruber woman said that the Amish novels she has read are written about "higher-class" Amish. "They don't do things like us," she said. Still, Johnson-Weiner reports, the Swartzentruber readers of Amish fiction she knows enjoy the novels a great deal. "They're good stories," a young Swartzentruber mother told Johnson-Weiner. The woman's sister, a mother of four, agreed, adding that she often found it hard to wait until Sunday, the only day she allows herself to read novels.[7]

Several more anecdotes add more glimpses into an appreciative Amish readership. "I can't stop reading them," one Amish woman told a *Wall Street Journal* reporter. "I usually better not start in the morning because then I sit around too long."[8] When researcher Beth E. Graybill asked an Old Order Amish grandfather about Amish novels, he replied in a deliciously understated nugget, "We would have some of these books in our homes."[9] Amish novels line the shelves of many Amish-owned stores in Pennsylvania, including one that has hosted book signings for author Cindy Woodsmall. Author Wanda Brunstetter told me that Amish readers of her books are legion. "All of my Amish friends, and their friends, and *their* friends read my books," Brunstetter said, during a gap in the otherwise steady stream of readers at a book signing in Bird in Hand, Pennsylvania. Amish women in northern Indiana have held book signings for Brunstetter in their homes, and she counts among her appreciative readers at least one Amish bishop in Indiana and an Amish minister in Lancaster, Pennsylvania. Beverly Lewis also says that appreciative Amish readers of her books are many. "I don't want to mislead you, Mrs. Lewis," one fan wrote. "All of us are reading them under the covers."[10]

"There's just something about reading a book about your own way of life," Amish reviewer Doretta Yoder wrote about one Amish novel; "It's so easy to relate." Yoder, associate editor of the *Connection,* a periodical that goes to Amish and Mennonite households in forty-three states and Canada, reviews books each month, many of them Amish fiction. In 2011 over 60 percent of the books reviewed in Yoder's "I Love to Read!" column were Amish romance novels. About Beth Wiseman's *Plain Paradise,* Yoder, who lives in Indiana, writes, "I just got my hands on the latest of Beth's books and already my mom and cousins are itching to have their turn at reading it! I think this is all I need to say to convince you that her books are well worth every dollar spent. Keep them coming, Beth!"[11] And an Ohio woman writing in *Calvary Messenger,* the Beachy Amish Mennonite monthly periodical, says, "We grow a bit crimson when someone asks us if our life is 'just like the books.' Yet we find ourselves embarrassingly and stealthily checking them out at the library to read."[12]

An Amish man in Lancaster County suggested to Erik Wesner, who maintains the Amish America website, that there may not be as many Amish readers of Amish fiction as the authors suggest. "There is a small percentage of Amish readers that read the Beverly and Wanda books, mostly young females," the Amish man told Wesner. "For the most part they are taken for exactly what they are—storybook novels. Therefore most Amish people really don't have any time to read them, let alone ponder their meaning. More popular with the Old Order Amish and Mennonites are the Carrie Bender books . . . also the series by [Linda Byler]."[13]

An Amish teenager with whom I spoke concurs that Amish readers of Amish fiction are mostly young teenagers. She used to read a lot of them when she was in early adolescence, and says that younger girls like her thirteen-year-old sister are the ones reading Amish fiction in her community in Pennsylvania. At that age, she says, "You'll just kind of read anything. Especially if it's romance." Then again, this teen mentions that her grandmother had a bookshelf full of Amish romance novels.[14]

No one yet knows how many Amish people are reading Amish fiction, or which anecdotal evidence—the mostly appreciative Amish voices, which we have just heard, or the mostly critical ones, which we turn to next—is more representative of reality. If the hypothesis of the first chapter is correct—

These racks inside the front door of an Amish-owned store in central Pennsylvania are stocked with Amish romance novels.

Photograph by author.

that the appeal of Amish romance novels increases relative to the advances of hypermodernity and hypersexualization—then it is likely that the novels do not hold the same allure for Amish readers as for non-Amish readers. If significant numbers of Amish people are reading Amish romance novels, however, it is possible that Amish fiction is now actually shaping Amish culture, a prospect we entertain in chapter 9.

For now, one more story suffices to illustrate the extent to which Amish fiction has insinuated itself into Amish communities. Scholar Nao Nomura, who was studying Amish quilts on a Fulbright scholarship, tells of visiting a very conservative Amish settlement in Minnesota. Speaking with a young Amish teenager in the community, Nomura mentioned that she was living in Lancaster County for the year as she did research on Amish quilts. The young Amish woman said that she herself had learned about the Lancaster County Amish only recently, since doing some reading about them. "What have you read?" Nomura asked, expecting her to mention some nonfiction book about the Amish or perhaps an Amish-published magazine.

"Oh, the novels by Beverly Lewis," the young woman replied.

Critical Amish Readers

Ada, an Old Order Amish woman in Ohio, took it upon herself to collect some data for me after hearing about my project. Pulling aside her Old Order, New Order, and Mennonite neighbors at a neighborhood ice cream social one summer evening, Ada asked them one by one whether they read Amish fiction. She seemed pleased to report her findings on a voice-mail message to me the next day, summarizing their opinions in a snappy troika: "I don't read them. I see them everywhere. I don't have them in my home."

My own conversations with Amish people echoed Ada's findings. Most of the Amish people with whom I spoke were aware of Amish romance novels, but few had anything good to say about them. In general, they approached the topic with a mixture of resignation, bemusement, and exasperation. "It's a mystery to a lot of us why they're so popular," an Amish farmer in Ohio told me, shaking his head. An Amish woman in Lancaster who serves meals to tourists in her home said, "People come here and tell me, 'I've read all the Amish books.'" Rolling her eyes as she recounted how such visitors often assume that they are well informed about Amish life, she added, "And I'm kind of inwardly groaning, thinking, 'Oh, no.'"

Some of the Amish criticism of the genre that I encountered seemed predicated on a general mistrust of fiction itself, a sense that reading novels—romances in particular—is a waste of time. "Who has time to read this stuff? I'm too busy to read these books," said one Amish woman. Another Old Order Amish woman in Lancaster tells me that while she used to read some Christian fiction, with seven children and a dairy farm and a small business of her own, she simply doesn't have much time to read. When she does read, she reaches for books on child-rearing or marriage or devotional inspiration. Her teenage daughter, who has shyly taken a seat on the couch as her mother and I chat, says that she and her friends don't read Amish-themed novels either. Many of them are reading *Before You Meet Prince Charming*, a courtship and chastity manual for young women. "I would much rather see them reading books like that than reading books that put fantasies in their heads," her mother adds.

That Amish-themed romance novels nurture in readers an unhealthy fantasy life is the argument made by Jennifer Anderson, a Beachy Amish woman writing in her church periodical. Anderson urges her Beachy sisters not to read romance novels, including Amish ones, because they "arouse feelings of lust and desire" and "activate the imagination impurely."[15]

General avoidance of the subgenre also characterized the words of an older Amish woman from Ohio, who explained to me on the phone, "We shy away from such books." "There are so many good missionary stories to read," she told me, adding, "Our church standard shuns against untrue stories." However, her district's leaders have not made specific statements against Amish novels. Statements such as this woman's, which describe a generalized Amish frown on Amish romance novels, may be what led two journalists to maintain that several Amish districts have "banned" Amish fiction. During my research, I found no evidence of any official churchly statements against the novels.[16] The *Ordnung* changes slowly and by communal ratification, so such an ecclesial declaration would probably take years in coming. Beverly Lewis reports that in the months following the publication of *The Shunning*, she received letters from Amish women in Ohio and Indiana who reported that their bishops were "'nervous' about the spiritual underpinnings in that novel and told their people not to read that book." But Lewis says that she is also not aware of any formal decree against that book or any of her other novels.[17]

A few Amish readers were adamant in their opposition to the genre. One young mother took umbrage with representations of the Amish in the novels that she has read, especially Beverly Lewis's early work. "I think they're kind of deceptive," she told me. "I wouldn't want my daughters reading them. They try to make the Amish look like it's only a tradition." She added that many of the Amish novels she has read, especially those with protagonists who rebel against the *Ordnung,* give outsiders a false sense of who the Amish are. "They seem to think we should long for all the things you [non-Amish people] have."[18] Jennifer Anderson, the Beachy Amish woman who skewered Amish novels in her piece in a church periodical, went a few steps further in her antipathy toward the genre. Amish romance novels "create a value system in our minds that is contrary to the Bible," she wrote. "Amish novels are not Christian."[19]

In general, however, I found few Amish people who perceived the genre as threatening or offensive to their communities. Some of the Amish people with whom I spoke were amused by inaccuracies they had found in the novels, which we'll examine in chapter 9, and most demonstrated a fairly tolerant attitude toward the genre and its authors. "If they [the authors] enjoy this and it's their livelihood and if it's classed as fiction, then who am I to come along and say, 'Well, this is wrong and that's wrong'?" one Amish woman asked.[20]

Several of the Amish people with whom I spoke dismissed the books on literary grounds. Sitting outside on a warm June evening, holding her son on her lap, a young Amish mother in Ohio who taught school for eight years is eager to chat about her favorite novels by Barbara Kingsolver and James Herriott. When I ask her about Amish romance novels, she talks first about the plot weaknesses of the ones she has read and then tells me her theory of why they're so popular: "They're light reading," she says, then raises her eyebrows significantly and leans forward. "You sure never have to go for the dictionary."[21]

A middle-aged Old Order Amish woman in Pennsylvania, who calls

The Shipping News, by E. Annie Proulx, the greatest book of all time and who loves the novels of Toni Morrison and Richard Russo, also charges the books with being mediocre literature. "I'm very picky about what I read," she tells me; "No Christian fiction holds my interest." When I ask whether her friends and family read Amish novels, she says no. "They're *big* fans of Karen Kingsbury and Francine Rivers," she says. "My mother reads and reads and reads them. But they don't read Amish." And although she hasn't heard of anyone in her community who loves Amish fiction, she says that her mother and several other older women have begun passing around Danielle Steel novels—a revelation that makes her daughter, who is sipping tea, clap a hand over her mouth and slap the table in silent mirth.[22]

I can't stop smiling at the image of Amish grandmothers sneaking around with Danielle Steel contraband either, and the idea of Amish women reading Toni Morrison I find equally lovely. These revelations underscore that the Amish are diverse enough to include several taste publics, each of which values distinct kinds of literature. One Old Order Amish woman I spoke to in her kitchen in Leola, Pennsylvania, summed up the view of the Amish taste public that has no time for Amish fiction. "I know there has to be a good reason that Amish novels are so popular," she told me bluntly, "and I am not that reason."[23]

Ambivalent Readers

Not all Amish readers of Amish fiction fall so clearly into either the appreciative-reader camp or the critical one. Speaking on her cell phone one rainy September morning, after having just put her niece down for a nap, seventeen-year-old Ruthie tells me that she's not a big fan of Amish fiction and that none of her friends are either. She read some Amish novels as a young teenager but hasn't read any for several years. When she does read an Amish novel, Ruthie says, "I don't really feel like I'm reading about my own culture. They [the characters] drive horse and buggies, and we dress pretty close to the same, but other than that, I just can't relate to them."[24] The characters talk about "courting" and "betrothal," concepts that she says are outmoded in her circles, where Amish youth go out to eat on Saturday nights "just like non-Amish couples." Several other things in the Amish novels she has read "just seem odd," Ruthie says, adding that she prefers novels by Dee Henderson, who writes inspirational romantic suspense.

But as we chat, Ruthie begins recalling how absorbed she got in the story line of one Amish novel. Knowing that I was writing about Amish fiction, Ruthie had offered to help me by reading a few of the novels and telling me her impressions. The previous week her sister loaned her the second in Beverly Lewis's Rose Trilogy, *The Judgment,* which is the story of two sisters: Rose, who is considering leaving the Amish, and Hen, who left her community and now wants to return. At the end of the second book, Rose has not decided whether she will stay or go. "She's very confused as to whether she wants to stay Amish or not, and I can definitely relate to that," seventeen-year-old Ruthie tells me. "I could relate to not knowing what you want to do in life, whether you want to get a higher education."

Ruthie has been finished with school for several years and now works several days at a local market. Standing on the cusp of adulthood, with its attendant decisions regarding baptism and church membership and marriage, Ruthie is candid about her more-than-occasional doubts regarding whether she wants to remain Amish. "In *The Judgment,* it's mainly family ties that held them back," Ruthie reflects. She says she wants to bring up her own children some day with the same values she has had and worries that even if she lived "a good Christian life" as a non-Amish person, her children might fall away from any faith at all. "It seems like the next generation always takes it further," she says.

Yet there is still an undertow of restlessness in her words, a niggling curiosity about what a non-Amish future might look like. Ruthie is generally chatty, but for a moment there is silence on the other end of the line. "I kind of want to read the next one, actually," she says. Despite her mild dislike of the genre, Ruthie confesses that she wants to find out what happens at the end of the series, especially whether or not Rose stays Amish. Perched on the edge of the same decision, Ruthie giggles a little sheepishly. "I guess the books are a little more captivating than I admitted to earlier."

After our conversation, I realize how curious I am, too, about whether Rose stays Amish or leaves. The next day I stop by my local Christian bookstore, where I find the last book of the Rose Trilogy on a display rack near the door. I thumb through the final pages until I figure it out: Rose stays. Whether Rose's fictional choice will have any bearing on Ruthie's actual one is unclear. But Ruthie's identification with the protagonist, grudging though it may be, suggests that it is possible.

The Only *Amish* Amish Novelist

As I spoke with Amish people who were critical of Amish fiction, they sometimes mentioned one author as an exception. The owner of an Amish bookstore in Geauga County, Ohio, told me that although his store doesn't stock Amish-themed novels "because they usually don't have the facts accurate," they do sell the novels of Linda Byler.[25]

No one else in the field can claim the bona fides of Byler. Although many of the Amish authors do diligent research and vet their manuscripts with Amish people before publication, as we will see in the next chapter, and although some have familial ties to Anabaptism and one—Jerry Eicher—is formerly Amish, Byler is the only currently Amish person writing Amish novels that are available to a general readership. Add the fact that some of Byler's novels are based on her own life experiences, and she has pretty much got the "authentic and accurate" competition sewn up.

Were "Amish" and "celebrity" not antipodes, one could use them both to describe Byler, what with the vanloads of Amish fans stopping by her house in Franklin County, Pennsylvania, and her books being sold in Walmart and Barnes & Noble. *Running Around (and Such)*, her first roman à clef marketed to a wide audience, sold 62,000 copies in its first year and a half. Her five novels, including the first two in the Sadie's Montana series, had sold more than 256,000 by mid 2012. While those sales are a fraction of Beverly Lewis's, they're impressive numbers given that her small publisher's marketing budget is trifling compared to that of Bethany House.[26]

Not long ago, Byler was a self-published author who stashed her inventory of books in her dining room and garage and filled handwritten orders herself. She started writing books in 2003, when a family-owned business failed and money was extremely tight. "So of course, I thought about what I could do to help financially," Byler says. "And Amish women can only do so much—we can clean houses or quilt or . . . well, what else can we do?

And I thought of writing."[27] Byler, a much-loved columnist for the Amish newspaper *Die Botschaft*, modeled her first book about a protagonist named Lizzie after Laura Ingalls Wilder's Little House on the Prairie books. It contains the fictionalized account of Byler's own life between the ages of five and nine. The book is filled mostly with stories from an Amish childhood—miniature ponies, a sister's rheumatic fever, a new teacher at school. By briefly explaining the way Amish do things, the book includes occasional nods to the possibility of a non-Amish reader.

When she had finished the manuscript, Byler traveled out to Carlisle Printing in Walnut Creek, Ohio, with the handwritten manuscript in a single composition notebook and hired the printer to do a first run of five thousand copies. She recalls lying awake at night after she returned home, wondering whether book sales would even begin to recoup the costs of printing. Five thousand copies cost about fifteen thousand dollars, a staggering amount of money for an Amish family already in financial crisis and not accustomed to carrying debt.

Byler needn't have worried. Carlisle Printing sent brochures about the book to Amish-owned bookstores around the country, and before long, orders were pouring in. The first book eventually sold about 12,500 copies, and Byler kept writing more books, about two a year, aging Lizzie as she went. "I remember coming from the mailbox with little handfuls of orders—oh, it was just a thrill!" Byler recalls. The Buggy Spoke series sold more than 60,000 copies in all. It is thus conceivable that a majority of Amish youth in the United States have not only heard of the Lizzie books but have read them.

I meet Byler one cold January morning in the offices of her publisher, Good Books. Exuding a self-effacing confidence, Byler is eager to chat about her work and about Amish fiction more generally. Byler's editor and publisher, Phyllis Pellman Good, joins us for the conversation. Phyllis and her husband, Merle, own a constellation of businesses in Intercourse, Pennsylvania, including a bookstore. Good Books is best known for its *New York Times*-bestselling cookbooks of slow-cooker recipes, but on its publishing backlist are a considerable number of books about Amish and Mennonite life.

Phyllis Pellman Good first became aware of Byler when staff members in the bookstore began raving to her about the self-published Amish novels that they were pulling off the shelves to read during their lunch breaks. "Suddenly we were hearing from about three different staff members— maybe more than that—who were telling us, 'These Lizzie books are fantastic!'" Good recalls. "We get lots and lots of submissions in this Amish-fiction genre, and we have just pretty categorically said no. We just didn't see our way clear to publish them. Then we read the Lizzie books and said, 'There is a gifted writer here. There is an authentic story here. Maybe there is an opportunity here for us and for Linda.'"

And the rest is history. Good Books editors revised the seven-book series into three volumes, which focus less on Lizzie's childhood and more on her adolescence and budding romantic life. So far, Good Books is the only publisher that can lay claim to the text emblazoned on the front cover of Byler's books: "A novel based on true experiences from an Amish writer!" *Wild Horses,* the first installment of Byler's new Amish-fiction series, Sadie's Montana, received a glowing review from *Publishers Weekly,* which says the novel is set apart from the rest of the subgenre by its "rich detail of Amish life and . . . the lack of melodrama."[28] The third book, *The Disappearances,* was released in September 2012.

If one has read a slew of Amish novels, Byler's books may feel a little like a hiccup. Her novels unapologetically violate several conventions of the Amish romance genre. The love interest, Stephen, doesn't appear until halfway through the first book, in chapter 20, and even then there's no chemistry. "He's different!" Lizzie tells her sister after she meets him. "He's so quiet, he gives me the creeps."[29] And thanks to Lizzie's frequent self-doubt and good-natured reports of herself as unattractive, readers may only rarely experience what Janice Radway says is one of the central attributes of a romance novel: what it feels like to be the object of desire in a courtship. The plots of the Lizzie books mosey along somewhere below the surface, and the narratives tilt toward the mundane, with lengthy riffs on Lizzie's homesickness as a *Maud* (house help) for other families, washing diapers with a wringer washer, learning to sew dresses, and butchering chickens. There are no shunnings, no buggy accidents, no violations of the *Ordnung* greater than too-transparent stockings and too many gathers in a dress sleeve. Instead, there are generous helpings of teenaged angst: about boys, pimples, and ultimately one's place in the world. Lizzie is impetuous, jealous of her sister, and given to eating four creme-filled doughnuts at a time. In fact, judging from the reviews on Amazon, some readers find the protagonist downright unattractive. "Lizzie is very self-centered and often ignorant of the wants, needs and expectations of others," wrote one reviewer. "She is a whiner, shirks her duties and plays the 'I'm ugly and no one loves me' card way too often. She irritated me and I wanted someone to tell her what's what."[30]

Lizzie is indeed not always likable, and she lacks the earnest piety that imbues many Amish protagonists. But there is a sprightly step to Byler's prose, a waggishness, even, which lends a picaresque quality to the narrative. One reader described Byler's novels to me as "bouncy." Lizzie's thoughts about everything from high heels to husbands are mostly irreverent, as in this passage, in which she notices handsome twins in her new school and thinks back to her mother's frequent lectures about choosing a marriage partner not for his good looks but for his character. "The way Mam sometimes made it sound, all the handsome boys weren't good husbands—just the homely ones. It caused Lizzie to fall into a great state of sadness most times when Mam gave them that lecture. . . . Well, Lizzie was too young to take this husband matter very seriously, but she certainly hoped one of these twins would be God's will, as Mam put it. She couldn't wait to talk to Mandy after school to ask her which twin she wanted."[31]

When she does try to be obedient or reverent, Lizzie mostly fails and usually ends up comparing herself to her older sister, Emma, whose many virtues seem effortless. "Concentrating seemed to be Lizzie's problem. Dat told them to thank the Lord for their food and to look down at their plates as they prayed. Lizzie often forgot to pray because she was peeping at someone or thinking other thoughts. . . . She tried hard though. Emma dropped her head far and moved her lips as she said her silent prayer. Lizzie often watched her sideways, fascinated by her goodness."[32] Lizzie matures throughout the course of the trilogy and gains a greater trust in God and commitment to her Amish faith. But even after she marries, the immediacy of her voice is not lost, and the earthiness of her early adolescent self remains.

Readers accustomed to the appealing protagonists, devotional qualities, and romantic tension of most Amish romance novels may find the Lizzie books a rough ride. Like Joseph Yoder's *Rosanna of the Amish*, the Lizzie books could be considered autoethnographies: reflexive texts of experience situated within a particular culture. Eric Miller, writing about the Lizzie books in *Christianity Today*, notes that, in some places, the series "has the feel of a translation."[33] If the usual Amish-fiction aesthetic parallels the smooth, idealized vision of Thomas Kinkade's country cottages and arbors, Byler's approximates the rustic oeuvre of Grandma Moses, one of Byler's heroes because of her late start in painting and her commitment to her artistic ideas regardless of how primitive they appeared to others.[34] "Byler's story is a romance, to be sure, a graceful celebration of Amish life," Miller writes. "But more deeply, it's a celebration of life itself, absent the melodrama of the other stories. A comic vision guides Byler's narrative, in which reconciliation and union are the final, unmerited, blessed end."[35]

The comic vision that guides Byler's prose is apparent in her person as well. As we finish the interview, I ask Byler what she thinks of the way that Good Books has packaged her novels, complete with the requisite pretty model on the front and whoopie pie recipes in the back. Like other publishers of Amish fiction, Good Books hired a design firm to do the front covers. Since hearing so much hilarity from Amish women about Amish-fiction covers' inaccuracies, from the mismatched Pennsylvania-Amish dress paired with Indiana-Amish covering to the bangs leaking out from the front of the covering, I am curious what Byler thinks of her own books. She has mentioned that she didn't much care for the covers of her self-published books, which she drew herself, with their roughhewn sketches of buggies and Flat Stanley-esque Amish girls. But I am curious whether the bust of a clear-skinned maiden rising above an idealized rural landscape strikes her as preferable. Byler's publisher has stepped out of the room for a moment, so I'm hoping that she can speak freely—although knowing Lizzie, Byler's fictional self, she is likely to speak her mind no matter who is around.

Byler picks up a copy of *When Strawberries Bloom,* the second in the Lizzie Searches for Love series, and holds it in the air for scrutiny. "Well, the cape? Oh my, it's pitiful how they put that on." She points out some error in how the model's *Halsduch* is draped, some false angle or scrunched-up lay of the fabric. I can't quite follow her explanation, and she acknowledges that it would seem a minor detail to an English person like me. And the model's hairstyle—is that accurate? I ask. "Yeah, well, she's really done sloppy, but

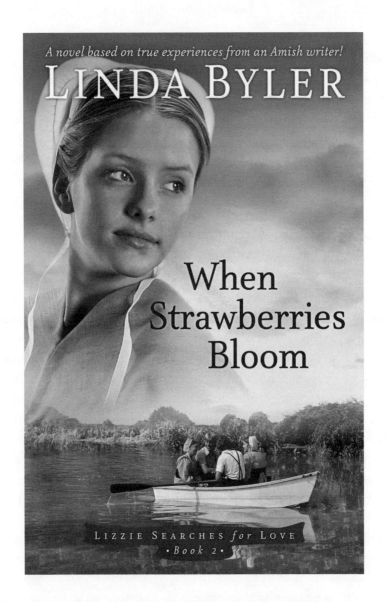

A novel based on true experiences from an Amish writer!

LINDA BYLER

When
Strawberries
Bloom

LIZZIE SEARCHES *for* LOVE
• Book 2 •

When Strawberries Bloom *(2011), by Amish writer Linda Byler, is an edited
and repackaged version of her self-published* Lizzie's Teen Years.
Used by permission of Good Books.

yeah," Byler says drolly. Then she waves her hand in the air as if to dismiss her critique. "But this is all fine, because these people do not know. I like the covers, actually."

As we leave, Byler tells me that friends and acquaintances, having seen her books in bookstores or at Walmart, sometimes ask whether the cover photo is of her when she was younger. "'Is that you? Is that you?' they ask a lot," Byler says. She huffs good-naturedly. "They should know it's not me because I'd never wear my *Halsduch* that way."

Toward the Authentic and Accurate

It is unclear how much traction Linda Byler gets from being an honest-to-goodness Amish author in a field of non-Amish authors. A marketing manager for one of the evangelical houses dismisses any threat Byler might pose to his own authors. "Of course she gets high marks where you're in close to Amish communities," he told me on the phone. "People in southeastern Pennsylvania or Holmes County, Ohio, they appreciate her writing. Now in Phoenix, people don't know and don't care."

To what extent terms like *authenticity* and *accuracy* even matter to most readers of Amish fiction is uncertain. When readers are looking for a good story, how much do they care about its facticity? And what does it even mean to say that a novel is authentic or accurate? What measure of fact is required of fiction, and how beholden are makers of fictional worlds to the vagaries of the real one?

At least some of these questions lie behind the most frequent inquiry I received from people when they heard about my research. "How accurate are the novels?" many people asked; if I heard it once, I must have heard it twenty times. Some readers of Amish fiction asked me for recommendations on which authors are writing the most authentic novels, so that they could read those and not waste their time on others. My friend Richard Stevick, a psychologist who has written a book about Amish youth culture, rendered the question into a command one morning over breakfast, when he told me firmly that I really *must* deal with this question of accuracy.[36]

So since Rich is an amiable bloke and rarely so bossy, I figured I should at least consider his point.

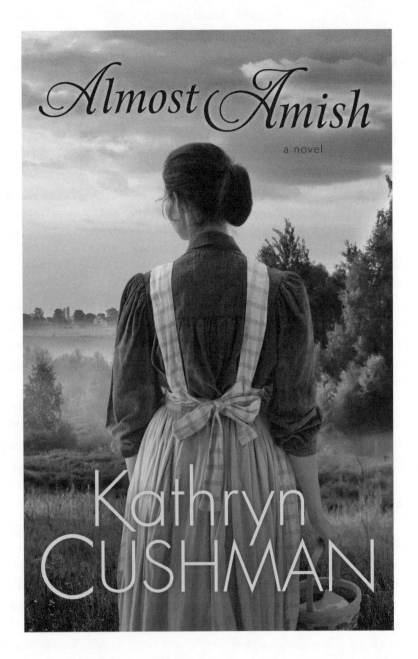

In Almost Amish *(2012), by Kathryn Cushman, the protagonist participates in a reality show in which she must "go Amish."*
Used by permission of Baker Publishing Group.

ॐ Chapter Nine ॐ

Something Borrowed,
Something True

Whenever anyone asked me whether Amish novels are accurate—
or in Rich's case, told me I'd better find out—I usually mumbled
something vague and entirely unhelpful. I would say it depends on whether
you're talking about a specific author or the entire subgenre, or whether
you're talking about authors getting details right or about authors "getting"
the Amish in a more macro sense. Occasionally I'd become evasive like
Bill Clinton in his 1998 grand-jury testimony. "That depends on what your
definition of 'accurate' is," I'd say and slink away. I doubt I ever gave anyone
the answer they were looking for, partly because I wanted to argue with the
question.

My resistance to the question relates, oddly enough, to the figurine of
the Amish woman that Ceil's husband expertly carved and generously proffered. Sitting beside my computer, extending her basket with an enigmatic
smile, she testifies that novels, like wood carvings, are works of the imagination and that creators of both must be granted some leeway when it
comes to this question of accuracy. Inquiring after the facticity of Amish
novels can suggest that accuracy and authenticity should be a novelist's
highest commitments. But Amish-themed novels require a different rubric
from sociological studies of the Amish or scholarly accounts of their history or theology—and those accounts are mediated, too, although to a lesser

degree than fiction. Just as Ceil's husband Jack made choices with regard to wood, grain, tool, and angle as he carved his Amish figurine, it is a novelist's prerogative to stylize and amend, to pick and choose among details, to amplify some attributes and minimize others.[1]

"It is hard for fiction to make mistakes," writes critic Terry Eagleton, "because one of the invisible instructions which accompanies it is: 'Take everything said here as intended.'" Writers of fiction strike a bargain, of sorts, with readers: I will tell you a story I've made up, and you will agree not to believe it. "You cannot lie in fiction, because the reader does not assume that you are intending to be truthful," Eagleton writes.[2] And if readers assume that Amish fiction offers an objective, documentary-like understanding of Amish life and thought, then they are violating the fictional bargain. As one author of Amish fiction told me, "I am a storyteller. I have never portrayed myself as an expert on the Amish. . . . I'm weaving a story that is meant to entertain. So it's not, 'Read my book and now you're going to know all you need to know about the Amish.'"

No one author should be held responsible for the composite impression created from a raft of Amish novels. Say, for instance, that one novelist wants to write about shunning. Say that other novelists also decide to write about shunning. Although Amish people in some settlements, especially more progressive ones, may during their entire lives know only one or two people who have been shunned, a reader of several Amish novels may walk away thinking Amish people are shunned as regularly as the cows are milked. Yet this not the responsibility of any particular author. Since plot possibilities lie most thickly in liminal spaces, novelists will likely be drawn to stories of *Rumspringa* and shunning and English-Amish romance, all of which play the line between belonging and exclusion.

In addition, the question operates from a modernist assumption that there is one accurate representation of Amish life to be had. Postmodern theory would remind us that there *is* no normative Amish man or woman, and to construct a novel based on some totalizing Amish metanarrative would be to ignore the heterogeneity of Amish life. More salient for our purposes—unearthing the cultural and religious work that Amish novels perform in the lives of readers—are questions of appropriation, exoticism, domestication, and whiteness, which we deal with later in this chapter.

Novelists cannot be released from all responsibility to the actual world, however, especially when they're writing stories about a living ethnic and religious culture to which they and most of their readers do not belong. Representing one culture to another comes with a host of ethical responsibilities, and the ancillary dangers—circulation of misinformation, appropriation of cultural symbols, assertion of control—are many.

We will examine some of these basic responsibilities of representation and dangers of appropriation in the second part of this chapter. But aside from those larger questions, it is clear that writing about another culture presents narrative hurdles of the most basic kind.[3] How would a married woman greet her brother-in-law? Is mealtime characterized by conversation or silence? What do adolescent boys talk about when adults aren't around? Sufficient research requires not only reading scholarship and history of Amish life but building relationships with Amish people, or at least obtaining some Amish informants. Even within postmodernism, it is possible to say that some representations approximate reality more than others, and that some authors do their research more carefully than others.[4]

Readers do trust authors in this regard, assuming the basic architecture of the narrative to be sturdy and solidly researched. The nature and dates of historic-sounding events, the customs and habits and dress and lifestyle of the characters: readers trust novelists of historical and ethnic fiction to clad their narratives with factual skin. Such fictions should be enveloped in fact, most readers would assert, so that by reading them they are not only entertained but informed, not only transported to a *different* place or time but to a *real* one. The standard of accuracy to which readers hold the books they read will vary; some readers will likely be quite forgiving of any mistakes, given that they are reading for pleasure, while others will be disappointed, having assumed that they were getting only accurate information about the Amish from the books.[5]

So even though I would much rather argue with the question of accuracy than answer it, what follows is a brief discussion of the accuracy of Amish romance novels. After examining whether Amish fiction can be considered factually *appropriate,* in the second half of the chapter we ask whether it is *appropriating.*

Researching the Amish

Many novelists of Amish fiction demonstrate impressive knowledge of the Amish, their practices, and the distinctions between Amish settlements. One Amish person wrote to Wanda Brunstetter that it was hard for her to believe that Brunstetter wasn't Amish herself, so authentic did her books feel, and an Amish reviewer wrote in the *Connection,* a periodical with a primarily Amish audience, "Wanda, you have definitely done your homework and I can tell you have a feel for our community."[6] The authors I spoke with were both solemnly committed to extensive research and humble about any claims to exhaustive knowledge of Amish life. Most rely on interlocking sources—contacts and friendships with Amish people, nonfiction scholarship on Amish life, and ethnographic observation when visiting Amish settlements. Several regularly read the *Budget* or another Amish newspaper and visit Amish friends and acquaintances—or, in the case of Jerry Eicher, Dale Cramer, and a few others, family. Several have lived with an Amish family for a period of time.

There are exceptions, such as the author who makes one research trip to Lancaster County, asks some questions of another Amish-fiction author, and then considers herself sufficiently informed. One author recounts that, when she confessed to her agent that she knew nothing about the Amish except that they drove buggies and wore "little white hats," the agent replied, "That's what research is for." Six weeks later, the author had submitted a partial Amish-fiction manuscript and been taken on as a client, and the agent had told her to "hurry up" and finish the book.

In general, however, as one editor told me about her authors, "They work *very* hard to get their facts straight. No one intends to be wrong." Many editors insist that their authors give due diligence to their research. "I encourage them to find a local contact," Zondervan editor Sue Brower tells me. "I don't think the fans will let you get away with bad information. If you have any of your Amish facts wrong, word gets out."[7]

Having manuscripts stamped with Amish credibility becomes critical as the category becomes clotted with more writers, and publishers are devoted to spreading the word about their authors' standards for accuracy. In addition to personal connections to the Amish or another Anabaptist group, as we saw in the preface, authors are adding other qualifications. One Amish-fiction author advertises her membership in the Lancaster Mennonite Historical Society on her website and in marketing copy for her books, although she both misnames the organization and fails to mention that it is open to anyone willing to pay the forty-dollar membership fee. The most common credibility mechanism among Amish-fiction authors, however, is the vetting of a manuscript with an Amish informant or friend before (or in some cases after) the book goes to press. Designed in the hope that the reader will catch inaccuracies about Amish culture or faith or improbable thoughts, dialogue, or action, the "Amish audit" has become de rigueur in the field. Cindy Woodsmall frequently mentions the fact-checking of her Amish friend Miriam Flaud, who has caught inaccuracies such as Lancaster Amish people riding bikes (instead of the more common scooters) and errors in Pennsylvania Dutch.[8] One author gives credit to a Mennonite college professor with Amish relatives who vets her manuscripts, and another author hires an Amish-Mennonite couple to read her books.[9] One new author advertises that her stories are "read and approved by two Amish readers in Lancaster County, Pennsylvania who critique everything through the lens of Amish experience." Amy Clipston told a reporter about an error that her Amish consultant caught: "I had them eating macaroni and cheese on Sunday after church, and she told me that they don't eat macaroni and cheese on Sundays."[10]

Obtaining an Amish imprimatur is an important step toward producing more accurate and authentic portrayals of the Amish. Yet corrections of culinary or transportation slipups do not an error-free manuscript make. One Amish woman who reads prepublication manuscripts for an Amish-fiction author suggested to me that although it's easy to fix small inaccuracies, such as details of dress or technology use in her community, it's more difficult to help an author create authentic-feeling dialogue and practices, a character's thought life, or a community's ethos. "People just don't have a grip on the culture," she told me, struggling to find words for her inchoate sense that the manuscripts she has read and vetted are a little off, somehow; "They just don't."

That question—whether any outsider can "have a grip on the culture"—is one that sociologists and anthropologists have batted about for years. Writers of Amish fiction, by and large, make admirable attempts and deserve credit for their research and efforts to faithfully mediate Amish culture to their readers. But they face a daunting task, one that occasionally stymies some of them.

Just the Facts: Major and Minor

Stephen Scott's knowledge of the Amish was as wide as his beard was long. A convert to the Old Order River Brethren, an Anabaptist group that allows cars and electricity but maintains conservative dress and other markers of separation from the world, Steve was sometimes mistaken for Amish. Having arrived in Lancaster County in 1969, after attending a Baptist college and becoming interested in plain sects, Steve stayed and ended up marrying the daughter of a River Brethren bishop. "I suppose I could write my own romance novel based on my experiences," he used to say, a characteristic smile parting his beard.

Steve died of a heart attack as I was writing this book. As a research associate at the Young Center for Anabaptist and Pietist Studies at Elizabethtown College, and known by some friends as "Mr. Anabaptist," Steve wrote six books and many articles about the Amish and the Anabaptists and contributed to encyclopedias, magazines, and journals. He sometimes lectured on the topic "How Factual Is Amish Fiction?" and was contacted by several Amish-fiction authors with questions about Amish practices and lifestyle.

Steve Scott took extensive handwritten notes on many of the Amish novels he had read, with chapter numbers in the margins and comments that reveal more than a little impatience with inaccuracies: misleading spellings of Pennsylvania German words, misrepresented ecclesial practices, improbable conversations between Amish people or reactions to events. Although some of the authors have evidently done a great deal of research on the Amish, Steve maintained that a "major misunderstanding of basic Amish beliefs and practices" exists within the genre.[11]

Criticism about inaccuracies in Amish fiction fall into at least two registers, what I'll call major and minor—although the relative importance of any of these is open to debate. Minor mistakes include things like mangled Pennsylvania German dialect and inaccurate portrayal of Amish use of technology. Major inaccuracies include misunderstandings of shunning, which we'll examine, and misrepresentation of Amish soteriology and the bishopric, which we looked at in chapter 5. We begin with minor errors, move to more major errors in the portrayal of shunning, and then take up the biggest breach of the subgenre thus far: the invention of a cultural practice that, as far as I can tell, does not exist.

Minor

The devil is in the details, and it is in details that Amish novels sometimes flounder. A quick sampling, from a variety of novels: one Amish person calls another "Mr." rather than using his first name; characters have family names like Benner, Friesen, Swartley, and Gaymen, which appear in Mennonite communities, not Amish ones;[12] two Amish adults not in *Rumspringa* sip cappuccino at a McDonald's on a Sunday afternoon; words like *bitte* and *mein Gott*, which are High German and not Pennsylvania Dutch, pepper the dialogue; letters sent between Amish people are written in Pennsylvania Dutch instead of English; the *Ordnung*, or unwritten code of behavior, is referred to as the "leadership" of the church and granted human consciousness, as in "the *Ordnung* would say he had no choice"; a contemporary Amish home in Paradise, Pennsylvania, is depicted as having no indoor plumbing.

In some books, inaccuracies like these are few and far between; in others, a critical mass of small mistakes can quickly accrue. Once when I asked Steve Scott to read a wedding scene from an Amish romance novel, he found seven errors in the space of two pages. The Amish people with whom I spoke often highlighted similar details in the novels they'd read: Amish surnames appear in the wrong Amish settlement, an Amish woman hugs a male who is not related to her, Amish characters leave their buggy beside the road but apparently never tie up their horse, Amish characters eat at restaurants more frequently than a wealthy English family on vacation.

More often, however, the Amish readers I spoke with mentioned an intangible feeling of dissonance, a sense that many of the books are slightly off key, that they haven't managed to capture the texture of Amish life. "They're just so artificial," one Amish teenager told an Amish man, who relayed her comment to me. Saloma Miller Furlong, who grew up Amish and has written a memoir about leaving the church of her childhood, concurs. "I have quite given up on reading Amish fiction, unless it is by someone who was Amish," Furlong wrote on her blog. "I don't care how careful someone is when writing about the Amish, there is just no way for someone in mainstream America to 'get it right,' because there are so many nuances about the Amish culture/life/religion that one only gets from having lived it. I don't often make blanket statements like this, but I've given enough Amish fiction books a try to be able to say that."[13]

Still, while some of the novels may get some facts or nuances wrong, these inaccuracies are generally invisible to anyone outside a relatively small crowd of Anabaptist cognoscenti: those with direct ligatures to the Amish, whether of friendship, kinship, ecclesiology, proximity, or past. In fact, it is likely that Amish fiction clears up more popular misconceptions about the Amish than it creates. To charge novelists with propagating misconceptions about the Amish based on a few erroneous details, such as the number of suspenders worn by men in a particular community, is to assume that their readers initially know enough about the Amish to have those perceptions corrupted. Rather, someone reading an Amish novel for the first time will likely gain more information about Amish life and culture—most of it accurate—than they had before reading the book.[14]

And if readers walk away thinking that the Amish in Lancaster County drive black buggies instead of gray, or that Amish people write letters in Pennsylvania German rather than English, has any real harm been done? To the extent that readers of these novels are looking for an "Amishish" experience rather than a watertight nonfiction analysis, the subgenre, in general, delivers.

Major: Shunning

The prominence of shunning in Amish fiction as a category is, as I pointed out earlier, problematic, although not the fault of any one novelist. One Old

Order Amish grandmother told me that during her lifetime she had known only one person who was shunned—although reading many Amish novels may make one think that shunning occurs in Amish communities as often as weddings or funerals do. Given how frequently shunning is represented in the pages of Amish fiction, as well as the complexity of this mechanism of ceremonial shaming, it is perhaps inevitable that it would at times be inaccurately portrayed.

Several novels suggest that excommunication occurs for minor infractions of the *Ordnung*, the unwritten rules of the church district, for things over which one has no control, or simply for things that would not result in shunning in most Amish communities: playing a guitar or humming a non-Amish song, studying the Bible, moving to a different Amish community after one has taken vows in one's home district, getting pregnant from a rape, or allowing one's live-in English niece to be too wild. In reality, shunning is usually reserved for members who repeatedly refuse to adhere to the *Ordnung*, and the *Bann* is rarely applied at the whim of the bishop or other church leaders, as portrayed in at least some Amish novels. In Adina Senft's novel *The Wounded Heart*, Amish protagonist Amelia is diagnosed with multiple sclerosis and wants to undergo a treatment in Mexico involving cow myelin, a procedure that her church doesn't condone. "The elders have as much as said they'd put me under the *Bann* if I went," she tells her friends. One friend says she'll help her raise money to get to Mexico in any way she can—even if it means that she has to "write a novel and sell sixty thousand copies." "Where did that girl get her outlandish ideas?" Amelia thinks to herself. "Then you'd be put under the *Bann* too."[15] According to Steve Scott, both scenarios—being immediately shunned for pursuing alternative medical treatment and for writing a novel—are unlikely in most Amish communities.

Shunning in most Amish communities means not eating, doing business, or accepting help from the offender. Talking with the one who is being shunned is encouraged, as is offering assistance to the person in the hopes that she might be won back to the church. "Members are encouraged to help, assist, and visit people under the ban," writes Donald B. Kraybill in *The Riddle of Amish Culture*. "Thus, shunning is an asymmetrical, one-way relationship. Members can help offenders, but offenders may not have the dignity of aiding a member."[16] Katie Lapp, who is brought under the *Bann* in Lewis's *The Shunning*, finds something else entirely. Her family refuses to speak with her or accept written notes from her, and they begin treating her as if she were invisible. Katie also remembers "her Mammi Essie telling about a man who had been shunned for using tractor power. None of the People could so much as speak to him or eat with him, lest they be shunned too. 'It's like a death in the family,' Essie told her."[17] In *The Confession*, the musical adaptation of Lewis's The Heritage of Lancaster County series, the shunning scene riffs on a courtroom drama in which a guilty verdict is handed down. Above the ominous chords of a bass guitar, the bishop's deep voice bellows out the shunning order—"From henceforth there will be no communication with this individual. Katie Lapp no longer exists in this community." A transparent curtain hangs between the actress playing Katie and the Amish congregants, who are backlit so their faces are in shadow. Choking down sobs, Katie rips off her covering and runs offstage.

Related to such portrayals of shunning is the fact that the *Ordnung*, or set of implicit and explicit directives that guide Amish practice in each district, is rarely portrayed as something that the community ratifies and that the bishop enforces. Nor is the *Ordnung* depicted as "organic, malleable, dynamic, and subject to varied interpretation by leaders," as several scholars suggest that it is.[18] In many of the novels, the *Ordnung* seems to issue from the figure of the bishop himself and appears as inflexible and oppressive as he is.

The enlargement of shunning's frequency, purview, and severity in Amish fiction, as well as the stiff representation of the *Ordnung*, might be seen as performing an additional religious task in the lives of evangelical readers, as we saw in chapter 4: reminding them whence they came. As Eric Miller writes in *Christianity Today*, in the 1960s and following decades, many evangelicals began shedding the fundamentalist layers that they found stifling. "If these writers find fault with the Amish on this count— order gone bad—it has a lot to do with their own stories."[19] In that sense, metastasized versions of shunning and the *Ordnung* may appeal to evangelical Christians as reminders of both their fundamentalism-wrapped history and their distance from it.

As Amish fiction as a category has magnified shunning beyond its actual size, it has also, by all appearances, manufactured a cultural practice out of thin air.

The Mythic Man Swap

Laura Hilton's three-book series The Amish of Seymour revolves around the supposed trading of men between Amish communities to widen the Amish gene pool. Hilton, who lives with her husband and five children in Arkansas, summarized her first novel, *Patchwork Dreams*, in a blog interview soon after the book came out: "Jacob Miller believes he was sent to the Old Order Community in Missouri to help out a distant cousin. Instead, he discovers he was part of an arranged swap—sending men from his Pennsylvania district to the Missouri district to bring new blood into the Amish community."[20] Jacob first learns from his Missouri host, Daniel, that he is a pawn in the bishops' scheme to reduce the incidence of genetic diseases caused by DNA slim pickings: "Our bishop put out a request for young men to be sent to our area to marry and settle down," Daniel tells Jacob. "Your name is on that list. Your daed told us that they were coming out early to get a start looking for property. To get first pick of the women." Jacob feels betrayed by his father, who put him in the "man swap" without Jacob's consent in order to remove him from a girlfriend with an affinity for the guitar. In Hilton's second book, another young man, Jacob's friend Matthew Yoder, is traded for the sake of genetic variety. Matthew appears first in *Patchwork Dreams*. "He came down to be part of the swap," Jacob says casually as he introduces Matthew to a friend.[21]

During a conversation with Hilton on *Amish Wisdom*, interviewer and novelist Suzanne Woods Fisher manages a generous tone even as she sounds dubious about the claim that Amish communities are trading young men like baseball teams trade players. "Did you ever meet anyone who had participated in something like that?" Fisher asks. No, Hilton responds. When Fisher asks gently after her research methods, Hilton recounts reading about the man swap in another Amish novel. Beverly Lewis's Abram's Daughters series includes the trading of men between Ohio and Pennsylvania Amish communities.[22]

Fisher retains her composure in the interview with Hilton, even as it's clear that she is perplexed by the use of another novel as a primary source. "There's nothing like original sourcing," Fisher says, after hinting ever so slightly that Hilton would do well to keep building her contacts among the Amish. "It's such a help, even as you're writing fiction, to know that you're writing credibly."[23]

Fisher's kindly submerged skepticism about the man swap is well-founded. When I ask experts on Amish life and Amish people themselves about whether Amish men are ever swapped, the response is mostly furrowed eyebrows and cocked heads. Amish scholar Donald B. Kraybill suggests that the tale sounds like several other legends circulating among English people about Amish sexual practices, such as one he heard recently: that Amish men encourage their oldest daughters to have sex with English men to introduce new genetic lines to their family. The man swap sounds similar, Kraybill says. Although an Amish man in Lancaster may work for a period of time in Ohio or Indiana and eventually marry a woman from that settlement, "it would never be arranged in order to deliberately introduce new genetic partners into the community. Frankly, it's quite laughable from a factual research perspective."[24] Another scholar of Amish life, Steven Nolt, agrees; "Particularly in smaller communities, people may have to travel to find a spouse, but that's not 'swapping' like she describes it," Nolt tells me.[25] No academic accounts of Amish history or life mention such a practice. When I ask one Amish man about the man swap, he first looks startled and then chuckles. The idea that Amish communities would essentially "dump chlorine into their gene pool," as he puts it, keeps him amused for the remainder of our interview.[26]

What the Amish man-swap legend demonstrates is not that Amish fiction is categorically untrustworthy or that Amish-fiction readers are inherently gullible. Many authors carefully consult scholarship about the Amish, conduct interviews with Amish friends or informants, and visit Amish communities. It does, however, illustrate the extent to which Amish novels are being read as nonfiction, and in this case even as primary research documents for an emerging author. Since many writers within a genre are also readers of the same, the content of early novels, assumed to be accurate, begins to generate new content.

The man swap also demonstrates the difficulty of writing about a culture to which one does not belong, as well as how easy it is to swap fiction and "fact," with most readers being none the wiser. Ultimately, for readers looking to swap the demands and distractions of hypermodernity for the comforts and coherence of an older order, trading truth for myth may seem an insignificant exchange indeed.

English Body, Amish Soul: Appropriating the Amish

Despite a few man-swap-sized exceptions, we could say that Amish fiction, in general and broadly conceived, is factually *appropriate* and offers many readers a fuller picture of Amish life than they previously possessed. Perhaps more salient than the question of whether Amish fiction is appropriate, however, is the manner in which it *appropriates*. When non-Amish novelists write fiction about the Amish for a mostly non-Amish audience, it is possible that they borrow something essential from the community, such that it now becomes the property not of the community in which it originated but of the mediator who extracted it.

Cultural appropriation is a term often applied to the dominant white culture's use and abuse of artwork, artifacts, styles, and motifs poached from minority racial and ethnic groups, such as American Indians. Some distinguish the term *appropriation* from *exchange* or *borrowing*, so that *appropriation* implies an imbalance of power and harm to the integrity of the appropriated community, and *exchange* or *borrowing* suggests relative equality and more neutral ethical tones. Philosopher James O. Young broadly defines cultural appropriation as "any use of something developed in one cultural context by someone who belongs to another culture."[27] In that sense, appropriation may be inevitable in any cultural exchange. If so, the issue becomes whether a subgenre like Amish fiction appropriates culture carefully or carelessly.

The Sanguine View: Appreciation, Not Appropriation

One could argue that cultural appropriation is not operative in Amish fiction, since one person's appropriation is another's heartfelt cross-cultural transaction. When a writer decides to use first-person prologues and epilogues in her novel, written in the voice of the Amish protagonist, is it appropriation or artistic prerogative? When a novelist closes her e-mail messages and newsletter entries with "Em Gott sei Friede" ("God's peace" in Pennsylvania German) and another signs off her website "Mitt liebe" ("With love"), is it appropriation or linguistic tribute?[28]

Authors of Amish fiction almost always use terms like "respect" and "admiration" and "love" when describing their feelings toward the Amish. "I deeply respect the Amish faith and enjoy exploring it in my stories," Mindy Starns Clark told an interviewer from the *Christian Post.* "I'm eager to continue correcting inaccuracies about the Amish, what they believe and why they live the way they do."[29] Cynthia Keller, author of two Amish Christmas novels, told one interviewer, "It's so important to me to do right by these people."[30] Another writer called them "an endearing people" whom she would never want to offend, and one author's website address is www .loveamish.com. While at times patronizing or panegyric in their language about the Amish, several of the writers hold nuanced understandings of conversing, writing, and publishing across cultures, and few would consider their work to be appropriative. They view their work as increasing readers' empathy for the Amish and creating bridges of cross-cultural sensitivity to a people from whom they say they have learned much and whom many outsiders misunderstand. "No one I have read is trying to diss the Amish," one editor told me. "They are always trying to honor" them.

Also, despite its use of an Amish setting and characters, an Amish novel is not an artifact extracted from a native burial site and transported to an urban museum. Nor are the Amish a subaltern or indigenous or racially minor people. Unlike American Indians and African Americans and other groups at the mercy of colonialism, the Amish have generally prospered in the land of the free. Although they were persecuted for their faith, the oppression took place in another land five centuries ago; the lack of a clear and current power differential between evangelical writers and their fictional Amish subjects may raise questions about whether the term *appropriation* even fits. It certainly makes it much less clear than the cultural appropriation that Lenore Keeshig-Tobias writes about in her essay "Stop Stealing Native Stories," in which she lambasts non-Native Canadians for telling

Native Canadian stories through documentaries, novels, and other media.[31] Speaking for the Other takes on a less sinister aura when that Other—in this case, the Amish—has not been clearly silenced but simply appears to have little interest in speaking for itself.

Furthermore, to suggest that novelists should *never* write cross-culturally or in the voice of a character different from themselves would be to condemn books like *Cry, the Beloved Country* or *At Play in the Fields of the Lord*. Fictionalizing the Other has a distinguished literary history—Faulkner did it in *Go Down, Moses*, William Styron did it in *The Confessions of Nat Turner*, and Kazuo Ishiguro did it in *Remains of the Day*. Fiction is often more about the Other than about oneself, and novelists' freedom to inhabit the skin of someone unlike themselves is a critical aspect of their work. Otherwise, cultural identity becomes a property that no outsider may transgress and literature itself becomes impoverished.[32] "I reject anything that limits the imagination," writer Neil Bisoondath fumed in a letter to the editor in the *Globe and Mail* regarding a debate over non-Native Canadians' telling Native stories. "No one has the right to tell me who I should or should not write about, and telling me what or how I do that amounts to censorship."[33]

The Critical View: Borrowing and Benefiting

Yet, while it is difficult to diagnose cultural appropriation in singular and isolated instances, the term gains resonance when one looks at an entire shelf of Amish novels, with face after face framed by a covering and a cape, or as one reads a raft of novels in which Amish characters perform for a mostly non-Amish readership. It is when looking at the phenomenon as a whole that one begins to ask questions about one culture's borrowing and benefiting from another culture's goods. Although no author of Amish fiction intends to assert dominance over the Amish by writing about them, the sheer number of Amish books written by evangelicals, and the success they are finding in the publishing marketplace, makes it fairly clear who is in charge.[34]

The impulse of white writers to tell Native stories, as Keeshig-Tobias recounts, and the impulse of evangelical women to tell Amish ones resemble each other enough to warrant some analysis. "Why are Canadians so obsessed with native stories anyway?" she asks. "Why the urge to 'write Indian?'"[35] The question would require little revision to be asked of the Amish-fiction phenomenon.

The reasons white Canadians want to "write Indian" and evangelicals want to "write Amish" are complex indeed. The metaphors of chapters 4–7 helped us find several answers to the question, and appropriation is also an instructive concept. As critical theorist Deborah Root notes, appropriation often grows out of a sense of cultural bankruptcy or inauthenticity of one's own culture of origin. In her essay in *Borrowed Power,* an anthology of writings about appropriation, Root writes of meeting several white men who considered themselves "white-skinned Indians." These Caucasian men identified themselves as American Indian, although they had no American Indian ancestors, and felt that their souls were in some sense American Indian. Their white skin, they believed, had them living in exile from their true identities. The longings of these Indian wannabes, who identified themselves with names like Aura, Coyote, Antelope, and Phoenix, suggest the extent to which American Indians, as well as the Amish, have come to signify authenticity and redemption. Having begun at least as early as the 1960s, when "a fantasy of Native people functioned as a metaphor for the rejection of mainstream, bourgeois, white society," Root writes, white people's appropriation of American Indian culture and identity still remains visible in jewelry, artwork, and spirituality. Indian wannabes are mostly well-intentioned, she says, and sincere in their desire to separate themselves from consumptive, alienated culture, even as they appropriate a rather random mashup of Indian and hippie symbols to signify their new allegiances. She writes with a measure of empathy for the white-skinned Indians she has become acquainted with. "I understand their desperation," Root says. "Western culture seems so bankrupt and uninteresting; of course they are going to grab onto something else."[36]

Few readers of Amish fiction are Amish wannabes in the manner of Root's "white-skinned Indians," but the sheer number of Amish novels containing English characters who discover their own Amish bloodline suggests the appeal of a similar "English-skinned Amish" fantasy. In at least five Amish novels or series, an English heroine not only encounters

the Amish without but discovers the Amish within.[37] In each book the heroine travels a distance—from Oregon, California, Philadelphia, New York, or
Virginia—to an Amish settlement in Pennsylvania on some item of business: to investigate a brother's disappearance, to find a birth mother, to
visit an investment property, to escape a stalker, or to pursue a naturopathic
remedy for cancer. In the process, she discovers her native Amish birth and
the story behind her removal from her tribe, which often involves the ille-
gitimate pregnancy of an Amish teenager and the baby's ensuing adoption
by an English couple.

In each case, the protagonist finds that her previously disheveled life
gathers into coherence and calm as she learns the truth of her essential
Amishness and, eventually, returns to her English life. "There was something about the blending of the Plain community with the rest of us, the
Amish cousins with the English, that felt healing and right," reflects Si-
enna, the protagonist of Mindy Starns Clark's *Secrets of Harmony Grove*.
In Beverly Lewis's Seasons of Grace series, grad student Heather Nelson
discovers that she was born to an Amish woman out of wedlock and given
up for adoption and that she is actually a half-sister of her Amish friend
Grace. Nurse-midwife Lexie Jaeger, the main character of Clark and Gould's
The Amish Midwife, also discovers that her Amish friend, Ada, is her sister.
By the time Lexie leaves Lancaster County, her shattered identity has been
healed. "I didn't need photos to recall the peacefulness of these rolling hills,
the warmth and vitality of the Amish homes, the complex and fascinating
people who shared my blood and my heart," she reflects; "All were pictures
I would never, ever forget. Put together, they hold my story. The story I had
found at last."[38]

It is telling that this narrative—an English protagonist learning that she
was born Amish—is now du jour. The inverse trajectory, in which an Amish
protagonist discovers that she was born English, has appeared much less
frequently in the years since Beverly Lewis's first series, in which Katie
Lapp, Amish Woman, learns that she is actually Katherine Mayfield, English Heiress.[39] More than fifteen years into the millennial Amish-fiction
wave, readers want the English protagonist to discover that she has an
Amish pedigree, not the other way around. The fantasy of discovering that

one is of true Amish stock resembles Root's discovery that white people often construct American Indian culture "as the imaginary space that can save us from ourselves."[40]

The frequency with which this tale is told—of an English protagonist discovering that her personal story is actually an Amish one—as well as the authors' own rehearsal of their Amish connections that we observed in chapter 1, could be read not as appropriative impulse but as a reaction against hypermodernity and a desire for belonging and community. Susan L. Trollinger writes that white, middle-class Americans have assimilated to mainstream culture largely by losing specific ethnic identities that previously offered a sense of personal and communal identity. "White middle Americans signify as the empty set," Trollinger writes, as a partial explanation for the attraction of tourists to an ethnically specific and historically rooted group such as the Amish.[41] At the end of this chapter we will examine the connections between whiteness and Amish fiction.

Many Amish novelists, perhaps cognizant of the dangers of appropriation, write from a relative remove in terms of narrative mode. Other than the occasional prologue and epilogue written in the voice of the protagonist, a form popularized by Beverly Lewis and taken up by several other novelists, most Amish novelists write in third person—either third-person multiple point of view, which allows the author to shift between the internal lives of several characters, or third-person limited, in which the author restrains the perspective to one point-of-view character. The third-person mode takes a less authoritative posture than first-person voice.[42] Writer Stephen Quigley says that complete cultural appropriation of identity occurs in fiction when a writer uses first person, which creates "the least amount of psychic distance between the reader and the main character." In first person, "it is easy for a reader to generalize that a given character's perceptions of the world are representative of the perceptions of the character's larger cultural group as to how they view and interact in the world. If a writer misrepresents an appropriated character, then damage is done to the appropriated culture."[43]

Quigley, who has written a novel set in Cambodia, does not let himself or other cross-cultural novelists off the hook. Although he used third person rather than first, he still made representational mistakes, he says, so that some of his Cambodian characters ended up as rather flimsy cultural stereotypes. Rather than claiming that he does not appropriate another cultural identity when he writes, or that he and all other authors should stop writing cross-culturally, Quigley calls himself an appropriator: one who recognize the risks of such writing but proceeds cautiously and with attention to the attendant ethical dilemmas. "Ultimately," he asserts, "the appropriator must realize a responsibility to the appropriated."[44]

In a rare instance of dissent on Thomas Nelson's Amish Living website, a reader of Amish fiction echoed Quigley's concern. After noting some inaccuracies she had found in some of the novels, she raised several questions. "Who speaks for the Amish when we get it wrong in our novels?" she wrote. "Are we in any way obliged to be as accurate as possible when weaving our tales of romance and angst? Do we owe the Amish that much, since we are, after all, profiting from their culture?"

An author published by Thomas Nelson responded with this post: "I can't speak for all the authors on this site, but before my books go to print, each one is proofed for accuracy by an Amish or ex-Amish reader. I don't think that ANY of us will ever put out a perfect novel about the Amish folks because we don't live with them on a day-to-day basis. But I do believe that most of us strive to portray them in as accurate a way as possible. I have Amish friends in Lancaster County that read my books and enjoy them. . . . I really do think that we all believe the Amish are an endearing group of people, and we'd never want to offend them. I certainly don't."[45] This author's description of her commitment to accuracy and her care to not offend this "endearing" sect demonstrates the extent to which the concept of accuracy—rather than the concept of appropriation—drives ethical discussions within the genre.

There are some indications, however, that issues of appropriation may be entering the conversation. This author does not indicate whether the Amish and ex-Amish readers who proof her manuscripts receive payment for their work. If they are paid, it may address at least part of the reader's concern about what is owed to the culture and who is profiting.[46] And some writers do pay Amish informants if they use a true story from that person's life in their books. In at least one instance, Beverly Lewis has paid an Amish person for use of a story in one of her novels, suggesting an awareness and sensitivity to the complications of writing cross-culturally.[47]

As Amish fiction matures, such ethical and literary complications may occupy more central places in discussions among writers and readers. A desire to write accurately and respectfully is a critical starting point. But until issues of appropriation also enter the conversation, the subgenre risks disregarding the cultural integrity, complicated history, and sometimes recondite spirituality of the people at the center of the books.

Appropriation is sometimes accompanied by *exoticism,* a process by which one culture is mediated for consumption by another, and *domestication,* by which the Other is rendered useful or "just like the rest of us."[48] These twin impulses within Amish fiction, while appearing to move in opposite directions, actually exist symbiotically. By both exoticizing (highlighting the charm and the dark side of the unfamiliar Other) and domesticating (creating familiarity with the charming Other), Amish novels commend themselves to readers as resources by which to explore difference and identity.

Exotic Domestics: Employing the Amish

Employing the Amish for one's own purposes tracks a long history. What has been called the "ideological malleability" of the Amish is manifest in twentieth-century history, from their function as guardians of American values in Depression-era America to their role as strict, authoritarian religionists for producers of 20/20 documentaries.[49] In that sense, exoticism and domestication track the same path: use of the Other for one's own purposes. Exoticism does so by privileging difference, and domestication by trading in sameness. Both, in the words of anthropologists Jacob Pandian and Susan Parman, make the "Other serve the needs of Us."[50]

The use of the Other is perhaps inevitable, as we have seen, in the writing of fiction. Mediation of another culture is also almost inescapably ideological, such that the mediator-author's concerns, anxieties, and longings are superimposed on the group about whom she is writing. It has undoubtedly happened in this book, as I have represented the readers, writers, and other producers of Amish fiction, and I am certain that at times the slip of my ideological bias has hung below the narrative hem. It almost certainly happens in Amish fiction itself, when authors create characters and plotlines that service their devotional, instructional, or ideological commitments.

Exoticism

The exotic, as an anthropological and literary concept, developed in colonial writing as European travelers, missionaries, and artists described people groups in far reaches of the empire to folks back home. The habits of the "natives" were scrutinized, their appearance aestheticized, and their Otherness dramatized. French artist Paul Gauguin is among the best-known exoticists; his sumptuous renderings of Tahitian subjects became known for their essentialist portrayals of Polynesian women as earthy, sexually alluring, mysterious creatures, and some historians have suggested that his paintings reveal grief for the passing of an ancient culture that he never really knew.[51] The exotic is usually constructed as anthropologists or artists or novelists "study down," examining people from groups less privileged or powerful than their own, groups considered more "traditional" than the one to which the observer belongs.

Exoticism, according to theorist Chris Bongie, is the "discursive practice intent on recovering 'elsewhere' values 'lost' with the modernization of European society." While Bongie situates exoticism as a force occurring at the end of the nineteenth century, he also examines how it foreshadows the exoticism inscribed in discourse at the end of the twentieth century. The exotic, or the allure of the Other, in the words of anthropologist Stephen William Foster, becomes "a compensation for the increasingly schematized patterns of life in industrial society, a memory bank of how and who we think we were in the 'primitive' reaches of the past."[52] The "we" in this phrase is problematic in relation to Amish fiction, since the Amish are not ancestors, either literal or figurative, of most Americans. Yet the Amish remain exotic figures in many representations in popular culture, often portrayed as essentially different from "the rest of us." The Amish are the ultimate exotics, in this sense: containers into which non-Amish readers can pour their own personal cocktail of anxieties and longings. Like American Indians, the Amish can become proxies for whatever quality hypermodern readers perceive as lacking in their own social location: family values, constancy, communality, forgiveness, sexual fidelity, frugality, technological discretion, a slower pace, or an ability to live in the moment.[53]

In that sense, as other observers have pointed out, the ways we construct the Amish reveal as much about who we are as they do about the Amish. Through their strangeness, we invent our own identities. Through travel to their exotic locations, we indict our own. "I think about how I can try to live my life like the Amish, and change my mindset to live more peaceful," writes one blogger, who says she "adores all Amish stories": "So this is my quest: to find out can I go from being a stressed out, angry, agitated doubtful believer to a strong, grateful, and encouraging human being to everyone around me."[54]

This blogger's comment embodies a characteristic exoticizing move—marking the nature of the Other as essentially "more" in any domain where we feel a lack. For residents of a hypermodern world, such as Meg, the protagonist in Cynthia Keller's *An Amish Christmas* who gets stranded with her family at an Amish farm over the holidays, the Amish become ciphers of authenticity, purveyors of redemption. Meg and her husband and children were Icarus-like overspenders, typical American consumers whose waxen wings of credit the recession has melted, and with them their marital and familial health. Forced to spend the holiday with Amish hosts after a car accident, they recover the meaning, love, and hope they have lost. At the end of the book, Meg's husband decides to become a broker for Amish furniture. "I also like the idea of supporting their work," he tells his wife. "It's kind of the least I can do for the community. They saved us—in more ways than one."[55]

This novel's construction of the Amish—as messianic figures for misguided English characters—harks at least as far back as Cora Gottschalk Welty's 1908 *The Masquerading of Margaret,* in which one character waxes rhapsodic about how wonderful it would be if "this great surging world would pause to listen and to learn at the feet of the Amish." It finds resonance in popular media throughout the twentieth century, such as the 1997 film *For Richer or Poorer.*[56] And although the story line lacks the racial and colonial scaffold of the sort of exoticism that theorist bell hooks describes, it fits within her heuristic of "eating the Other." "The Other is coded as having the capacity to be more alive," writes hooks—"as holding the secret that will allow those who venture and dare to break with the cultural anhedonia [the inability to feel pleasure] . . . and experience sensual and spiritual renewal."[57]

One of the ways Amish fiction exoticizes the Amish is through Pennsylvania Dutch–inflected dialogue.[58] Most Amish novels include at least a dusting of words and phrases taken from Pennsylvania Dutch, thus mirroring the distinctive diction often used by local-color writers like Helen Reimensnyder Martin in the early twentieth century. Authors often choose those dialect words that are most similar to English words, so the meaning is not lost—for example, "He's a *gut mann,* your Isaiah," the protagonist in Kathleen Fuller's novella *What the Heart Sees* tells her friend Sarah Lynne; "He is, *ya,*" Sarah Lynne replies. Or authors provide immediate translation through the English paraphrase of another character—"*Ich hab ken half draa grict!*" the protagonist's son wails in Wanda Brunstetter's *Lydia's Charm,* and then his mother asks, "What couldn't you catch hold of?" Some authors choose to represent dialect speech in other ways as well, such as dropping the final "g" of words ending in *-ing;* for example, the father in Brunstetter's novel *The Hope Chest,* as he teases his daughter, says, "Should I be askin' your *mamm* to start makin' a weddin' quilt?"[59]

Linguist Karen Johnson-Weiner notes that dialect in popular novels about the Amish is often a combination of Pennsylvania Dutch words and outmoded English syntax. One Amish mother I spoke with suggested that the speech patterns in the Amish novels she has read called to mind a Western accent rather than anything recognizably Amish. Another Amish woman told me that the characters in a Beverly Lewis novel she read recently were always talking "half Amish." A Mennonite blogger expressed more blatant disgust: "WHY does she [Beverly Lewis] always write the dialogue in this bizarre hick-pioneer-midwestern-redneck lingo, dropping g's all over the place and putting in these strange phrases that have absolutely no counterpart in Dutch? . . . Please hear me on this: AMISH PEOPLE DO NOT TALK LIKE THAT."[60]

Readers almost certainly know that the "half Amish" speech—a dash of dialect, outdated syntax, and accented diction—is a code to remind them that the entire dialogue would be written in Pennsylvania Dutch were they themselves, the readers, conversant in it. Since novels can't have subtitles, however, toggling back and forth between English and Pennsylvania Dutch remains the most frequent strategy for reminding readers of the characters' Otherness. Johnson-Weiner writes that such linguistic devices "hint at the social isolation of the Amish protagonists" and mark them as a "people out of touch with everyday events and strangers in their own land."[61]

Domestication

Even as the Amish are exoticized in fiction, film, and other media, they are *domesticated* as well: made useful for the person mediating them or made suitable for one's purposes. The extent to which the Amish have been domesticated within Amish fiction is apparent in author Mindy Starns Clark's description of her workshop "Amish 101," offered at the 2010 American Christian Fiction Writers Conference; the seminar explored, among other things, why the Amish world "is such a perfect fit for Christian fiction."[62]

Whether the martyr-filled history, pacifist commitments, rejection of higher education, and churchly authority of the Amish is indeed a "perfect fit" for blockbuster inspirational novels is arguable. Clark's claim is accurate in the sense that, as the authors of *The Amish Way* write, the Amish do generally believe in "free-market capitalism, political democracy, and conservative family values."[63] But the Amish are also quite peculiar relative to dominant Christian culture, and domestication requires the muffling of such inconvenient differences. In many Amish novels, the picturesque qualities of Amish life—buggies, quilts, barn raisings—are exaggerated, while the elements less savory to modern minds—the nonresistant stance, the eighth-grade ceiling on education, the holy kiss, the sometimes grueling manual labor—are downplayed or completely ignored.

Especially revealing of the domesticating posture of Amish fiction is one aspect of Amish life that is essentially erased in much of the subgenre. Few contemporary Amish-themed novels deal with the issues of nonresistance, conscientious objection, or opposition to war.[64] Although most Amish people are not politically activist in terms of protesting war or advocating peacemaking as a solution to global conflict, the belief that violence is wrong remains central to the theological and spiritual character of their communities. Many Amish people are active supporters of the Mennonite Central Committee, which programmatically opposes armed conflict, and the Amish have at various points in history become troublesome to governments because of their refusal to join the military, to the point of arrest, imprisonment, and torture.[65] In eras when the military draft is not employed, the political implications of Amish nonresistance may be submerged. Still, nonresistance remains a constitutive aspect of Amish life.

Commitment to nonresistance pervades Amish discourse and practice, informing everything from their refusal to litigate to their eschewal of self-defense of any kind. Patriotism, or any sense of duty to one's country, is also almost entirely absent from Amish writings, sermons, and conversations. No American flag is hung in any Amish-run schoolhouse, no pledge of allegiance recited, no "Star-Spangled Banner" sung. No military officers are held up as heroes, no care packages for soldiers are packed. There was almost certainly no cheering among the Amish when Baghdad fell, or when Saddam Hussein was captured, or when Navy SEALs killed Osama bin Laden. The place of nonresistance within Amish consciousness can hardly be overstated.

But this is not information a reader would garner from Amish novels. "Peace," in most of Amish fiction, is a private matter, an intangible spiritual approach to life, rather than a robust ethic with potentially life-altering consequences during wartime. Although her first nonfiction book is titled *Amish Peace,* novelist Suzanne Woods Fisher mentions the centuries-old Amish opposition to war only in a brief reference to an Amish man's conscientious-objector status during the Vietnam War. Amish "peace" is rendered as a quality of the soul, obtainable through devotions, reordering one's priorities, and making minor adjustments: "Building a margin of error into your schedule—for unexpected things like traffic jams—can be a simple and effective way to add peace to your life."[66]

The invisibility of nonresistance within most Amish novels is not any one particular novelist's fault. Romance novels are, by definition, about the personal and the private, and they shouldn't be held responsible for representing the totality of Amish theology and history. Amish people are indeed prone to talk about the internal peace their way of life brings them, and it is possible that when speaking with outsiders, they privatize the concept more than they do in worship services and writings. The minimal reference to this central facet of Amish identity in Amish fiction simply represents one way that the Amish have been domesticated, whittled down to a charming size. As the "Amish Store" at the Christian Book Distributors website suggests, "Warm bread, freshly baked shoofly pies, lush rolling hills, and handmade quilts are hallmarks of the Amish way of life."[67] The attraction of the Amish clearly rests not in their war-opposing selves but in their domestic—and domesticated—ones.

This elision of Amish nonresistance points to what the novels domesticate the Amish into: good Americans. Readers want protagonists "who value very traditional American values, in the sense of honesty and hard work and doing the right thing and looking out for each other," says Andrea Doering, an editor at Revell. "So you feel like you are really among friends, among people who value what you value." Literary agent Chip MacGregor agrees. "It [Amish fiction] speaks to the best of American values of God, work, family, and achievement," he told one reporter.[68]

Championing the Amish as quintessential Americans tracks a long history, at least back to the 1930s.[69] In *Selling the Amish,* Susan L. Trollinger suggests that Amish-themed tourism offers a view of the Amish that celebrates the myth of U.S. dominance and the essential goodness of the nation. The Americanization of the Amish extends to Amish fiction's general erasure of complicated Amish notions about patriotism, citizenship, and nonresistance, such that the Amish begin to look a lot like "us." "Maybe it doesn't really matter if he's Amish or not," Lilly's mother tells her in *Autumn's Promise,* when Lilly, a non-Amish teen, tells her that she is dating Robert Miller, an Amish man. Her mother goes on: "And though a year ago I never would have imagined saying this, I don't think the Amish are much different from us."[70]

While exoticism and domestication may seem to run in fundamentally different directions, they are complementary impulses. Both employ the Other for one's own project, whatever it may be, and both reveal as much about the mediator as about the mediated. So whether as exotic subjects, on which difference has been writ large, or domesticated ones, on which difference has been carved away, the Amish have proved useful to novelists and readers, and never more so than in the past five years.

Us or Other? Racing the Amish

Forged in postcolonial theory, both concepts—exoticism and domestication—raise issues of racial and ethnic difference. Although analyzing the role of race in Amish fiction is a little like calculating wind speed on a day with no breeze—how do you measure something that's not there?—it is salient to this discussion insofar as it reveals the subgenre's general lack of engagement with contemporary conversations about race and ethnicity.

With few exceptions, Amish fiction is populated almost entirely by white characters. An occasional African American or other person of color appears, such as veterinarian Dr. Robinson in Suzanne Woods Fisher's 1960s-era *The Waiting* and Kendrick in Cindy Woodsmall's *When the Morning Comes*. Dale Cramer's The Daughters of Caleb Bender series, set in Mexico in the 1920s, is the most notable exception in a mostly white field. *Paradise Valley*, the first book in the series, revolves around interactions between Amish and Mexican characters and a growing awareness on the part of the Amish characters that the German landowner who has welcomed them is a virulent racist who thinks all Mexicans are lazy, unreliable, and immoral. A budding romance between the sister of the Amish protagonist and an indigenous Mexican hired hand, and the school that she begins for both Amish and Mexican children, carry the plot far beyond the confines of whiteness within which most Amish novels exist.

Apart from these examples, Amish fiction is almost entirely devoid of racial and ethnic diversity. One African American author of inspirational romances, Cecelia Dowdy, who sometimes reviews Amish-fiction titles on her Christian fiction blog, told me that she had toyed with the idea of writing an Amish novel with African American main characters and Amish secondary characters. "I tried to write it and was blocked," Dowdy recounts; "it just didn't work. I doubt I'll try that again."[71] Another writer, posting on Thomas Nelson's Amish Living website, sent out a plea to others trying to write Amish fiction: "Please, please, please will someone write about African-Americans and the Amish-Mennonites."[72]

The invisibility of racial difference in Amish fiction is a reflection of actual Amish communities, of course, in which nonwhite members are rare.[73] Apart from the occasional interracial adoption, the Amish are almost entirely German and Swiss in ethnic origin, so for authors to invent black Amish protagonists would stretch plausibility. Authenticity almost demands an all-white or mostly white cast. Yet the whiteness of Amish fiction is notable because it incarnates the racialized reality of fiction in the wider CBA marketplace. In her study of evangelical romance novels, Lynn Neal found a genre dominated by white characters, as well as frustration on the part of African American readers of inspirational fiction who found that "stories depicting women of color in realistic and relevant ways remain in short supply."[74] "I find it interesting that there's such interest in publishing Amish fiction, but not quite so much in publishing books featuring characters of other cultures," one African American reader and writer of inspirational romance, Patricia Woodside, told me. "Many African American authors of inspirational fiction find that they must either publish with 'secular' [American Booksellers Association] publishers or self-publish. The thought is that ABA (American Booksellers Association) books tend to be a bit edgier, and that CBA readers wouldn't be interested in them."[75]

A marketer at one publishing house that publishes Amish fiction confirms the racialized reality of the CBA market. "People want to look at that cover and feel like they're going to enter into a relationship with the characters," he said on the phone. "The more you make them feel like they can relate to that character, the stronger that character is to them." He recounted a recent disagreement among his colleagues regarding whether to put an Asian woman on the cover of a novel that contains an Asian protagonist. "Most of our market, they don't know someone who is Asian," he said. "They can't enter into that. And that's going to hurt us in sales. People have to be able to feel like they can connect to that cover model." The reliably white cover models of Amish fiction, even while dressed in exotic garb, likely hold more appeal to the assumed readers within the CBA market than if the Amish had originated in Asia or Africa instead of Europe.

Race is now commonly understood as ideological construct rather than biological fact. Yet whiteness in America, largely invented and often invisible, exerts tremendous force on individual identity and social structures and becomes an assumed and neutral norm against which others are measured. Ethnic groups like the Irish—and, we could theorize, the Amish—slide between nonwhiteness and whiteness in the popular imagination, as historian Noel Ignatiev points out in *How the Irish Became White*. It is possible that, like the Irish in the twentieth century, the Amish have moved from the nonwhite column to the white one in the American imagination or even, as writer Julia Kasdorf argues, to a "whiter-than-white" or "ultrawhite" category. Amish communities function in some sense as "internal colonies amid whiteness," Kasdorf claims—hamlets with breeding boundaries so tightly drawn that a certain racial and ethnic purity is achieved.[76]

Amish fiction, then, absent post-9/11 conversations about race, ethnicity, and religious difference, may reveal a largely white readership anxious about race, nervous about their movement away from iconic, normative status, and eager to escape to a whitewashed world. Marcia Z. Nelson, religion editor at *Publishers Weekly*, suggests that had the attacks of September 11 not occurred, Amish fiction might not have gained such traction. Since then, Nelson says, there has been "this sort of cultural anxiety that is now a permanent subtext in our culture, and that we notice every time we go to the airport." She believes readers may read Amish fiction in part to escape the "particular tensions brought about by multicultural diversity."[77]

Alternatively, the Amish may still be sufficiently Other, even "nonwhite," in many people's minds. Steve Scott recounted a time when he called a hardware store in Berne, Indiana, and asked whether they carried any items specifically for Amish buyers. "No, just things we white people use," came the reply.

Richard Brodhead's argument—that reading regional fiction about "safe" native communities like Tennessee mountain people or the Amish was a way for Americans who defined themselves as "white" to rehearse cross-cultural interactions—may still explain Amish novels' popularity. If so, Amish fiction may function for contemporary white readers as Brodhead suggests regional fiction did for readers in the previous century: as a way to bring themselves "within hearing distance" of increasing racial and ethnic diversity without actually encountering it.[78]

Amish Fiction and the Future

We come at last to the question that many writers and agents and publishers are asking themselves: does the thrill of the chaste have staying power?

Are the fictional Amish maidens lining bookstore shelves as sturdy as the wooden carving of the Amish woman who sits beside me, or will they go the way of the protagonists of 1990s inspirational chick lit, whom few readers now remember? Chapter 10 addresses these questions, as well as a few others: what are the effects of the genre on its readers, both English and Amish? What might this study of Amish novels commend to future scholarship on similar literatures?

And the most random but perhaps most revealing question of all: in the first decade of the twenty-first century, when a Christian librarian in Oklahoma challenges her elderly cousin to turn off the television and read a book, to what kind of novels is that cousin likely to turn?

Something New (2012), by Dianne Christner, set in a conservative
Mennonite community in Ohio, represents a growing subgenre of
Mennonite-themed inspirational fiction.
Used by special permission of Barbour Publishing Inc.

❦ Chapter Ten ❦

Happily Ever After

A family friend leans over her plate at dinner when she hears about my Amish novel research. Margaret has read a few Amish novels, and she is intrigued and a little confused. Like several other people with whom I spoke, she thinks at first that I am *writing* an Amish romance novel. No, I clarify; I am writing *about* them.

"So let me get this straight." Margaret pauses, her forefinger raised above her chicken and rice. "You are writing a book about *us,* who are *reading* the books that *other* people write about the Amish?" It is obvious that this project strikes her as a tad funny, amusing in both its degrees of separation from the Amish and the endless ripples of research that it suggests. Margaret is courteous, but I think I detect an unspoken question that is keeping the smile on her lips as she picks up her fork. Did I now expect someone else to write a book about the book that I was writing about the books that have been written about the Amish?

Although my project continued to make more sense to me than it did to Margaret, questions like the ones that plague scholars and writers of all stripes began to visit me as I neared the end of this project. What *is* the significance of all this research? Does it propose anything of consequence? Could *Thrill of the Chaste* bring anything to bear on future investigations of inspirational romance fiction and representations of the Amish, or is it just so much academic malarkey?

After laying out several forecasts regarding the future of Amish fiction, this chapter turns to the possible consequences of Amish fiction on non-Amish and Amish readers. We will then entertain the questions that entertained my friend: how, or if, this analysis actually matters. Finally, we will turn our attention to that librarian, her reading challenge, and her cousin's newfound love for a certain kind of fiction.

Migrations of Amish Fiction

From all indications, Amish fiction is nowhere near its expiration date. During 2012, a new Amish novel appeared on the market about every four days, and a new Amish series commenced about every two weeks. An April 2012 *New York Times* bestseller list for trade fiction contained two Amish romance titles: Beverly Lewis's *The Fiddler,* with an initial print run of 240,000 copies, came in at number eight, right below Kathryn Stockett's blockbuster *The Help.* Wanda Brunstetter's *The Half-Stitched Amish Quilting Club* was number twenty-four.[1]

Editor Sue Brower of Zondervan told me that because Amish fiction has been so widely embraced by Christian baby boomers, she doesn't see it declining until the boomers reach their eighties and nineties. For the youngest boomers, that is still more than forty years away. Thomas Nelson vice president and fiction publisher Allen Arnold suggests that the Amish-fiction market is showing signs of "maturation, not saturation," and Bill Westfall of Barbour Books told me that when he asks Barbour's key buyers to predict Amish fiction's future, "They tell me they just don't see an end to it."[2] In February 2012, Barbour Books editor Rebecca Germany told *Publishers Weekly,* "I don't see the interest in people like the Amish going away anytime soon."[3]

While the market appears to be enduring, it may also be getting glutted. Some publishers and agents told me that it is becoming harder for new authors to break into the field, although they still predict robust sales for authors who are already in. "A year ago they [Amish-fiction manuscripts] were a little easier to sell than they are now," one literary agent told me in 2011; "Publishers have become more picky, because so many people are writing them." Another agent told me that several editors have advised him, "I think we have enough Amish right now." Kim Moore of Harvest House told *Publishers Weekly* that the genre is "no longer white hot"—although she attributes that not to decreasing interest but to the scores of books now available.[4]

A few authors who previously billed themselves as authors of Amish fiction have begun using more general descriptors for themselves and their writing. Beth Wiseman's website header used to include her photograph superimposed on top of an Amish-looking rural scene, complete with barn and buggy; by March 2012, the background was simply blue. An emerging writer, aware that the possibility of saturation of the Amish market may disadvantage debut authors, changed her website tagline in August 2011 from "Lighthearted Romance with an Amish Flavor" to the more general "Contemporary Romance Writer." "The truth is, Amish fiction may not endure or it may become too glutted (if it isn't already)," Sarah Forgrave wrote in a blog post about what she called her "re-branding." "And if that's the case, I've got lots more stories in me that don't touch Amish culture at all. Could I plant them in Amish settings if the market calls for it? Sure. But at this point, that remains to be seen."[5] Thomas Nelson senior editor Natalie Hanemann told *Publishers Weekly* in February 2012 that she had seen sales level off during the previous three years, and Germany of Barbour agreed that the market is "a bit flooded."[6]

Although the Amish-fiction supply might actually be catching up to the demand, the genre's already long lifespan and proven sales record suggests that it will stick around, in some form, for a long time to come. The agent who told me that Amish-fiction manuscripts are getting harder to sell also told me that she is still looking for them. "At this point I feel that I always will be," she said. "It's not a fad, it's not going anywhere. It's not going to disappear," one marketer told me, suggesting a parallel between Amish fiction in the CBA market and Regency fiction in the ABA market, which has retained a steady market share of commercial fiction.[7] "I don't see it growing at this point, but I don't see it declining, either," he told me. "I think it's stable. It's going to remain a nice, profitable niche."

If Amish fiction's appeal is pegged to a hypermodern, hypersexed culture, as I have argued, more than to the recession or other discrete events, then as long as readers experience the epoch and the culture as excessively modern and immoderately sexualized, Amish fiction will remain a viable genre.

As hypermodernity advances, sects like the Amish—rooted in centuries-old traditions and faith and marked by highly visual cultural distinctives—will likely garner even more attention. Similarly, if hypersexualization of mass culture continues, "clean" genres like inspirational fiction—and überclean ones like Amish fiction—will likely become even more popular as more readers, not just evangelical Christians, scout around for alternative media.

Nevertheless, because the Amish-fiction market is increasingly subdivided among a mounting populace of titles and authors and publishers, finding ways to turn a profit may take some creativity, especially for publishers of lesser-known authors. Like the Amish themselves, who have responded to development and other pressures by moving to rural areas where no Amish settlement existed before, new Amish novels and series are migrating to new territory, both geographic and narrative. Forthcoming and continuing series are set in Amish communities in Maine, Montana, Colorado, and Kentucky, and several new series delve farther back into Amish history than previous novels—Pennsylvania in 1777, Kansas in 1881, antebellum Virginia. The Amish angel and Amish vampire series represent routes of this migration, as do the growing number of Amish westerns and Amish quilting novels. Five such growing edges of Amish fiction deserve our attention. Although the jury is still out on the lasting success of these adjunct genres and subgenres, all appear to be benefiting from the Amish-fiction trend while staking out territory slightly apart from it.

Exposé Amish Fiction

The dialectic between fictional representations of the Amish as fallen saints and saving remnant that we saw in chapter 2 is still operative. Judging from my conversations with two aspiring Amish novelists, the pendulum may be swinging.[8] These authors warned me that their books would be different from most Amish novels on the market. "I'm writing my Amish fiction the way [another Christian writer] has challenged us writers at writers' conferences to do: to expose the Amish lifestyle as, not Christian, but a cult," one author wrote in an e-mail to me. "They are a community of 'works get you to heaven,' not salvation through Jesus' atoning work on the cross alone. So,' that's one of the main themes of my book." When I corresponded with her, this author, having published Christian fiction for young readers and served as a homeschool consultant, was seeking an agent for her manuscript.

A similar caveat came my way from another author who has an agent for her Amish-fiction manuscript. Soon after our conversation, this author signed a three-book deal for her Amish series. "I must warn you in advance that my Amish novel is not like many of those in the genre on the market," this author wrote to me before our interview. "The inspiration for my characters was found among my former[ly] Amish friends. As such, there is quite a bit more truth about the Amish lifestyle and quite a bit less sugar coating." Her novel, based on the composite stories of her formerly Amish friends, tells the story of a young woman's difficult adjustment to English life and the stringent shunning she experienced from her Amish friends and family.

Although she isn't ready to call the Amish a cult, this author, who refers to her work as "honest-driven Amish fiction," is frustrated by the tenor of the current genre, which she thinks perpetuates a myth of Amish life as simple, healthy, and desirable. She tells me that many of the formerly Amish people she knows, most of whom were raised Swartzentruber or Andy Weaver Amish, two of the more conservative affiliations, have experienced sexual abuse, punishment for reading an English Bible, coercion to remain in the community, and, even if they had not taken baptismal vows, extreme shunning. "They're being rejected because they want a deeper walk with the Lord," this author tells me on the phone. "Their understanding of the Bible when they first come out is very limited."

Whether these authors' books are the first in a new round of backlash Amish fiction remains to be seen. While Clara Bernice Miller's books, which contained similar assumptions, sold well in the 1960s, contemporary readers may not care for books that so jar their generally positive impressions of and identification with the Amish. If Amish fiction is popular because evangelical Christian readers, living within what they perceive to be hypermodern and hypersexed times, need the Amish to be saints, will they want to read books in which the Amish are sexually abusive, cultic sinners?

One of the authors told me that even her formerly Amish friends, most of whom have bitter memories from their childhoods, like to read the very Amish novels that she says idealize the Amish. "In spite of the fact that they've left, they have heart ties," this author says. "They loved the farm-ing, they loved the animals. It's one of several ironies about being formerly Amish—they still want to read about the life they had."

Amishesque Fiction

"Amish fiction" has become a synecdoche for all manner of fiction about conservative ethnoreligious communities, and the number of communities represented, and the novels written about each, will likely increase. The Amish tab under the category "fiction" on the Christian Book Distributors website includes links to novels about Quakers, Shakers, and Mennonites. Authors are now writing inspirational novels and novellas that center on Mennonites, Shakers, Puritans, Moravians, the Amana Colonies, Quak-ers, and Mormons.[9] Mennonite fiction, in particular, seems to be gaining ground. It is possible that Amish fiction will continue splintering into even more plain Christian sects, such as the Hutterites, the Huguenots, the Old German Baptist Brethren, and the Old Order River Brethren, producing novels that gain momentum from the Amish brand while remaining dis-tinct from the crowd.

The number of novels featuring minor Amish characters in an otherwise English cast is also growing. Kimberly Stuart's *Operation Bonnet* is one such vaguely Amish novel, as is Kathryn Cushman's *Almost Amish*. Three recent installments in Summerside Press's Love Finds You series (*Love Finds You in Paradise, Pennsylvania, Love Finds You in Lancaster County*, and *Love Finds You in Sugarcreek, Ohio*) feature English-dominated plots with a dash of Amishness. In *Love Finds You in Paradise, Pennsylvania*, the Amish serve as matchmakers for the English point-of-view characters, a lawyer and a vet-erinarian. An editor at Zondervan told *Publishers Weekly* that she is seeing more Amish novels that feature "other characters who might have different lifestyles, but interact with the Amish in their day-to-day lives."[10] These two types of Amishesque novels—those about religious sects that resemble the Amish in some way and those with an Amish backdrop—will likely expand.

Amish Fiction for a General Audience

Industry insiders disagree about whether Amish fiction can exist as a recognizable subgenre outside the cozy home that inspirational Christian fiction and the CBA market have thus far provided it. Several marketing managers told me that Amish fiction appeals to a particular Christian reader, one who would not pick up a novel written by a non-Christian or produced by a non-Christian publisher. They suggest that Jodi Picoult's *Plain Truth*, published by Washington Square Press in 2007 and garnering the same lucrative sales that all Picoult's novels do, is an anomaly in the Amish-fiction market, an outlier in an otherwise faith-filled field. One author of Amish fiction told me that she finds Picoult to be an "exquisite writer" but thinks that her books are part of a trend in commercial fiction "toward really dark books that explore the underbelly of humanity."[11]

But there are indications that evangelical publishers' immunity from competition outside the CBA domain may be in the past. Christians aren't the only readers looking for the chaste fictional mold that has coalesced around the Amish. Several recent novels from Berkley and NAL Trade, imprints of Penguin, are manifestations of this, as are titles from Ballantine, an imprint of Random House; Zebra, an imprint of Kensington; and Gallery, an imprint of Simon & Schuster. These and similar books tend to be more vaguely inspirational, with fewer references to the Christian faith of the main characters and lacking in any devotional element. Cynthia Keller's 2010 *An Amish Christmas* contains the word "God" only twice: when one non-Amish character says "Oh my God" in embarrassment and another uses "Dear God" in dismay. Nowhere in the novel do the words "Jesus," "Christian," or "faith" appear.[12]

Whether general trade publishers can reach the loyal readers of Amish fiction, most of whom like faith referenced a lot more frequently and God referred to a lot more respectfully, or whether they are cultivating new audiences located outside the Christian fiction market remains to be seen. "The Amish can transfer over into the rest of the market, because there is a market for nice clean books without explicit sex or violence," Marcia Z. Nelson, religion editor at *Publishers Weekly*, told me. "I think it will remain anchored there [in a CBA readership], but there are a lot of people interested in a wholesome, nostalgic read." And Andrea Doering, an editor at Revell, suggests that the commercial success of Amish fiction is persuading other publishers to join the game. "Once the cash register starts ringing, a lot of people get interested and start wondering what in the world this is," Doering says. "They begin to wonder how replicable it is, and how much they can take it and parlay it into something else."[13]

Whether the Amish are destined to the albeit lucrative ghettos of commercial and Christian fiction, or whether they could cross over to literary fiction, remains to be seen. A few such novels already exist: Graywolf Press, a literary independent press, published Michael Lowenthal's 2002 novel *Avoidance*, which tells the story of a gay Harvard student who lives with an Amish family while researching shunning practices, and Tristan Egolf's 2005 *Kornwolf* was reviewed in the *New Yorker*.[14] Literary novels and memoirs about Mennonites appear to be thriving. Rhoda Janzen's candid memoir *Mennonite in a Little Black Dress* (Holt, 2009) garnered both critical and commercial success; and Canadian Mennonite novelist Miriam Toews's 2011 bildungsroman about a Mexican Mennonite woman, *Irma Roth*, was greeted with wide critical acclaim. Canadian Mennonite literary fiction dates back to Rudy Wiebe's 1962 *Peace Shall Destroy Many*.[15] It is possible that as the reign of hypermodernity spreads, readers loyal to literary fiction may also long for Amish- and Mennonite-themed narratives.

Digital Amish Fiction

Like most genres, Amish fiction is being stamped with the signature of the digital publishing revolution. One-fifth of American adults read at least one e-book during the past year, and the ranks are growing swiftly—from 17 percent in mid-December 2011 to 21 percent in February 2012.[16] Amish books are now widely available for Kindle, Nook, and other e-readers, and several readers I interviewed read their Amish novels exclusively on their e-readers.

A significant aspect of this trend is that the doors to publication for would-be Amish authors unwilling or unable to publish via traditional routes have been thrown open. Since August 2010, more than 120 Amish novels, novellas, and short stories have been self-published or published digitally by author-owned presses; none of these books were included in the graph in chapter 1. While at first glance these numbers may appear neg-ligible considering the rapid-fire production of Amish books by traditional publishers, this transformation of publishing channels allows self-styled authors with some business savvy to compete quite seriously against the giants in the field.

For example, an Amazon bestseller list for Christian romance fiction in May 2012 listed eight Amish romance novels among the top twenty titles. Of those eight Amish novels, only one—*Leaving Lancaster,* written by Kate Lloyd and published by David C. Cook—was produced by a traditional pub-lisher. The other seven novels—six of them written by a Florida paralegal in her spare time—were published by companies owned by the authors them-selves. Four of the paralegal's Amish e-novels beat out books by Christian fiction matriarchs Karen Kingsbury, Tracie Peterson, and Francine Rivers.[17] The digitization of reading will likely continue to widen opportunities for more writers to gain an audience for their Amish-themed books.

Amish Nonfiction and Memoirs

The crowding of new authors into the subgenre has at least some readers raising the bar of authenticity and accuracy, and it is possible that a drive for credible information about the Amish will at times supersede readers' desires for fiction. There is some indication that this is already happening and that at least some readers are expanding their tastes from Amish fiction to Amish nonfiction. Many Amish-fiction authors, most notably Suzanne Woods Fisher, have turned to writing nonfiction treatments of the Amish in addition to novels; Fisher has written four books of nonfiction about the Amish.[18]

Amish-themed novels also seem to be paving the way for memoirs by the Amish or the formerly Amish. Several recent ones demonstrate the ris-ing cache of Amish autobiographical writing. Ira Wagler's coming-of-age narrative *Growing Up Amish,* about his Old Order Amish childhood, was released in June 2011 by Tyndale, a Christian publishing house. Sales of the book "well exceeded our expectations," editor Carol Traver told me; Wagler's memoir appeared three times on the *New York Times* bestseller list for e-books and went into its fifth printing within the first six months. Saloma

Miller Furlong's memoir *Why I Left the Amish* was published by Michigan State University Press in January 2011, and another memoir claiming the same initial title as Wagler's (*Growing Up Amish: Insider Secrets from One Woman's Inspirational Journey*) appeared in 2008 from Morgan James Publishing, a well-disguised vanity press. Now that at least sixty writers are producing Amish fiction, many readers will want to be assured that the authors of the Amish-themed books they're reading know more about the Amish than that they drive buggies and wear bonnets. Eli Hochstetler, owner of Gospel Bookstore in Berlin, Ohio, says that tourists coming into his store are increasingly turning toward nonfiction books, many of them self-published, which have been written by Amish people. Hochstetler's observation suggests that Amish fiction may be lubricating the gears of reader interest for other Amish-themed books and that publishing houses may begin seeking out Amish-produced memoirs and nonfiction.[19]

Consequences of Amish Fiction

The discussion of appropriation and exoticism and domestication and whiteness in chapter 9 may suggest that Amish fiction is a hopeless venture, with literary and representational dangers at every turn. Writers shouldn't make the Amish out to be *too* different from "the rest of us," I have said, but they shouldn't make them out to be too similar, either. If exoticism and domestication are the only options, authors may be damned if they do, damned if they don't.

But I have hope for Amish fiction, at least for its possibilities for non-Amish readers. If conversations about appropriation begin to take place among readers and writers, and if readers are willing to move beyond snap judgments of the Amish as Other, it is possible that the subgenre will fulfill its possibilities for a non-Amish audience. "We should perhaps not too quickly discount the idealized images of the Amish that pervade mainstream culture," historian Paul Boyer has written. "As Thoreau argued, it is good for societies to think about alternative social models, even if the process involves distortions and misperceptions."[20]

Making the Familiar Strange: Effects on English Readers

At its best, Amish fiction can help non-Amish readers view their familiar world as strange, a task that is as taxing and rare for many Americans as shoveling manure or stoking a woodstove. Few white Americans, Diane Zimmerman Umble and David Weaver-Zercher have written, have spent much time "thinking of themselves as Other, luxuriating instead in the assumption that their way of life is normal and therefore best."[21] By entering an Amish world, fictive though it may be, readers may begin to see themselves and their world of origin through the eyes of the Amish, and taken-for-granted customs of hypermodern life may become suddenly contingent and unstable. In that sense, reading Amish fiction can become an exercise in anthropological relativism, of making "the familiar strange, and the strange familiar," as T. S. Eliot suggested good poetry does.

In Cynthia Keller's *An Amish Christmas*, for example, we begin to view the English protagonist's former life from the critical distance she gains through being stranded over the holidays with Amish hosts. A few days into her stay, things that Meg had never questioned—a nightly ritual involving her five-color-coded calendar, obsessive attention to dinner party place settings, morning makeup routines—stop making sense. "By this point, the notion of wearing a face full of makeup struck her as faintly ridiculous, as if she were slathering dirt on herself," Keller writes. Later Meg listens in as her children reflect on their non-Amish lives at home: "'One thing is,' Will said, 'it was kind of boring at home. I mean, everybody's on the computer or their phone all the time, and you have to do that or you're just out of things. I didn't used to think that, but now I kinda do.'" In Suzanne Woods Fisher's *The Choice*, when Veronica McCall takes off in her little red convertible, we observe her harried, avaricious existence—and perhaps our own—through the eyes of the Amish man Eli. Veronica's character is a little overdrawn, but the lives of most readers resemble hers more closely than we may care to admit. "'Englisch,' Eli muttered, shaking his head as he passed by Carrie to head into the house."[22]

If readers can not only follow Amish protagonists but be followed by them, they may find themselves questioning the dictates of their own social order, their conformity to the *Ordnung* of hypermodernity, and the costs that accrue from such allegiances. Dwelling within an all-Amish world, even for the relatively short period of time it takes to read a book, may lead readers to see themselves as Other.[23] It's a strenuous metacognitive task, this viewing oneself as Other, but if readers are willing to try out a new optic, Amish fiction can help them to achieve it. Readers may express this idea in ways that seem simplistic or appropriative to some observers, and many might indeed get stuck at the exoticizing or domesticating stage. But when Amish fiction can truly make the familiar strange and the strange familiar, it can become an antidote to the myopic gaze of hypermodernity.

Making the Strange Familiar: Effects on Amish Readers

For Amish and other plain readers of bonnet fiction, the results of Amish fiction may be more mixed. What does gazing at someone's carving of you do to your definition of yourself? What shifts in culture, theology, and identity occur as Amish people read themselves through the eyes of non-Amish writers? When a young Amish woman in Minnesota uses Amish novels as a nonfiction source about the Amish in Lancaster County, as Nao Nomura learned, Amish fiction may indeed be manufacturing Amish identity. And when a young Amish woman in Lancaster County, who is considering leaving her community, reads an Amish novel in which the heroine mulls over the same thing, Amish fiction may be assembling an Amish future.

On one hand, Amish fiction may fortify Amish culture, as some have noted that Amish-themed tourism does. By clarifying boundaries between the Amish and the outside world, tourism may encourage Amish people themselves to remain separate. Amish fiction may serve a similar function for Amish communities—demarcating the boundaries of an Amish life and reinforcing for Amish readers, via the validation of outsider interest, that their culture is worth preserving.

But tourism represents Amish people largely to non-Amish ones. Amish novels, created almost entirely by non-Amish people, are now representing the Amish to the Amish. Now that Amish fiction has found an Amish readership, in a case of the observer altering the observed, novelists of Amish fiction may be literally producing Amish notions of spirituality and theology. What evangelical romance novels do for readers more generally, Amish novels may do for Amish readers: augment their spiritual lives, such that their Christian commitments are reinforced and their inner lives enriched.[24]

In privileging the personal devotional life, however, Amish fiction may also weaken Amish readers' ties to their community. In *The Riddle of Amish Culture*, Donald B. Kraybill writes that "a shift toward individual belief, subjective experience, and emotionalism would cultivate individualism and undermine the total package of traditional practices."[25] While not writing specifically about Amish fiction, Kraybill's words suggest that Amish fiction's portrayal of personal spirituality may enervate an Amish reader's commitment to Amish culture, which depends on the continuance of churchly and community authority in members' lives.

In a diatribe against Amish romance novels in her church periodical, one Beachy Amish critic suggests something similar: that the emphases contained in Amish novels "undermine the authority of the home and church, blot out true reasons for joining the church, and teach that becoming a Christian in one short dramatic prayer is going to take away all problems and we live happily ever after."[26] In that sense, Amish fiction may operate like a Trojan horse within Amish communities, clad as innocent literature but releasing narratives of individualized piety that counteract the bonds of this collectivist society. The ultimate irony would be if the novels became corrosive agents to the very culture about which their authors articulate such affection.[27]

In addition to rewriting Amish spirituality, Amish novels, if they are read by Amish people, may affect Amish notions of romance. While Amish perspectives on romance vary between affiliations, families, and individuals, Charles Hurst and David McConnell maintain that Amish romantic relationships generally place less emphasis on emotion than non-Amish romantic relationships do, and more on an integration of expressive and instrumental components. Romantic Amish relationships, they suggest, more closely approximate what sociologist Francesca Cancian describes as colonial-era romance, characterized as much by shared economic activity as by romantic feelings. "Amish love is based on respect rather than emotion," said one Amish man with whom I spoke, and an Amish woman's comment in the Amish publication *Family Life* seems to confirm this: "Although romance may have its part in a healthy marriage, let's not mistake tinsel for gold," she writes. "Gifts of flowers and candy may be a token of love and appreciation, but a helping hand with the work or with the children are deeds that speak of true love and devotion."[28]

Cancian argues that as industrialization cordoned off male spheres of influence from female ones, love became defined as a feminine virtue, valued for its emotive bonds more than its economic ones. This "feminization of love" tends to ignore the "practical, material aspects of love such as giving help or sharing activities" in favor of "tenderness and expressing feelings."[29] Romance novels, almost by definition, highlight the expressive aspects of love, and the novels themselves could be seen as a product of the feminization of love.[30] Some Amish novels emphasize the instrumental aspects of marital relationships, while others trade mostly in the affective and emotive. If real-life Amish courtship and marriage relationships prioritize instrumental aspects of love more than non-Amish relationships do, then it is possible that the reading of Amish novels by the Amish will begin changing cultural understandings of romance.[31] Intuiting this possibility, the same Beachy Amish Mennonite woman who warned that Amish novels undermine the authority of the church also cautioned her sisters about the damage that Amish romance novels might do to their marriages. Reading the novels may alter marital expectations, Jennifer Anderson writes, to the extent that "our husbands now have to be 'the man of our dreams,' and good-looking to be good husbands." Amish novels "set inaccurate and unchristian views of love and marriage," Anderson claims, which "focus on the physical and what a person can get out of it."[32]

Transactional reading theories remind us that novels can't exert total control over any of their readers, Amish ones included, and Amish readers are as able as non-Amish readers to resist aspects of the texts they read. Amish and other plain readers may choose to enjoy aspects of Amish romance novels, such as the story line, while opposing others, such as the novels' constructions of spirituality or romance. In addition, cultural change often occurs over the course of generations, so that the full effect of Amish novels on Amish culture may not be apparent for a long time. Thus, claiming that Amish fiction poses a present and measurable threat to Amish life would be histrionics at this point; suggesting that it may alter Amish culture is not.

Consequences of *Thrill of the Chaste*

As a study of a subgenre of inspirational fiction about a people group that make up less than one-tenth of 1 percent of the U.S. population, this book has a very narrow purview. The field of Amish fiction, though fertile, remains a relatively small plot on the literary landscape, and it would be hubris on the part of any surveyor to claim otherwise. Even as Amish romance novels were reforming the terrain of Christian fiction, I still regularly encountered people who, when they heard about my project, asked, "Amish fiction? What's that?"

Yet rarely has such a large corpus of fictional work about one culture been produced by members of another. "Ethnic" fiction is usually written by those considered "ethnic" themselves, with prominent authors' names sometimes standing in for the categories—Louise Erdrich for American Indian fiction, for example. Whether entire bodies of fiction gain strength or suffer harm when famous "ethnic" authors become proxies for those literatures is a valid question. Either way, however, the phenomenon throws into relief this publishing conundrum in which *non*-Amish authors' names, such as Beverly Lewis, have become placeholders for "Amish fiction." If hypermodernity fledges more genres such as Amish fiction, in which writers within one culture represent subjects from another, issues of commodification, appropriation, and the ethics of cross-cultural mediation will become even more critical. *Thrill of the Chaste* commends to future scholarship the lenses of cultural criticism and transactional reading theory through which to view those processes.

In addition, I have surveyed only one segment (albeit the largest) of Amish-themed fiction: inspirational novels. The many Amish-themed mysteries from writers like P. L. Gaus, the Amish science fiction titles, the emerging LGBT Amish fiction, the nonevangelical Amish titles, the growing corpus of Mennonite fiction and Quaker fiction: these and other Amish-related genres are ripening for study. Future studies of such literature would do well to examine not only the texts themselves but also the production strategies with which the books are conceived, published, and sold. Even as a genre such as Amish fiction is produced within a hypermodern publishing climate, it offers readers the opportunity to declare themselves independent from hypermodern allegiances and affections. As more chaste fictions develop around similar people groups, researchers should listen to readers' words about their beloved books and observe the ways in which their comments may signal not just personal reading preferences but the longings and anxieties of an entire discourse community. As we have seen, literature can serve as a semaphore for the subculture that produces and consumes it, a flag by which it expresses concern regarding contemporary cultural directions.

Thrill of the Chaste also suggests two words of caution: one for evangelicals themselves, and one for those who represent them. First, when evangelicals seek inspiration from and alliance with other Christians at odds with a hypermodern, hypersexed culture, they risk overlooking the singularity and cultural integrity of those with whom they identify. In a hypermodern economic realm, drawing spiritual sustenance from a sect like the Amish can come uncomfortably close to profiting from it, and the use of the Other to metabolize one's own cultural or religious anxieties may ultimately do a disservice to the represented group. Theologian Vincent Miller warns that religious beliefs can easily be "reduced and abstracted," turned into sentiments that function "solely to give flavor to the already established forms of everyday life or to provide compensations for its shortcomings."[33] Writers and publishers who deliver one religious culture to another would do well to reflect on this dilemma: that is, whether their work extracts religious symbols and customs for decorative or therapeutic purposes. Hopefully this study has offered some theoretical tools for such self-examination.

Similarly, a caveat goes to those who seek to represent evangelical readers and writers to those outside of evangelicalism. Evangelical Christians are sometimes portrayed as monolithically rightist in their politics, closed-minded in their worldview, and sanctimonious in their morality. In this study I have attempted to illuminate some of the internal logic of evangelicalism, its priorities and longings, and to offer one more jumping-off point for future studies of evangelical reading tastes and practices. Yet I may also have fallen prey to the same domesticating and exoticizing impulses that the genre itself must confront vis-à-vis the Amish. Nonfiction accounts of evangelical readers are in as much peril of distortion or misinterpretation of a culture and its affections and practices as fictional accounts of the Amish

are. Even as I have tried to represent the readers and writers of Amish fiction fairly and with respect, like authors of Amish fiction, I too risk oversimplification and caricature. As a Mennonite, I may also view Amish fiction
with a misplaced sense of custodianship. Now that so many people, mostly
non-Anabaptists, are writing about my ecclesial cousins, criticism from a
Mennonite like me may reflect a knee-jerk mistrust of outsiders writing
about "my" people.

Yet while I remain personally ambivalent about the subgenre, I am not
ready to accuse all of its readers of unproductive nostalgia and fantasy-filled
escapism. For who can say why we read what we do, or why we love it? What
claims can be made about any particular narrative, why it delights some and
bores others? One can apply the calipers of literary analysis or ethnography
or cultural studies to a genre like this, probing and pinching to squeeze
meaning from its sudden popularity, sense from its inexplicable fame. In
the end, the consummate appeal of Amish fiction will remain clear to those
who love it, inscrutable to those who don't.[34]

Most of the readers and writers and others whose stories I have told in
this book can let me know whether I've been fair to the genre they love. But
one reader, whom I dearly wish I could have met, will not have that chance.
When my mother's cousin Ruth Ann, a retired librarian in Oklahoma, told
me a story of this recently deceased gentleman, his recently acquired reading habit, and the recently published novels that he devoured each week, I
knew that it was his story with which this book must end.

A Nonagenarian and His Novels

Hydro, Oklahoma, population 960, is an exposed little town on the high
plains of the western part of the state. The four months following Thanks-
giving 2010 were the driest on record for Oklahoma since 1921.[35] From my
visit there one summer about ten years ago, I remember mostly hot pave-
ment and sere front lawns. But when Ruth Ann's Amish grandfather Valentine Swartzendruber visited Hydro in the summer of 1904, looking for
fertile farmland, Hydro must have at least approximated the liquid claims
of its name. Her grandfather returned to his failing farm in Missouri with
two forty-pound watermelons, proof to his wife and children that Hydro

farmland could support them. He moved his family there, and unlike the many who left the Dust Bowl in the 1930s, the Swartzendrubers stayed.

Ruth Ann's older cousin, Glenn Swartzendruber, was a farmer for much of his life. Like her, he was a grandchild of Valentine and a Mennonite. Unlike her, Glenn did not like to read. For the last several years of his life, Glenn lived in an assisted living facility, where Ruth Ann would visit him once a week. On one visit she made to his home a short time before he moved into assisted living, Ruth Ann noticed that his television was on, as usual. She recalls sitting on the couch that evening and suddenly summoning the nerve to say, "Glenn, why don't you turn off that TV and read a book instead?" She doesn't remember thinking much would come of it, but apparently Glenn took her advice. He began checking out books from their church library, and when he moved to assisted living, Ruth Ann brought him books once a week. Once he started reading, he didn't stop.

Ruth Ann made sure that Glenn was supplied with books. He read about one novel a week, making his way through several chapters each day except on Sundays, when he would read only his Bible. Ruth Ann kept a list of the books she supplied to him so that she wouldn't bring him duplicates. That list is four pages long, with two columns of type on each page. While a smattering of genres show up on Glenn's reading list, a quick glance reveals his favorite kind of fiction: Amish romance novels.

During the last three years of his life, Glenn read almost ninety Amish-themed novels. He loved books by Wanda Brunstetter and Beverly Lewis, Ruth Ann recalls, but also enjoyed the work of Cindy Woodsmall, Beth Wiseman, Kim Vogel Sawyer, and others. Despite the proliferation of Amish-fiction titles in recent years, Ruth Ann was starting to have difficulty finding Amish novels that he hadn't read, and they often had to wait their turn for the new titles they would put on hold at the library. Ruth Ann says he would comment on how the books took him back to the rural Mennonite and Amish communities of his childhood, to the farmland he worked until he no longer could. He occasionally found inaccuracies in the books, Ruth Ann says, but they didn't bother him greatly; mostly he was pleased to have found fiction that reminded him of home.

Glenn died in May 2011, at age ninety-two. He was survived by two daughters and several grandchildren and great-grandchildren. The funeral program shows a photograph of him wearing a plaid shirt, an impish grin, and a hat that reads "Warning: Farming May be Hazardous to Your Wealth." The last novel that Glenn read before he died was *The Thorn*, the first in Beverly Lewis's The Rose Trilogy.

That a nonagenarian, living in a nursing home in what some have called the New Dust Bowl, was a faithful reader of Amish fiction demonstrates several things that we would do well to remember. Glenn's reading habit reminds us that Amish fiction stretches beyond an evangelical female audience, that the appeal of the books can't simply be pegged to gender or brand of Christian faith. Glenn's love for the genre reminds us that many readers, regardless of their demographic, are seeking imaginative transport away from a hypermodern, hypersexualized context. In fact, Glenn was only one of many appreciative readers of Amish fiction that I kept hearing about as I wrapped up my research. A college friend who lived in Bolivia told me that the Old Colony Mennonites—both men and women—who frequent a Mennonite-run lending library in Santa Cruz are loyal readers of Amish romance novels.[36] A friend of a friend in the checkout aisle in Target grabbed my elbow and told me, "My mother and aunts *love* Amish books!" A physician with degrees from Harvard and the University of Pennsylvania shared that he enjoys listening to the audio versions of Beverly Lewis's novels, and the copyeditor of this book e-mailed to say that she is an Amish-fiction reader, too.

Many readers mourn the passing of the old world, regardless of whether they, like Glenn, ever experienced it: the rhythms of the family farm, the consolations of community, the disciplines of faith, the clarity of preindustrial gender and sexual norms, the coherence of an offline life. The fictional source to which they go may be a nostalgic throwback, a "happily ever after" fantasy, or an appropriated fiction. It may be Christian literature's version of, as Stephanie Coontz has written of the idealized past, "the way we never were."[37]

Or Amish-themed fiction may be a coping strategy in a helter-skelter, anonymous world, a portal through which readers can view an alternative vision, however sentimentalized or hagiographic that vision may be. It is possible that Amish fiction is a kind of social commentary, gently packaged and sealed with a chaste kiss, which indicts *progress* and *freedom* and *technol-*

ogy and *convenience* and all the other shibboleths of hypermodernity. Finding themselves ambivalent residents of this age, readers become "fraught with misgivings and sorrows," writes philosopher Albert Borgmann; "in these sentiments a genuine alternative quietly asserts itself."[38] By living an ersatz Amish life, for episodes as long as a book or a series lasts, readers get to rehearse one alternative to hypermodernity and its vicissitudes. In the pages of Amish fiction, retired farmer Glenn, librarian Ceil, at-home mom Pam, novelist Suzanne, real estate executive Deanna, and college-student Betsy can try on a life without Facebook or college or cars or life insurance premiums or *American Idol*. In twenty-first-century America, this is a radical surrogacy indeed.

These readers' love of Amish romance novels may illustrate a penchant for commodified escapism or regressive nostalgia. But it might also represent a profound sense that the new millennium and its attendant developments have not yet delivered on their promises, a sense that rehearsing a fictional alternative to supercharged contemporary life is better than doing nothing at all. The consummate allure of Amish novels to people like Glenn and Ceil and Pam and others may represent less what historian Eric Miller calls the "immaturity of nostalgia" than "the intelligence of hope."[39]

Sitting beside his window overlooking I-40, the pulsing interstate that bisects Oklahoma, and tucking into the latest Amish novel his cousin dropped off for him, Glenn may not be a symbol of nostalgia or elegy at all. He may instead represent readers' desire for a sane, coherent, and communal future, a world in which the drought of hypermodernity has ended.

Notes

Preface

1. The Amish refer to non-Amish people as "English" or "Englischers."

2. At least five male authors are writing Amish romances: Jerry Eicher, Dale Cramer, Murray Pura, Gilbert Morris, and Patrick Craig.

3. Mennonites are one branch of the Anabaptists and are historically and theologically related to the Amish, as we will see in chapter 3. Some Mennonite women and all Amish women wear an organza or cotton covering (*Kapp*), cloth veiling, or other head covering because of the apostle Paul's admonition in 1 Corinthians 11 that women should cover their heads when they pray.

4. *Schuslich:* restless. *Dopplich* (or *doppich*): clumsy or awkward.

5. Tamela Hancock Murray, "Bonnet Fiction—Here to Stay?" in *From the Heart* (blog), March 3, 2010, http://hartlineliteraryagency.blogspot.com/2010/03/bon net-fiction-here-to-stay-by-tamela.html (site discontinued).

6. "About Beverly," Beverly Lewis website, www.beverlylewis.com/index .php?option=com_content&view=category&layout=blog&id=11&Itemid=138, accessed June 27, 2012; "About Amy," Amy Clipston website, www.amyclipston .com/about.html, accessed June 27, 2012; Cindy Woodsmall website, www .cindywoodsmall.com/about-cindy/biography/, accessed June 27, 2012; Shelley Shepard Gray, interview by Scott Simon, "Amish Romance: More Faith and No Sex in This Slice of Christian Fiction," *Weekend Edition Saturday*, October 16, 2010, www.npr.org/blogs/monkeysee/2010/10/15/130589491/amish-romance -novels-more-faith-no-sex-and-strong-sales; "About VC," *Vannetta Chapman* (blog), http://vannettachapman.wordpress.com/about/, accessed June 27, 2012.

7. Walbert, *Garden Spot*, 3.

8. Marx, *Machine in the Garden*, 6.

9. Lewis, *The Crossroad*, 17.

10. Several article-length scholarly treatments of Amish-themed fiction do exist. See the articles in the "Serial Fiction" issue of *Center for Mennonite Writing Journal* 2, no. 4 (July 2010), www.mennonitewriting.org/journal/2/4/, esp. Beck, "Mennonite and Amish Serial Fiction." See also Graybill, "Chasing the Bonnet"; and Johnson-Weiner, "Pow-Wow Healers." Other studies that deal with some aspect of Amish-themed fiction include Weaver-Zercher, *Amish in the American Imagination* (chap. 4); Neal, *Romancing God* (chap. 5); and Gandolfo, *Faith and Fiction* (chap. 4).

11. Throughout this study, I refer to readers of Amish fiction and the Amish themselves primarily by their first names only or else do not refer to them by name at all. Some were open to having their last names used, but others preferred to have only their first names used. For the sake of consistency, I excluded most last names.

12. Slovic, *Going Away to Think*, 28.

13. Throughout this book, I use both *genre* and *subgenre* to refer to Amish romance fiction. This flexibility reflects what I heard in my research: while some editors suggest that Amish fiction is now large enough to be considered its own genre, other observers point out that Amish romance fiction is actually a subsubgenre (with Christian fiction as the genre and Christian romance fiction as the subgenre within which it is housed). Genre theorists frequently point out that few texts would fit clearly into one genre even if the characteristics of that genre could be agreed upon. Thus, rather than relying on a strict taxonomy of genre, I use the terms interchangeably to reflect the fluidity of genre itself. For more on genre studies, see John Frow, *Genre* (New York: Routledge, 2006).

14. Some Amish writers do produce fiction, some of it with romance elements, that is read mostly by other Amish or plain people. Several novels published by Amish-owned Pathway Publishers in Aylmer, Ontario, contain romance themes—see, for example, Sara M. Weaver, *Beyond the Past* (Aylmer, ON: Pathway, 1972). Serialized fiction in *Young Companion*, a monthly periodical for Amish teens, sometimes narrates stories of romance. These stories do not always have "happy" endings, however, a fact that stands in fascinating counterpoint to the satisfying resolutions of most Amish novels.

15. Other writers of Amish-themed mysteries that do not contain a romance element include Barbara Workinger, Earlene Fowler, and Madelyn Alt.

16. For more on representations of the Amish in fiction, see Kraybill, Johnson-Weiner, and Nolt, *The Amish*, chap. 20.

17. Amy Clipston, "A Trend or a New Subgenre?" *Author Jennifer Hudson Taylor* (blog), March 15, 2010, http://jenniferswriting.blogspot.com/2010/03/bonnet-fiction-trend-or-new-subgenre.html (site discontinued).

18. Carol Johnson, conversation with author, April 19, 2011.

19. Beverly Lewis, conversation with author, January 28, 2011.

20. Regis, *Natural History of the Romance*, 14; Radway, *Reading the Romance*, 64.

Chapter One. Slap a Bonnet on the Cover

1. The sales of Amish fiction appear to be somewhat regional in nature: that is, bookstores close to Amish settlements tend to stock Amish-themed novels to a greater extent than stores located far from Amish communities. One Christian bookstore manager in southern California assured me that sales of Amish novels there were brisk, however, and a regional sales representative for an evangelical publisher said Amish fiction sells well in most of his region, which stretches from the southern United States to New England.

2. Steve Oates, quoted in Miller, "Love, Amish Style," 25.

3. Beverly Lewis's Amish novels have sold 17 million copies. Steve Oates, e-mail to author, March 20, 2012. Wanda Brunstetter's books have sold 6 million copies. Shalyn Sattler, e-mail to author, April 25, 2012. Cindy Woodsmall's Amish books (all novels except one book of Amish nonfiction, coauthored with Amish woman Miriam Flaud) have sold 1 million copies. "Cindy Woodsmall Reaches Publishing Milestone: 1 Million Copies Sold," CBA Industry Brief, May 2, 2012, www.cbanews.org/article.php?id=4613#.

4. *The Thorn*, the last title in Lewis's The Rose Trilogy, sold 280,000 copies between September and December 2010. See Miller, "Love, Amish Style," 25.

5. Amish novels by several other authors have appeared on *New York Times* bestseller lists, although many were likely hitting sales that could have placed them there years ago. Since many Christian bookstores only started reporting sales figures to Nielsen Bookscan, data provider for the publishing industry, in the past several years, titles that were doing extremely well in the Christian market and garnering impressive sales simply went unnoticed by mainstream bestseller lists. Sales numbers for Amish books are difficult to obtain, in part because many publishers are reluctant to release numbers.

6. CBA Fiction Bestsellers, September 2011, www.cbaonline.org/nm/docu
ments/BSLs/Fiction_Inspirational.pdf, accessed October 1, 2011; CBA, or the
Association for Christian Retail, was formerly the Christian Booksellers Association.

7. "Amish" was already a category for certain publishers and retailers, including Christian Book Distributors. But "Fiction / Amish & Mennonite" first appeared as a Book BISAC (Book Industry Subject and Category) code, created by
the Book Industry Study Group (BISG), on BISG's 2011 list of subject headings,
released in September 2011. See the BISG list of fiction headings at www.bisg
.org/what-we-do-0-100-bisac-subject-headings-list-fiction.php.

8. Andrea Doering, conversation with author, March 17, 2011. John Bomberger, CEO of Choice Books, a Christian book distributor, echoed Doering in a
conversation on October 5, 2011: "Already we're talking about Amish as its own
category. It seems like Amish fiction is a category itself, not a subcategory."
Zondervan's Sue Brower told me essentially the same thing on November 18,
2011: "We used to think in terms of historical and contemporary. I think Amish
is now its own genre."

9. Hillary Manton Lodge said that her editor at Harvest House asked "if I
could write Amish, couching it with the fact that they were looking for 'Sassy
Amish.'" Hillary Lodge, comment on "The Amish," *Cecelia's Christian Fiction
Blog*, March 15, 2009, http://ceceliadowdy.blogspot.com/2009/03/amish.html.

10. As of March 2012, LGBT Amish romances on the market were Yolanda
Wallace, *Rum Spring* (Valley Falls, NY: Bold Strokes Press, 2010); Shelter Som-
erset, *Between Two Worlds* and *Between Two Promises* (Frisco, TX: Dreamspinner
Press, 2011); Andrew Grey, *Love Means . . . No Shame* and *Love Means . . . No Fear*
(Frisco, TX: Dreamspinner Press, 2009, 2010); and Jay Hughes, *The Shunned*
and *The Forbidden* (Ravenous Romance, 2010).

11. See Morgan, "Getting Dirty in Dutch Country," 69; and David Wright,
"Carrie Bradshaw—In a Bonnet?" ABC News, May 26, 2009, http://abcnews
.go.com/Nightline/story?id=7676659&page=1&page=1. Hamilton Nolan, "Can
Bonnet Porn Save Publishing?" *Gawker*, September 9, 2009, www.gawker
.com/5355481/can-bonnet-porn-save-publishing.

12. Kraybill, Johnson-Weiner, and Nolt, *The Amish*, chap. 9.

13. Beth Wiseman, interview, in Golden Keyes Parsons, *Where Hearts are
Free* (Nashville: Thomas Nelson, 210), 350. Wiseman did release a non-Amish
women's fiction book in March 2012, and wrote on her website that her plan is
to "alternate between Amish novels and contemporary stories." "About Beth,"
https://bethwiseman.com/about-beth/, accessed February 27, 2012.

14. Jane Love, religious books buyer for Barnes & Noble, told a reporter that Amish fiction accounts for fifteen of the chain's top one hundred religious fiction titles. See Alter, "They're No Bodice Rippers."

15. Lipovetsky, *Hypermodern Times*, 30, 32.

16. Ibid., 39.

17. Ibid., 59.

18. Kammeyer, *Hypersexual Society*, 12. Baudrillard's use of the term also connotes the way that, within a hyperreal world, simulated experiences of sex displace actual sexual coupling. For Baudrillard's original use of the term, see Jean Baudrillard, *Fatal Strategies* (Los Angeles: Semiotext[e], 2008), 30 (originally published in 1983 in French).

19. See Paul, *Pornified*; Levy, *Female Chauvinist Pigs*; McNair, *Striptease Culture*. For specific instances, see Oppliger, *Girls Gone Skank*, 135.

20. McNair, *Striptease Culture*, 61; Traci Lords quoted in Frank Rich, "Finally, Porn Does Prime Time," *New York Times*, July 27, 2003, www.nytimes .com/2003/07/27/arts/finally-porn-does-prime-time.html?pagewanted=all& src=pm; Paul, *Pornified*, 11.

21. "Fifty Shades Trilogy Tops 10 Million Sold," *Publishers Weekly*, May 22, 2012, www.publishersweekly.com.

22. In *Sex and the Soul*, Freitas uses the descriptor "purity culture" in reference to the culture on evangelical Christian college campuses. For a fascinating examination of evangelical constructions of chastity, see Christine J. Gardner, *Making Chastity Sexy: The Rhetoric of Evangelical Abstinence Campaigns* (Berkeley: University of California Press, 2011). See "Father-Daughter Purity Ball," www.purityball.com/, accessed June 27, 2012.

23. Lipovetsky, *Hypermodern Times*, 32 (emphasis mine).

24. Trollinger, *Selling the Amish*, 110.

25. Shaker-themed romance novels within inspirational fiction include four novels written by Ann Gabhart and published by Revell: *The Believer, The Seeker, The Outsider,* and *The Blessed*.

26. Miller, "Why We Love Amish Romances," 39.

27. Johnson-Weiner, "Selling the Past," 3. "Selling the Past" contains an important discussion of "Amishness" and commerce and of the extent to which producers, both Amish and non-Amish, actually construct Amishness as they design Amish-looking products for sale to non-Amish consumers.

28. "The Shunning," The Deuce of Clubs Book Club, www.deuceofclubs .com/books/290the_shunning.htm, accessed June 27, 2012.

29. See Wimsatt and Beardsley, "The Intentional Fallacy" and "The Affec-

tive Fallacy," in *The Verbal Icon*, 3–39. These essays are signature texts of New Criticism.

30. This idea comes from cultural critic Crystal Downing, conversation with author, March 15, 2011.

31. Eagleton, *Literary Theory*, 43.

32. Nell, *Lost in a Book*, 4.

33. See Louise Rosenblatt, *The Reader, the Text, the Poem: The Transactional Theory of the Literary Work* (Carbondale: Southern Illinois University Press, 1978).

34. Eagleton, *After Theory*, 96.

35. Ibid., 88.

36. Williams, *Raymond Williams Reader*, 11, 268.

37. Gans, *Popular Culture*, 6, xiv.

38. Ibid., 143.

39. Eagleton, *Literary Theory*, 9.

40. Ohmann, "Shaping of a Canon," 219; Nell, *Lost in a Book*, 41.

41. Cavallo and Chartier, *History of Reading*, 319.

42. Eliot, "Silly Novels by Lady Novelists," 442.

43. Mock, "Love and Marriage."

44. Associated Press, "Christian Literature Has Expanded, from Amish to Vampires," *Los Angeles Times*, July 17, 2009, http://articles.latimes.com/2009/jul/17/entertainment/et-christian-books17.

45. Regis, *Natural History of the Romance*, xi, quotation on 207.

46. Radway, *Reading the Romance*, 11. Radway is not without her opponents, and in a 1991 edition of *Reading the Romance*, she writes an introduction outlining different directions she would have taken were she writing the study in the 1990s. See Radway, "Writing *Reading the Romance*," in *Reading the Romance*, 2nd ed. (Philadelphia: University of North Carolina Press, 1991). Feminist critic Tania Modleski levels numerous charges against Radway's ethnographic methodology and claims, including that Radway, in Modleski's opinion, "winds up condescending to the very people she wants to rescue from critical scorn"; see Modleski, *Feminism without Women*, 44.

47. Ceil Carey, conversation with author, April 12, 2011.

48. I have borrowed the idea of an "ur–bonnet book" from Pamela Regis, who calls E. M. Hull's *The Sheik*, published in 1919, the "ur–romance novel of the twentieth century." Regis, *Natural History of the Romance*, 115.

49. Staff member of Dauphin County Historical Society, conversation with

author, April 4, 2011. After consulting the 1906 copy of the Harrisburg City Directory, the staff member told me that one Frederick Martin, a musician, is listed as owning a home at 1168 Mulberry Street, Harrisburg, Pennsylvania. Additionally, Helen Reimensnyder Martin told the *Ladies Home Journal* that she had "had just two homes in all my life—the one in which I was born, reared, and married and the one my husband and I built soon after our marriage and have dwelt in ever since." "Our Family Album," *Ladies Home Journal* 44 (January 1927): 28.

50. Seaton, "Helen Reimensnyder Martin's 'Caricatures,'" 88.

Chapter Two. The DNA of Amish Romance Novels

1. An Amish operetta, *Love Will Find a Way*, with music by Hugo Marks and lyrics by Charles Howell and David McNeal, appeared in 1903. The plot anticipates that of *Sabina* and features an Amish maiden, Martha Churchly, being courted by English suitor Jack Huntley. *Sabina* remains the first novel, however, containing Amish characters and setting and romance themes.

2. Martin, *Sabina*, 63.

3. Ibid., 26.

4. Ibid., 29.

5. Brodhead, *Cultures of Letters*, 115, 135. Readers of local-color writing were rarely inhabitants of the culture being written about, Brodhead clarifies, a point that Martin herself made: "The Pennsylvania Dutch don't like my stories. That is, the educated descendants of the Pennsylvania Dutch don't like them. The people of whom I write generally are people who read nothing, not even newspapers." Helen R. Martin, quoted in Grant Overton, *The Women Who Make Our Novels* (New York: Moffat, Yard, 1922), 219.

6. Brodhead, *Cultures of Letters*, 137, 133–34.

7. Martin, *Sabina*, 233.

8. This is despite Martin's claim that she did not deal with feminism or socialism in her work "because the folks she writes about are not aware of such questions." Seaton, "Helen Reimensnyder Martin's 'Caricatures,'" 89.

9. Martin, *Sabina*, 51, 231. Martin was likely influenced by Charlotte Perkins Gilman, author of the famed short story "The Yellow Wallpaper" and an early leader of the women's movement, claims historian Marlene Epp. Gilman's conviction that women's emancipation rested on the imperative of economic independence was reflected in the sensibilities of Martin's protagonists, Epp writes,

most of whom "are supporters of suffrage, are educated, and value career options for women other than marriage." Epp, "A Brief Look."

10. Another local-color writer who narrated the lives of Pennsylvania Germans was Elsie Singmaster. Singmaster's short story "The Amishman" appeared in *Ladies Home Journal* in April 1925, 18–19, 211–15. For more on Singmaster, see Hill, *Heart Language*. Hill suggests that Singmaster's work represented the Amish much more sympathetically than Martin's did, tying Pennsylvania German life to "American ideals of peace, justice, and individual opportunity." Hill, *Heart Language*, 3.

11. Welty, *Masquerading of Margaret*, 184–85.

12. Cultural theorist Crystal Downing first proposed this idea in her application of the pastoral convention to several films featuring the Amish. See Downing's essay "Witnessing the Amish," 25–41.

13. See Gifford, *Pastoral*, for three distinct definitions of the pastoral. I generally use the term in Gifford's second sense—as "any book or poem that affirms the essential goodness of rural areas and lifestyles and people as contrasted to urban ones" (1–2).

14. Welty, *Masquerading of Margaret*, 35, 31.

15. Ibid., 36, 39, 16.

16. Ibid., 68, 91; Downing, "Witnessing the Amish," 38.

17. Weaver-Zercher first identified this dialectic in *Amish in the American Imagination*, tracing it through various manifestations in popular culture. Both poles of the dialectic contain themes of sin, redemption, and warning, he writes, and "both draw sustenance from the other by participating in an ongoing dialectic of idealization and demythologization." Weaver-Zercher, *Amish in the American Imagination*, 185.

18. Welty, *Masquerading of Margaret*, 148, 213.

19. Kasdorf, "Why We Fear the Amish," 69.

20. Beth Wiseman, interview with Michele Cushatt, "Interview with Beth Wiseman," *Family Fiction*, April 11, 2011; "Just Like Us," *Family Fiction*, May–June 2011, 13–16.

21. Eli Bontrager, "'Straw in the Wind' Criticized by Authority on Amish Customs," *Middlebury (IN) Independent*, February 11, 1937. See Bender, "Three Amish Novels," and 1973 correspondence between David Luthy and Ruth Lininger Dobson, Amish Historical Library, Aylmer, Ontario. "Your book presents the Amish as a ridiculous and ignorant people," wrote Luthy, an editor at an Amish publishing company and a convert to the Amish; "It is true the Amish

oppose the novel and so do I." Dobson wrote detailed letters addressing his concerns, at first sounding bewildered by his accusation ("My family had great respect for the Amish. I was taught that") and, in later letters, matching the ire of her Amish correspondent ("Are you prepared to say that no Amish man *ever* resembled Moses?").

22. Joseph W. Yoder, quoted in Kasdorf, "Introduction," 11. Multiple questions regarding Yoder's claims to accuracy have been raised, including his self-identification as someone who "still belong[s] to the Amish church" and his genealogical facticity. Nevertheless, the book, which Kasdorf calls indigenous local-color writing, demonstrates "one sincere and creative response to an ongoing bias and ignorance regarding this group." Kasdorf, "Introduction," 22.

23. Yoder, *Rosanna of the Amish*, 207, 208, 195.

24. Ibid., 320; John Umble, review of *Rosanna*.

25. Several Amish-themed romantic short stories appeared in magazines during the first half of the twentieth century, including Brook Hanlon's short story "The Shunning," in *American Magazine* 152, no. 6 (December 1951): 38–40, 83–87.

26. Miller, *Katie*, 20, 72, 179, 278.

27. Ibid., 276.

28. For more on the Amish mission movement, see Steven M. Nolt, "The Amish 'Mission Movement' and the Reformulation of Amish Identity in the Twentieth Century," *Mennonite Quarterly Review* 75, no. 1 (2001): 7–36. See also Kraybill, *Riddle of Amish Culture*, 36–38. For a discussion of Amish studies scholar John Hostetler's evolving perspectives on this issue, see Weaver-Zercher, *Writing the Amish*.

29. Donald B. Kraybill first used the term "Anabaptist escalator" in Kraybill and Olshan, *Amish Struggle with Modernity*, 72. Kraybill also credits Leo Driedger for his use of the term "Anabaptist identification ladder." Driedger, "The Anabaptist Identification Ladder: Plain-Urbane Continuity in Diversity," *Mennonite Quarterly Review* 51, no. 4 (October 1977): 278–91. The term has been used not only to describe movement between Anabaptist groups but, more generally, to describe the continuum of Amish groups, from the most closed, world-rejecting Amish affiliations such as the Swartzentrubers to the more liberal New Order Amish; see Hurst and McConnell, *Amish Paradox*, chap. 3. Roger Finke and Rodney Stark identify a parallel movement in other faith cultures; see *The Churching of America, 1776–2005: Winners and Losers in Our Religious Economy*, rev. ed. (Piscataway, NJ: Rutgers University Press, 2005), esp. chap. 7.

30. David Kline has published three books of nature writing: *Great Possessions: An Amish Farmer's Journal* (San Francisco: North Point Press, 1990); *Scratching the Woodchuck: Nature on an Amish Farm* (Athens: University of Georgia Press, 1997); and *Letters from Larksong: An Amish Naturalist Explores His Organic Farm* (Wooster, OH: Wooster Book Company, 2010).

31. David Kline, conversation with author, January 15, 2011. The phone in a phone shanty is often shared by several Amish families. That Miller's novels were published by Mennonites, close ecclesial relatives of the Amish who have at times been quite invested in positively portraying the Amish, may at first glance be surprising. For one explanation of this, see Weaver-Zercher, *Amish in the American Imagination*, 140.

32. Ibid., 137.

33. Miller, *Katie*, 72.

34. Carol Johnson, conversation with author, April 19, 2011; and Neal, *Romancing God*, 26–30.

35. Blodgett, *Protestant Evangelical Literary Culture*, 47.

36. Carol Johnson, conversation with author, April 19, 2011. For more on Janette Oke's prairie romances, see Neal, *Romancing God*, esp. 26–30.

37. Ibid., 22.

38. Quoted in Rabey and Unger, *Milestones*, 172.

39. Radway, *Reading the Romance*, 33.

40. Ibid., 40.

41. Regis, *Natural History of the Romance*, xi. For a comprehensive history of the romance novel, see also Radway, *Reading the Romance*.

42. The man on the cover of Cheryl Reavis's *A Crime of the Heart* is vaguely Amish-looking, but the covers of these other general-market Amish romances contain no sign of Amishness.

43. Neal, *Romancing God*, 77.

44. On her website, Beverly Lewis says that her grandmother, Ada Ranck Buchwalter, "left her Old Order Mennonite upbringing to marry a Bible College student." In one guest entry on a Christian fiction blog, Lewis constructs her grandmother's experience as one of shunning. "My maternal grandmother . . . experienced a heart-breaking shunning that lasted her entire life (from age 17 onward), when she opened her heart to a relationship with the Lord Jesus and married a ministerial student (outside the Plain community). This man became my grandfather (Omar Buchwalter) and he and my courageous grandmother Ada Ranck Buchwalter pastored churches in WA, FL, and later returned

to their homeland of Lancaster, PA, where my mother and her 8 siblings grew up. Because of Ada's bold move toward a personal relationship with Christ, I am one of the many benefactors on the whole vast side of Ada's and Omar's family tree." "Guest Blogger—NT Times Bestselling Author Beverly Lewis!" *Cecelia's Christian Fiction Blog*, March 24, 2009, http://ceceliadowdy.blogspot.com/2009/03/guest-blogger-ny-times-bestselling.html. Lewis also narrates her family history on the online radio program *Amish Wisdom*. Beverly Lewis, interview by Suzanne Woods Fisher, *Amish Wisdom*, podcast audio, April 21, 2011, http://toginet.com/podcasts/amishwisdom/?s=amishwisdom.

Stephen Scott, research associate at the Young Center for Anabaptist and Pietist Studies, suggested in an unpublished paper that Ada Ranck and her husband, Omar Buchwalter, *both* grew up Mennonite. Scott claimed that both Ranck and Buchwalter were not Old Order Mennonite but rather members of Lancaster Conference Mennonite churches, which would have been quite conservative in the early 1900s but with no formal practices of shunning. "It is quite conceivable that the Ranck family felt very strongly that Ada should not leave the Mennonite Church and may have expressed their disapproval," Scott wrote. "But this has also been true of people strongly grounded in any denomination if a family member leaves the fold." Scott also takes issue with Lewis's construction of her grandmother's opening of her heart "to a relationship with the Lord Jesus" as if that were something foreign to her Mennonite faith; Ada's mother's obituary, for example, suggests that before she died, she often repeated her favorite hymn, "Jesus, Lover of My Soul." "It rather sounds like Ada's mother, Beverly's great-grandmother, had a 'personal relationship with Christ.'" See Scott, "Popularity of Amish Fiction."

45. Quotations in this section from Carol Johnson, conversation with author, April 19, 2011.

46. "Peretti Delivers 'Monster' of a Thriller," McClure/Muntsinger Public Relations, February 15, 2005, http://mmpublicrelations.com/recent-monster_announcement.html.

47. Weaver-Zercher, *Amish in the American Imagination*, 152.

48. Steve Oates, conversation with author, January 27, 2011.

49. Beverly Lewis, *The Beverly Lewis Amish Heritage Cookbook* (Grand Rapids, MI: Bethany House, 2004); Beverly Lewis, *Amish Prayers: Heartfelt Expressions of Humility, Gratitude, and Devotion* (Grand Rapids, MI: Bethany House, 2011); "New Amish Musical to Celebrate Its 100th Performance," July 27, 2011, http://theconfessionmusical.wordpress.com/.

50. Steve Oates, e-mail to author, March 20, 2012.

51. Steve Oates, conversation with author, January 27, 2011.

52. Gayle Roper's original trilogy released by Multnomah included *The Key* (April 1998), *The Document* (October 1998), and *The Decision* (December 1999). The books were edited, retitled, and released by Harvest House as *A Stranger's Wish* (February 2010), *A Secret Identity* (September 2010), and *A Rose Revealed* (February 2011).

53. Andrea Doering, conversation with author, March 17, 2011.

54. Cindy Woodsmall, "Author Spotlight," *Suzanne Woods Fisher* blog, August 5, 2011, http://suzannewoodsfisher.blogspot.com/2011/08/author-spotlight-cindy-woodsmall.html; Andrea Doering, conversation with author, March 17, 2011.

55. Sue Brower, conversation with author, November 18, 2011; Mary Sue Seymour, "An Agent's Tips for Your Manuscript," American Christian Fiction Writers blog, January 30, 2012, www.acfw.com/blog/?p=2427.

56. For more on the Nickel Mines shooting, see Kraybill, Nolt, and Weaver-Zercher, *Amish Grace;* Chip MacGregor, conversation with author, May 16, 2011.

57. Alisa Valdes-Rodriguez, "The Rise of Traditionalist Fiction in America," *Huffington Post*, June 14, 2011, www.huffingtonpost.com.

58. CBA, formerly known as the Christian Booksellers Association, is now known as the Association for Christian Retail but retains the acronym CBA. It is a nonprofit trade organization serving thousands of Christian retailers, distributors, publishers, and music labels. The name of the annual convention also changed in 2005, from CBA International Convention to International Christian Retail Show. See "CBA Historical Timeline, 1950–2006," www.cbaonline.org/nm/timeline.htm. Levi Miller, e-mail message to author, February 26, 2011; Welty, *Masquerading of Margaret*, 36.

59. Although *Ben's Wayne* is not strictly a romance according to the definitions advanced by Radway and Regis, it contains a love story—albeit a tragic one, in which the protagonist's girlfriend is killed in an auto accident. See L. Miller, *Ben's Wayne* (Intercourse, PA: Good Books, 1989). Carol Duerksen, conversation with author, August 23, 2011. Knepp and Duerksen have written and self-published two Amish-themed series—the Jonas Series and the Skye Series—as well as a duology about an Amish woman, Kate Weaver, and a children's book. Knepp and Duerksen's books have sold quite well among the Amish themselves. Most have a romance element.

60. Patricia Weaver, e-mail message to author, April 21, 2011.

61. Levi Miller, e-mail message to author, April 20, 2011; "About Herald Press," www.mpn.net/about/hp.html, accessed June 27, 2012.

62. Ervin Stutzman, quoted in Rich Preheim, "Leaders: Deep Trouble at MPH," *Mennonite*, February 5, 2002, 19; see also John Sharp, "End of an Era," *Mennonite*, June 2011, 12–17.

63. Levi Miller, conversation with author, April 20, 2011. Through a series of measures including a churchwide fund-raising effort dubbed the "Barn Raising Campaign," the publishing house rallied and paid off its debt in 2006.

64. Miller, *Consuming Religion*, 3.

65. Schechner, *Performance Studies*, 45.

Chapter Three. An Evangelical and an Amishman Walk into a Barn

1. Schultze and Woods, *Understanding Evangelical Media*, 22.

2. I am playing a little fast and loose with the term *discourse community* to describe the Amish, in that scholars usually imply that a measure of choice is inherent in belonging to any particular discourse community. Amish adults, although they have chosen to be baptized and join the church, have almost always been raised Amish rather than having converted from another background. The term *discourse community*, which emerges from linguistics, is in some circles being replaced by *communities of practice*, which comes from sociocultural theory. For a discussion of some of these issues, see Erik Borg, "Discourse Community," *ELT Journal* 57, no. 4 (October 2003): 398–400.

3. Some scholars locate the roots of modern evangelicalism much deeper in history, either in the 1920s or even in nineteenth-century Protestant orthodoxy. For a long view of evangelicalism's history, see Hunter, *American Evangelicalism*, chap. 3.

4. Smith, *American Evangelicalism*, 10. My cursory summary of evangelicalism's history is shaped largely from Smith's account. For a more detailed history of twentieth-century evangelicalism, see Smith, *American Evangelicalism*, chap. 1. For a concise tour of the landmark events that shaped modern evangelicalism, see Mark Noll, "Where We Are and How We Got Here," *Christianity Today*, October 2006, 42–49. For a helpful history and discussion of the convergences and differences between evangelicalism and fundamentalism, see Marsden, *Understanding Fundamentalism and Evangelicalism*.

5. Christian Smith makes this point very well in *Christian America?* esp.

chaps. 1–3. For a historical tracing of this concept of the United States as a "Christian nation," see John Fea, *Was America Founded as a Christian Nation? A Historical Introduction* (Louisville, KY: Westminster John Knox, 2008).

6. Loconte and Cromartie, "Let's Stop Stereotyping Evangelicals."

7. Bebbington, *Evangelicalism in Modern Britain*, 2–17. See Marsden, *Understanding Fundamentalism and Evangelicalism*, 5–6, for another definition. For more on the beliefs and practices of evangelical Christians, see the work of Christian Smith, esp. *American Evangelicalism* and *Christian America*.

8. For more on evangelical understandings of the family, see Smith, *Christian America*, chap. 5.

9. Wright, "They Like You"; Beth Wiseman's website, http://bethwiseman .com/?page_id=15.

10. For more on evangelical media, see Heather Hendershot, *Shaking the World for Jesus: Media and Conservative Evangelical Culture* (Chicago: University of Chicago Press, 2004); and Schultze and Woods, *Understanding Evangelical Media*.

11. Depending on how you do the numbers, the Bible still holds pole position. When you count all segments of Christians as defined by the ECPA—active, professing, liturgical, private, and cultural—the Bible ekes out a five-point lead (23% of Christian book purchases, compared with Christian fiction at 19%). See "Fiction Nearly Rivals Bible Purchases," *Christian Retailing Update*, September 9, 2010, www.christianretailing.com/index.php/newsletter/latest -etailing/21992-fiction-nearly-rivals-bible-purchases.

12. Michael Covington, "The Truth about Fiction (It's Better Than You Might Think)," ECPA Wire, October 1, 2010, www.ecpa.org/news/54961/The-Truth -About-Fiction-Its-Better-Than-You-Might-Think.htm.

13. In her study of readers of Christian romance novels, Rebecca Barrett-Fox writes that readers of the genre are largely "white middle- and lower-class and range in age widely . . . [and] self-identify as born-again Christians or simply 'Christian.'" See Barrett, "Higher Love," para. 4.

14. Gallagher and Lundin, *Literature through the Eyes of Faith*, 143; Schultze and Woods, *Understanding Evangelical Media*, 284.

15. See, for example, Hunter, *American Evangelicalism*, 7–9.

16. Statistics taken from Kraybill, Johnson-Weiner, and Nolt, *The Amish*. For more on Amish population patterns, see *The Amish*, chaps. 1, 8, and 9. Hurst and McConnell note that many Old Order Amish people suggest that the "social distance between Old Order Amish and non-Amish is far less than that

between Old Order and Swartzentruber Amish." Hurst and McConnell, *Amish Paradox*, 55. The Swartzentruber Amish are among the most conservative affiliations.

17. Kraybill, *Riddle of Amish Culture*, 88, 16. See also Kraybill, Johnson-Weiner, and Nolt, *The Amish*, chap. 9. Some estimates place the retention rate at about 80 percent. The rate of retention also varies among affiliations, with the "lower" groups tending toward higher rates of retention of youth than more progressive ones (see Hurst and McConnell's example from Holmes County, Ohio, in *Amish Paradox*, 79–80).

18. For much more in-depth explication and analysis of Amish history and life, see Kraybill, Johnson-Weiner, and Nolt, *The Amish;* Kraybill, *Riddle of Amish Culture;* and Steven M. Nolt, *A History of the Amish,* rev. ed. (Intercourse, PA: Good Books, 2004). See also Donald B. Kraybill, *Concise Encyclopedia of Amish, Brethren, Hutterites, and Mennonites* (Baltimore: Johns Hopkins University Press, 2010); and Steven M. Nolt and Thomas J. Meyers, *Plain Diversity: Amish Cultures and Identities* (Baltimore: Johns Hopkins University Press, 2007). A brief overview of various aspects of Amish history and life is available at the Amish Studies website maintained by the Young Center for Anabaptist and Pietist Studies at Elizabethtown College, www2.etown.edu/amishstudies/Index .asp.

19. Trollinger, *Selling the Amish*, 28.

20. Discourse about the Amish frequently demonstrates as much about the mediators themselves as about the Amish, such that the Amish become a foil by which to indict the culture to which the mediator belongs. See Weaver-Zercher, *Amish in the American Imagination,* especially the introduction. For a concise summary of the Amish rise to iconic status in North America, see Weaver-Zercher, "Amish."

21. Institute for the Study of Global Anabaptism, www.goshen.edu/insti tutes/anabaptism/. For more on global Mennonitism, see the Global Mennonite History Series, which was initiated at the Mennonite World Conference in 1997. Three volumes (on Mennonites in Africa, Europe, and Latin America) are currently available from Good Books and Pandora Press. For more on Anabaptist responses to and interactions with evangelicalism, see Norman Kraus, ed., *Evangelicalism and Anabaptism* (Eugene, OR: Wipf & Stock, 2001).

22. Steve Oates, conversation with author, January 27, 2011. Although many Mennonites apparently read Amish fiction, the ones I spoke with tended to be critical of the Amish novels they had read because of concerns about accuracy

and representation. Many Mennonites who live near Amish settlements have a fairly high degree of knowledge about Amish life and culture and thus are suspicious of attempts by non-Anabaptists to write about it. They may also feel protective of a people with whom they feel a measure of affiliation. One Mennonite woman I spoke with, who almost exclusively reads Christian fiction, told me that she had little interest in reading Amish novels and was turned off by the "little models with their coverings" on the front covers.

23. The Beachy Amish emerged in the 1920s in Somerset County, Pennsylvania, and although they have "Amish" in their name, they tend to associate more with conservative Mennonite groups. For more on the Beachy Amish, see Nolt, *History of the Amish*.

24. Gray, *Autumn's Promise*, 288.

25. Whether this portrayal of Mennonites is accurate is another matter entirely: Melanie Springer Mock, a Mennonite English professor, suggests that Mennonites as portrayed in Amish novels "often come off as far more evangelical and pious than I have ever experienced them myself." Mock, "Love and Marriage."

26. *Contact zone* is a term coined by Mary Louise Pratt to refer to "social spaces where cultures meet, clash, and grapple with each other." Pratt, *Imperial Eyes*, 7. Pratt's definition includes an imbalance of power and a history of imperialist contact between the two cultures, which the evangelical-Amish contact zone of Mennonite discourse may or may not include. Still, the concept is useful here insofar as it illuminates the hybrid nature of Mennonite faith as represented in Amish novels.

27. Morgan, "Getting Dirty in Dutch Country," 70.

28. The Amana Colonies were utopian communities, as were the Shakers. Both groups were established in the eighteenth- and nineteenth-century United States and grew out of German Pietism. The Amish trace their roots to sixteenth-century Anabaptism, which birthed the Mennonites. The Amish and the Swiss Brethren (Mennonites) divided in Switzerland and in Alsace (France) in 1693 over several issues, including how to treat former members.

29. "Romantic Times Gives Beverly a Career Achievement Award," on Beverly Lewis's website, http://beverlylewis.com, accessed June 27, 2012. One writer of Amish fiction, Shelly Sabga, writes both general and Christian romances—although she writes under one name for her Amish romances (Shelly Shepard Gray) and another one for general romances (Shelley Galloway).

30. Doreen Owens Malek, "Mad, Bad, and Dangerous to Know," 75; Barrett-Fox, "Christian Romance Novels."

31. Kuyper is quoted in Trachtenberg, "HarperCollins Acquires." *Christian Retailing*, an industry journal for Christian bookstores, uses the figure $4.6 billion to quantify the Christian-products industry.

32. Morgan's piece angered romance readers for a variety of reasons. See online reader comments in "Romance Fiction: Getting Dirty in Dutch Country," http://app.businessweek.com/UserComments/combo_review;jsessionid=71E4477D56B61D828CB34600E908DB36.nyo6tls?action=all&style=wide&productId=107291&productCode=spec.

33. Steve Oates, conversation with author, January 27, 2011.

34. Amish romance novels existed before *The Shunning*, as we saw in chapter 2, but they didn't gain sales momentum or adhere to any common conventions until after 1997. Harlequin's Love Inspired Suspense line did bring out one Amish-themed series in 2007, Patricia Davids's Three Sisters Inn, but none of the protagonists were Amish: merely the setting and a few peripheral characters were.

35. Miller, "Love, Amish Style," 25; Jodie, conversation with author, April 11, 2011.

36. Gregory Wolfe, editor of *Image: Art, Faith, Mystery*, suggests that Christian art is often characterized by a "fear of the imagination": "The underlying message conveyed by these products is that they are safe; they have the Christian seal of approval. But this is a devil's bargain: in exchange for safety, these products have given up their imaginative power"; see Gregory Wolfe, "Art, Faith, and the Stewardship of Culture," *Image* 25: 96–105.

37. For a discussion of the Amish as a brand, see Kraybill, Nolt, and Wesner, "Enterprise Success in Amish Communities," esp. 125–26.

38. Amish woman, conversation with author, February 15, 2011.

39. Nelson, "Recipe for an Amish Novel," 3.

40. Gans, *Popular Culture*, 32.

41. Neal, *Romancing God*, 190.

42. Ibid., 192.

43. Gans, *Popular Culture*, 33.

44. Jodie and Louise, conversations with author, April 11, 2011.

45. John Mort, review of *Levi's Will*, by Dale Cramer, *Booklist*, Amazon, www.amazon.com, accessed June 27, 2012; review of *A Place of Peace*, by Amy Clipston, *Publishers Weekly*, www.publishersweekly.com, accessed June 27, 2012.

46. Miller, *Miriam's Heart*, 209; Lewis, *The Longing*, 309.

47. Williams, *Raymond Williams Reader*, 177.

48. Lipovetsky, *Hypermodern Times*, 30.

Chapter Four. Taking the Amish to Market

1. *Amish Wisdom,* http://toginet.com/shows/amishwisdom, accessed June 27, 2012. I was a guest on *Amish Wisdom* on August 18, 2011, speaking about my editorial work on the 30th anniversary edition of *Living More with Less.*

2. "Lazy, Hazy Days of Summer," *Suzanne Woods Fisher,* http://suzan newoodsfisher.com/, accessed June 27, 2012.

3. These statistics come from R. R. Bowker, a provider of bibliographic information. In 2010, 47,392 new works of fiction appeared; in 2002, 25,102 fiction books were published. See www.bowkerinfo.com/pubtrack/AnnualBook Production2010/ISBN_Output_2002-2010.pdf. In 1993, a Bowker report says, 7,721 novels were published. See www.bowker.com/bookwire/decadebookpro duction.html, accessed March 2011. E-books, social media, the rise of self-publishing, and a new generation of what writer Marc Prensky has called "digital natives" are drivers of this instantaneity. See Prensky, "Digital Natives, Digital Immigrants," *On the Horizon* 9 (2001): 1–6.

4. Heim, "Surviving the E-books Earthquake." While it's hard to measure whether what Heim calls consumer impatience has actually risen along with the number of titles, a glance at Amish-fiction author Facebook pages does reveal a readership anxious for some speedy turnaround from their favorite scribes. "When is your next book coming out?" wrote one reader on Cindy Woodsmall's Facebook page. "I have already read all the others!! Im having withdrawls! Lol! I just LOVE your books!" "Hurry up June 28th," a woman posted on Shelley Shepard Gray's Facebook page. "I'm so ready for The Protector." "I think I've read all your books," another reader posted, along with two smiley-face emoticons. "I need a new one."

5. Suzanne Woods Fisher, conversation with author, February 11, 2011; Shelley Shepard Gray, interview by Suzanne Woods Fisher, *Amish Wisdom,* June 16, 2011, http://toginet.com/podcasts/amishwisdom/?s=amishwisdom. Not all of Gray's books were Amish titles. Writing under the pen names Shelley Galloway and Shelley Shepard Gray, Shelley Sabga has written for Harlequin, HarperCollins's imprint Avon Inspire, Avalon, and Abingdon.

6. Lipovetsky, *Hypermodern Times,* 30, 34; Agger, *Speeding Up Fast Capitalism,* 38. Agger's book is a sequel to his *Fast Capitalism* (Champaign: University of Illinois Press, 1989), a book on the same topic.

7. Julie Bosman, "Writer's Cramp: In the E-Reader Era, a Book a Year Is Slacking," *New York Times,* May 12, 2012, www.nytimes.com/2012/05/13/business/in -e-reader-age-of-writers-cramp-a-book-a-year-is-slacking.html?pagewanted=1&

_r=1&ref=books; Peter Straus quoted in Alex Clark, "The Lost Art of Editing," *Guardian*, February 11, 2011, www.guardian.co.uk/books/2011/feb/11/lost-art-ed iting-books-publishing; Lisa Scottoline quoted in Bosman, "Writer's Cramp."

8. Suzanne Woods Fisher, conversation with author, February 11, 2011.

9. Suzanne Woods Fisher, conversation with author, May 13, 2011.

10. Moore, *Selling God*, 38, 6. Radway suggests that the consumptive quality of reading is characteristic of romance reading in particular; see *Reading the Romance*, 18 and chap. 1, "The Institutional Matrix: Publishing Romantic Fiction."

11. Radway, *Reading the Romance*, 19–20.

12. Ibid., 20. Critic Richard Ohmann makes a similar point in "Shaping of a Canon."

13. Raymond Williams advanced this theory. He is not the only theorist to note this, of course—Karl Marx did so first—and Williams himself has posited nuanced arguments with this claim elsewhere. Yet he professes a continued belief in the essence, if not the details, of Marx's theory.

14. Williams, *Raymond Williams Reader*, 264.

15. Lipovetsky, *Hypermodern Times*, 39.

16. Sociologist Wendy Griswold offers another metaphor for culture: a four-part diamond of cultural creators, cultural receivers, cultural objects, and the social world. See Griswold, *Cultures and Societies in a Changing World*, 2nd ed. (Newbury Park, CA: Pine Forge Press, 1994), 11, 15.

17. In one sense, Amish fiction is functioning as Richard Brodhead says regional fiction functioned in the late nineteenth century: as a genre that granted literary access to writers who were having difficulty gaining entrance. Brodhead writes that by making "the experience of the socially marginalized into a literary asset," regional fiction created "a writer's role that women were equipped to perform, especially women from small towns and peripheral locations." Brodhead, *Cultures of Letters*, 117.

18. See Pratt, *Imperial Eyes*, 7; see also chaps. 3 and 4 in the same work.

19. Miller, *Consuming Religion*, 77.

20. Epstein, *Book Business*, 106. Literary agent Peter Matson is quoted in Julie Bosman, "Nurturer of Authors Is Closing the Book," *New York Times*, May 8, 2011, www.nytimes.com/2011/05/09/books/robert-loomis-book-editor-retiring -from-random-house.html?_r=1&scp=1&sq=editor%20retire&st=cse.

21. Trachtenberg, "HarperCollins Acquires." The $200 million purchase was finalized after a lengthy government review. See "HarperCollins Completes Nelson Purchase," *Publishers Weekly*, July 11, 2012, www.publishersweekly.com.

22. Lynn Garrett, "Stunned Reaction to HarperCollins's Acquisition of

Thomas Nelson," *Publishers Weekly,* November 4, 2011, www.publishersweekly
.com.

23. Miller, *Consuming Religion,* 84.

24. The Amish Living site now requires users to sign in in order to both view and comment on items on the site.

25. One such request on Amish Living generated 142 replies, some from as far away as Germany and Australia, most from other members with the same desire for an epistolary friendship with someone plain. Posts in response to "Amish Penpals," Lisa Hidlay, Amish Living, http://amishliving.com/forum/topics/amish-penpals?id=4089131%3ATopic%3A2086&page=1#comments, accessed November 10, 2011.

26. For more on Thomas Nelson, especially its acquisition by HarperCollins, see Trachtenberg, "HarperCollins Acquires."

27. Levine et al., *Cluetrain Manifesto,* xiv, xvii.

28. Jaffe, *Join the Conversation,* 48, 24.

29. Terry Glaspey, conversation with author, May 27, 2011.

30. "20,000 Bloggers Have Caught the BookSneeze Bug," January 11, 2011, http://news.thomasnelson.com/2011/01/11/20000-bloggers-have-caught-the
-booksneeze-bug/.

31. Suzanne Woods Fisher, conversation with author, February 11, 2011.

32. Miller, *Reluctant Capitalists,* 4; quotes on 159, 143.

33. Steve Oates, e-mail to author, March 20, 2012.

34. Melissa Endlich, conversation with author, June 3, 2011.

35. Don Cusic, *Encyclopedia of Contemporary Christian Music: Pop, Rock, and Worship* (Santa Barbara, CA: Greenwood Press, 2010), 59. In addition, as mentioned in chapter 2, in 2005 CBA changed the name of its annual convention from "International Convention" to "International Christian Retail Show"; it advertises that there are "hundreds of worldwide suppliers of Christian products."

36. "50 Years of Christian Retailing," Strang Communications, www.chris
tianretailing.com/history.php, accessed June 27, 2012; "Media Information on Christian Retail," Association for Christian Retail, www.cbaonline.org/nm/me
dia.htm.

37. David Weaver-Zercher makes this point in *Amish in the American Imagination,* 3.

38. Karen Johnson-Weiner explores this concept of "Amishness" in "Selling the Past."

39. For more on the symbolic capital of the Amish brand, see Kraybill, Nolt, and Wesner, "Enterprise Success in Amish Communities," 125–26.

40. John Bomberger, conversation with author, October 5, 2011.

41. See Bado-Fralick and Norris, *Toying with God.* Historian Laurence Moore makes a similar point, noting that his history of religion's role in commercial culture should not be read as a "tale of declension" and that without the commodification of religion, Christian churches in the United States would be as empty as those in Western Europe. See Moore, *Selling God,* 6, 10. Suzanne Woods Fisher, conversation with author, February 11, 2011; Michele Cushman, "Interview with Beth Wiseman," American Christian Fiction Writers website, April 11, 2011, www.fictionfinder.com/author_interview/read/interview_with _beth_wiseman.

42. Miller, *Consuming Religion,* 32.

43. Ibid., 27, 32; Lipovetsky, *Hypermodern Times,* 59.

44. Miller, *Consuming Religion,* 79.

45. Ibid., 84.

46. Amish Living, http://thomasnelson.promo.eprize.com/fiction/, accessed November 20, 2011.

47. For an investigation of the American wedding industry, see Rebecca Mead, *One Perfect Day: The Selling of the American Wedding* (New York: Penguin, 2007). This point has implications for accuracy and authenticity in the subgenre, which we examine in chapter 9, as well as for Amish fiction's possible effects on Amish readers, which we deal with in chapter 10.

48. Lipovetsky, *Hypermodern Times,* 30.

49. Religion scholar Leigh Schmidt warns against reducing the story of contemporary spirituality to the now well-worn metaphors of spiritual smorgasbords and buffets, "as if religious seekers were little more than spiritual gluttons gobbling up anything and everything that they can heap on their plates." See Schmidt, *Restless Souls: The Making of American Spirituality from Emerson to Oprah* (New York: HarperSanFrancisco, 2005), 21.

50. Suzanne Woods Fisher, conversation with author, February 11, 2011; Chip MacGregor, "The Passion in Writing," October 8, 2010, http://chipmacgregor .typepad.com/main/2010/10/the-passion-in-.html, accessed May 15, 2011 (site discontinued).

51. Miller, *Consuming Religion,* 144.

Chapter Five. Is Amishness Next to Godliness?

1. Lipovetsky, *Hypermodern Times*, 32.

2. Fish, *Is There a Text*, 14. Although Fish's theory is often applied to critical and academic interpretive communities, Radway and others have expanded the notion to communities of readers surrounding particular genres of popular literature. Fish has come under fire from many critics, but his basic idea remains helpful in understanding how readers operate from particular assumptions.

3. Brunstetter, *Lydia's Charm*, 273, 375.

4. Barrett, "Higher Love," para. 7.

5. Neal, *Romancing God*, 108, 12.

6. Lipovetsky, *Hypermodern Times*, 33.

7. Martin, *Sacred Doorways*, 2.

8. This idea comes from Anthony Ugolnik in *The Illuminating Icon:* "'Symbol' implies that a thing is *other* than itself; Orthodox Christian 'symbols,' however, *participate* in the reality they convey" (45).

9. Titus Burckhardt, foreword to Leonid Ouspensky and Vladimir Lossky, *The Meaning of Icons* (Crestwood, NY: St. Vladimir's Seminary Press, 1982), 7; Nes, *Mystical Language of Icons*, 12.

10. Linda Barlow and Jayne Ann Krentz make a similar point about coded language in general romances in their chapter "Beneath the Surface: The Hidden Codes of Romance," in Krentz's *Dangerous Men and Adventurous Women*, 27: "We suggest that in order to understand the appeal of romance fiction, one must be sensitive to the subtle codes, contained in figurative language and in plot, that point toward a uniquely feminine sharing of a common emotional and intellectual heritage."

11. Onasch and Schnieper, *Icons*, 31. For an intriguing discussion of the use of images in Orthodox and non-Orthodox Christianity, see Ugolnik, *Illuminating Icon*, chap. 2.

12. Ugolnik, *Illuminating Icon*, 102.

13. Ceil Carey, conversation with author, April 11, 2011.

14. Kristin J., "Finding Spiritual Inspiration in Amish Fiction Novels," blog post on Amish Living website, June 7, 2011.

15. Beverly Lewis, conversation with author, January 28, 2011.

16. Mary Ellis, interview by Suzanne Woods Fisher, *Amish Wisdom*, July 29, 2010, http://toginet.com/podcasts/amishwisdom/?s=amishwisdom.

17. Neal, *Romancing God*, 163. Rebecca Barrett makes a similar point in "Higher Love," paras. 8–10.

18. Beverly Lewis, conversation with author, January 28, 2011.

19. Brent Curtis and John Eldredge, *The Sacred Romance: Drawing Closer to the Heart of God* (Nashville: Thomas Nelson, 1997). For a fuller discussion of the ways in which God as lover is inscribed in evangelical Christian writing, see Neal, *Romancing God*, 172–73. For exploration of the language of romance in contemporary worship music, see Jenell Williams Paris, "I Could Sing of Your Love Forever: The American Romantic Ideal in Contemporary Praise and Worship Music," in *The Message in the Music,* ed. Robert Woods and Brian Walrath (Minneapolis: Augsburg Press, 2007).

20. Woodsmall, *When the Heart Cries,* 254–55, 325–26.

21. Lewis, *The Longing,* 314.

22. Lewis, *The Shunning,* 67; Lodge, *Simply Sara,* 84, 273.

23. Neal, *Romancing God,* 159; Paul Boyce, "Byzantine Iconography—A Brief Overview," Byzantine Icon Art website, www.csg-i.com/icons/html/overview.htm.

24. Shelley Shepard Gray, "Don't Smirk: Amish Love Stories Inspire Me," CNN Living, September 7, 2010, http://articles.cnn.com.

25. Constantine Cavarnos, *Orthodox Iconography* (Belmont, MA: Institute for Byzantine and Modern Greek Studies, 1986), 31.

26. Roper, *Stranger's Wish,* 182–83; Lodge, *Simply Sara,* 185.

27. Miller, "Why We Love Amish Romances," 40.

28. Ibid., 40. For more on the fundamentalist-modernist controversy, see David Harrington Watt, *A Transforming Faith: Explorations of Twentieth-Century American Fundamentalism* (New Brunswick, NJ: Rutgers University Press, 1991), esp. chap. 2.

29. Lewis, *The Mercy,* 28.

30. Ibid., 40–41.

31. Beverly Lewis, conversation with author, January 28, 2011.

32. Roper, *Stranger's Wish,* 133–34.

33. Ceil Carey, conversation with author, April 10, 2011; Lewis, *The Shunning,* 131; Lewis, *The Reckoning,* 280. While Lewis's early heroines frequently end up Mennonite or Beachy Amish or New Order Amish, her more recent protagonists often remain Old Order. Rose, the heroine in her 2011 novel *The Mercy,* considers becoming New Order because her boyfriend is; but ultimately Rose decides to remain Old Order.

34. For more on this distinction between "the new birth" and being "born again," see Kraybill, Johnson-Weiner, and Nolt, *The Amish,* chap. 4.

35. Kraybill, Nolt, and Weaver-Zercher, *Amish Way,* 39.

36. Another Amish woman I spoke with in Indiana echoed this. "Once it gets into religion, that's the part I don't like them to write about," she told me, because, from her perspective, the authors don't understand Amish faith. "I don't want to put anyone down, but I will not touch Beverly Lewis's books," she said.

37. Adina Senft, "Interview with Adina Senft & Giveaway," *Sugarpeach*, September 28, 2011, http://sugarpeach.wordpress.com/2011/09/28/interview-with-adina-senft-giveaway/.

38. There are many examples of Old Order Amish people expressing themselves in evangelical language, including the Old Order Amish woman Marlene Miller, speaking with Suzanne Woods Fisher on *Amish Wisdom* on October 5, 2011: "Accept Jesus Christ as your personal Savior, and let him come in and live in your life," Miller said. "Don't try to handle it all yourself. . . . Get Christ when you're young."

39. Clipston, *Gift of Grace*, 197.

40. Ibid., 225.

41. Woodsmall, *When the Heart Cries*, 268.

42. Lodge, *Simply Sara*, 159.

43. Hilton, *Patchwork Dreams*, 106; Woodsmall, *When the Heart Cries*, 264.

44. Lewis, *The Crossroad*, 134–35.

45. Reid, *Promise of an Angel*, 50. For nonfiction descriptions of Amish bishops' work and the process by which they are called, see Kraybill, *Riddle of Amish Culture*, chaps. 4 and 5; and Kraybill, Johnson-Weiner, and Nolt, *The Amish*, chap. 10.

46. Neal, *Romancing God*, 12; Randi Sider-Rose, website of Immanuel Icons, http://immanuelicons.org/about.html.

Chapter Six. An Amish Country Getaway

1. The number 11 million comes from the Pennsylvania Dutch Convention and Visitors Bureau, http://pressroom.padutchcountry.com/lancaster-informa tion/lancaster-statistics.asp. For more in-depth discussion of Lancaster County Amish-themed tourism, see Walbert, *Garden Spot;* and Weaver-Zercher, *Amish in the American Imagination,* esp. chap. 3.

2. Quotations in this section are from Deanna, conversation with author, May 9, 2011.

3. Clifford, *Predicament of Culture*, 13.

4. Miller, "Why We Love Amish Romances," 41.

5. Robert F. Berkhofer Jr., in his book *The White Man's Indian: Images of the American Indian from Columbus to the Present* (New York: Vintage Books, 1979), 76, suggests that the "noble savage" trope was often utilized in literature to "criticize existing social institutions and to propose reforms."

6. Steve Oates, conversation with author, January 27, 2011.

7. See Graybill, "Amish Women, Business Sense."

8. Gerrig, *Experiencing Narrative Worlds*, 10–11. Janice Radway also noted that romance novels served as "a means of transportation . . . to the exotic" for the readers she studied; see Radway, *Reading the Romance*, 61.

9. Quoted in Radway, *Reading the Romance*, 89.

10. This editor's words echo the criticism of evangelical romance fiction that religion scholar Lynn Neal found in her study of that genre. She summarized the critics' perspective this way: "These women, unable to handle the tragedies of life, even in fiction, retreat to a world of make-believe and feel-good emotions. . . . Proponents of this interpretation fear that the escapist impulses and sentimental endings of the genre foster a dangerous apathy in regard to the real world." Neal, *Romancing God*, 102.

11. Grossman, "Literary Revolution in the Supermarket Aisle."

12. Lipovetsky, *Hypermodern Times*, 30–31. Other scholars investigating hypermodernity or fast capitalism include philosopher Albert Borgmann, writer Heather Menzies, and sociologist Ben Agger. It is critical to note that Lipovetsky himself does not discount the possible positive outcroppings of hypermodernity and does not equate it with nihilism or declension. See Lipovetsky, *Hypermodern Times*, 67–69.

13. Lipovetsky, *Hypermodern Times*, 45.

14. Amish-themed products and tourism were actively being generated and consumed prior to hypermodernity; see Weaver-Zercher, *Amish in the American Imagination*, chap. 3. Modernity also made room for desire for products and experiences associated with traditional or "folk" groups. Hypermodernity, as is its wont, merely intensified modernity's attention to cultures seen as having an unbroken connection to the past.

15. Lipovetsky, *Hypermodern Times*, 58.

16. Sociologist Donald B. Kraybill argues that the Amish can actually be viewed as a modern people, in that they have exercised a great deal of self-conscious choice with regard to what technologies and practices to accept and reject. See Kraybill, *Riddle of Amish Culture*, 320. Amish scholar John Hostetler made a similar point when he wrote that "Amish communities are not relics of

a bygone era. Rather they are demonstrations of a different form of modernity."
Hostetler, *Amish Society*, 4th ed. (Baltimore: Johns Hopkins University Press,
1993), ix.

17. Chase and Shaw, *Imagined Past*, 4. Linguist Karen Johnson-Weiner first
applied Chase and Shaw's idea of talismans of the past to the Amish in "Selling the Past."

18. Lipovetsky, *Hypermodern Times*, 64; Gray, *Autumn's Promise*, 254; Cramer,
Paradise Valley, 307; Lewis, *The Shunning*, 282.

19. "PTC STUDY: Sexualized Teen Girls Are Tinseltown's New Target," December, 15, 2010, www.parentstv.org/FemaleSexualization/Study/PR_101215_Sexu
alization_Study.pdf; Levy, *Female Chauvinist Pigs*, 26.

20. Miller, "Love, Amish Style," 25; Tricia Goyer, "Over-sexualization of
Young Girls," *Tricia Goyer: Authentic Fiction, Real-Life Truth* (blog), February 12,
2011, http://triciagoyer.blogspot.com.

21. Oppliger, *Girls Gone Skank*, 2.

22. Radway, *Reading the Romance*, 189.

23. Eicher, *Wedding Quilt for Ella*, 29.

24. Lewis, *The Telling*, 289; Gray, *Autumn's Promise*, 219.

25. Gandolfo, *Faith and Fiction*, 68.

26. Ludic and intellectual experiences are not always at odds, of course, but
some readers experience them as such. Victor Nell explores the notion of ludic
reading in *Lost in a Book*. The concept of ludic reading, he writes, reminds us
that reading is "at root a play activity, intrinsically motivated and . . . engaged in
for its own sake" (2).

27. Facebook message from Kimberly, March 12, 2011.

28. Radway, *Reading the Romance*, 196.

29. Jodie, conversation with author, April 11, 2011.

30. See Donald Horton and R. Richard Wohl, "Mass Communication and
Parasocial Interaction," *Psychiatry* 19 (1956): 215–24. See Gandolfo, *Faith and
Fiction*, 68.

31. Gandolfo, *Faith and Fiction*, 67; Suzanne Woods Fisher, conversation with
author, May 13, 2011. Romance novelist Jayne Krentz notes that reader identification with protagonists is much more complex than people often assume.
Female readers of romances, and the writers themselves, often articulate identifying with the hero instead of or in addition to the heroine. "Both reader and
writer slip easily in and out of the skins of the two main characters as the
romance progresses," writes Krentz. *Dangerous Men and Adventurous Women*,
introduction, 7.

32. See Regis, *Natural History of the Romance,* chap. 3.

33. Gerrig, *Experiencing Narrative Worlds,* 79 (emphasis mine).

34. Jodie, conversation with author, April 11, 2011; Betsy, conversation with author, September 14, 2011. A recent study from the University of California–San Diego, published in the journal *Psychological Science,* found that knowledge of how a short story turns out actually enhanced readers' enjoyment of the narrative. See "Spoiler Alert: Stories Are not 'Spoiled' by Spoilers," Association for Psychological Science, August 10, 2011, www.psychologicalscience.org.

35. Beverly Lewis, interview by Jeanne Dennis, "Heritage of Truth," http:// heritageoftruth.com/archives/899.

36. Radway, *Reading the Romance,* 65–66.

37. Nell, *Lost in a Book,* 59.

38. Radway, *Reading the Romance,* 198.

39. Brunstetter, *A Sister's Hope,* 296–97; Wiseman, *Healing Hearts,* in *An Amish Love,* 377; Reid, *Promise of an Angel,* 289.

40. Neal, *Romancing God,* 104; Romans 8:28 (King James Version).

41. Neal, *Romancing God,* 104; Roach, "Getting a Good Man."

42. Quoted in David Wood, "Albert Borgmann on Taming Technology: An Interview," *Christian Century,* August 23, 2003, 24.

43. Borgmann, *Technology and Contemporary Life,* 197.

44. Borgmann, *Crossing the Postmodern Divide,* 116.

45. See Gifford, *Pastoral,* 1–2. For more on the pastoral ideal in literature, see also Marx, *Machine in the Garden;* and Paul Alpers, *What Is Pastoral?* (Chicago: University of Chicago Press, 1997). For applications of the pastoral ideal to the Amish in particular, see Downing, "Witnessing the Amish"; Walbert, *Garden Spot,* 15–19; and Weaver-Zercher, *Amish in the American Imagination,* chap. 5.

46. Clark and Gould, *Amish Midwife,* 59.

47. Lewis, *The Crossroad,* 79–80.

48. Kraybill, *Riddle of Amish Culture,* 245; Hurst and McConnell, *Amish Paradox,* 175. For an analysis of the migration of Amish labor from farm to nonfarm businesses, see Kraybill and Nolt, *Amish Enterprise;* see also Kraybill, *Riddle of Amish Culture,* chap. 10; and Kraybill, Johnson-Weiner, and Nolt, *The Amish,* chap. 15.

49. For a discussion of the iconography of the "little red schoolhouse" and its connection to representations of the Amish, see Weaver-Zercher, *Amish in the American Imagination,* 48–81.

50. Marx, *Machine in the Garden,* 9, 10.

51. Romance writer Rosslyn Elliott makes a similar point in "Amish Fiction

and the American Pastoral," *Rosslyn Elliott* (blog), October 11, 2010, http://ink hornblue.blogspot.com/2010/10/amish-fiction-and-american-pastoral.html. See also Adina Senft, "It's Not about the Bonnet," *Romance Writers' Report*, October 2011, 20–24, in which Senft makes the case that Amish fiction operates as pastoral literature.

52. Marx, *Machine in the Garden*, 5, 27; Fisher, *The Waiting*, 250.

53. Woodsmall quoted in David Wright, "Carrie Bradshaw—in a Bonnet?" ABC News, May 26, 2009, http://abcnews.go.com/Nightline/story?id=7676659 &page=1; Sarah, conversation with author, October 4, 2011; Neal, *Romancing God*, 77, 86.

54. Brunstetter, *On Her Own*, 284; Wiseman, *Plain Proposal*, 269; Brunstetter, *Lydia's Charm*, 374.

55. Neal, *Romancing God*, 82–87.

56. "Frequently Asked Questions," Beverly Lewis website, www.beverlylewis .com; Beverly Lewis, conversation with author, January 28, 2011; post on Amish Country Holiday Book Tour Facebook page, November 3, 2011.

57. Amish Living, www.amishliving.com/forum/topics/thankful-for-the -amish-fiction.

58. Natalie Warren, "Young Women's Desires to Become Amish," Amish Living, August 26, 2011, http://amishliving.com/forum/topics/young-women -s-desires-to-kbecome-amish?xg_source=activity.

59. Commenters, Amish Living, posts in response to question by Richard, July 15, 2011, http://amishliving.com/forum/topics/would-you-or-could-you-eve r?id=4089131%3ATopic%3A112562&page=1#comments.

60. Boym, *Future of Nostalgia*, xiii; Lipovetsky, *Hypermodern Times*, 59.

61. Boym, *Future of Nostalgia*, xvi. Social psychologist Janelle Wilson suggests that nostalgia can become a "sanctuary of meaning" for individuals living in a time "when so many threats and obstacles to constructing and maintaining a coherent and consistent self abound." Wilson, *Nostalgia*, 8.

62. See Downing, "Witnessing the Amish," 39.

63. Young, "Making a Choice," 122.

64. Neal, *Romancing God*, 12.

Chapter Seven. Virgin Mothers

1. Quotations in this section come from Betsy, conversation with author, September 14, 2011.

2. Freitas, *Sex and the Soul*, 114.

3. Lewis, *The Mercy*, 300.

4. Neal, *Romancing God*, 86; Lisa Brown, "Amish Fictional Characters Are Inspiring," April 25, 2011, http://amishamerica.com/amish-fiction-characters -stereotypes/comment-page-1/#comments.

5. Michelle Thurlow, in her examination of Beverly Lewis's novels, makes a similar point about Lewis's gender politics being a mix of conservative and progressive ideas. See Thurlow, "A Whisper of Satin: The Infant Dress Leitmotif," *CMW Journal* 2, no. 10 (July 15, 2010), www.mennonitewriting.org/journal/2/4/ whisper-satin/#all.

6. Exceptions to this four-part template pepper the field: Mary Ellis's protagonist Abigail is married when the novel begins; Beth Wiseman's Levina, in *Healing Hearts,* has adult children who have already left home; and the voices of male point-of-view characters in many of the novels surface as frequently and prominently as those of the female protagonists.

7. Regis, *Natural History of the Romance*, 35. This is not unilaterally true; some Amish heroines are married or widowed, some have had sexual intercourse in the past, and an occasional heroine has been the victim of rape. Some marry during the course of the novel, thus presumably losing their virginity— although, as we will see, that loss is never narrated.

8. For an examination of the virgin martyrs, see Karen Winstead, *Virgin Martyrs: Legends of Sainthood in Late Medieval England* (Ithaca, NY: Cornell University Press, 1997). For more on constructions of Queen Elizabeth I, see John N. King, "Queen Elizabeth I: Representations of the Virgin Queen," *Renaissance Quarterly* 43, no. 1 (Spring 1990): 30–74; and Frances A. Yates, *Astraea: The Imperial Theme in the Sixteenth Century* (reprint, London: Routledge, 1999).

9. Wendell and Tan, *Beyond Heaving Bosoms*, 37.

10. Malek's books differ from Amish romance novels because their virginal heroines, during the course of the novel, give their virginity to a man worthy of such a gift; if Amish heroines lose their virginity during the course of an Amish novel, it is almost always within the context of marriage and is never narrated in any detail. In other words, general-market romance tends to narrate the loss of virginity, while Amish fiction narrates the maintenance of it (or at least of chastity). Still, Malek's theory speaks to the power of virginal heroines in Amish fiction.

11. Malek, "Loved I Not Honor More," 117.

12. Miller, *Miriam's Heart,* 12.

13. Woodsmall, *When the Heart Cries*, 10. In his book *Growing Up Amish*, Richard Stevick suggests that Amish culture contains an ambivalence regarding physical beauty. Stevick argues that Amish culture places less emphasis on physical attractiveness than many cultures, even as Amish individuals say that appearance does indeed have a bearing on the choice of mate. See Stevick, *Growing Up Amish*, 182–83.

14. Barrett, "Higher Love," para. 19.

15. Woodsmall, *When the Heart Cries*, 12; Lewis, *The Thorn*, 260, 340.

16. Suzanne Woods Fisher, conversation with author, May 13, 2011.

17. Lev Grossman, "Finding Passion in Jane Austen," *Time*, August 3, 2007, www.time.com.

18. For an extensive treatment of the custom of bundling, see Stevick, *Growing Up Amish*, 188–97.

19. For more on popular representations of bundling during the past century, see Weaver-Zercher, *Amish in the American Imagination*, 53–55. Long, *Arms of Love*, 165–68.

20. Long, *A Marriage of the Heart*, in Wiseman, Fuller, and Long, *An Amish Love*, 88; Ellis, *Forsaken*, 225, 226. *Forsaken* was published by an independent, general publishing house, but characters frequently quote Scripture and the author, Leanna Ellis, has published several previous novels with a Christian publishing house. "Book Description," in *Jacob's Return*, Amazon, www.amazon.com/Jacobs-Return-ebook/dp/B004ZH8O2A, accessed May 3, 2012.

21. Freitas, *Sex and the Soul*, 80.

22. Lewis, *The Betrayal*, 353.

23. Economist Martha Farnsworth Riche first used the term *postmarital* to describe contemporary North American society in her piece "The Postmarital Society," *American Demographics*, November 1988.

24. Cherlin, *Marriage-Go-Round*, 5; "New Marriage and Divorce Statistics Released," The Barna Group, March 31, 2008, www.barna.org. Bradford Wilcox makes a similar point in his chapter "How Focused on the Family?" in *Evangelicals and Democracy in America*, 251–75.

25. For a nonfiction exploration of Amish marriage by an Amish-fiction author, see Suzanne Woods Fisher, "Plain Talk about the Amish: How to Make a Marriage Last," *Christian Post*, September 29, 2011, http://blogs.christianpost.com/amish-principles-for-families/2011/09/plain-talk-about-the-amish-how-to-make-a-marriage-last-29/.

26. For more on Amish gender roles, see Kraybill, Johnson-Weiner, and Nolt, *The Amish*; Kraybill, Nolt, and Weaver-Zercher, *Amish Way*, chap. 8; and

Hurst and McConnell, *Amish Paradox*, chap. 4. For a fascinating exploration of Amish gender roles, see Marc A. Olshan and Kimberly D. Schmidt, "Amish Women and the Feminist Conundrum," in Kraybill and Olshan, *Amish Struggle with Modernity*, 215–29. Primary sources on Amish understandings of marital roles include "The Husband's Role," a serial article with multiple authors that appears in several issues of *Family Life:* April 2004, 13–18; May 2004, 9–14; June 2004, 12–16; "How a Wife Can Improve Her Marriage" *Family Life,* October 2007, 19–20; "Building a Christian Marriage," *Family Life,* May 2004; and a two-part series "by some husband's wife," "She Will Do Him Good," *Family Life,* February 2002, 14–17; and *Family Life,* March 2002, 11–15.

27. Lewis, *The Reckoning*, 279.

28. Brunstetter, *Plain and Fancy*, 342, 365.

29. Lewis, *The Postcard*, 141–42.

30. Sarah, conversation with author, October 4, 2011; 1 Corinthians 11:3, 10 (New Revised Standard Version).

31. Sarah, conversation with author, October 4, 2011.

32. Gallagher and Smith, "Symbolic Traditionalism," 229.

33. Fisher, *The Waiting*, 276; Gray, *Autumn's Promise*, 255–56.

34. Neal, *Romancing God*, 135.

35. The name of the movement, "Quiverfull," may or may not be used by those within it. "Quiverfull" refers to a passage in the Psalms: "Like arrows in the hands of a warrior are sons born in one's youth. Blessed is the man whose quiver is full of them" (127:4–5, New International Version). The QuiverFull! Digest, an online forum, bills itself as a resource for "Christian couples who eagerly accept their children as blessings from God and eschew birth control, natural family planning, and sterilization." www.quiverfull.com/digest.php. For a book-length treatment of this phenomenon, see Joyce, *Quiverfull*.

36. For more on changing evangelical perspectives on birth control, see Mark Oppenheimer, "Many Evangelicals See Something to Admire in Candidates' Broods," *New York Times,* January 20, 2012, www.nytimes.com.

37. Kraybill, *Riddle of Amish Culture*, 88.

38. For more on Amish understandings of children, see Kraybill, Nolt, and Weaver-Zercher, *Amish Way*, chap. 7.

39. Miller, *Miriam's Heart*, 213.

40. Wilcox, "How Focused on the Family?" 253.

41. Fuller, *Marriage of the Heart*, in Wiseman, Fuller, and Long, *An Amish Love*, 128.

42. Lewis, *The Shunning*, 16.

43. Woodsmall, *When the Soul Mends*, 336; Ellis, *Abigail's New Hope*, 278.

44. Pamela Regis summarizes this criticism in *Natural History of the Romance*, 11.

45. Modleski, *Feminism without Women*, 43.

46. Mock, "Love and Marriage," 9–10; Amanda Hess, "Amish Romance Novels Provide Stolen Kisses, but Not 'Women's Rights,'" *Washington City Paper* (blog), September 9, 2009, www.washingtoncitypaper.com.

47. For treatments of the connection between traditionalist gender ideology and conservative politics, see Linda Kintz, *Between Jesus and the Market: The Emotions that Matter in Right-Wing America* (Durham, NC: Duke University Press, 1997); and Joyce, *Quiverfull*.

48. Neal, *Romancing God*, 13; Barrett-Fox, "Christian Romance Novels," 14–15.

49. Regis, *Natural History of the Romance*, 15–16. Penelope Williamson, an author of romance novels, writes that in her books "the fantasies are uniquely *feminine*, and the story is essentially the *heroine's*." Williamson, "By Honor Bound," in Krentz, *Dangerous Men and Adventurous Women*, 126.

50. Since Amish romance shares certain characteristics with general-market romance novels, the arguments of Jayne Ann Krentz and other romance writers could also be applied to this defense of Amish romance novels. Krentz and her coauthors argue that romance novels are "inherently subversive" and that they "invert the power structure of a patriarchal society because they show women exerting enormous power over men." Krentz, *Dangerous Men and Adventurous Women*, 5.

51. Cramer, *Paradise Valley*, 125; Lewis quoted in Gorski, "Contemporary Amish Fiction."

52. Radway, *Reading the Romance*, 61. For more on Radway's delineation of the combative and compensatory functions of romance-novel reading, see "The Act of Reading the Romance: Escape and Instruction," in *Reading the Romance*, chap. 3. Several of the romance writers whose essays are anthologized in Krentz, *Dangerous Men and Adventurous Women*, make a similar point about the liberation inherent in the act of picking up a romance novel.

53. Brunstetter, *Lydia's Charm*, 376.

54. Neal, *Romancing God*, 103.

Chapter Eight. Amish Reading Amish

1. Quotations from Ceil Carey, conversation with author, April 11, 2011, and e-mail to author, April 29, 2011.

2. For a comprehensive account of Amish affiliations, from the conservative Swartzentruber Amish to much more change-minded groups, see Kraybill, Johnson-Weiner, and Nolt, *The Amish*, chap. 8.

3. American Library Association, "National Bookmobile Day 2011," www.ala .org, accessed March 13, 2012.

4. Trollinger, *Selling the Amish*, 26.

5. Quotations from Marty LaVigne, conversation with author, June 24, 2011.

6. In *Plain Secrets: An Outsider among the Amish*, in which journalist Joe Mackall writes about the Swartzentruber Amish in Ashland County, Ohio, Mackall recounts one Swartzentruber woman's enjoyment of the Herald Press books by Carrie Bender (a pseudonym for an Old Order Mennonite writer in Lancaster County). See *Plain Secrets* (Boston: Beacon Press, 2007), 176–78.

7. Johnson-Weiner, e-mail message to author, October 26, 2011.

8. Quoted in Alter, "They're No Bodice Rippers."

9. Quoted in Graybill, "Chasing the Bonnet."

10. Quoted in Sachs, "Amish Romance Novels."

11. Doretta Yoder, review of *On Her Own*, in "I Love to Read!" *Connection*, January 2008, 42; Doretta Yoder, review of *Plain Paradise*, in "I Love to Read!" *Connection*, May 2010, 44.

12. Anderson, "Happily Ever After," 26.

13. "Ask an Amishman," Amish America website, Erik Wesner, March 2, 2009, http://amishamerica.com/ask-amish-man/.

14. Amish teenager, conversation with author, October 24, 2011.

15. Anderson, "Happily Ever After," 26.

16. Journalist Andrea Sachs writes in *Time* that Beverly Lewis's books have been "banned by some Amish leaders in Ohio because of theological differences," and Ann Rodgers says in the *Pittsburgh Post-Gazette* that Amish communities "in Pennsylvania and elsewhere have actively discouraged them or banned them." See Sachs, "Amish Romance Novels"; Rodgers, "In Amish Romance Novels."

17. Beverly Lewis, e-mail to author, January 9, 2012.

18. Amish woman, conversation with author, June 23, 2011.

19. Anderson, "Happily Ever After," 29.

20. Amish woman, conversation with author, January 31, 2011.

21. Amish woman, conversation with author, June 23, 2011.

22. Amish woman, conversation with author, January 31, 2011.

23. Amish woman, conversation with author, March 21, 2011.

24. Quotations in this section from Ruthie, conversation with author, September 28, 2011.

25. Amish bookstore owner, e-mail to author, November 21, 2011.

26. Interestingly enough, one of Linda Byler's daughters was a pen pal of Beverly Lewis's for several years. Interview with Beverly Lewis, *Amish Wisdom*, April 21, 2011, http://toginet.com/podcasts/amishwisdom/?s=amishwisdom.

27. Quotations in this section from Linda Byler, conversation with author, January 31, 2011.

28. Review of *Wild Horses*, by Linda Byler, *Publishers Weekly*, accessed July 12, 2012, www.publishersweekly.com.

29. Byler, *Running Around*, 166.

30. Charlene L. Amsden, "Mixed Feelings," review of *Running Around (and Such)*, Amazon, November 17, 2010, www.amazon.com.

31. Byler, *Running Around*, 70–71.

32. Ibid., 239.

33. Miller, "Why We Love Amish Romances," 41.

34. American artist Thomas Kinkade, known for his idyllic renderings of houses, gardens, and other items of Americana, trademarked the term "Painter of Light." Kinkade is known as "America's most-collected living artist," and his company claims that 1 in 20 American homes contain some form of his art.

35. Miller, "Why We Love Amish Romances," 41.

36. See Stevick, *Growing Up Amish*.

Chapter Nine. Something Borrowed, Something True

1. This argument echoes the one that Merle Good of Good Books made in the immediate aftermath of *Witness*, the 1985 blockbuster directed by Peter Weir. While many Mennonites derided *Witness* as an inauthentic and even offensive portrait of Amish life, Good defended it at least partially, suggesting that critics should remember the difference between the storyteller's and the sociologist's tasks: while the sociologist looks for "*typical* behavior," the storyteller seeks out "the *exception*." "Often by studying the *edge*, a storyteller shows us more about the *center*." See Good, "Reflections on *Witness* Controversy," *Gospel Herald*, March 5, 1985, 161–64.

2. Eagleton, *After Theory*, 90, 89.

3. For more on the tangle of representational dilemmas regarding mediators of Amish life and culture, see Weaver-Zercher, *Amish in the American Imagination;* Weaver-Zercher, *Writing the Amish*.

4. Postmodernism is often portrayed too simplistically in this regard, as a rel-

ativist approach to reality. But as Linda Hutcheon suggests, for postmodernists "past events existed empirically, but in epistemological terms we can only know them today through texts. Past events are given meaning, not existence, by their representation in history." Hutcheon, *The Politics of Postmodernism* (New York: Routledge, 1989), 82.

5. Janice Radway, in her study of romance readers in the 1980s, found that readers of romance novels did assume that the romances they were reading were historically, geographically, and culturally accurate. "Although the books [romance novels] are works of fiction, the women use them as primers about the world," Radway wrote. "The romance for them is a kind of encyclopedia, and reading, a process of education." Radway, *Reading the Romance*, 60.

6. Wanda Brunstetter, conversation with author, September 12, 2011; Doretta Yoder, review of *A Cousin's Challenge*, in "I Love to Read! Doretta's Book Review," *Connection*, April 2010, 44.

7. Sue Brower, conversation with author, November 18, 2011.

8. Cindy Woodsmall and Miriam Flaud recently cowrote a nonfiction book, *Plain Wisdom: An Invitation into an Amish Home and the Hearts of Two Women* (Colorado Springs: WaterBrook Press, 2011).

9. New author Jennifer Beckstrand's agent writes, "Her stories are read and approved by two Amish readers in Lancaster County, Pennsylvania." "Published Authors," The Seymour Agency, www.theseymouragency.com/Published-Au thors.html. Beth Wiseman writes on her website, "I have Amish connections and friends in Pennsylvania and Colorado who read the manuscripts prior to publication to make sure the books are in line with the Old Order Amish ways." "About Beth," Beth Wiseman website, http://bethwiseman.com/?page_id=15.

10. Amy Clipston, quoted in Howard Dukes, "Amish Culture Setting for Novels," *South Bend Tribune*, November 6, 2011, www.southbendtribune.com/enter tainment/inthebend/sbt-amish-culture-setting-for-novels-20111106,0,1279044 .story.

11. Scott, "How Factual Is Amish Fiction?"

12. Ibid.

13. Saloma Miller Furlong, "Amish Fiction," *About Amish* (blog), May 1, 2011, http://aboutamish.blogspot.com/2011/05/amish-fiction.html. Furlong suggests that intangible elements such as an individualistic worldview, as seen, for example, in a ten-year-old Amish character who muses, through a metaphor, on his essential separateness from his community, indicate the authors' lack of understanding of Amish life and thought.

14. I owe this argument partially to David Weaver-Zercher, who outlines a similar one in his discussion of *Witness* in *Amish in the American Imagination*, chap. 5.

15. Senft, *Wounded Heart*, 151.

16. Kraybill, *Riddle of Amish Culture*, 138. For helpful insights into shunning, see Kraybill, Nolt, and Weaver-Zercher, *Amish Grace*, chap. 11.

17. Lewis, *The Shunning*, 132. Steve Scott suggests a further problem with this passage: "Aside from the inaccuracy about shunning, the matter of tractor power would not even be an issue in Lancaster." Stephen Scott, e-mail to author, October 25, 2011.

18. For a detailed description of how the *Ordnung* forms and functions in Amish districts, see Kraybill, Johnson-Weiner, and Nolt, *The Amish*, chap. 7.

19. Miller, "Why We Love Amish Romances," 40.

20. Laura Hilton, "Interview/Giveaway with Author Laura Hilton," interview by Penny Zeller, April 21, 2011, http://pennyzeller.wordpress.com/2011/04/21/interviewgiveaway-with-author-laura-hilton/.

21. Hilton, *Patchwork Dreams*, 22–23, 175.

22. In Lewis's series, one of Abram's daughters ends up marrying Eli, "the thirty-eight-year-old who had come from Ohio with the other traded men." Jake, who has been sent to Ohio in the swap, returns because, in the words of another character, "It's got his goat, bein' traded for other men." Lewis, *The Revelation*, 28, 38.

23. Laura Hilton, interview by Suzanne Woods Fisher, *Amish Wisdom*, March 31, 2011.

24. Donald B. Kraybill, e-mail to author, July 7, 2011.

25. Steven Nolt, e-mail to author, July 7, 2011.

26. Beverly Lewis assured me in an e-mail of August 2, 2011, that man swaps do exist and that she knows of several instances of men being traded between communities. Such trades are generally kept "hush hush," she said, and suggested that I might not be able to find anyone willing to tell me about them. She was right: I was not able to find any confirmation of engineered swapping of men. Even if such trades exist, it's unlikely that they begin, as Hilton's narrative does, with a young Amish man being hauled to a new community in a white van, a man who "wasn't quite a prisoner, but . . . might as well have been." Hilton, *Patchwork Dreams*, 13.

27. Young, *Cultural Appropriation and the Arts*, 5.

28. "Em Gott sei Friede" is one rendering of "In God's peace." The spelling "mit" is more common than "mitt," although orthography is less rigid in Pennsylvania German than in High German.

29. "Author Mindy Starns Clark Talks about All Things Amish," *Christian Post*, February 22, 2011, www.christianpost.com.

30. Cynthia Keller, interview by Jennifer Vido, Fresh Fiction, November 5, 2010, http://freshfiction.com/page.php?id=2919.

31. See Keeshig-Tobias, "Stop Stealing Native Stories."

32. For a discussion of the ethnic subject in literature, see Benjamin D. Carson, "Re-Imagining the Contact Zone: Ethnic Theory and the Fiction of Clarence Major, Maxine Hong Kingston, Ana Castillo, and Gerald Vizenor" (PhD diss., University of Nebraska, 2005), partially available at http://digitalcom mons.unl.edu/dissertations/AAI3176772/.

33. Neil Bisoondath quoted in Coombe, "Properties of Culture," 76–77.

34. Two Amish-fiction authors use the term *takeaway* to describe what non-Amish readers can learn from the Amish, and one of them gives talks titled "Amish Takeaway: What We Can Learn from the Plain Community." Although they are referring to *takeaway value*, or lessons about faith and life that people can apply to their lives, the term suggests the appropriative muscle that is at work in the category.

35. Keeshig-Tobias, "Stop Stealing Native Stories," 73.

36. Root, "'White Indians,'" 232.

37. These novels are *Shadows of Lancaster County* and *The Secrets of Harmony Grove* by Mindy Starns Clark, *The Amish Midwife* by Clark and Leslie Gould, *The Hope of Refuge* by Cindy Woodsmall, and the Seasons of Grace series by Beverly Lewis. (The Seasons of Grace series also has an Amish protagonist, but Heather Nelson's story of discovering that she was an Amish baby born out of wedlock and put up for adoption fills a large role in the narrative.)

38. Clark, *Secrets of Harmony Grove*, 358; Clark and Gould, *Amish Midwife*, 321.

39. One exception is Beth Wiseman's character Linda, in *Plain Paradise*, whose English mother left her with an Old Order Amish family seventeen years earlier.

40. Root, "'White Indians,'" 232.

41. Trollinger, *Selling the Amish*, 126.

42. A few exceptions: *The Amish Nanny* by Mindy Starns Clark and Leslie Gould is written in the voice of Ada Rupp, an Amish woman, and Hillary Manton Lodge writes in a first-person ex-Amish voice in *Simply Sara*.

43. Quigley, "Ethics of Cultural Appropriation," 55, 57.

44. Ibid., 61.

45. Comments of Beth Wiseman, in response to a post by Sadie Crandle, "Accuracy = Research . . . But Does It Matter?" Amish Living, November 9, 2010, www.amishliving.com/profiles/blogs/accuracy-research-but-does.

46. The one Amish fact-checker with whom I spoke does not get paid by the author who sends her manuscripts; it is possible that other authors do pay the Amish or ex-Amish fact-checkers who vet their manuscripts.

47. Beverly Lewis, interview by Suzanne Woods Fisher, *Amish Wisdom*, April 21, 2011.

48. I owe this definition of exoticism to writer Alden Jones from her piece, "This Is Not a Cruise," in *The Smart Set from Drexel University*, www.thesmartset .com/article/article08060708.aspx.

49. Weaver-Zercher, *Amish in the American Imagination*, 195–96.

50. Pandian and Parman, *Making of Anthropology*, 4.

51. See "Gauguin: Maker of Myth," National Gallery of Art Press Office, www .nga.gov/press/exh/3011/index.shtm.

52. Bongie, *Exotic Memories*, 5; Foster, "Exotic as a Symbolic System," 21. For an interesting exploration of the position of one social scientist, John Hostetler, between academia and the group he studied and once belonged to, see Simon Bronner, "Plain Folk and Folk Society," in Weaver-Zercher, *Writing the Amish*, 56–97.

53. For more on this idea, see Boyer, "Understanding the Amish"; and Weaver-Zercher, *Amish in the American Imagination*, esp. the introduction. Boyer traces some other groups in American history—American Indians, African Americans, and Quakers—who have been idealized by critics of American culture. Boyer suggests that the idealization of Quakers in fiction tended to feature Quakers of the past rather than Quakers of the present, who by the mid-twentieth century had mostly disposed of distinctives in dress and speech. Ironically, Boyer says, Quakers' activism against the nuclear arms and militarism "diminished their utility as an idealized group that could be invoked to criticize mainstream American culture." Boyer, "Understanding the Amish," 370. For more on Quakers in fiction, see Anna B. Caulfield, *Quakers in Fiction: An Annotated Bibliography* (Northampton, MA: Pittenbruach Press, 1993).

54. Kym Elizabeth, blog post, http://kymelizabeth.blogspot.com/, accessed November 20, 2011.

55. Keller, *An Amish Christmas*, 228.

56. Welty, *Masquerading of Margaret*, 91. See Downing, "Witnessing the Amish."

57. hooks, *Black Looks*, 26.

58. There are others, including the depiction of powwowing in at least one novel as a common contemporary health-care practice among the Amish (it is actually quite rare).

59. Fuller, *What the Heart Sees*, in Wiseman, Fuller, and Long, *An Amish Love*, 136; Brunstetter, *Lydia's Charm*, 13; Brunstetter, *The Hope Chest*, 430.

60. Johnson-Weiner, "Language and Otherness," 1; Dorcas Smucker, "Another Amish Novel Rant/Critique," *Life in a Shoe* (blog), July 18, 2011, http://dorcassmucker.blogspot.com/2011/07/another-amish-novel-rantcritique.html.

61. Johnson-Weiner, "Language and Otherness," 5.

62. *American Christian Fiction Writers* blog, June 20, 2010, www.acfw.com/blog/?p=697.

63. Kraybill, Nolt, and Weaver-Zercher, *Amish Way*, 14.

64. Exceptions include Murray Pura's Snapshots in History series, Serena Miller's *An Uncommon Grace*, Kelly Long's historical novel *Arms of Love*, and Suzanne Woods Fisher's *The Waiting*, in which an Amish character goes to Vietnam as a conscientious objector. *Fields of Grace*, a historical Mennonite romance by Kim Vogel Sawyer, also deals with pacifist Amish responses to a military draft. Dale Cramer's work also offers two exceptions. *Levi's Will* deals with the protagonist's decision to leave his Amish community and join the military, and *Paradise Valley* raises issues of the refusal of the Amish to defend themselves and their families. In several of these novels, including Pura's *The Face of Heaven*, *Levi's Will*, and *Paradise Valley*, the Amish commitment to nonresistance is portrayed as innocently misguided. See, for example, Cramer, *Paradise Valley*, 350.

65. For more on Amish understandings of nonresistance and the peril in which it has at times placed them, see Donald B. Kraybill, ed., *The Amish and the State*, 2nd ed. (Baltimore: Johns Hopkins University Press, 2003).

66. Fisher, *Amish Peace*, 86.

67. Christian Book Distributors, www.christianbook.com/Christian/Books/cms_content?page=259746&sp=69515%22, accessed November 7, 2011.

68. Andrea Doering, conversation with author, March 17, 2011; MacGregor quoted in Sarah Hamaker, "Amish Fiction: Bonnet Books Rise in Popularity," *Crosswalk.com*, March 4, 2011, www.crosswalk.com/culture/books/amish-fiction-bonnet-books-rise-in-popularity.html.

69. In the 1930s, a national controversy surrounding one-room school-houses versus consolidation employed the Amish as guardians of traditional American virtues. For a history of the midcentury controversy surrounding the Amish and the "little red schoolhouse," see Weaver-Zercher, *Amish in the American Imagination*, chap. 2.

70. Trollinger, *Selling the Amish*, 70–74; Gray, *Autumn's Promise*, 129.

71. Cecelia Dowdy, e-mail to author, October 11, 2011.

72. Comment by Theodora, on Amish Living's "Amish Writers" forum, August 18, 2011. With regard to one of the few representations of African Americans in Amish romance novels, Theodora added, "Carrie Bender's portrayal of Af-Amer in *Summerville Days* was absolutely offensive to me (all us black folks don't know what corn is and have a parent on crack and we sing songs with the word 'darkie' in it and we don't know how to behave—wow, does she really believe what she wrote?). I was a little sad because I liked Ms. Bender's other books yet I didn't know she felt that way about me as a black person until I read *Summerville Days*—sigh. But this is why we need to write about it."

73. For a brief discussion of Amish perspectives on race, see Hurst and McConnell, *Amish Paradox*, 268.

74. Neal, *Romancing God*, 92.

75. African American Christian fiction tends to occur in urban or suburban settings, Woodside notes, and more frequently includes elements that CBA publishers may prohibit, such as alcohol and divorce. These are usually included not for any salaciousness quotient, Woodside says, but because "those are real things that happen and African American readers want a bit more realism in their fiction." Woodside, e-mail to author, October 2, 2011.

76. Noel Ignatiev, *How the Irish Became White* (New York: Routledge, 2008); Kasdorf, "Why We Fear the Amish," 69. Kasdorf's treatment of race with regard to representations of the Amish in contemporary poetry is an excellent primer on issues of whiteness and mediations of the Amish. Kasdorf's continuum of stereotypical qualities associated with Amish people, on page 70 of her chapter in *The Amish and the Media*, would offer an interesting rubric by which to measure portrayals of the Amish in Amish fiction. For more on the Amish and whiteness, see Trollinger, *Selling the Amish*, chap. 5.

77. Marcia Z. Nelson, conversation with author, April 11, 2011.

78. Brodhead, *Cultures of Letters*, 133.

Chapter Ten. Happily Ever After

1. At least twenty-three Amish romance series began in 2012, and those numbers don't include continuing series. "Paperback Trade Fiction," *New York Times* bestseller list, April 29, 2012, www.nytimes.com/best-sellers-books/trade-fiction -paperback/list.html?category=trade-fiction-paperback&pagewanted=print. The print-run figure comes from Crosby, "Sizzle, Sizzle," 3.

2. Sue Brower, conversation with author, November 18, 2011; Marcia Z. Nelson, "American Christian Fiction Writers Meet amid Strong Reader Interest," *Publishers Weekly,* September 28, 2011, www.publishersweekly.com; Bill Westfall, conversation with author, October 18, 2011.

3. Quoted in Crosby, "Sizzle, Sizzle," 3.

4. Ibid.

5. Sarah Forgrave, "Why I'm Re-Branding Myself," *Sarah Forgrave* (blog), August 28, 2011, http://sarahforgrave.com/2011/08/28/why-im-re-branding-my self/.

6. Quoted in Crosby, "Sizzle, Sizzle," 3.

7. Regency novels are set in Great Britain during the early nineteenth century. They tend to follow particular conventions and emphasize manners, differences in class, and chaste romances.

8. In Amish nonfiction, especially ex-Amish memoirs, the demystifying force has been at work for some time. Memoirs of formerly Amish people such as Ruth Irene Garrett's *Crossing Over: One Woman's Escape from Amish Life* (New York: HarperOne, 2003) and Chris Burkholder's *Amish Confidential: The Bishop's Son Shatters the Silence* (Louisville, CO: Argyle Publishing, 2005), demonstrate this.

9. Writing about Mennonites are Kim Vogel Sawyer, Nancy Mehl, Gail Sattler, Dianne Christner, and Amy Wallace; Ann Gabhart is writing about Shakers; Jody Hedlund writes about Puritans; Melanie Dobson has written about Moravians; Judith Miller and Melanie Dobson write about the Amana Colonies; Quaker fiction is being written by Lauralee Bliss, Ramona Cecil, Rachael Phillips, Claire Sanders, Suzette Williams, Ann Schrock, Jennifer Hudson Taylor, and Suzanne Woods Fisher; and Allison Pittman is writing Mormon fiction.

10. Crosby, "Sizzle, Sizzle," 3.

11. Picoult's book includes infanticide committed by an Amish grandmother in a misguided and bizarre attempt to get her daughter to remain Amish. Several readers of Picoult's book who have intimate knowledge of Amish life told

me that Picoult's research into and knowledge of Amish faith and practices is almost without fault.

12. See Keller, *Amish Christmas,* 135 ("Oh my God, Mom!") and 148 ("'Dear God,' James breathed"). The few references to Amish spirituality in the book include the first line of the Lord's Prayer (91) and an after-dinner ritual in which the Amish characters sing "a song primarily about gratitude" (115).

13. Marcia Z. Nelson, conversation with author, April 11, 2011; Andrea Doering, conversation with author, March 17, 2011.

14. "Briefly Noted," a review of *Kornwolf, New Yorker,* February 27, 2006, 83. Some might include Jodi Picoult's *Plain Truth* in the category of literary fiction, but it is more frequently considered commercial fiction.

15. Toews's simultaneously released memoir about her father's manic depression, *Swing Low,* also received much critical attention. For a bibliography of Mennonite writing in the United States, see Ervin Beck, "Mennonite/s Writing in the U.S.," www.goshen.edu/english/ervinb/bibliographies/menno_us_bib/ BeckBib.html.

16. Lee Rainie et al., "The Rise of E-Reading," Pew Internet and American Life Project, April 4, 2012, http://libraries.pewinternet.org/2012/04/04/the -rise-of-e-reading/.

17. Amazon bestseller lists are updated hourly. The list referred to in this chapter appeared at 9:00 a.m. on May 2, 2012. Slots one, three, four, and five on this May 2 Amazon Christian romance fiction bestseller list were occupied by Amish novels by Samantha Jillian Bayarr. Books by Christian fiction stars Karen Kingsbury, Tracie Peterson, and Francine Rivers trailed behind at numbers nine, eleven, and twelve, respectively.

18. Other novelists of Amish fiction who have written Amish nonfiction include Beverly Lewis (*Amish Prayers* and a cookbook), Cindy Woodsmall (*Plain Wisdom,* coauthored with Miriam Flaud), Mindy Starns Clark (*A Pocket Guide to Amish Life*), and Wanda Brunstetter (*A Celebration of the Simple Life* and the Amish Friends Cookbook series).

19. Carol Traver, e-mail to author, November 3, 2011; Eli Hochstetler, conversation with author, June 24, 2011. One example is Marlene Miller's memoir of becoming Amish called *Grace Leads Me Home* (Sugarcreek, OH: Carlisle Printing, 2011).

20. Boyer, "Understanding the Amish," 376.

21. Umble and Weaver-Zercher, *Amish and the Media,* 257. Umble and Weaver-Zercher credit Crystal Downing's argument in "Tongue in Check: Paralleling the Taliban with the Amish" as a source for this idea.

22. Keller, *An Amish Christmas*, 172, 190; Fisher, *The Choice*, 41.

23. One could argue that viewing oneself as Other, and allowing oneself to be viewed in this way, is in itself a very Amish thing to do. According to Downing, *Gelassenheit*, which is the Amish principle of "yieldedness" or submission, actually "radicalizes the concept of Otherness . . . by establishing the Amish themselves as the Other." In other words, rather than forcing others to submit to their ideology, the Amish "submit themselves to the forces of a dominant discourse which needs to see them as Other." Downing, "Tongue in Check," 203–4.

24. Lynn Neal makes this point about evangelical romance novels in *Romancing God*. This would be a parallel development, of sorts, to the one that G. C. Waldrep identifies in the work of Pathway Publishers, an Old Order Amish-owned publishing house that produces books and periodicals for Amish readers. Waldrep suggests that, in addition to the influence of New Order and para-Amish groups, Pathway has had a significant spiritual renewal effect on Old Order Amish groups. See Waldrep, "The New Order Amish and Para-Amish Groups: Spiritual Renewal within Tradition," *Mennonite Quarterly Review* 82, no. 3 (July 2008): 395–426.

25. Kraybill, *Riddle of Amish Culture*, 37. For more on this relationship between personal spirituality and ecclesial authority, see Kraybill, Johnson-Weiner, and Nolt, *The Amish*, chap. 4.

26. Anderson, "Happily Ever After," 28–29.

27. Amish minister Joseph F. Beiler first employed the Trojan horse as a metaphor for tourism in "The Tourist Season," *Gospel Herald*, June 8, 1976, 482. Marc Olshan also used the image to describe the growth of cottage industries among the Amish, which "carries with it a potential for forcing the realignment of Amish life to accord with the dictates of commerce." Olshan, "The Opening of Amish Society," in Kraybill and Olshan, *Amish Struggle with Modernity*, 146.

28. Hurst and McConnell, *Amish Paradox*, 123; "A wife [name withheld]," "How a Wife Can Improve Her Marriage," *Family Life*, October 2007.

29. Cancian, *Love in America*, 5.

30. Radway makes a similar point when she claims that romance novels, by perpetuating the divide between public and private spheres, wherein romance is assigned to the private sphere, leave unchallenged "the male right to the public spheres of work, politics, and power." *Reading the Romance*, 217.

31. Little research on Amish definitions of romance exists. For one of the few treatments of Amish romantic relationships, see Stevick, *Growing Up Amish*, chap. 9.

32. Anderson, "Happily Ever After," 28, 26.

33. Miller, *Consuming Religion*, 105–6.

34. Jayne Ann Krentz suggests something similar about general-market romance novels: "It is different to explain the appeal of romance novels to people who don't read them. . . . In a sense, romance writers are writing in a code clearly understood by readers but opaque to others." Krentz, "Beneath the Surface: The Hidden Codes of Romance," in Krentz, *Dangerous Men and Adventurous Women*, 15.

35. Justin Juozapavicius, "2011 Drought: Oklahoma Sees Driest 4 Months since 1921," *Huffington Post*, April 6, 2011, www.huffingtonpost.com.

36. Old Colony Mennonites in Bolivia migrated from Mexico in the 1960s. There are an estimated 130,000 Low German Mennonites living in settlements stretching from Canada to South America, located in Mexico, Bolivia, Belize, Paraguay, and several states and provinces. For more on Old Colony Mennonites, see Royden Loewen, "To the Ends of the Earth: An Introduction to the Conservative Low German Mennonites in the Americas," *Mennonite Quarterly Review* 82, no. 3 (July 2008): 427–48.

37. See Coontz, *The Way We Never Were: American Families and the Nostalgia Trap* (New York: Basic Books, 2000).

38. Borgmann, *Crossing the Postmodern Divide*, 115.

39. Miller, "Why We Love Amish Romances," 41.

Bibliography

Agger, Ben. *Speeding Up Fast Capitalism: Cultures, Jobs, Families, Schools, Bodies.* Boulder, CO: Paradigm, 2004.

Alter, Alexandra. "They're No Bodice Rippers, but Amish Romances Are Hot." *Wall Street Journal*, September 9, 2009, http://online.wsj.com/article _email/SB125244227154093575-lMyQjAxMDI5NTAyOTQwNDkyWj. html#articleTabs%3Darticle.

Anderson, Jennifer. "Happily Ever After: The Fairy Tale World of Amish Romance Novels," *Calvary Messenger*, April 2012, 26–29.

Bado-Fralick, Nikki, and Rebecca Sachs Norris. *Toying with God: The World of Religious Games and Dolls.* Waco, TX: Baylor University Press, 2010.

Barrett, Rebecca Kaye. "Higher Love: What Women Gain from Christian Romance Novels." *Journal of Religion and Popular Culture* 4 (Summer 2003), http://www.usask.ca/relst/jrpc/art4-higherlove.html.

Barrett-Fox, Rebecca. "Christian Romance Novels: Inspiring Convention and Challenge." Unpublished paper, in author's files.

Bebbington, David W. *Evangelicalism in Modern Britain: A History from the 1730s to the 1980s.* London: Unwin Hyman, 1989.

Beck, Ervin. "Mennonite and Amish Serial Fiction: An Informal Bibliography." *Center for Mennonite Writing Journal* 2, no. 4 (July 15, 2010), http://www .mennonitewriting.org/journal/2/4/mennonite-and-amish-serial -fiction/.

Bender, Elizabeth Horsch. "Three Amish Novels." *Mennonite Quarterly Review* 19, no. 4 (October 1945): 273–84.

Blodgett, Jan. *Protestant Evangelical Literary Culture and Contemporary Society.* Westport, CT: Greenwood Press, 1997.

Bongie, Chris. *Exotic Memories: Literature, Colonialism, and the Fin de Siècle.* Stanford, CA: Stanford University Press, 1991.

Borgmann, Albert. *Crossing the Postmodern Divide.* Chicago: University of Chicago Press, 1992.

————. *Technology and Character of Contemporary Life: A Philosophical Inquiry.* Chicago: University of Chicago Press, 1987.

Boyer, Paul S. "Understanding the Amish in Twenty-First-Century America." *Mennonite Quarterly Review* 82, no. 3 (July 2008): 359–76.

Boym, Svetlana. *The Future of Nostalgia.* New York: Basic Books, 2002.

Brodhead, Richard H. *Cultures of Letters: Scenes of Reading and Writing in Nineteenth-Century America.* Chicago: University of Chicago Press, 1995.

Brunstetter, Wanda. *The Hope Chest.* Uhrichsville, OH: Barbour Books, 2007.

————. *Lydia's Charm.* Uhrichsville, OH: Barbour Books, 2010.

————. *On Her Own.* Uhrichsville, OH: Barbour Books, 2007.

————. *Plain and Fancy.* In *Lancaster Brides.* Uhrichsville, OH: Barbour Books, 2003.

————. *A Sister's Hope.* Uhrichsville, OH: Barbour Books, 2008.

Byler, Linda. *Running Around (and Such).* Intercourse, PA: Good Books, 2010.

Cancian, Francesca M. *Love in America: Gender and Self-Development.* New York: Cambridge University Press, 1990.

Cavallo, Guglielmo, and Roger Chartier. *A History of Reading in the West.* Boston: University of Massachusetts Press, 1999.

Chase, Malcolm, and Christopher Shaw, eds. *The Imagined Past: History and Nostalgia.* New York: Manchester University Press, 1989.

Cherlin, Andrew. *The Marriage-Go-Round: The State of Marriage and the Family in America Today.* New York: Knopf, 2009.

Clark, Mindy Starns. *Secrets of Harmony Grove.* Eugene, OR: Harvest House, 2010.

Clark, Mindy Starns, and Leslie Gould. *The Amish Midwife.* Eugene, OR: Harvest House, 2011.

Clifford, James. *The Predicament of Culture: Twentieth-Century Ethnography, Literature, and Art.* Cambridge, MA: Harvard University Press, 1988.

Clipston, Amy. *A Gift of Grace.* Grand Rapids, MI: Zondervan, 2009.

Coombe, Rosemary J. "The Properties of Culture and the Possession of Identity: Postcolonial Struggle and the Legal Imagination." In *Borrowed Power: Essays on Cultural Appropriation,* edited by Bruce Ziff and Pratima Rao, 74–96. New Brunswick, NJ: Rutgers University Press, 1997.

Cramer, Dale. *Paradise Valley*. Minneapolis: Bethany House, 2011.

Crosby, Cindy. "Sizzle, Sizzle . . . Fizzle, Fizzle . . ." *Publishers Weekly Religion Update*, February 2012, 1–6.

Downing, Crystal. "Tongue in Check: Paralleling the Taliban with the Amish." *CrossCurrents* 53 (2003): 200–208.

———. "Witnessing the Amish: Plain People on Fancy Film." In Umble and Weaver-Zercher, *Amish and the Media*, 25–42.

Eagleton, Terry. *After Theory*. New York: Basic Books, 2003.

———. *Literary Theory: An Introduction*. Anniv. ed. Minneapolis: University of Minnesota Press, 2008.

Eicher, Jerry. *A Wedding Quilt for Ella*. Eugene, OR: Harvest House, 2011.

Eliot, George. "Silly Novels by Lady Novelists." *Westminster Review* 66 (October 1856): 442–61.

Ellis, Leanna. *Forsaken*. Naperville, IL: Sourcebooks, 2011.

Ellis, Mary. *Abigail's New Hope*. Eugene, OR: Harvest House, 2011.

Epp, Marlene. "A Brief Look at the Writings of Helen Reimensnyder Martin, 1868–1939." Unpublished paper on file at the Heritage Historical Library, Aylmer, ON.

Epstein, Jason. *Book Business: Publishing Past, Present, and Future*. New York: Norton, 2002.

Fish, Stanley. *Is There a Text in This Class? The Authority of Interpretive Communities*. Cambridge, MA: Harvard University Press, 1982.

Fisher, Suzanne Woods. *Amish Peace: Simple Wisdom for a Complicated World*. Grand Rapids, MI: Revell, 2009.

———. *The Choice*. Grand Rapids, MI: Revell, 2010.

———. *The Waiting*. Grand Rapids, MI: Revell, 2010.

Foster, Stephen William. "The Exotic as a Symbolic System." *Dialectical Anthropology* 7, no. 1 (September 1982): 21–30.

Freitas, Donna. *Sex and the Soul: Juggling Sexuality, Spirituality, Romance, and Religion on America's College Campuses*. New York: Oxford University Press, 2008.

Gallagher, Sally K., and Christian Smith. "Symbolic Traditionalism and Pragmatic Egalitarianism: Contemporary Evangelicals, Families, and Gender." *Gender and Society* 13, no. 2 (April 1999): 211–33.

Gallagher, Susan V., and Roger Lundin. *Literature through the Eyes of Faith*. New York: HarperSanFrancisco, 1989.

Gandolfo, Anita. *Faith and Fiction: Christian Literature in America Today*. Westport, CT: Praeger, 2007.

Gans, Herbert. *Popular Culture and High Culture: An Analysis and Evaluation of Taste*. Rev. ed. New York: Basic Books, 1999.

Gerrig, Richard. *Experiencing Narrative Worlds: On the Psychological Activities of Reading*. New Haven, CT: Yale University Press, 1993.

Gifford, Terry. *Pastoral*. London: Routledge, 1999.

Gorski, Eric. "Contemporary Amish Fiction Gains a Following." *Boston.com*, July 17, 2009, http://articles.boston.com/2009-07-17/lifestyle/29258276_1 _christian-fiction-christian-publishing-christian-perspective/2.

Gray, Shelley Shepard. *Autumn's Promise*. New York: Avon Inspire, 2010.

Graybill, Beth E. "Amish Women, Business Sense: Old Order Women Entrepreneurs in the Lancaster County, Pennsylvania Tourist Marketplace." PhD diss., University of Maryland–College Park, 2008.

————. "Chasing the Bonnet: The Premise and Popularity of Writing Amish Women." *Center for Mennonite Writing Journal*, July 15, 2010, http:// www.mennonitewriting.org/journal/2/4/bonnet-fiction/.

Grossman, Lev. "Literary Revolution in the Supermarket Aisle: Genre Fiction is Disruptive Technology," *Time*, May 23, 2012, http://entertainment .time.com.

Heim, Tami. "Surviving the E-books Earthquake." *Christian Retailing*, January 21, 2011, http://christianretailing.com/index.php/features/industry-issues/ 22598-surviving-the-e-books-earthquake.

Hill, Susan Colestock. *Heart Language: Elsie Singmaster and Her Pennsylvania German Writings*. State College: Pennsylvania State University Press, 2009.

Hilton, Laura V. *Patchwork Dreams*. New Kensington, PA: Whitaker House, 2011.

hooks, bell. *Black Looks: Race and Representation*. Boston: South End Press, 1992.

Hunter, James Davison. *American Evangelicalism: Conservative Religion and the Quandary of Modernity*. New Brunswick, NJ: Rutgers University Press, 1983.

Hurst, Charles E., and David L. McConnell. *An Amish Paradox: Diversity and Change in the World's Largest Amish Community*. Baltimore: Johns Hopkins University Press, 2010.

Jaffe, Joseph. *Join the Conversation: How to Engage Marketing-Weary Consumers with the Power of Community, Dialogue, and Partnership*. Hoboken, NJ: Wiley, 2008.

Johnson-Weiner, Karen. "Language and Otherness: Popular Fiction and the Amish." In *The Language and Culture of the Pennsylvania Germans: A*

Festschrift for Earl C. Haag, edited by W. D. Keel and C. R. Beam, 73–83. Lawrence, KS: Society for German-American Studies, 2010.

———. "Pow-Wow Healers, Dumb Dutchmen, and Salt of the Earth: The Portrayal of Old Order Amish in Popular Literature." Paper presented at the Amish, the Old Orders, and the Media Conference, Young Center for Anabaptist and Pietist Studies, Elizabethtown College, Elizabethtown, PA, June 15, 2001.

———. "Selling the Past: Authenticity, Amishness, and New Traditions in the Marketplace." Unpublished paper, in author's files.

Joyce, Kathryn. *Quiverfull: Inside the Christian Patriarchy Movement*. Boston: Beacon Press, 2009.

Kammeyer, Kenneth. *A Hypersexual Society: Sexual Discourse, Erotica, and Pornography in America Today*. New York: Palgrave Macmillan, 2008.

Kasdorf, Julia Spicher. Introduction to *Rosanna of the Amish: The Restored Text*, by Joseph W. Yoder, 11–23. Edited by Julia Kasdorf and Joshua R. Brown. Scottdale, PA: Herald Press, 2008.

———. "Why We Fear the Amish: Whiter-than-White Figures in Contemporary Poetry." In Umble and Weaver-Zercher, *Amish and the Media*, 67–90.

Keeshig-Tobias, Lenore. "Stop Stealing Native Stories." In *Borrowed Power: Essays on Cultural Appropriation*, edited by Bruce Ziff and Pratima Rao, 71–73. New Brunswick, NJ: Rutgers University Press, 1997.

Keller, Cynthia. *An Amish Christmas*. New York: Ballantine, 2010.

Kraybill, Donald B. *The Riddle of Amish Culture*. Rev. ed. Baltimore: Johns Hopkins University Press, 2001.

Kraybill, Donald B., Karen M. Johnson-Weiner, and Steven M. Nolt. *The Amish*. Baltimore: Johns Hopkins University Press, 2013.

Kraybill, Donald B., and Steven M. Nolt. *Amish Enterprise: From Plows to Profits*. Baltimore: Johns Hopkins University Press, 1995, 2004.

Kraybill, Donald B., Steven M. Nolt, and David L. Weaver-Zercher. *Amish Grace: How Forgiveness Transcended Tragedy*. San Francisco: Jossey-Bass, 2007.

———. *The Amish Way: Patient Faith in a Perilous World*. San Francisco: Jossey-Bass, 2010.

Kraybill, Donald B., Steven M. Nolt, and Erik J. Wesner. "Sources of Enterprise Success in Amish Communities." *Journal of Enterprising Communities* 5, no. 2 (2011): 112–30.

Kraybill, Donald B., and Marc A. Olshan, eds. *The Amish Struggle with Modernity*. Hanover, NH: University of New England, 1994.

Krentz, Jayne Ann, ed. *Dangerous Men and Adventurous Women: Romance Writers on the Appeal of the Romance*. Philadelphia: University of Pennsylvania Press, 1992.

Levine, Rick, Christopher Locke, Doc Searls, and David Weinberger. *The Cluetrain Manifesto: The End of Business as Usual*. Tenth anniv. ed. New York: Basic Books, 2009.

Levy, Ariel. *Female Chauvinist Pigs: Women and the Rise of Raunch Culture*. New York: Free Press, 2005.

Lewis, Beverly. *The Betrayal*. Minneapolis: Bethany House, 2003.

———. *The Crossroad*. Minneapolis: Bethany House, 1999.

———. *The Longing*. Minneapolis: Bethany House, 2008.

———. *The Mercy*. Minneapolis: Bethany House, 2011.

———. *The Postcard*. Minneapolis: Bethany House, 1999.

———. *The Reckoning*. Minneapolis: Bethany House, 1998.

———. *The Revelation*. Minneapolis: Bethany House, 2005.

———. *The Shunning*. Minneapolis: Bethany House, 1997.

———. *The Telling*. Minneapolis: Bethany House, 2010.

———. *The Thorn*. Minneapolis: Bethany House, 2010.

Lipovetsky, Gilles. *Hypermodern Times*. Malden, MA: Polity Press, 2005.

Loconte, Joseph, and Michael Cromartie. "Let's Stop Stereotyping Evangelicals." *Washington Post*, November 8, 2006, www.washingtonpost.com/wp-dyn/content/article/2006/11/07/AR2006110701228.html.

Lodge, Hillary Manton. *Simply Sara*. Eugene, OR: Harvest House, 2010.

Long, Kelly. *Arms of Love*. Nashville: Thomas Nelson, 2012.

Malek, Doreen Owens. "Loved I Not Honor More: The Virginal Heroine in Romance." In Krentz, *Dangerous Men and Adventurous Women*, 115–20.

———. "Mad, Bad, and Dangerous to Know: The Hero as Challenge." In Krentz, *Dangerous Men and Adventurous Women*, 73–80.

Marsden, George. *Understanding Fundamentalism and Evangelicalism*. Grand Rapids, MI: Eerdmans, 1991.

Martin, Helen Reimensnyder. *Sabina: A Story of the Amish*. New York: Century, 1905.

Martin, Linette. *Sacred Doorways: A Beginner's Guide to Icons*. Cape Cod, MA: Paraclete Press, 2002.

Marx, Leo. *The Machine in the Garden: Technology and the Pastoral Ideal in America*. 35th anniv. ed. New York: Oxford, 2000.

McNair, Brian. *Striptease Culture: Sex, Media, and the Democratisation of Desire*. London: Routledge, 2002.

Miller, Clara Bernice. *Katie.* Scottdale, PA: Herald Press, 1966.

Miller, Emma. *Miriam's Heart.* New York: Harlequin, Love Inspired, 2011.

Miller, Eric. "Why We Love Amish Romances." *Christianity Today,* April 2011, 38–41.

Miller, Laura. *Reluctant Capitalists: Bookselling and the Culture of Consumption.* Chicago: University of Chicago Press, 2006.

Miller, Lisa. "Love, Amish Style." *Newsweek,* December 13, 2010, 25.

Miller, Vincent J. *Consuming Religion: Christian Faith and Practice in a Consumer Culture.* New York: Continuum, 2004.

Mock, Melanie Springer. "Love and Marriage, Horse and Carriage." Paper presented at West Region Christianity and Literature Conference, California Baptist University, Riverside, CA, March 2010.

Modleski, Tania. *Feminism without Women: Culture and Criticism in a "Postfeminist" Age.* New York: Routledge, 1991.

Moore, R. Laurence. *Selling God: American Religion in the Marketplace of Culture.* New York: Oxford University Press, 1994.

Morgan, Spencer. "Getting Dirty in Dutch Country." *Bloomberg Businessweek,* July 25–August 1, 2010, 69–71.

Neal, Lynn S. *Romancing God: Evangelical Women and Inspirational Fiction.* Chapel Hill: University of North Carolina Press, 2006.

Nell, Victor. *Lost in a Book: The Psychology of Reading for Pleasure.* New Haven, CT: Yale University Press, 1988.

Nelson, Marcia. "Recipe for an Amish Novel." *Publishers Weekly,* February 28, 2011, 3.

Nes, Solrunn. *The Mystical Language of Icons.* Grand Rapids, MI: Eerdmans, 2004.

Ohmann, Richard. "The Shaping of a Canon: U.S. Fiction, 1960–1975." *Critical Inquiry* 10, no. 1 (September 1983): 199–223.

Onasch, Konrad, and Annemarie Schnieper. *Icons: The Fascination and the Reality.* New York: Riverside Books, 1997.

Oppliger, Patrice. *Girls Gone Skank: The Sexualization of Girls in American Culture.* New York: McFarlane, 2008.

Pandian, Jacob, and Susan Parman. *The Making of Anthropology: The Semiotics of Self and Other in the Western Tradition.* New Delhi: Vedams ebooks, 2004.

Paul, Pamela. *Pornified: How Pornography Is Damaging Our Lives, Our Relationships, and Our Families.* New York: St. Martin's Griffin, 2006.

Pratt, Mary Louise. *Imperial Eyes: Travel Writing and Transculturation*. New York: Routledge, 1992.

Quigley, Stephen. "The Ethics of Cultural Appropriation of Identity in Fiction: A Writer's Choices in Cross-Cultural Writing." *Writer's Chronicle*, March–April 2011, 54–61.

Rabey, Steve, and Monte Unger. *Milestones: 50 Events of the 20th Century That Shaped Evangelicals in America*. Nashville: Broadman & Holman, 2002.

Radway, Janice A. *Reading the Romance: Women, Patriarchy, and Popular Literature*. Chapel Hill: University of North Carolina Press, 1984.

Regis, Pamela. *A Natural History of the Romance Novel*. Philadelphia: University of Pennsylvania Press, 2003.

Reid, Ruth. *The Promise of an Angel*. Nashville: Thomas Nelson, 2011.

Roach, Catherine. "Getting a Good Man to Love: Popular Romance Fiction and the Problem of Patriarchy." *Journal of Popular Romance Studies* 1, no. 1 (August 2010), http://jprstudies.org/2010/08/getting-a-good-man-to -love-popular-romance-fiction-and-the-problem-of-patriarchy-by-cathe rine-roach/.

Rodgers, Ann. "In Amish Romance Novels, Racy Takes a Back Seat to Values." *Pittsburgh Post-Gazette*, August 16, 2009, http://www.post-gazette.com/ pg/09228/991202-44.stm.

Root, Deborah. "'White Indians': Appropriation and the Politics of Display." In *Borrowed Power: Essays on Cultural Appropriation*, edited by Bruce Ziff and Pratima Rao, 225–33. New Brunswick, NJ: Rutgers University Press, 1997.

Roper, Gayle. *A Stranger's Wish*. Eugene, OR: Harvest House, 1998.

Sachs, Andrea. "Amish Romance Novels: No Bonnet Rippers." *Time*, April 27, 2009, http://www.time.com/time/magazine/article/0,9171,1891759,00 .html.

Schechner, Richard. *Performance Studies: An Introduction*. 2nd ed. New York: Routledge, 2006.

Schultze, Quentin J., and Robert H. Woods Jr., eds. *Understanding Evangelical Media: The Changing Face of Christian Communication*. Downers Grove, IL: InterVarsity Press Academic, 2008.

Scott, Stephen. "How Factual Is Amish Fiction?" Unpublished paper, Young Center for Anabaptist and Pietist Studies, Elizabethtown, PA.

———. "The Popularity of Amish Fiction." Unpublished paper, Young Center for Anabaptist and Pietist Studies, Elizabethtown, PA.

Seaton, Beverly. "Helen Reimensnyder Martin's 'Caricatures' of the Pennsylvania Germans." *Pennsylvania Magazine of History and Biography* 104, no. 1 (January 1980): 86–95.

Senft, Adina. *The Wounded Heart*. Nashville: FaithWords, 2011.

Slovic, Scott. *Going Away to Think: Engagement, Retreat, and Ecocritical Responsibility*. Reno: University of Nevada Press, 2008.

Smith, Christian. *American Evangelicalism: Embattled and Thriving*. Chicago: University of Chicago Press, 1998.

———. *Christian America? What Evangelicals Really Want*. Berkeley: University of California Press, 2000.

Stevick, Richard A. *Growing Up Amish: The Teenage Years*. Baltimore: Johns Hopkins University Press, 2007.

Trachtenberg, Jeffrey A. "HarperCollins Acquires Religion-Book Publisher." *Wall Street Journal*, November 1, 2011, http://online.wsj.com/article/SB1 0001424052970203707504577010283227448426.html.

Trollinger, Susan L. *Selling the Amish: The Tourism of Nostalgia*. Baltimore: Johns Hopkins University Press, 2012.

Ugolnik, Anthony. *The Illuminating Icon*. Grand Rapids, MI: Eerdmans, 1989.

Umble, Diane Zimmerman, and David Weaver-Zercher, eds. *The Amish and the Media*. Baltimore: Johns Hopkins University Press, 2008.

Umble, John. Review of *Rosanna of the Amish*, by Joseph W. Yoder. *Mennonite Quarterly Review* 15, no. 2 (April 1941): 143–47.

Walbert, David. *Garden Spot: Lancaster County, the Old Order Amish, and the Selling of Rural America*. New York: Oxford University Press, 2002.

Weaver-Zercher, David. "Amish." In *American Icons: An Encyclopedia of the People, Places, and Things That Have Shaped Our Culture*, edited by Dennis R. Hall and Susan Grove Hall, 1:15–21. Westport, CT: Greenwood Press, 2006.

———. *The Amish in the American Imagination*. Baltimore: Johns Hopkins University Press, 2001.

———, ed. *Writing the Amish: The Worlds of John A. Hostetler*. State College: Pennsylvania State University Press, 2005.

Welty, Cora Gottschalk. *The Masquerading of Margaret*. Boston: C. M. Clark, 1908.

Wendell, Sarah, and Candy Tan. *Beyond Heaving Bosoms: The Smart Bitches' Guide to Romance Novels*. New York: Touchstone, 2009.

Wilcox, W. Bradford. "How Focused on the Family? Evangelical Protestants, the

Family, and Sexuality." In *Evangelicals and Democracy in America*, edited by Steven Brint and Jean Reith Schroedel, 1:251–75. New York: Russell Sage Foundation, 2009.

Williams, Raymond. *The Raymond Williams Reader.* Edited by John Higgins. Malden, MA: Blackwell, 2001.

Wilson, Janelle L. *Nostalgia: Sanctuary of Meaning.* Cranbury, NJ: Rosemont, 2005.

Wimsatt, William Kurtz, Jr., and Monroe C. Beardsley. *The Verbal Icon: Studies in the Meaning of Poetry.* Lexington: University of Kentucky Press, 1954.

Wiseman, Beth. *Plain Proposal.* Nashville: Thomas Nelson, 2011.

Wiseman, Beth, Kathleen Fuller, and Kelly Long. *An Amish Love: Three Amish Novellas.* Nashville: Thomas Nelson, 2010.

Woodsmall, Cindy. *When the Heart Cries.* Colorado Springs: WaterBrook Press, 2006.

———. *When the Soul Mends.* Colorado Springs: WaterBrook Press, 2008.

Wright, Bradley R. E. "They Like You," *Christianity Today,* August 2011, 21–25.

Yoder, Joseph W. *Rosanna of the Amish: The Restored Text.* Edited by Julia Kasdorf and Joshua R. Brown. Scottdale, PA: Herald Press, 2008.

Young, Brittany. "Making a Choice: Virginity in the Romance." In Krentz, *Dangerous Men and Adventurous Women*, 121–24.

Young, James O. *Cultural Appropriation and the Arts.* Hoboken, NJ: Wiley-Blackwell, 2010.

Index

Page numbers in italics refer to figures and tables.

advertising. *See* marketing

African Americans, 212, 225–26, 290n72, 290n75. *See also* race

Agger, Ben, 81

Amana Colonies, 266n28. *See also* fiction, Amana Colonies–themed

American Indians, 211–14, 219, 245

Amish, the: as brand, 9, 70, 236; as cult, 234–35; history of, 63–64, 129, 266n28; as innocents, 12–13, 113, 118, 156–57; effects of Amish romance novels on, 180–91, 242–44; as exotic, 15, 32, 130–31, 218–22, 224; as not fully Christian, 116–23, 234–36; opinions of Amish romance novels, 73, 99, 124–25, 180–91; population of, 7, 63, 245; publishing by, 191–97, 252n14, 293n24; as quintessential Americans, 218, 224; as role models, 113–16, 119, 126, 146

Amish, Beachy, 38, 65, 115–16, 125, 165, 184, 187–88, 243–44, 266n23

Amish, New Order, 38–40, 115–16, 141, 186

Amish, Old Order, xv, 7, 39–40, 115, 120–24, 183–84, 186–89, 239. *See also* Amish, the

Amish, Swartzentruber, 38, 183, 235, 259n29, 264–65n16, 283n6

Amish Living (website), 92–94, 101, 112, 151, 217, 225, 270n24

Amish Reader (website), 92–94

Amish romance novels. *See* romance novels, Amish

Amish Wisdom (radio show), xiii, 79–80, 113, 209–10

Anabaptism, xiv, 4, 38, 52, 58, 99, 191, 203–4, 206; history of, 62–65

"Anabaptist escalator," 38–40, 118, 259n29

Anderson, Jennifer, 184, 187–88, 243–44

appearance. *See* attractiveness, physical

appropriation, xv, 13, 200–201, 211–18, 240, 242, 245–46, 249, 287n34

Association for Christian Retail (CBA), 5, 51–54, 80, 97, 148, 226, 233, 237, 262n58

attractiveness, physical, 159–60, 193, 280n13
authors of Amish fiction. *See specific authors*

Bann, the. See shunning
Barbour Books, 49, 52, 104, 230, 232–33
Barrett-Fox, Rebecca, 68, 109, 160, 172
Baudrillard, Jean, 10
Bebbington, David, 60
bed courtship, 161–62
Bender, Carrie (pseudonym), 52, 182, 184
bestseller lists, 5–7, 45, 67, 80, 232, 239, 253n5
Bethany House, 41–42, 45–46, 48, 52–53, 65, 67–68, 131, 134, 191
Bible, 108, 114, 118–21, 143, 151, 165, 188, 235, 248; centrality within evangelicalism, 60–61; references within Amish romance novels, 120, 121, 175, 207; sales of, 61, 264n11
bishops, 35, 74, 111, 122, 124–27, 170, 183, 187, 205, 207–9
Blair, Annette: *Jacob's Return*, 70, 72, 73, 90, 162; *Thee, I Love*, 44, 70, 71, 72
Blodgett, Jan, xii
Bloom, Allan, 20–21
Bloomberg Businessweek, 7, 56, 67–69
bodice-rippers, 44, 58, 69. *See also* romance novels
Bomberger, John, 99, 254n8
Bongie, Chris, 219
bonnet. *See* covering, prayer
bonnet fiction. *See* romance novels, Amish
bonnet rippers, 66. *See also* romance novels, Amish: terminology for
book clubs. *See* book discussion groups; book distributors
book discussion groups, 92, 106–10, 143, 175. *See also* Gals and Books
book distributors: Choice Books, 98–99; Christian Book Distributors, 73, 80, 223, 236; Crossings Book Club, 49, 73, 98
bookmobile, Holmes County, 14–15, 180–82
booksellers, 3, 7, 14, 41, 82, 84, 96–98, 102; Christian, 73, 97–98
Borgmann, Albert, 134, 144–45, 250
Borntrager, Mary Christner, 52, 182
Boyer, Paul, 240, 288n53
Boym, Svetlana, 152
brides, 6, 101–2, 154
Brodhead, Richard, 30–31, 227, 269n17
Brower, Sue, 50, 202, 232, 254n8
Brunstetter, Wanda, xi, 49, 51, 76, 162, 181–84, 202, 248; sales of books by, 5, 232, 253n3
Brunstetter, Wanda, works of: *The Hope Chest*, 221; *Lydia's Charm*, 104, 107–8, 110, 149, 170, 175, 221; *On Her Own*, 149, 170; *Plain and Fancy*, 164–65; *A Sister's Hope*, 142
bundling. *See* bed courtship
Byler, Linda, 64, 184, 191, 197; biography of, 191–93; Buggy Spoke series, 178, 192; Lizzie Searches for Love series, 159, 192–95, 196; Sadie's Montana series, 193; sales of books by, 191–92, 197; *When Strawberries Bloom*, 195, 196

capitalism, 10, 17, 40, 77, 81–82, 84, 87–88, 100, 102, 222
Chapman, Vannetta, xi
chastity: the Amish and, 12–14, 157; in Amish romance novels, 69, 76, 136,

148–50, 157–58, 161, 163, 279n10; definitions of, 12, 156; evangelical understandings of, 11–12, 28, 60, 69, 156, 187. *See also* "clean reads"; purity culture; virginity

Cherlin, Andrew, 163, 167

Choice Books. *See under* book distributors

Christian Booksellers Association (CBA). *See* Association for Christian Retail

Christian fiction, ix–x, 4, 7, 9, 13, 106, 222, 237–38, 245; conventions of, 23, 106, 138, 142; history of, 41–42, 51; influence on popular fiction, 70; readers of, 22–23, 77, 157, 187, 189; sales of, 45, 61, 239

Christian publishers. *See* publishing, Christian

Christian romance novels. *See* romance novels, evangelical

Christmas, 6–7, 78, 101–2

Christner, Dianne, 230

Christy Awards, 20, 80

Clark, Mindy Starns, 50, 76, 212, 222; *The Amish Bride* and *The Amish Midwife* (coauthored with Leslie Gould), 146, 154, 163, 215; *Secrets of Harmony Grove*, 215

"clean reads," 12–13, 65, 91, 112, 148, 234, 237

Clipston, Amy, xi, 76, 95, 203; *A Gift of Grace*, 76, 124

colonialism, 86–87, 212, 219–20

commodification, 88, 98–103, 245; of the Amish, 54, 90, 98–102, 152, 246; of Amish romance novels, xiv, 10, 77, 82–103; of books, xiv, 82–83, 88, 96–98; of religion, 53, 82–83, 88, 99–101, 271n41

community, 14, 24, 39, 74, 94, 111, 121, 151, 216, 249

complementarianism. *See* gender roles: complementarianism; marriage: evangelical understandings of

Confession, The (musical), 22, 46, 208

conversational marketing. *See under* marketing

conversion. *See* Jesus: personal relationship with; salvation

coverings, prayer, x, 38, 45, 51, 53, 69–70, 76, 101, 118, 136, 157, 159, 164, 202, 208, 251n3; on front covers of Amish romance novels, xv–xvi, 3–4, 48–49, 70, 90, 165–66, 195, 213

Cramer, Dale, x, 202, 225; *Levi's Will*, 76, 289n64; *Paradise Valley*, 76, 135, 173, 289n64

Crossings Book Club. *See under* book distributors

cultural criticism, 12, 14, 19–21, 24, 83, 245, 247

cultural studies. *See* cultural criticism

cultural theory. *See* cultural criticism

Cushman, Kathryn, 198, 236

divorce, 60, 163–64, 169, 290n75

Dobson, Ruth Lininger, 35, 54, 125, 258–59n21

Doering, Andrea, 6, 49–50, 224, 238

domestication, xv, 24, 103, 200, 218, 222–25, 240, 242, 246

Dowdy, Cecelia, 225

Downing, Crystal, 33, 152–53, 256n30, 293n23

Duerksen, Carol, 52, 262n59

Dutch, Pennsylvania: as ethnic group, 25, 30, 162, 257n5, 258n10; as language, x, 64, 74, 203–6, 212, 221–22, 287n28

Eagleton, Terry, 16, 18–21, 200
e-books, 22, 81, 97–98, 130, 133, 238–39, 268n3
editors, xiii–xiv, 7, 41–45, 49–51, 57, 61, 84–86, 88–92. *See also specific editors*
Eicher, Jerry, 138, 182, 191, 202
Ellis, Leanna, 6, 280n20
Ellis, Mary, 113, 123, 181; *Abigail's New Hope*, 171; *Sarah's Christmas Miracle*, 78
Endlich, Melissa, 97
epilogue, 107, 149, 164–65, 212, 216
e-readers. *See* e-books
escapism, 132, 247, 250. *See also* reading: as transport
ethnicity: and Amish romance novels, 30–34, 221–22, 225–27; in fiction, 201, 216–17, 245; in the United States, 130, 211–14, 216–17. *See also* race
Evangelical Christian Publishers Association (ECPA), 5, 51, 61, 68, 80
evangelicalism: aesthetics within, 20, 62, 66, 74–75; chastity within, 11–12, 60, 156–57, 159; characteristics of, 37, 57–62; concerns of, 9, 11, 167; discourse of, 19, 39, 58–62, 157–58; diversity within, 57–59, 61–62; gender within, 8, 45, 164, 166–68, 172, 175; history of, 58–59, 118, 208; interactions with Amish, 34, 38, 40, 53–54, 62, 66, 212, 246; media of, 61–62, 68, 234; piety within, xiv, 27, 37, 40, 113–14, 119–21; representations of, 60, 246; sense of being disliked, 60–61. *See also under* family; marriage; motherhood; salvation
evangelical romance novels. *See* romance novels, evangelical
evangelism, 36–38, 60
excommunication. *See* shunning

exoticism, xv, 24, 200, 218–22, 224–25, 240, 242, 246

Facebook, xiii, 94–95, 101, 150, 250, 268n4
faith: Amish romance novels as strengthening readers', 107, 112–16, 126, 150; characteristics of Amish, 62–64, 121–23, 242–43; characteristics of evangelical, 37, 58–61, 113–21. *See also* evangelicalism: piety within; God; Jesus; romance novels, Amish: spirituality within; romance novels, evangelical: spirituality within; salvation
familism, 169. *See also* family: evangelical understandings of
family: Amish understandings of, 63, 124, 169; evangelical understandings of, 8, 60, 151, 156, 167, 169–72, 219, 222
farms, xi, 146–48, 168, 172, 236, 247–49
fast capitalism, 81. *See also* hypermodernity
feminism, 31–32, 44, 57, 83, 166, 171–74, 176
fiction, Amana Colonies–themed, xv, 3, 67, 236, 291n9. *See also* Amana Colonies
fiction, Amish-themed: angel, 6, 234; digital, 238–39; exposé, 234–36; gay and lesbian, 4, 6, 238, 245; historical, 6, 76, 162, 234; literary, 238, 292n14; mysteries, xv–xvi, 4, 6, 245, 252n15; quilting, 6, 74, 234; science fiction, xv, 245; suspense, 6, 76, 267n34; vampire, 6, 17, 90, 141, 162, 234; Wild West, 6, 234. *See also* romance novels, Amish

fiction, Mennonite-themed, xv, 3, 5, *230*, 236, 238, 245, 291n9. *See also* Mennonites

fiction, Moravian-themed, xv, 3, 236, 291n9

fiction, Mormon-themed, xv, 236, 291n9

fiction, Puritan-themed, xv, 3, 236, 291n9

fiction, Quaker-themed, xv, 3, 80, 236, 245, 288n53, 291n9. *See also* Quakers

fiction, Shaker-themed, xv, 3, 13, 236, 291n9

Fish, Stanley, 106

Fisher, Suzanne Woods, x, 79–82, 95–96, 100, 103, 123, 126, 161, 223, 239; as host of *Amish Wisdom*, 79–80, 113, 209–10; sale of books by, 79–81, 97

Fisher, Suzanne Woods, works of, 80, 239, 291n9; *The Choice*, 140, 167, 241; *The Waiting*, 148, 225

focal things, 144–45, 152

forgiveness, 50, 74, 112–13, 123, 163, 219

formalism. *See* New Criticism

Foster, Stephen William, 219

Freitas, Donna, 11, 155–56, 162

Fuller, Kathleen, 95, 170, 181, 221

fundamentalism, 59–60, 106, 118, 168, 208. *See also* evangelicalism

Furlong, Saloma Miller, 206, 239–40

Gallagher, Sally K., 166–68

Gallagher, Susan V., 62

Gals and Books (book discussion group), 106–10, 112, 120, 127, 138–39, 143, 175, 179

Gandolfo, Anita, xii, 138–40

Gans, Herbert, 20, 74–75, 180

Gaus, P. L., xv, 4, 182, 245

Gelassenheit, 64, 293n23

gender roles: complementarianism, 158, 163–68; headship, 164–68; in symbolic traditionalism, 166–68. *See also* evangelicalism: gender within; feminism; womanhood, Christian

genre fiction, 16–17, 23, 74–75, 111, 132, 142, 252n13

German, Pennsylvania. *See* Dutch, Pennsylvania

Gerrig, Richard, 132, 141, 150

Gifford, Terry, 146, 258n13

Glaspey, Terry, 94

globalization, 10, 90, 106, 130–31

God: Amish romance novels as connecting readers to, 100, 110, 112, 126–27; characters' trust in, 74, 113–14, 142–43, 165, 194; as judge, 37, 116–18, 124; as lover, 114–16; will of, 39, 107–8, 113, 142–43, 172, 194

Good, Phyllis Pellman, 192–93

Good Books, 192–93, 195, *196*

Gould, Leslie, *The Amish Bride* and *The Amish Midwife* (coauthored with Mindy Starns Clark), 146, *154*, 163, 215

Goyer, Tricia, *128*, 131, 136

Gray, Shelley Shepard, xi, 80, 116, 266n29, 268nn4–5; *Autumn's Promise*, 65–66, 135, 138, 167, 224

Graybill, Beth E., 132, 183

Grossman, Lev, 132, 161

Harlequin, 42, 44, 67–68, 70, 83; Love Inspired, 68, 70, 97–98, 267n34

HarperCollins. *See* Nelson, Thomas; Zondervan

Harvest House, 48–49, *78*, 92, 94, *154*, 232–33, 254n9

headship. *See under* gender roles

Herald Press, *39*, 40, 46, 51–54, 182, 283n6

heroines. *See* protagonists in Amish romance novels

Hill, Grace Livingston, 42

Hilton, Laura, 125, 209–11, 286n26

hooks, bell, 220

hypermodernity: and the Amish, 13, 28, 32, 102, 135, 157, 219; Amish romance novels as benefiting from, 10, 77, 82–84, 89–90, 101–2; Amish romance novels as dissenting from, xiii, 9–10, 14, 28, 51, 54, 77, 84, 127, 132–35, 144–45, 184, 186, 216, 233–35, 241–42, 249–50; definition of, 10, 12, 133; and the economy, xiv, 10, 81, 84, 102; and evangelicalism, 19; the individual within, 110, 135; and the past, 134, 152; publishing within, 10, 81–84, 89–90, 93, 245–46; religion within, 100–2, 110, 134–35

hypersexualization: and Amish romance novels, xiii, 9, 11–12, 14, 19, 28, 51, 132, 136–37, 163, 185–86, 233–34, 246, 249; definition of, 10–12; and evangelicalism, 11, 14, 19, 136–37, 246; in popular culture, 10–11, 51, 135–36

icons: Amish romance novels as, xiv, 77, 103, 111–14, 117, 127; characteristics of, 110–11, 113, 116–17, 127

inspirational fiction. *See* Christian fiction; romance novels, evangelical

interpretive community, 106, 108, 111, 127

Jaffe, Joseph, 93–94

Jesus, 99, 103, 164, 237; and the atonement, 60, 123, 234; personal relationship with, 37, 113–21, 123, 165, 260–61n44, 274n38; and the Sermon on the Mount, 63

Johnson, Carol, 41–42, 44–46, 48, 52

Johnson-Weiner, Karen, 14, 183, 221

Kammeyer, Kenneth, 10–11

Kasdorf, Julia, 34, 36, 227, 259n22

Katie (Miller), 37–40, 45

Keeshig-Tobias, Lenore, 212–14

Keller, Cynthia, 131, 212, 220, 237, 241

Kingsbury, Karen, 107, 189, 239

Kindle. *See* e-books

Knepp, Maynard, 52, 262n59

Kraybill, Donald B., xii, 38, 207, 210, 243, 275n16

Lancaster County, x–xi, 25, 38, 46, 64, 118–20, 123, 129–30, 140, 168, 186, 202–3, 206, 217, 242; in Amish romance novels, xii, 6, 27, 45–46, 146–47, 215, 236

Lewis, Beverly, xvi, 38, 51–52, 54, 112, 118–19, 121–23, 149–50, 162, 173, 181–84, 186, 216–17, 221, 248–49; biography of, x, 45, 67, 114, 118–19, 121, 260–61n44; sales of books by, ix, 5, 45–49, 97, 191, 232

Lewis, Beverly, works of: Abram's Daughters series, 163, 209, 286n22, 286n26; Annie's People series, 155; Courtship of Nellie Fisher series, 76, 115; Heritage of Lancaster County series, 45–49, 66, 164, 215; Home to Hickory Hollow series, 232; *The Postcard / The Crossroad*, xii, 125–26, 146–47, 165; the Rose Trilogy, 118, 141–42, 156, 160, 190–91; Seasons of Grace series, 107, 138, 163, 215, 249; for young readers, 45. See also *Confession, The; Shunning, The*

Lipovetsky, Gilles, 10, 12, 77, 81, 84, 101–2, 105, 110, 133–35, 152 literary agents, xiv, 50, 84–88, 102, 133–34, 202, 232–33. *See also specific agents*

local-color writing. *See* regional fiction

Lodge, Hillary Manton, 116–17, 125

Long, Kelly, 76, 162

Love Comes Softly. See Oke, Janette

Lundin, Roger, 62

Lydia's Charm. See under Brunstetter, Wanda, works of

MacGregor, Chip, 50–51, 103, 224

"man swap," 209–11, 286n22, 286n26

marketing: of Amish romance novels, 41, 51–54, 57, 64, 82, 88–90, 92–96, 233; conversational, 93–95; contemporary theories of, 93–96; "prosumers" and, 93, 94; and social media, 92–96

marriage, 156, 163, 171–73; in Amish romance novels, xiv, 12, 66, 76, 107, 113, 125, 138, 140–42, 156–58, 163–68, 170–72, 194, 209–10; Amish understandings of, 187, 243–44; in early Amish romance novels, 29, 31–32, 35, 37; in evangelical romance novels, 41–42; evangelical understandings of, 156, 163–69

Marshall, Catherine, 42

Martin, Helen Reimensnyder, 25–34, 54, 221

Marx, Leo, xii, 147–48

memoir, Amish-themed. *See* nonfiction, Amish-themed

Mennonites, x, xiii, 38, 45, 51–53, 62, 99, 122, 186, 193, 203, 247, 260–61n44; as authors of Amish romance novels, 35, 38–40, 51–52, 118; characteristics of, 62, 64–65, 251n3; as characters within Amish romance

novels, 65–66, 115–16, 121, 135, 164, 171, 266n25; history of, 28, 62, 64–65, 129; and opinions of Amish romance novels, 35–36, 99, 186, 203, 221, 265–66n22; as readers of Amish romance novels, 46, 65, 175, 184, 248–49. *See also* fiction, Mennonite-themed

midwives, 74, 101, 170

Miller, Clara Bernice, 27, 36–41, 45–46, 52, 54, 118, 235

Miller, Emma, 76, 159, 169

Miller, Eric, 13, 117–18, 131, 195, 208, 250

Miller, Laura, 96

Miller, Levi, 51–54, 57

Miller, Lisa, 69, 136

Miller, Vincent, 53, 88, 90, 100–101, 103, 246

Mock, Melanie Springer, 22, 171–72

modesty, 11, 13, 60, 136, 159–60

Moore, Laurence, 82–83

Morgan, Spencer, 67–69

motherhood: in Amish romance novels, xiv, 31–32, 35, 157–58, 165, 168–71; Amish understandings of, 168; evangelical understandings of, 168–72. *See also* family; marriage

Neal, Lynn S., xii; on aesthetics and subculture of evangelicalism, 74–75; on content of evangelical romance novels, 42, 114, 116–17, 143, 153, 157, 176, 226; on readers of evangelical romance novels, 44–45, 109, 126, 143, 149, 175

Nell, Victor, 16, 21

Nelson, Marcia Z., 227, 237–38

Nelson, Thomas, 89, 92–93, 95, 232–33. *See* Amish Living (website)

New Criticism, 14–19

Nickel Mines school shooting, 9, 50, 123
Nolt, Steven, 210
Nomura, Nao, 186, 242
nonfiction, Amish-themed, 80, 223, 239–40
nonresistance: in Amish romance novels, 222–24, 289n64; in Anabaptist theology, 63, 65, 101, 222–24
nostalgia, xii, 51, 83, 152–53, 237–38, 249–50, 278n61
novelists, Amish. *See specific authors*
novels, Amish. *See* romance novels, Amish; *and specific authors and titles*

Oates, Steve, 46, 48, 52, 65, 68, 131
Oke, Janette, ix, 41–44, 70, 139–40
online discussions of Amish romance novels. *See* Amish Living (website); Amish Reader (website)
Oppliger, Patrice, 136
Ordnung, the, 64, 118, 126, 187–88, 207–8; as depicted in Amish romance novels, 65, 121, 193, 205, 207–8
oversexualization. *See* hypersexualization

pacifism. *See* nonresistance
paperbacks, mass-market, 44, 88–89, 97
parasocial relationships, 137, 139–40
pastoral, the, xii, 83, 258n13; in Amish romance novels, 28, 32–33, 36, 144–48, 152–53
patriarchy. *See* gender roles; marriage
Paul, Pamela, 11
peace. *See* nonresistance
Peretti, Frank, ix–x, 45
Picoult, Jodi, 237, 291–92n11, 292n14

Plano, Illinois, 103, 105–10, 127
plot: in Amish romance novels, 27, 73–76, 107–8, 113–14, 135, 161, 163, 188, 193, 200, 236; in evangelical romance novels, 12, 109
prairie romance, ix, 41–42, 43, 45
Pratt, Mary Louise, 86–87, 266n26
pregnancy, 41, 115, 142, 149, 163, 207, 215
production. *See* publishing
protagonists in Amish romance novels, 6, 67, 114, 157–58, 194; agency of, 135, 157, 167, 172–73, 257–58n9; "English" (non-Amish), 33–34, 146, 158, 164, 167, 214–16, 236, 241; family and romantic lives of, 30–31, 33–36, 142–43, 149, 156, 162, 164–65, 168–71; male, xii, 29, 147, 279n6, 279n10; reader descriptions of, 13, 75, 125, 167, 194; reader relationship or identification with, 110, 139–40, 191, 241, 276n31; spiritual lives of, 37, 65–66, 113–21, 273n33; virtues of, 13, 25, 113, 158–60, 224; voice of, 212, 216–17; work lives of, 131, 170–71
publishing: Christian, 28, 41–42, 49–53, 68–70, 84, 88–96; consolidation within, 88–90; fast pace of, 10, 80–82, 84; production strategies within, xiv, 83–84, 88, 90, 98, 245; romance, 42, 44–45, 67–73
purity culture, 11–12, 67, 160, 162–63. *See also* chastity; "clean reads"; virginity

Quakers, 129, 288n53. *See also* fiction, Quaker-themed
Quigley, Stephen, 216–17
quilts, 46, 92, 99, 101, 111, 222, 224
Quiverfull, 168–69, 281n35

race, 130, 212–14, 216, 225–27, 241, 288n53; in Amish romance novels, xv, 34, 61, 225–27, 290n72; in evangelical romance novels, 226, 290n75; as ideological construct, 130, 226

Radway, Janice A., xvi, 23, 36, 42, 83, 137, 139, 142, 174, 193, 256n46, 285n5, 293n30

Random House, 50, 89, 237. *See also* WaterBrook

reader-response theory. *See* reading theory, transactional

readers of Amish romance novels, xii–xiii, 11, 13–14, 17–19, 23–24, 34, 54, 67, 174–75, 227; Amish, 119, 180–91, 205–6, 208, 242–44; characteristics of, 52, 61, 65, 68, 133, 249; comments on the novels, 75, 112–14, 120, 123, 131–32, 136–39, 148–51, 166, 217; effects of the novels on, 240–44; interactions among, 94, 106–11, 127; male, 22, 247–50; opinions of the Amish, 50–51, 61, 84, 113, 134, 169; as "prosumers," 94–95; and suspense, 140–42

readers of evangelical romance novels, 22, 42, 44–45, 49, 62, 74, 100, 113–14, 149–50, 175

readers of general romance novels, 42, 44, 83, 137, 139, 142

reading: as communal practice, 82, 94, 106–11, 127; as devotional practice, 90, 112–16; as escape, 132, 227; gender and, 21–23, 94, 109, 173–74, 249; history of, 21, 28, 82; as ludic experience, 14, 138; as private practice, 82; as transport, 128, 131–33, 137, 150, 201

reading theory, transactional, xii–xiii, 14, 18–19, 24, 175, 244–45

Reading the Romance (Radway). *See* Radway, Janice A.

recession, 4, 9, 50–51, 83, 90–91, 106, 233

regional fiction, 29–30, 33–34, 227, 269n17

Regis, Pamela, xvi, 22–23, 36, 140, 173

Reid, Ruth, 6, 126, 143

religion. *See* evangelicalism: piety within; faith; God; Jesus; romance novels, Amish: spirituality within; romance novels, evangelical: spirituality within; salvation

representation. *See* appropriation; domestication; exoticism

Revell, 6, 49, 80, 224, 238

Rivers, Francine, 107, 189, 239

romance: in Amish culture, 243–44; in Amish romance novels, xvi, 69, 114–16, 142–43, 148–50, 155, 160–63, 170; colonial-era, 243–44; divine, 114–16

romance novels: conventions of, 67, 140–42, 272n10; criticism of, 21–23, 83, 171; definitions of, xvi, 36; as freeing for women, 173–74, 282n50; history of, 42, 44–45; media treatment of, 23, 66–67; popularity of, 67–68, 83; readers of, 23, 42, 139, 142, 174, 193; sexuality within, 42, 44–45, 69

romance novels, Amish: accuracy of, 182, 191, 195, 197, 199–211, 217–18, 284n1; conventions of, 67, 74–75, 91, 111, 127, 137–43; criticism of, 8, 15–17, 73–76, 91, 155, 171–72, 186–91; diversity among, 6–7, 75–77, 162, 169; endings of, 74, 140–43; in evangelical romance novels, 226, 290n75; front covers of, 3, 44, 48–49, 54, 70, 73, 90, 159, 165–66, 195, 197, 226; future

romance novels, Amish (*cont.*)
of, 227–28; gender within, 163–68,
169–76; genres related to, 3–4, 234–
38; media treatment of, 7, 15, 66–73;
myths about, 66–77; sales of, 3–7,
48–54, 67, 68, 92, *185*, 232–34, 238,
253n1; series, 6–7, 140, 142; spirituality within, 107, 112–27, 242–43; subgenres of, 6; terminology for, xv–xvi.
See also fiction, Amish-themed; readers of Amish romance novels; *and
specific authors and titles*
romance novels, evangelical, xii, 157;
chastity within, 28; conventions
of, 23, 74; criticism of, 62, 132, 142,
275n10; gender and, 153, 160, 172;
history of, 28, 36–42; readers' relationships surrounding, 109–10; spirituality within, 114, 116–19, 242–43; as
women's ministry, 109
Roper, Gayle, 48–49, 117, 120, 141
Rosanna of the Amish (Yoder), 35–36,
146, 194–95
Rosenblatt, Louise, 18
Root, Deborah, 214, 216
Rumspringa, 28, 63, 135, 200, 205
rurality, xiv, 22, 27–30, 32–33, 40, 42,
45, 145–48. *See also* pastoral, the

Sabina: A Story of the Amish (Martin),
25–34
salvation: Amish understandings of,
121–23, 243; evangelical understandings of, 37, 40, 60, 117, 119–23, 126–
27, 234
Sawyer, Kim Vogel, 248
Schultze, Quentin, 58, 62
Scott, Stephen, 204–5, 207, 227, 261–
62n44
Senft, Adina, 123, 207

sexuality: in Amish romance novels,
12–13, 67–68, 70, 148–50, 156–57,
160–63, 169; in evangelicalism, 11–13,
44–45, 60, 136–37, 157, 162–63, 169;
in general romance novels, 42, 44–
45, 69. *See also* chastity; hypersexualization; purity culture; romance
shunning, 27, 74, 124–26, 193, 200,
205–9, 235, 260–61n44. *See also
Shunning, The*
Shunning, The, xiv, 2, 25, 27–28, 40,
45–49, 66, 68, 116, 121, 135, 170, 187–
88, 208; sales of, 5, 46–48. *See also*
Lewis, Beverly
simplicity, 7–10, 14, 24, 32–33, 65, 70,
83, 113, 147, 151, 235
Sinful Moments Press, 70, 72
Smith, Christian, 58–59, 166–68
spirituality. *See* evangelicalism: piety
within; God; Jesus; romance novels,
Amish: spirituality within; romance
novels, evangelical: spirituality
within; salvation
Steel, Danielle, 16, 70, 189
Stevick, Richard, 197, 199
Stich, Jon, *56,* 66–67
submission. *See* gender roles
suspense: strategies of, 137, 140–42, 155;
as subgenre of Amish fiction, 6, 76,
267n34

Tan, Candy, 158
taste cultures, 20, 23–24, 66, 74–75, 91,
180, 189
taste publics. *See* taste cultures
theology. *See* Amish, the; evangelicalism; faith; God; Jesus
theory. *See* cultural criticism; reading
theory, transactional
tourism: Amish-themed, 46, 64, 129–

32, 181, 186–87, 216, 224, 242; of the imagination, 132; of memory, 10, 134

Trollinger, Susan L., 12, 216, 224

Umble, Diane Zimmerman, 241

virginity: the Amish as emblems of, 12–13, 156–57; in Amish romance novels, 12, 38, 113, 156–63, 279n10; evangelical understandings of, 11, 156–57, 162–63; in general romance novels, 158–59, 279n10; in history, 12, 158

Wagler, Ira, 239–40
Walmart, 96–98, 102, 130, 180, 191, 197
WaterBrook, 50, 89
Weaver-Zercher, David L., xii, 113, 241
weddings, 53, 102, 116, 205, 207. *See also* brides
Welty, Cora Gottschalk, 32–34, 51, 54, 220
Wendell, Sarah, 158
whiteness, 28, 61, 211, 213–14, 216, 241; in Amish romance novels, 32–34, 200, 225–27. *See also* race
Wilcox, W. Bradford, 169

Williams, Raymond, 19–20, 76, 83–84, 89
Wiseman, Beth, 7, 95, 100, 233, 248, 254n13; *Healing Hearts* (novella), 142–43; *Plain Paradise*, 184; *Plain Proposal*, 149
Witness (film), 46, 64, 161, 284n1
womanhood, Christian, xiv, 15, 77, 153, 157–58, 167–68, 172, 174–5
Woodiwiss, Kathleen, 42, 44
Woods, Robert, Jr., 58, 62
Woodsmall, Cindy, 80, 89, 118, 120–21, 149, 183, 203, 248; biography of, xi, 49–51; sales of books by, 5, 50, 52
Woodsmall, Cindy, works by: Sisters of the Quilt series, 66, 115, 160, 170–71; *When the Heart Cries*, 107, 115, 117–18, 124–25, 140, 160; *When the Morning Comes*, 225
writers' conferences, 49–50, 86, 103, 222, 234

Yoder, Doretta, 184
Yoder, Joseph W., 35–36, 194–95, 259n22

Zondervan, 50, 89, 94, 202, 232, 236

Young Center Books in Anabaptist & Pietist Studies
Charles E. Hurst and David L. McConnell, *An Amish Paradox:
Diversity and Change in the World's Largest Amish Community*
Rod Janzen and Max Stanton, *The Hutterites in North America*
Karen M. Johnson-Weiner, *Train Up a Child: Old Order Amish
and Mennonite Schools*
Peter J. Klassen, *Mennonites in Early Modern Poland and Prussia*
James O. Lehman and Steven M. Nolt, *Mennonites, Amish,
and the American Civil War*
Steven M. Nolt and Thomas J. Meyers, *Plain Diversity:
Amish Cultures and Identities*
Douglas H. Shantz, *A New Introduction to German Pietism:
Protestant Renewal at the Dawn of Modern Europe*
Tobin Miller Shearer, *Daily Demonstrators: The Civil Rights Movement
in Mennonite Homes and Sanctuaries*
Richard A. Stevick, *Growing Up Amish: The Teenage Years*
Susan L. Trollinger, *Selling the Amish: The Tourism of Nostalgia*
Diane Zimmerman Umble and David L. Weaver-Zercher, eds.,
The Amish and the Media
Valerie Weaver-Zercher, *Thrill of the Chaste: The Allure of
Amish Romance Novels*

Center Books in Anabaptist Studies
Carl F. Bowman, *Brethren Society: The Cultural Transformation of
a "Peculiar People"*
Perry Bush, *Two Kingdoms, Two Loyalties: Mennonite Pacifism in
Modern America*
John A. Hostetler, ed., *Amish Roots: A Treasury of History, Wisdom, and Lore*
Julia Kasdorf, *The Body and the Book: Writing from a Mennonite Life*
Donald B. Kraybill, ed., *The Amish and the State*, 2nd edition
Donald B. Kraybill, *The Riddle of Amish Culture*, revised edition
Donald B. Kraybill and Carl Desportes Bowman, *On the Backroad to
Heaven: Old Order Hutterites, Mennonites, Amish, and Brethren*
Donald B. Kraybill and Steven M. Nolt, *Amish Enterprise: From Plows to
Profits*, 2nd edition

Werner O. Packull, *Hutterite Beginnings: Communitarian Experiments during the Reformation*

Calvin Redekop, ed., *Creation and the Environment: An Anabaptist Perspective on a Sustainable World*

Calvin Redekop, Stephen C. Ainlay, and Robert Siemens, *Mennonite Entrepreneurs*

Benjamin W. Redekop and Calvin W. Redekop, eds., *Power, Authority, and the Anabaptist Tradition*

Steven D. Reschly, *The Amish on the Iowa Prairie, 1840 to 1910*

Kimberly D. Schmidt, Diane Zimmerman Umble, and Steven D. Reschly, *Strangers at Home: Amish and Mennonite Women in History*

Diane Zimmerman Umble, *Holding the Line: The Telephone in Old Order Mennonite and Amish Life*

David Weaver-Zercher, *The Amish in the American Imagination*